Success as a Real Estate Agent

3rd Edition

by Dirk Zeller
Founder of Real Estate Champions

for
dummies®
A Wiley Brand

Success as a Real Estate Agent For Dummies®, 3rd Edition

Published by: **John Wiley & Sons, Inc.**, 111 River Street, Hoboken, NJ 07030-5774, www.wiley.com

Copyright © 2017 by John Wiley & Sons, Inc., Hoboken, New Jersey

Published simultaneously in Canada

For general information on our other products and services, please contact our Customer Care Department within the U.S. at 877-762-2974, outside the U.S. at 317-572-3993, or fax 317-572-4002. For technical support, please visit https://hub.wiley.com/community/support/dummies.

Wiley publishes in a variety of print and electronic formats and by print-on-demand. Some material included with standard print versions of this book may not be included in e-books or in print-on-demand. If this book refers to media such as a CD or DVD that is not included in the version you purchased, you may download this material at http://booksupport.wiley.com. For more information about Wiley products, visit www.wiley.com.

Library of Congress Control Number: 2017934018

ISBN 978-1-119-37183-0 (pbk); ISBN 978-1-119-37185-4 (ePub); ISBN 978-1-119-37188-5

Manufactured in the United States of America

10 9 8 7 6 5 4 3 2 1

Contents at a Glance

Table of Contents

Introduction

Welcome to the third edition of *Success as a Real Estate Agent For Dummies!* You're about to move into the big leagues, populated by the most successful real estate agents.

Real estate sales is the greatest business in the world. In my more than 30 years as a business owner and entrepreneur, I've yet to find a business equal to real estate sales when it comes to income potential versus capital investment. In any marketplace, a real estate agent has the opportunity to create hundreds of thousands of dollars in income. (I coach many agents and teams who earn more than $3 million per year.) An agent's income is especially significant when viewed against the capital investment required by the business. Most agents need as little as $2,000 to start up their practices. Compare that to any other business and you'll find that most involve sizeable investments and burdensome loans to buy equipment, lease space, create marketing pieces, develop business strategies, and hire employees — all to achieve what is usually a smaller net profit than what a real estate agent can achieve in the first few years. It's almost too good to be true!

Because of technological advances, including the Internet and social media, a new agent can create the appearance of success, marketplace stature, and marketing experience far beyond the early stages of a real estate career. This gives new agents better odds at carving out a career for themselves. The timing of your decision to enter the field of real estate or advance your career could not be better. The industry has seen a steady and exciting improvement in sales and opportunity in the last few years. New agents are entering real estate sales in very high numbers. Real estate is in a strong growth phase in which home values have risen back to peak pre-recession market pricing.

Real estate sales paved the way for me to become a millionaire at a very young age. It has provided a solid income, many investment opportunities, an exciting lifestyle, and a platform from which I've been able to help many others achieve their own goals and dreams in life.

About This Book

This book is about becoming a successful real estate agent, for sure. It's also about acquiring sales skills, marketing skills, time-management skills, people skills, technology skills, and business skills. It's about gaining more respect, achieving more recognition, making more money, and closing more sales. It's a guide that helps you achieve the goals and dreams you have for yourself and your family.

I'm delighted to share with you the keys I've found for real estate success and to help you avoid the mistakes I've made along the way. (I'm a firm believer in the idea that we often benefit more from failures than from successes — but that doesn't mean you have to repeat my failures.)

The techniques, skills, and strategies I present throughout this book are the same ones I've used and tested to perfection personally and with thousands of coaching clients and hundreds of thousands of training program participants. Although technology has had an expanding influence on the real estate market in the past decade, the foundational skills of sales, time management, marketing, and people skills have not changed as much. This is not a book of theory but of "real stuff" that works and is laid out in a hands-on, step-by-step format. You'll also find time-tested scripts in most sales-oriented chapters. These scripts are designed to move prospects and clients to do more business with you. (If you're a junior member of the grammar police, you may find that some don't perfectly align with your expectation of the English language. The objective of sales scripts, though, is not perfect sentence structure but rather maximum persuasion of the prospect or client.)

If you apply the information contained in this book with the right attitude, and if you're consistent in your practices and in your success expectations, your success in real estate sales is guaranteed.

Throughout this book I incorporate a number of style conventions, most aimed at keeping the book easy to read, with a few aimed at keeping it legally accurate:

>> Throughout this book, I use the term *real estate agent* rather than *Realtor* unless I'm talking specifically about members of the *National Association of Realtors* (NAR). *Realtor* is a registered trademark owned by the NAR, which requires that the term appear either in all capital letters or with an initial capital R. For your information, all Realtors are real estate agents, but only those real estate agents who are members of and subscribe to the association's strict code of ethics are Realtors.

>> The word *agency* describes the relationship that a real estate agent has with members of the public, or as they're sometimes called, *clients.* When clients list a home for sale, they enter a contractual relationship with the agent who will

represent their interests. That agreement is called an *agency relationship.* Every state and province has a unique set of laws stipulating how consumers and real estate agents work in an agency relationship. These agency laws have been reworked and clarified over decades. Throughout this book, when I refer to agency agreements, I'm describing the real estate agent's relationship with buyers or sellers, depending upon whether the agent is the listing agent or the selling agent.

>> Bulleted and numbered lists present important information in a quick-skim format. Watch for lists marked by numbers or check marks. They contain essential facts to remember, steps to take, or advice to follow.

>> Whenever I introduce a new term, I *italicize* it and follow it up with a brief definition.

Foolish Assumptions

As I compressed a career's worth of real estate experience and coaching advice into these pages, I had to make the following assumptions about you, the reader:

>> You're already a licensed real estate agent. If you haven't yet taken the real estate license exam, consider the book *Real Estate License Exams For Dummies,* 3rd Edition, by John A. Yoegel (Wiley, 2017).

>> You're looking to rev up your real estate business, whether you're just starting out or have been in the business for a while. You may be deciding which real estate company to join. Or you've already launched your career with a good company and are now looking for advice on how to climb the success curve faster and higher. Or maybe you're interested in refining specific skills, such as prospecting, selling, running your business more efficiently, or building customer loyalty.

Icons Used in This Book

This wouldn't be a *For Dummies* book without the handy symbols that sit in the outer margin to alert you to valuable information and advice. Watch for these icons:

REMEMBER

When you see this icon, highlight the accompanying information in your brain. Jot it down, etch it in your memory, and consider it essential to your success.

TIP

The light bulb marks on-target advice and tried-and-true approaches that save time, money, and trouble as you achieve real estate success.

WARNING

When there's a danger to avoid or just a bad idea to steer clear of, this icon sits in the margin issuing a warning sign.

Beyond the Book

In addition to the material in the print or e-book you're reading right now, this product also comes with some access-anywhere goodies on the web. Go to www.dummies.com and search for "success as a real estate agent" to find these goodies. To view this book's Cheat Sheet, simply go to www.dummies.com and search for "**Success as a Real Estate Agent For Dummies Cheat Sheet**" in the Search box.

Where to Go from Here

The beauty of this book is that you can start wherever makes the most sense for you.

If you're a newcomer to the field of real estate sales, I suggest that you start with Part 1, in which I consolidate all the start-up information that you're likely to be looking for.

If you've been in the trenches for a while and simply aren't having as much success as you'd like, start with Chapter 3 or 4 and go from there.

If you're pressed for time, facing a crucial issue, or grappling with a particular problem or question, turn to the table of contents or index to look up exactly the advice you're seeking.

Wherever you start, get out a pad of yellow sticky notes, a highlighter pen, or your note-taking app and get ready to make this book — and all the information it contains — your own key to success. I send you off with my very best wishes!

1

Showing Up for Your Own Success Story

Get an overview of the skills you need to swing the odds for success your way. Find out the basic fundamentals that place agents on the right path to reach their target.

Navigate the process of evaluating, choosing, and joining a real estate company.

Discover how to act and work like a top-producing agent to make your goals a reality.

Research and understand the marketplace in which you're working.

Chapter **1**

Skills and Strategies of a Successful Agent

E ach agent defines success slightly differently. Some agents set their goals in dollars, some are attracted to the opportunity to be their own bosses and build their own businesses, and some want the personal control and freedom that a real estate career allows. Achieving success, however, requires the same basic fundamentals regardless of what motivates your move into real estate. Agents who build successful businesses share four common attributes:

» **They're consistent.** They perform success-producing activities day in and day out. Instead of working in spurts — making 50 prospecting calls in two days and then walking away from the phone for two weeks — they proceed methodically and steadily, day after day, to achieve their goals. And, instead of slamming their Facebook friends with a barrage of posts over a two-week span, they consistently post, engage, respond, and add value multiple times a week. They balance the personal postings that create a window into their personal life with business postings periodically to deliver interesting and relevant value.

» **They believe in the law of accumulation.** The law of accumulation is the principle that says with constant effort everything in life, whether positive or negative, compounds itself over time. No agent becomes an overnight success, but with consistency, success-oriented activities accumulate momentum and power and lead to success every time. I read an article on Warren Buffett recently. It said 90 percent of his wealth was accumulated after he was 50 years old! That's compounding!

>> **They're lifelong learners.** The most successful agents never quit improving. Their passion for improvement is acute, and they commit the time, resources, and energy it takes to constantly enhance their skills and performance. You're reading this book because you have a desire to be better, but that quest can't stop with this book. It must continue with additional reading, watching, listening, and attending events to improve your skills, strategies, and systems.

>> **They're self-disciplined.** They have the ability to motivate themselves to do the activities that must be done. Successful agents show up daily and put in a full day of work on highly productive actions such as prospecting, lead generation, and lead follow-up. They make themselves do things they don't want to do so they can have things in life that they truly want. Personal discipline is a fundamental building block for success. One of the greatest things about being a real estate agent is being an independent contractor. You're the master of your domain. You're the only one who can "require" you to show up to work. That also has a downside if you can't force or discipline yourself to do the harder success-producing actions.

MY OWN INAUSPICIOUS BEGINNING

As an original dummy in real estate sales, I'm the perfect author for this book. On my very first listing presentation, I went to the wrong house. Can you imagine arriving at the wrong address for your first presentation? The worst part is that the man who answered the door let me in. To this day, I'm not sure why he let me in and let me begin my listing presentation. I was nearly halfway through my presentation before I figured out the mistake! He just sat quietly listening to me talk about listing his home. He actually did have an interest in selling his home in the near future, so he just listened. I finally realized I was in the wrong house when I glanced over and saw the address on a piece of mail on the table. I had transposed a number on the address, which put me in the wrong house. All the while, the real seller was waiting for me down the street. The good news was that I successfully listed the man's home a few months later.

In the end, it really doesn't matter where you start in your career or what mistakes you make in the early stages. Everyone makes mistakes in new endeavors. What matters most is having a plan or process that keeps you moving down the track toward your goals. Most people would have quit with such a rocky start as mine. However, the sure way to lose is to quit. The only way you win is to keep going.

You're already on the road to real estate success, demonstrated by the fact that you picked up this book to discover what it takes to become a great agent. This first chapter sets you on your way to success by providing an overview of the key skills that successful real estate agents pursue and possess.

Having Goal Objectives and Sales and Income Targets

One of the first steps toward success is knowing what you want out of your real estate career. However, "financial independence" is not a specific enough answer.

I've been in real estate, either working in direct sales or teaching, speaking, training, writing, or coaching people, for nearly 30 years. I've spoken to sales audiences on five different continents. I've met hundreds of thousands of agents, and nearly every one started selling real estate with the same goal of financial independence. Countless times I've asked the question, "Tell me, how do you define financial independence?" What I usually hear in response is some variation of "So I don't have to worry about money anymore."

REMEMBER

The key to eliminating money worries is establishing a financial goal — an actual number — that you need to accumulate in order to achieve the quality of life you want to enjoy. Financial independence boils down to a number. (It can be a gross number, net income, created annually or monthly from your asset base.) Set that number in your mind and then launch your career with the intention to achieve your goal by a specific date.

By having your financial goal in mind, you find clarity and can see past the hard work that lies ahead of you. When you have to endure the rejection, competition, disloyal customers, and challenges that are inevitable along the way, your knowledge about the wealth you're working to achieve helps you weather the storms of the business.

I must share that this focusing on your financial independence number is more real to me today than ever. I realize these steps I just shared with you I did myself 30 years ago. I created a plan as I exactly have described for you. I have worked that plan for 30 years and it has compounded to the point where I don't have to work. The financial piece of the puzzle has been accomplished. I choose to work because I enjoy what I do, not because I need the money it brings. That is true freedom and financial independence. I wish that for you as well.

Acting Like a Top Producer from Day One

Real estate agents join doctors, dentists, attorneys, accountants, and financial planners in the ranks of licensed professionals who provide guidance and counsel to clients. The big difference is that most real estate agents don't view themselves as top-level, highly paid professionals. Many agents, along with a good portion of the public, perceive themselves as real estate tour guides, as home inventory access providers, or even as mere cogs in the wheel of the property sale transaction. The best agents, however, know and act differently.

The Internet and the open access to real estate information have accentuated the view that agents are simply home access providers. Consumers in the real estate market are able to find so much information online that they often view themselves as the experts and agents as simply the key masters. The increasing strength online of third-party sources of real estate information like Zillow, Trulia, and Realtor.com has created another gap between agents and consumers. I'm not advocating a return to the dark ages of MLS books the size of a local telephone book with property information printed biweekly. That is certainly a bygone era. But, to succeed in these technological times, we must expand our offerings and showcase that our services go well beyond basic real estate information and access into homes. We must clearly communicate with the online consumers what they don't have access to, what information they are lacking, along with our benefits and value — even in their early researching period.

REMEMBER

Real estate agents are fiduciary representatives and financial advisors — not people paid to unlock front doors of houses for prospective buyers. A *fiduciary* is someone who is hired to represent the interests of another. A fiduciary owes another person a special relationship of honesty, commitment, exclusivity in representation, ethical treatment, and protection. Build your real estate business with a strong belief in the service and benefits you provide your clients, and you'll provide a vital professional service while being recognized as the valuable professional you are.

Serving your professional representation

Real estate agents represent the interests of their clients. As an agent, you're bound by honor, ethics, and duty to work on your client's behalf to achieve the defined and desired results. This involves the following functions:

>> **Defining the client's objective:** To serve as a good fiduciary representative, you need to start with a clear understanding of the objectives your client is aiming to achieve through the sale or purchase of property. Too many agents get into trouble by starting out with uncertainty about the interests of the people they're representing.

>> **Delivering counsel:** In the same way that attorneys counsel clients on the most effective way to proceed legally, it's your job to offer similarly frank counsel so that your clients reach the real estate outcomes they seek. That counsel can vary based on the clients' goals and objectives, as well as the state of the marketplace. You will counsel a client differently in a seller's market than in a buyer's market. Turn to Chapter 3 to understand how market conditions influence what to say and do.

An attorney may encourage a client to proceed with a lawsuit when the client has a high probability of winning, or she may recommend an out-of-court settlement when odds point toward a court loss that could leave the client with nothing but legal bills to pay. Likewise, you need to be able to steer your clients toward good decisions regarding the value of their homes, the pricing strategies they adopt, the marketing approaches they follow, and the way their contract is negotiated in order to maximize their financial advantage.

>> **Diagnosing problems and offering solutions:** A good agent, like a good doctor, spends a great deal of time examining situations, determining problems, and prescribing solutions. In an agent's case, the focus is on the condition and health of the home a client is trying to buy or sell. The examination involves an analysis of the property's condition, location, neighborhood, school district, curb appeal, landscaping, market competitiveness, market demand, availability for showing, and value versus price. The diagnosis involves an unvarnished analysis of what a home is worth and what changes or corrections are necessary.

Some say that agents should present all the options available to their clients and then recommend the course of action they feel is best. By doing this, agents allow their clients to make the final decision. Although many experts praise the virtues of this approach, I prefer the diagnostic and prescriptive approach because it positions you better as the expert. When clients make poor choices such as setting the wrong price on their home or making an initial offer that is too low, you may still receive some or all of the blame even though they chose the wrong option. No matter the style of your counsel to a client, whether more advisory or assertive, your success in guiding your clients to a successful outcome is based on your expert analysis and application of the variables to the marketplace.

Many agents get into trouble because they lack the conviction to tell clients the truths they don't want to hear. If a home is overpriced or not ready for showing, or if an offer is too low for seller consideration, it's the agent's job to speak up with sound advice. In these situations, you could get blamed for a poor outcome. You may also run the risk of doing all this work and not getting compensated for the time you invested.

To prepare yourself for the task, flip to Chapter 12, which helps you determine and advise sellers regarding a home's ideal price; Chapter 13, which helps you counsel clients regarding changes they need to make before showing their property; and Chapter 15, which helps you counsel clients through the final purchase or sale negotiation.

>> **Troubleshooting:** Unavoidably, many times you have to be the bearer of bad news. Market conditions may shift, and the price on a seller's home may need to come down. A buyer may need to sweeten initial offers to gain seller attention. A loan request may be rejected, or you may need to confront sellers because the animal smells in their home may be turning buyers away. Or, a home that buyers really want may end up selling to someone else.

TIP

At times like these, your calm attitude, solution-oriented approach, and strong agent-client relationship will win the day. Chapter 16 is full of advice for achieving and maintaining the kind of relationship excellence that smoothes your transactions and leads to long-lasting and loyal clients.

Making the right financial decisions

When you help clients make real estate decisions, your advice has a long-lasting effect on your clients' financial health and wealth. Their decisions based on your counsel will affect their short-term equity as well as their long-term financial independence. According to a study by the Society of Actuaries, the equity in one's home on average represents 70 percent of one's total assets. In most cases, home equity is the single largest asset that people own. Your ability to guide clients to properties that match their needs and desires, that fit within their budgets, and that give them long-term gain from minimal initial investment impacts their financial health and wealth for years to come.

REMEMBER

Your influence as a wealth advisor reaches far beyond clients who are in a position to own investment real estate. In your early years, many of your clients may be first-time buyers who are taking their first steps into the world of major financial transactions. Advise them well and they'll remain clients and word-of-mouth ambassadors for years to come. See Chapter 16 for more information about keeping clients for life.

Avoiding the role of Designated Door Opener

Before the advances of the Internet, the consumer's only avenue to information about homes for sale was through a real estate agent. Every other week, agents received phonebook-sized periodicals presenting information on properties for sale, with each new entry accompanied by a small, grainy, black-and-white picture. I know that seems hard to imagine in our information-rich technological world.

AGENTS AS NECESSARY EVILS: A MIND-SET THAT COMES AND GOES

The mind-set that agents are overpaid and unnecessary to the real estate sale process continues to gain traction. This mind-set gains momentum especially when a robust market leads to low home inventories and the quick sale of homes that often receive multiple offers during the short time they're on the market. Sellers feel that their home will sell no matter who lists it, so they go cheaper.

This mind-set has increased in intensity and breadth with expanded online access to real estate information. It has been further developed as companies like Zillow and Trulia grant broader information services in the real estate industry segment.

When times are booming, a segment of consumers and new homebuilders begins to question the value of the agent's services against the associated fees. During the best of market times, some homebuilders even go so far as to sell their houses without allowing agent representation — or compensation.

The silver lining is that when times are good, so many properties are moving that the few listings affected by the agent-is-unnecessary mind-set hardly limit opportunity. Plus, booms don't last forever. When the market swings back and forth, as it will many times during your career, you need to be prepared to adjust your offerings. The ability to master your present marketplace trends while working to prepare for the next market shift is the skill of elite agents.

Today, consumers can go online instead of going to a real estate office to launch their real estate searches. With a few keystrokes and mouse clicks, they have access to a greatly expanded version of the kind of information that agents used to control. There are tens of thousands of sites that offer access to real estate information and access to properties for sale. However, when consumers discover a home they want to see, they must contact either the owner or an agent to gain inside access. This is where things get tricky.

Fifteen years ago, only 8 percent of buyers found the home they wanted to purchase on their own through the Internet. Last year, 44 percent of buyers found their home online themselves and then contacted a real estate agent. The consumer is clearly doing more online research and finding what they want.

WARNING

Often a consumer signs off the web and contacts an agent to get inside the home, as if the agent is simply an entry device. As an agent, you need to demonstrate special skills to engage the customer. Then you need to add value to your skills by having inside market knowledge, keeping up with trends in the marketplace, being aware of technological advances, and having other properties you know about that might be similar to the property that has created the inquiry. With this added know-how, you have an edge over other agents, which allows you to convert the inquiry into a committed buyer client for your business.

Securing Customers and Clients

Imagine that you're on the game show *Jeopardy!*, and you're given just seconds to provide the most important response of your career. Imagine that you're asked to write down the question that prompts the answer: *The function that makes or breaks a real estate agent's success.* (If this book contained music, you know what tune would be playing right now.) Okay, time's up. How did you respond?

The moneymaking reply is: *What is creating customers?* How did you score?

Did you answer: *What is customer service?* If so, you gave the same answer that more than 95 percent of new agents give. In fact, more than 90 percent of experienced agents don't win points with their answers, either. Only a rare few agents see customer creation as the golden approach that it is.

Rule #1: It's about lead generation

You have to be excellent at customer development *and* customer service. However, in terms of priority, you have to first be exemplary at lead generation. Following are a few reasons:

>> **You can't serve customers if you don't create customers in the first place.** And because customer-service excellence results from customer-service experience, customer development is a necessary prerequisite to outstanding customer service.

>> **Most consumers have been provided with such poor service that their expectations are remarkably low.** When service providers do what they say they'll do in the agreed-upon timeframe, consumers are generally content with the service they receive. An Internet-based customer, which is a growing segment, wants ease of service, faster service, and lower-cost service. The truth is that competing on the first two is better than the lower-cost service model. The real estate industry is more personalized in the service it renders than many other Internet-based businesses. Responsiveness is one of the keys to success in the Internet realm. Certainly you want to develop the kind of expertise that delivers exemplary, outstanding service, but if you commit from the get-go to do what you said you'd do when you said you'd do it, your delivery will be better than most.

REMEMBER

>> **Between creating customers and delivering service, customer creation is the more complex task.** Customer creation requires sales skills and ongoing, consistent, persistent prospecting for clients. It requires marketing, promotion, and branding of yourself and your service offerings. To develop customers inexpensively and effectively, you have to gain the level of skill and comfort necessary to pick up the phone and call people you know (or even people you don't know) to ask them for the opportunity to do business with them or to refer you to others who may be in the market for your service. It also requires a level of encouragement and interaction via social media avenues. You need to be able to engage with Facebook to connect with people you know. You also need to be effective in marketing your message online through targeted ads and boosted posts. Additionally, you must be watching for clues about life changes (think: new baby, kids going off to college, divorce) in those social-media interactions and platforms.

>> **If you attract the right kinds of customers into your business, your clients will match well with your expertise and abilities, and service will become an easier and more natural offering.** If you attract the right type of customers, you'll also reap greater quantity and quality of referrals.

Developing sales ability to win customers

REMEMBER

The single most important skill for a real estate agent is sales ability, and sales ability is how you win customers. Your sales ability is based on how effective you are in generating prospects, following up on those prospects to secure appointments, preparing for those appointments, conducting the appointments to secure an exclusive agency contract, and then providing service to that recently created client. People also base your ability on how quickly you can accomplish all of this.

Because you're holding this book, I'm willing to bet that you've either just come out of training to receive your real estate license or you're in the early days of your career. In either case, decide right now to master the skills of selling in order to fuel your success.

In my view, sales skills in the real estate industry are at the lowest level I've seen in 30 years. So much effort and emphasis has been placed on technology and social-media training in real estate that companies and agents have lost their way through the sales skills and sales strategies that are foundational to success in a sales-based industry.

You might be a younger new real estate agent. That means you are more native to technology. It also means you naturally communicate through technology platforms, but may lack the face-to-face interpersonal skills that older real estate agents grew up with. Typically, selling in real estate is done, even in the technological world, face-to-face. According to NAR, 67 percent of buyers buy through the first agent they meet with.

It's hard to believe that probably 95 percent of agents lack top-level sales skills. In my career in training and coaching, I've met hundreds of thousands of agents. Very few, even at the top echelon of earnings, have had any formalized sales training. Whenever I speak to agents, I always ask the audience how many have taken any formalized sales training, and I usually see only a few hands out of the hundreds in the room.

The other reason I know sales skills are lacking is that I coach some of the best and highest-earning agents in the world, and even they believe their sales skills can use improvement. Many agents record their prospecting sessions or listing presentations, but I have yet to meet one who feels that they've nailed their sales skills. The difference between these high-earning agents and other agents is that the high-earning agents realize that sales skills are vital to success, and they continuously seek excellence in this area.

HOW TIMES HAVE CHANGED

Years ago, salespeople were taught that a great presentation involved making the case, going for an early and repeated close, and then bullying the client into submission to secure the deal. Believe it or not, some trainers in the real estate industry still teach this antiquated sales model, which resembles verbal judo more than client development.

Look at the following breakdown of a great presentation today, compared to what one looked like in days long past.

Today's presentation time allocation	Time allocation in days long past
40% Building trust and confirming needs	10% Building rapport
30% Presenting your benefits and advantages	20% Qualifying
20% Discussing price	30% Presenting
10% Closing or getting confirmation	40% Closing

The big difference: Today's best agents spend nearly three-quarters of the presentation giving prospects a reason to say yes — by focusing on the prospect's situation and needs and how the agent can provide the best solution. Yesterday's agents spent virtually no time defining their clients' situations or their own unique solutions. Instead, they spent nearly three-quarters of the presentation making the sale and going for a high-pressure close. We've come a long way!

TIP

To follow the high-earning agent's example, make it your priority to develop and constantly improve your sales skills for the following reasons:

>> **To secure appointments:** Chapter 8 provides practically everything you need to know about winning leads and appointments through prospecting and follow-up activities.

>> **To persuade expired and for-sale-by-owner listings to move their properties to your business:** Chapter 10 is full of secrets and tips to follow as you pursue this lucrative and largely untouched field.

>> **To make persuasive presentations that result in positive buying decisions:** Chapter 12 helps you with every step from pre-qualifying prospects to planning your presentation. It's packed with tips for perfecting your skills, addressing and overcoming objections, and ending with a logical and successful close.

A real estate market won't dictate your success

According to the National Association of Realtors, more than 40 percent of agents didn't close a single transaction last year, and another 20 percent closed only one transaction. This clearly demonstrates the lack of sales and lead-generation skills in the industry.

WARNING

In robust market conditions, leads are abundant and relatively easy to attract, especially buyer leads. But when the market slows, as it inevitably will, real estate success becomes less automatic. Only great sales skills guarantee that you — rather than some other agent — will win clients no matter the market conditions. The best agents make more money in a challenging market than they do in a robust market.

REMEMBER

Regardless of economics, every market contains real estate buyers and sellers. No matter how slow the economy, people always need and want to change homes. Babies are born. Managers get transferred. Couples get married. People divorce. And with these transitions, real estate opportunities arise for those with the strategies to target those opportunities and the skills to sell their unique value.

The way to build immunity to shifting market conditions is to arm yourself with skills in prospecting, lead follow-up, presentations, objection handling, and closing.

The Reasoning and Rationale for Being a Strong Listing Agent

In real estate, there's a saying that "you list to last." In your early days, you're likely to build your business by working primarily with buyers. But in time, you begin to develop your own listings, and after that you begin your climb to real estate's pinnacle position, which is that of a listing agent.

REMEMBER

Typically a larger percentage of referral business will be buyer based. This means that you need to eventually develop a method outside of referrals to create and attract listings.

To create long-term success, a high quality of life, and a strong real estate business, set as your goal to eventually join the elite group — comprised of fewer than 5 percent of all agents — who are listing agents. The advantages are many:

>> **Multiple streams of income:** Listings generate interest and trigger additional transactions. Almost the minute you announce your listing by putting a sign in the ground, uploading the property on your website, and placing the listing in the MLS — syndicating the listing to sites like Zillow, Trulia, Realtor.com, and thousands of others — you'll start receiving calls, emails, and texts from active buyers; calls from neighbors; inquiries from drive-by traffic; and queries from people wanting to live in the area. These leads or inquiries represent current and future business opportunities that only arise when you have a listing with your name on it.

>> **Promotional opportunity:** A listing gives you a reason to advertise and draw the attention of prospects whom you can convert to clients or future prospects. And when your listing sells, you can spread the word of your success with another round of communication to those in the neighborhood, on social media, and throughout your sphere of influence.

>> **A business multiplier:** Talk to any listing agent and you'll have this fact confirmed: One listing equals more than one sale.

>> **Creates quality of life:** Being a strong listing agent creates quality of life as well. By my fourth year in real estate I was on pace to sell 150 homes. I also was in construction of a vacation home in Bend, Oregon. Joan, my wife, was a general contractor. She needed to be onsite on Fridays to meet with subcontractors. I shifted to working Mondays through Thursdays, and taking Fridays, Saturdays, and Sundays off. It was totally unheard of for an agent to take weekends off then, and even now.

I would have not have been able to accomplish the high level of sales and time off without being a strong listing agent. I didn't work a buyer the rest of my real estate sales career. They typically want to see property on weekends. I was enjoying my lifestyle at my vacation home playing golf, snowshoeing, hiking, and biking.

>> **A free team of agents working for you:** The moment you post your listing, all the other agents in your area will go to work on your behalf. And the best part is that they don't require payment until they deliver a buyer, and then they'll be paid not by you but by your seller through the commission structure.

Much of the information in this book focuses on developing listings, because to achieve top-level success, listings are the name of the game.

Choosing Your Avenue to Success

Agents typically follow one of these four basic approaches in the quest to achieve real estate success:

>> **Become a workaholic.** More than 80 percent of agents who generate a reasonable income achieve their success by turning their careers into a 7-day-a-week, 24-hour-a-day job. They answer emails, texts, private messages, and business phone calls day and night; they make themselves constantly available to prospects and clients; and they work on demand with no restraints or boundaries because of technology. That can lead to burnout.

>> **Buy clients.** The second-most-frequent pathway to success is to buy business through excessive marketing campaigns. Marketing can be a valuable tool, but you must monitor, track, and count the results. You have to be consistent in your marketing and branding. You can't start and stop campaigns. Some agents buy their way to top-level real estate success by investing in large branding or marketing campaigns — you will get called, texted, and emailed endlessly with both online and offline marketing and lead generation. The challenge is the risk-versus-reward position, and earlier in your career the risk is even greater. Others buy their way to the top by discounting their commissions. By offering themselves at the lowest prices, these agents eliminate the need to emphasize their skills, abilities, and expertise.

>> **Take the shady road.** Another avenue to real estate financial success is to abandon ethics and just go for the deal and the resulting money. Unlike the vast majority of agents who advise and advocate for their clients, agents who take this route choose not to be bound by ethics or any codes of conduct. They put their own needs first and put their clients' best interests in distant second place. Fortunately, these agents are few and far between.

>> **Build a professional services business.** The fourth and best pathway is to create a well-rounded, professional services business not unlike that of a doctor, dentist, attorney, or accountant. The balance of the two connected and complementary segments of prospecting, lead generation, lead conversion, and marketing is essential to reach this level. Fewer than 5 percent of all agents follow this route, yet the ones who do are the ones who earn the largest sums of money — some exceeding $1 million annually while also having high-quality lives and time for friends and family. Plus, when they're ready to bow out of the industry, they have a business asset they can sell to another agent. (See the sidebar "Mining gold from your professional services business" for more details on creating an asset you can sell.)

This is the route I urge you to follow. Each of the following chapters in this book tells you exactly how to build your own professional services business.

REMEMBER

MINING GOLD FROM YOUR PROFESSIONAL SERVICES BUSINESS

The best professionals provide ongoing services to clients who wouldn't think of taking their business elsewhere. These professionals develop reputations and client loyalty that reside in their company name, even after the founding professionals move on to other ventures or into retirement. Doing more than just earning an income and building a clientele, these professionals build an asset that they can sell, which allows them to receive compensation from the value of the successful businesses they've built.

As a favorite example, my father was a dentist for 30 years. When he decided to retire, he sold his practice to another dentist. He sold his building and equipment, but most important, he sold his patient roster, which raked in the majority of the money he received.

A real estate agent who builds a well-rounded, successful business can enjoy a similarly lucrative sale. In fact, your objective should be to build the kind of business that you can sell at the completion of your real estate career.

I worked with a coaching client a few years ago as she prepared her business for sale. She tracked lead-making strategies, lead conversion rates, client satisfaction, listings, buyers, and net profit. Then, for two years, we worked together to improve all the facets of her business until they were fine-tuned to perfection. She was among the minority 5 percent of agents who built a truly well-rounded business. The result: Her real estate practice sold for well over $1 million. How's that for a goal?

Chapter **2**

Selecting the Right Company

Before you sign on with a real estate company, you need to take time to look well beneath the surface and beyond first impressions to determine whether the company is, in fact, the right one for you. Do the company's core values and culture align with yours? Are its technology platforms and systems cutting edge, standard for the market, or lagging behind? Does its brand help you stand out in the marketplace?

Most agents, whether new or experienced, don't invest enough time in evaluating and analyzing companies, owners, key managers, and their direct broker manager in their office before they commit to a real estate firm. In this chapter, I help you to do the homework, compare the opportunities, make the choice, and establish a winning partnership.

Real Estate Office of the Future

Real estate offices have evolved from the sprawling buildings where every agent had his own workstation, cubical, or private office. Although some offices are still arranged this way, the vast majority of real estate offices are morphing into a more stop-and-go model. Agents on the go share spaces, tools and resources. Many agents work probably remotely from a home office. Their activities are mobile because of technological advances in access to information and paperless documents and transactions. Even agents who need staff or help for administrative functions are hiring virtual assistants, who can work from any location.

I have a client who has a team of agents and administration staff who all work remotely. They sell over 50 million dollars of real estate a year, but everyone works from a home office. They don't even have space at the real estate company.

In today's offices, you may notice the absence of a large meeting or training space. Many companies have cut back on their training offerings or switched to online training classes, so they have repurposed that unused space.

These changes can mean fewer laborious meetings and more time to generate business. Many tools and educational offerings are available in real-time, online environments. This office of the future helps you be more mobile and more effective with your time. You don't need to feel compelled to come in each day or even every week.

SPACE AGE

Real estate offices today are using a more open-space concept . . . think Starbucks or your neighborhood cafe. They often contain a bullpen rather than a large number of private offices. A "bullpen" is an area with a large number of cubicles where most agents work. Everyone shares the space in these new offices, which also have private workspaces available. Usually conference rooms are available for client and prospect meetings. Today's spaces are also more client-centric. They are more comfortable and inviting than the offices of old, where cubicles and private offices were lined up in a rigid row.

Weighing All Your Options

An agent choosing an agency isn't a whole lot different than a consumer choosing an agent. All the choices look good (often they all look very much the same!), and they all offer a wide variety of opportunities. What's more, they all tell you that they're the best. So how do you choose?

TIP

Choose by weighing benefits. What advantages can you count on in terms of training, continuing education, lead-generation opportunities, opportunities to host open houses, social-media positioning, lead generation, and market share by joining one company over another company? You should also check the search engine optimization of the company website for your market. Also check common search terms for your area. If you live in Wichita, Kansas, I would look at "Wichita real estate," "Wichita homes for sale," and other common search terms. Does your company rank on the first page or even at all? Additionally, check on strategic alliances or marketing partnerships the company may have with third-party lead generators like Zillow, Trulia, and Realtor.com.

A larger portion of buyers is going to these third-party sites. What type of relationship does your broker or national brand have with these companies? Do your listings get enhanced positioning? Do your listings get exclusive positioning where you are the only agent who is highlighted for your listings?

Check the technology tools and systems that are provided for free as well as for a fee. The new breed of agents needs to keep up with the technology options and tools coming out each month. Does the broker you're considering lead the field, or is it running in place? It's fair to ask the broker you're interviewing with, "What's in it for me? Why should I come to your company and your office?" The clearly delivered response will tell you a lot about the company.

As you assess company choices, use the upcoming advice to evaluate how office attributes and company size match with your own interests and priorities.

Choosing residential or commercial

Differences abound in real estate companies. The biggest difference being whether the product the company focuses on is residential or commercial. While real estate sales practitioners can legally sell any type of real estate, whether residential properties or commercial properties or even businesses, frequently a company will either specialize in residential or commercial real estate.

Residential

A residential company will primarily sell homes, town homes, condos, and small-plex properties. Agents are not precluded from other real estate activity in the commercial realm but they often leave that market to specialists.

Commercial

Commercial real estate companies tend to focus on larger commercial deals. They frequently leave the small-plex properties, such as duplex, triplex, and four-plex properties, to the residential agents and companies because of lower sale prices and lower demand for complex financing options. A buyer can receive conforming financing for up to a four-plex property. This means that the same sources that finance a primary residence can and do provide up to four-plex financing. These loans are easier to obtain than commercial loans on apartments, office buildings, and strip malls. They also require a lower down payment than the typical commercial loan requires. There is an underserved niche in small plexes that might be worthwhile to focus on.

Commercial companies in large and mid-size markets do the majority of the commercial leases of retail, industrial, and office space. They are the ones who handle the listing and sale of apartment complexes, office buildings, retail centers, industrial buildings, and land.

What makes a great office?

When I look at a real estate office, I evaluate how they rank based on the following list of attributes:

TIP

>> **Energy and enthusiasm:** It takes passion to succeed at essential real estate activities like prospecting, lead generation, and lead follow-up. If you surround yourself with agents who lack energy and enthusiasm for the business, it will affect your performance.

When trying to determine whether an office has energy and enthusiasm, find out whether agents are excited to come to work. Also find out whether the office has a public board where agents record their listings and sales for the other agents to see. If the office does have a board like this, look to see if it's full or empty. Are only a few names covering the entire board, or are all the agents represented? These boards are less common these days because agents don't come into the office daily, so you may have to ask for a spreadsheet of pending sales activity, which gives you the same information. Also, if you can start with other new agents, it can help with camaraderie and commonality. When the going gets tough, and it will . . . it's good to have a buddy.

>> **Reputation:** Although you can't count on your company's reputation to do your work for you, you can bet that your company's positive reputation will help you open doors.

>> **Experienced manager:** As a newer agent, you'll benefit greatly from a manager who knows the ropes and has experience taking agents to higher levels of production. Ask the following questions: What is the manager's track record in raising agent productivity? How long does it typically take the manager to reach different production thresholds with agents? The right answers can dramatically affect your career arc.

REMEMBER

You're looking for a manager who has a track record of building successful agents from new agents. Effective managers have low failure rates with new agents and see more than 40 percent of their new agents become successful. That percentage may seem low, but according to the National Association of Realtors (NAR), fewer than 20 percent of agents last more than two years in the business. A manager who can give you timeframes and statistics on his agents' success is a serious candidate for your manager. Most of them can't tell you these stats.

>> **Listings inventory:** Does the company offer you the opportunity to establish some income over the early months by working someone else's inventory while you're creating your own? Can you post the inventory of other agents in marketing, social media, or online to generate interest and calls? What are the company's online lead-generation strategies with its listing inventory? Do those inquiries go to the agent who listed the property, or does the company spread them around to all agents? As a newer agent, you ideally want a company that spreads the wealth. As an established, successful agent, you want the opposite. An established inventory gives you the opportunity to create buyers and income by working open houses, ad calls, and sign calls.

>> **Training focus:** Look into how well the company handles the two major areas of training: initial training (so you can earn an income) and ongoing training (so you can build and grow your business). Training options have exploded in the past few years, especially with online classes and programs, videos, webinars, and other opportunities.

Most companies are still behind the curve in online training. Online training can mean either live or recorded sessions. In having personally taught more than 3,000 live online sessions, I can attest that a wonderfully designed live online program can space the learning out so you will be able to build a successful career.

WARNING

When they're selecting an agency, most new agents don't focus enough on the company's training programs because they get wrapped up in the "what's my split" game. If, through good training, you're able to master the skills you need to excel, your income is unlimited. However, if you don't, you have no chance.

CHECK OUT PREMIER ONLINE TRAINING

Online training is convenient because it can be accessed from your home office and can be synchronous or asynchronous. If you want to check out cutting-edge online training, visit my website at www.realestatechampions.com. We are truly the experts in this medium, having developed content for Coldwell Banker, Century 21, ERA Real Estate, Berkshire Hathaway Home Services, and many other national and international brands, as well as our own proprietary programs.

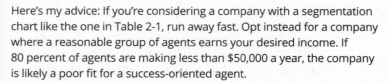

Every company says it offers good training. It's your job to look under the hood to see for yourself. To do that, ask these three questions:

- **What's the loss ratio for new agents?** The *loss ratio* is the number of agents who fail after completing the training program. This ratio tells you the effectiveness of the company's new-agent training program. That is the true number of new-agent success.

- **What is the per-person production ratio?** The average production by the salespeople in the company tells you whom you're likely to be surrounded by on a day-to-day basis. It clearly illustrates the results of the training programs. You're looking for results. To have training for the sake of training or to claim you have training is worthless. The question is what results are achieved in terms of income and quality service to clients. A company that claims to have excellent training but has low agent performance is fooling itself and its agents.

- **How do the agents segment into income brackets?** The answer tells you whether the company's ongoing training is building the capabilities of all agents or only a few. As an example of a breakdown you want to avoid, check out Table 2-1, which shows how agents in a 200-agent company segment into earning categories.

Here's my advice: If you're considering a company with a segmentation chart like the one in Table 2-1, run away fast. Opt instead for a company where a reasonable group of agents earns your desired income. If 80 percent of agents are making less than $50,000 a year, the company is likely a poor fit for a success-oriented agent.

TIP

TABLE 2-1

Agent Segmentation by Income Bracket

Income Segment	Number of Agents
$500,000+	1
$250,000+	2
$200,000+	2
$100,000+	5
$50,000+	10
$25,000+	100
$25,000 or less	80

Bending or breaking the rules

Real estate agents follow two basic sets of rules:

>> **The regulatory body that governs real estate in your state establishes one set of rules.** This group sets regulations regarding how to handle the earnest money you collect from purchasers, what the deadlines are for the paperwork that is involved with each transaction, who is to receive original copies, and what timeline the legal aspects of the transaction are to follow. The regulatory group is generally focused on consumer protection.

>> **The second set of rules that most agents follow is the code of ethics established by the NAR.** The code of ethics dictates how agents with NAR member companies should conduct business and how they should deal with prospects, clients, and other agents. Obtain a copy of the code of ethics from your broker, your local real estate board, or online at www.realtor.org.

However, individual agencies also have their own sets of rules. The following sections fill you in.

The rules of the house

Most company rules are based on the absolutes presented by state laws and regulations and by the NAR code of ethics, but some rules vary from office to office.

WARNING

To protect themselves, some companies shorten the legally dictated timeframes to ensure that agents turn in paperwork to brokers with time to spare. When paperwork is submitted to the principal broker, it gets recorded with a date that provides evidence of receipt. The state regulatory body can audit a real estate company's files at any time and, if paperwork doesn't conform to regulations, can levy fines or, worse, close the firm down until lapses are corrected.

When you're interviewing with a company, request a copy of its rules, its operational/procedural manual, or its new-agent handbook to find out how it expects you to work, and then actually read it before you make a commitment to joining the company. If the company can't produce one, read the lack of response as a clue about its level of organization.

A penny for you, a penny for me: Commission split arrangements

Media reports advise consumers that seller/agent commission fees are negotiable. Likewise, buyer/agent commission fees are negotiable, as well. You're the one who determines your fees. Some agents charge higher fees because they're worth more. They can sell to the consumer a higher level of value, so they can increase their fees.

New agents all seek a universal formula for commission splits, but none exists. Each broker establishes a unique formula, usually beginning with a split that apportions 50 percent of the commission to you and 50 percent to your broker, moving gradually upward in your favor over time as you achieve different earning levels.

The following list presents some of the most common commission options you may see in the industry:

>> **The graduated split:** The graduated split is the most common compensation package. You start at a 50/50 split, which is increased to 60/40 and upward incrementally as you become more productive and your earnings reach company-established levels for graduation.

>> **The graduated split capped:** Some companies put an annual cap on the revenue the company derives from the graduated split arrangement. After they collect the established amount of company commission income, the rest is yours. A per-transaction fee that doesn't cap often accompanies this commission type. This is fair, in my view, because although you receive all your income beyond the cap, the company still has costs for each transaction beyond your cap.

>> **The graduated split rollback:** Under this increasingly popular compensation arrangement, which is structured primarily for the benefit of the company, you receive a graduated split, but at the end of each year you roll back to 50/50 or some other established allocation. With this type of rollback, the company has a better chance of making a decent net profit from all earnings. Too often, company expenses and profits are covered by too small a group of agents. By rolling splits back at the beginning of each year, companies ensure that their costs are covered by commission revenue received early in the year. It also motivates agents to increase productivity in the early months to increase their splits over the rest of the year.

WARNING

>> **100 percent commission:** Colloquially, this is known as the rent-a-desk arrangement. Agents on 100 percent commission pay a flat amount monthly to rent space and purchase a few services from the company. From there, they cover all their own costs and retain 100 percent of all the commissions they generate.

You need to be well established and pretty darned successful to do well under this system, and for that reason I don't recommend it for new agents. The risk is too great for beginners because of their lack of experience in creating leads and opportunities for income.

Brokerage fees: Don't bite the hand that feeds you

After compensation arrangements are in place, most brokers add fees to help cover their expenses. Among the most common fees to expect are transaction fees, fees to cover errors and omissions insurance, and franchise fees.

>> **Transaction fees:** Many brokers charge agents a per-transaction fee of somewhere between $150 and $500 to cover the cost of processing the paperwork that accompanies a real estate sale.

PASSING THE BUCK

I started charging my clients a transaction fee of $150 in 1993. At that time, I was among the first in the country to do so, joined by only a few other high-producing agents. Over the years, I raised the amount to $495. Today, it's the real estate companies that are charging the transaction fees to the agents. However, with a little advance planning and sales tact, you can pass the transaction fees along to your clients.

The first step in being able to charge a transaction fee is believing that you're worth the additional money. You can't charge the fee if you don't believe in your extra value because you won't be able to defend why you're worth more. Everyone is quick to point out that real estate commissions are negotiable. If that's the case, why not charge more? If your service is better, your skills are better, and the outcome for your clients is achieved with less risk, you're worth more money.

To show my value, I explain to clients that when I first started real estate sales, agents had three-page agreements, whereas now some agreements are more than 50 pages long with disclosures included. I also note that agents now manage multiple inspections (such as radon testing, pest inspections, and so on) when before only one inspection was performed. Transactions involve more processing than ever before.

REMEMBER

» **Errors and omissions (E&O) insurance fees:** Many brokers charge an E&O insurance fee on a per-deal basis, which often adds $100 to $250 to each transaction to cover premium costs. E&O insurance protects professionals should they make a mistake in service or representation. In such an event, the insurance company covers legal fees and settlement costs.

» **Franchise fees:** If you join a real estate franchise, expect to pay approximately 6 percent of your gross revenue every time you complete a transaction. The percentage is established by the franchise contract. It doesn't graduate or fluctuate based on your productivity.

What really matters? Looking at size, online presence, training, and market share

Personally, I think size can make up for other deficiencies in real estate companies, and here's why:

» **Companies with a large number of agents create a large listing inventory.** As a newer agent, you'll find it easier to get other agents to let you post and advertise on their properties, leverage their properties online on your own website, market behind their inventory with direct mail, and work open houses for them if they have 15 rather than 2 listings apiece.

» **Large companies enjoy economies of scale, allowing them to provide a greater degree of service at a lower price per agent.** As a result, they can offer more training, more marketing, and more exposure than smaller companies can afford to provide in most cases.

» **Because of their size, large companies can negotiate better rates for online marketing ads; website-development costs; click-through ad banners; SEO costs; third-party online lead generators like Zillow, Trulia, and Realtor.com; and mortgage rates.** However, large companies follow no hard-and-fast rule for how they direct their savings. Some companies decide to turn a larger profit margin for the company. Others — the ones you'll most want to join — pass on the benefits to their clients and agents.

» **Large companies hold a dominant portion of market share in their communities.** As a result, they have the most prominent reputations and earn the greatest slice of regional business. They tend to have more inbound business, which can really help a newer agent.

TIP

In the end, you should base your choice on the office attributes rather than on the size of the real estate office. However, when two companies have equal attributes, let size tip your decision.

Prioritizing your needs and expectations in a company

Before you can determine whether a company is a good match for you, you have to be clear about your own values and expectations so you can see if they're shared and supported by the company you choose to work with.

Know your values

Ask yourself: What are your core values? What beliefs and principles guide your life? What would you hold dear even if it proved to be a competitive disadvantage in the marketplace? Even if the marketplace or business climate changed, what aspects of how you work are nonnegotiable?

Here's an example. In my company, Real Estate Champions, one of our core values is "exceptional execution of the fundamentals." I believe in and have seen the truly astounding results that occur when people apply the fundamentals of sales and business consistently, without reliance on shortcuts or miracle marketing systems. In truth, our company commitment to the fundamentals means that we attract fewer people. Obviously, it's easier to sell agents on magic formulas that require no work, energy, discipline, or rigorous activity. But in spite of the competitive disadvantage it presents, our company belief in disciplined fundamentals doesn't ever change. It's a core value, and it's a truth we adhere to.

REMEMBER

When choosing an agency, know what you stand for, what you honor, and what you believe in. After you study yourself, you can then study the values of the company you're considering to ensure that your belief systems align.

Establish your expectations

What do you expect from yourself over the next 6 to 12 months? What do you expect from your company over the same time period? What will your new company expect from you? What does it consider to be the minimum standard for new-agent production? What does it consider to be average, or good, production? What do you need to earn in income to make this worthwhile for you? What is the most that anyone has ever produced in the company? What is the most anyone has done in your market?

Also, beyond expectations for the next year, I suggest looking a few years down the road. What is the progression of income and units likely to be over the next few years?

Before you choose a company, align your expectations with the company's by taking these steps:

>> **Set your goals and expectations for the upcoming year.** Establish your targets for gross income, number of transactions, number of listings taken and sold, and number of buyer sales.

>> **Know the expectations and typical production levels that exist within the company you're considering.** If your targets are high, you need to join a company where established inventories and support systems help you jump-start your business for quick success. If your aims are lower, you need to be sure that they match company expectations for new agents.

TIP

After you establish your goals, keep them in front of you at all times. Carry them with you. Put them on your screen saver; program them into your smartphone; and write them on index cards and stick them on your sun visor, bathroom mirror, TV set, or anywhere else they'll catch your eye repeatedly throughout the day.

Creating Your Agency Short List

With all the options for where to "hang your license," you want to shrink your list down to your top two or three firms quickly so you can really study each one. The upcoming section helps you winnow it down.

Completing your homework

Follow these steps as you research each of your top-choice companies:

1. **Rank your top-choice agencies based on your views as a consumer.** Before you color your opinion with facts or market statistics, ask yourself: What is each company's reputation? Based only on information available to the general public, what impression does the company make? I tell you to do this because when you join a firm, you automatically acquire this reputation.

2. **Engage the thoughts of your friends and family.** You can post a question on your Facebook page about which company your friends would select to represent themselves as sellers and buyers. You will get a host of answers and consumer feedback. Try to get them to focus on companies, not specific agents. Imagine how valuable it would be to know that a large portion of your sphere of influence has had a bad experience with a company you're considering.

3. **Evaluate each company's market share.** Determine the portion of all real estate business that each firm captures in its geographic area. Then figure out what percentage of the market it commands in the specialized area in which

you'll be working. (See the sidebar "Determining market share" for some how-to information.)

Like many real estate agents, I knew I couldn't cover my whole market area of Portland, Oregon. I knew I needed to specialize in specific bedroom communities and suburbs in order to serve my clients well. In selecting a company, I first evaluated the firm's overall Portland market share to discover its general market strength, but then I also evaluated the market share it held in the suburban communities I selected.

DETERMINING MARKET SHARE

Before selecting a real estate company, find out how well it competes in its market area by determining the share of the market it commands. (If the company you're considering has more than one office, work out the numbers for the office you're likely to join.)

To assess market share, first get answers to the following questions:

- How many listings did the company you're considering take last year? How many listings did it sell? How many houses did it fail to sell?
- How many buyer-represented sales did it make?
- How many agents work at the company?

Then obtain similar statistics for the entire market area. By dividing the firm's performance by the total market area performance, you discover the firm's market share. For instance, if the market area produced 1,000 listings and 400 came from a single company, that company has a 40 percent market share (400 / 1,000 = .40).

To obtain information, begin by asking each company to provide you with its statistics. Any company with a competitive advantage knows and wants to share its statistics, and many are also willing to provide comparisons between themselves and their competition.

Also check with your local board of real estate agents, where you can access several varieties of information, including the total number of agents in the marketplace and the number of agents per company.

The multiple listing service, or MLS, which compiles information on all homes for sale, shares information on sales, listings, pending transactions, and homes that failed to sell — on a market, company, and individual office basis.

For another good resource, consult your local business journal. Most produce annual lists ranking companies by industry, and nearly all have special sections devoted to the real estate business.

4. **Assess how production is distributed within each company.** Ask whether a number of agents contribute to the company's success or whether a few agents or even just one person carries production.

WARNING

I have a coaching client who creates 27 percent of the revenue and 42 percent of the listings in her office. Her leaving would be a huge blow to the company and the agents whose income is reliant on her presence and listings. I advise new agents to steer away from this type of situation.

5. **Go online to evaluate presence.** Use search engines to see the ranking of the company's website. The higher the ranking, the more the leads. Also search on key real estate sites like Zillow, Trulia, and Realtor.com to figure out the company's position on sites with listing inventory. You can evaluate the listing quality, as well as price ranges, locations, marketing materials, virtual tours, and so on. Review the online profiles of agents in the company on the third-party sites. Do they have a lot of reviews? Are their profiles complete and well written? By doing your reconnaissance on a few agents in the company, you will be able to see if the company is helping these agents online.

6. **Drive around your market area to determine each company's visibility.** In today's technological world, you can do much of your research online, but if you're still stumped, count the number of signs you see for each firm you're considering. Also, evaluate the quality and array of homes presented by each company. You may discover that a firm has a lot of signs, but they're all concentrated in a small geographic area or a specific price range. Beware of these firms because they could limit your opportunity. For example, if a company's business is concentrated at the lower end of the marketplace, securing higher-priced listings may be more difficult.

7. **Evaluate each company's marketing.** Monitor media exposure for at least a few weeks to gain a good perspective of the scope and nature of a company's marketing campaign and its exposure. Check out Craigslist postings for frequency, as well as strategy and information. Check out their Facebook page, Instagram accounts, and Twitter feeds. Review what has been tweeted and posted in the last few months and what responses, shares, and retweets they have generated.

Is the company using traditional methods of marketing as well? Print media, such as newspapers and home magazines, aren't as effective as they used to be, but some sellers still want their homes to appear in them. While monitoring the media, do the following:

- Study the ads carefully. Is the company using classified or display ads? What is the size and exposure? Do the ads feature individual agents? Could you see yourself in these ads?

- Go to the grocery store and pick up copies of real estate magazines. Are the companies you're considering featured? What do their ads look like? Are they linking it with Call Capture or text-back features?

REMEMBER

If you see marketing that is paid for by individual agents of your selected company, each featuring his or her own listings, you have proof that you'll be working with agents who are willing to invest in themselves and their businesses.

If you see marketing strategies featuring the listings of a number of agents from your selected company, you know that agents who don't have enough listings to fill a whole page (like you in the early days) can achieve advertising visibility by buying into a company ad on a per-slot basis.

8. **Visit the company's website.** More than 90 percent of all consumers now search the web for properties. Is the company's website easy to use? Are the listings easy to find and navigate? Are agents featured on individual pages within the company site?

Does the site have a forced registration? *Forced registration* is when someone comes to the site to look at properties but they are forced to register their information to continue. These are effective lead-creation strategies that will help you generate leads.

TIP

Act like an online shopper and find out whether the site performs well in online searches. Go to major search engines and directories, such as Google, Yahoo!, MSN, and Bing, and conduct a search for real estate in your market area. How well a company's site ranks in the search results affects the number and quality of leads you may generate.

Ask 12 key questions

Your moment in front of a prospective broker is a pivotal one: The broker is sizing you up to determine whether you fit well in the company. Instead of treating the session like a job interview, use it to ask questions and obtain information that enables you to understand the unique attributes of the agency. Ask the following questions:

1. **What is your training program for new agents?** The old-school approach of "Here's your desk. Here's your phone. Go get 'em." won't prepare you for success. You're looking for a legitimate, established, multi-week training program that extends beyond contract writing and gets into the fields of prospecting, lead follow-up, online and offline lead generation, skills and strategies, sales presentations, objection handling, and closing techniques.

2. When was the last time you updated your training program?

Follow this question with: What did you change about the program? Growing companies regularly update training and techniques. If a company is still teaching the philosophies and techniques of the 1970s in today's dramatically changed environment, that's about all you need to know.

3. How many new agents do you train annually?

REMEMBER

Companies that regularly recruit and train new agents usually have better training programs than those that don't.

Find out the success rate of the agents who complete the program. Ask what percentage of trained agents continues with the company for at least one year. What percentage lasts two years?

REMEMBER

As you evaluate the responses, remember that the North American real estate industry is having a growth period. There are more new agents entering real estate sales than in years past. The market has some influence on the volume of new agents and the success that they achieve.

4. Can I talk with a few of your agents?

TIP

Try to get the perspectives of four to five agents, including a fairly new agent, an agent who is struggling to produce, a solid producer, and a top-performing agent. This diverse group provides a wonderful view of the company's training, education, support, and pathway to success or failure.

5. How will you help me generate business?

Ask this question and then wait. Give the broker time to think, and expect to hear responses that fall all over the map. Some make specific mention of open houses and floor time. (*Floor time* is when agents are assigned times to take inbound leads, whether online or offline, or meet with walk-in prospects. The task is usually assigned on a rotating schedule in shifts that last several hours.) Some discuss the frequency and scope of marketing efforts. Some offer to pay for business cards. Some send marketing materials announcing your association with the company to those in your sphere of influence.

Use the answers to this question to assess

- Whether the company is committed to helping you succeed.
- Whether the company has a system or process that works to generate business for new agents.

6. Whom do I turn to when I have a question or problem?

REMEMBER

As you climb the steep learning curve ahead of you, you need to know who will help you find solutions to your problems. You need assurance that the person will be accessible. Make sure to ask whether this person is available during regular office hours.

7. What type of computer and software is provided for me?

Some companies make numerous high-quality computers available to agents. Some companies support agents with company database management programs, intranet sites, Internet sites, and even electronic marketing pieces or e-cards. With other companies, you're completely on your own to purchase the technology tools you need. You'll need your own computer, tablet, and smartphone, as well.

8. Do you have regular office meetings?

Most companies have moved away from weekly sales meetings, and, based on the assessment of our coaching clients, most weren't very useful anyway. When brokers or managers prepare and conduct staff training, however, the meetings rise to a whole different level of effectiveness. So, be sure to ask whether the meetings are training or informational sessions. Are they done online, or do you need to be present in the office?

9. Do you have an agent coaching program?

TIP

The hottest, fastest way to improve performance is through coaching. Coaching provides structure, accountability, performance measuring, training, and expert guidance. Find out whether the company you're considering embraces coaching as a way to increase agent performance.

10. What does it cost me to have my license with you?

Most agents enter real estate with limited cash to invest in a new business. Yet they need to fund business cards, errors and omissions insurance, MLS fees, Board of Real Estate Agents dues, and licensing fees — which can easily total more than $1,000. Some of these costs must be paid up front, and others can be withheld from your first commission check.

11. What's my commission split?

WARNING

Save this question until late in your interview. Certainly the answer affects your immediate-term income, but I think far too many agents put undue emphasis on the commission split as they make the decision to "hang their license" with a certain company.

Whether you receive a 50/50 split or a 60/40 split for the first year means very little over the course of your career. What's more important to your success is the investment the company is willing to make in terms of your training, education, services, leads, and opportunities. The company deserves a return for the investment it's making and the risk it's taking.

12. Why should I select this company?

In essence, you're asking: Why should I join your company over all my other options? What makes your company better, different, and more successful?

Raise a caution flag if the broker hesitates, struggles, or rambles with the answer. If the broker can't convincingly display belief and conviction that the company is better, you may have a similarly difficult time answering if a prospect later asks you the same question.

Left-side/right-side your research

After you complete your interviews with company brokers, put your assessments down on paper. On a single sheet, list all your final company candidates, along with their one-to-ten rankings in each of the following key areas:

- ≫ Initial training
- ≫ Ongoing education
- ≫ Marketplace reputation
- ≫ Market share
- ≫ Office environment
- ≫ Marketing
- ≫ Web presence
- ≫ Lead generation
- ≫ Other agents in the company or office
- ≫ Competence of the broker or manager

TIP

As you compare companies, weigh a few areas more heavily than the others. Especially in the early phase of your career, put special emphasis on a company's training and education offerings. As a close second, pay attention to how much the company is prepared to help you with lead generation and online marketing.

And the winner is?

As you add your scores for each company, give extra points to companies that rate particularly high in training and lead generation.

Then compare your findings with your initial, first-take impression of each company's consumer reputation. Do those with the best reputations also rank the highest in your assessment?

If two companies rank extremely closely in your assessment, you may want to re-interview the brokers or other high-ranking managers. Explain that you're deciding between two companies. I even suggest that you inform each company of your other top contender. This enables them to describe their benefits in direct comparison to the other company, which in turn gives you an indication of their ability to train you in selling based on their presentation against a direct competitor. Then, once again, ask why you should select their company over the other. And carefully weigh the answer.

TIP

When you make the final selection, send hand-written thank-you notes to the companies you didn't select. Thank them for the considerable time and help they provided you. This act alone will position you in the top 5 percent of agents they've ever met. It also keeps the door open in case you seek to work with another firm in the future.

Getting Off to a Fast Start

REMEMBER

When joining a new team, your objective is to blend in with the team. As an inexperienced agent, you should expect scrutiny from your associates. Many will greet you with a wait-and-see attitude for the simple reason that fewer than one in five agents succeeds in the long term while the rest wash out of real estate sales. Your fellow agents are waiting to see which category you'll fit into.

Building a relationship with your manager

I rarely see a broker or manager with high expectations of a new agent. Instead, they focus on potential. They believe that a new agent can become a top producer, but they cautiously reserve judgment until they see the quality of the agent's action. The key to success is to quickly move from "potential" to "performance."

Even though they're cautious of judging your performance, your manager is on your side, rooting and pulling for you to realize your goals, dreams, and potential.

The best way to build a relationship with your manager is to achieve results by taking the following steps along the way:

1. **Involve your manager as you set your goals.**

As you establish specific, concrete, attainable, and exciting goals, ask your manager for input regarding what you should do daily, weekly, and monthly to achieve your desired outcomes.

2. **Seek your manager's input as you lay out an activity plan.**

Gain advice regarding which avenues you should follow to achieve success and what you should do daily to bring you closer to your goals.

3. **Ask your manager to help monitor your activities.**

REMEMBER

By asking your manager to monitor and coach your performance, you separate yourself from 90 percent of the other real estate agents. Although nearly all agents want to improve, few are willing to make the changes necessary for success.

4. **Request a weekly meeting.**

Aim to sit down with your manager at the same time and on the same day each week. Some weeks the meeting may last only 15 minutes, during which time your manager can review your performance based on the contacts made, leads generated, appointments booked, appointments conducted, and properties listed or sold. Other weeks you may work on specific training topics.

5. **Ask for help with marketing and lead generation.**

Creating prospect opportunities can really separate the high producers from the marginal ones. Although service may be the same or similar, the person with the most leads usually wins.

Understanding your manager's role in your success

Of course you hope for a positive manager who supports you with a high level of encouragement, but even a negative manager can play a positive role in your success. It's counterintuitive, but when a sad-sack manager tells you that you can't accomplish your aims, the comment often ignites conviction and taps into a huge reservoir of "I'll show you" attitude.

A number of years ago, I coached an agent in Medford, Oregon, named Sheila Gunderson. She had a burning desire to close $24 million in sales over the next year. This amount was up from a current sales volume of about $10 million and was well above the top performance level of any Medford agent to date.

Together we constructed a business plan outlining how she would achieve her $24 million goal. With total excitement she took it to her broker. He laughed, telling her that no one in the market area had ever come close to $24 million, and asked her, "Who do you think you are?"

When I heard her manager's comments, I immediately knew that they would only fuel Sheila's fire. And they did. She blew right past the $24 million that she had projected and closed the year at more than $27 million, adding more than $17 million in sales to her previous year's performance.

TIP

Whatever input your manager gives you — even if it's negative — use it to fuel your fire.

Earning respect from your manager

Follow this simple formula to earn respect from anyone, including your manager:

» **Do what you said you would do.** Get to your office early each day, whether it's your home office or real estate office, and be proactive about prospecting and generating leads. The vast majority of agents wait for business to come to them and then make excuses for why it never shows up. Take action instead.

» **Improve your knowledge and education.** The vast majority of agents attend training courses to earn continuing education credit (or CE credit), rather than to master specific new skills or abilities.

I can't even count how many times I've been asked whether the training course I teach is CE-credit approved. I always answer with the same response and follow-up question. My response is that my course isn't CE certified because those who evaluate courses don't grant CE credit to courses that teach attendees how to make more money. My follow-up question is always, "Do you really want a CE-credit course, or do you want a course that teaches agents how to make more money?"

TIP

To earn your manager's respect, attend courses and education sessions that teach you how to make more money. Then implement what you discover after the session.

Forming partnerships inside your company

To get the real estate job done, you'll form many partnerships — some of which will last as long as a single deal and others of which will last for years and years. In this section, I take a look at those who will join you in the dance of real estate sales.

Earning respect from your peers

The sales arena — and certainly the real estate sales arena — is a magnet for those with big egos. To earn the respect of other real estate agents, you have to perform and succeed. Your peers will base their respect for you on how they feel you perform in the following three areas:

» **Production growth:** When you produce, you get noticed. In fact, many of your associates will notice your success even before you see a commission check because they'll notice your name on the company listings board.

At first, they may attribute your success to luck, thinking "He got good lead calls" or "He hit a hot streak," but as your listings keep appearing, their respect will build.

REMEMBER

Few agents perform consistently over the long haul. Most have a good month, quarter, or year, but only a rare few constantly finish at the top of the income list. However, when you do, your peers will most definitely notice and share their respect.

>> **Business ethics:** Because the commissions can be large, many people feel that acting unethically is acceptable. For many agents, money, or the opportunity to make money, too often exposes character flaws.

Be an exception. Maintaining your values even in the most competitive situations enhances your own self-respect, while also earning the respect of your peers.

>> **Life balance:** Agents notice and respect other agents who have their priorities in order, who manage not to be controlled by their businesses, and who carve out good chunks of time to spend with their friends and families. Few agents manage to earn a large income while also protecting their personal time. You'll be recognized and respected as one of the best agents in the country if you can strike this important balance. (Check out Chapter 17 for more on making the most of your time.)

Working with agents in your office

Nearly all agents are independent contractors earning no base salary and depending entirely on their own skills, actions, and activities to create income. This pay structure breeds competition within the industry and within each company. The trick is to balance that competition with cooperation.

WARNING

Striking this balance isn't always easy. Invariably, you end up competing with agents inside your own firm for clients and dollars. One example is finding that the agent in the next cubicle is working on the same lead you are. This situation is usually the result of a prospect who chose to work with several agents at one time but who didn't reveal the lack of allegiance to any of them. Later, when one agent writes the contract — after both agents showed the home — well, you can imagine the office arguments I've seen. This situation certainly presents a moment where a good broker makes a difference. A good broker can mediate the issues between the agents, making sure that the client is getting good service while handling the interpersonal issues between the agents.

To succeed in this competitive office environment, follow this advice:

>> **Use the other agents as mentors.** Nearly all agents owe a debt to some other agent who helped them along the road to success, and they feel a sense of obligation to repay the favor by being similarly helpful to a new agent like

you. Find a mentor. When you do, be respectful of the mentor's time, take action on the mentor's advice or counsel, report back on the success you achieve, and say thanks over and over again.

>> **Hold open houses for other agents.** Open houses can be burdens on the schedules of busy agents. Open houses are still popular, and many sellers expect agents to conduct one. In low-inventory markets they become solid lead generators because buyers came to them hoping to find a home. More buyers today fit into the DIY philosophy. Offer to serve as a stand-in host, supporting your associates while also giving yourself an opportunity to create prospects and business.

>> **Ask other agents to work with you on listings.** If you lack skill or experience in a certain price range or geographic area, you risk losing a listing to a more established agent. Be preemptive instead. Ask a more established agent in your firm to co-list the property with you. Through this short-term partnership, you capture the opportunity to expand your business while you learn and earn. Don't focus on "what percentage" you're giving away. Focus on how much you can learn.

Cooperating with agents in your marketplace

More than 90 percent of all real estate transactions come through the MLS, which exposes their availability to agents throughout the marketplace. As a result, you're constantly working jointly with agents from other firms to achieve sales. As you work with these agents, form cooperative relationships by following this simple advice:

>> **Deal with the other agents honestly and fairly.** Give them the information they need about your client or property without giving too many details. Always remain aware of the fiduciary responsibility and privacy protection you owe your client.

TIP

>> **Involve brokers when necessary.** If problems arise between you and the other agent, enlist the help of your broker. If paperwork comes back too slowly or you feel you're not getting the full facts, get your broker, or the other agent's broker, involved. Move quickly if you sense that a lack of cooperation is affecting your client's security in keeping the transaction together.

Developing strategic partnerships

Mortgage originators and loan officers lead the list of strategic partners who can help you get real estate deals done. These people play an essential role in securing your clients' loans. They can help you expand your business through several avenues:

>> **They can help you serve lower-credit clients.** Mortgage originators who are skilled and have a broad line of loan products are open to loan requests from a broadly diverse economic segment, which increases your pool of prospects.

>> **Some mortgage originators invest in joint marketing efforts.** These programs may consist of sending mailers to your sphere of past clients or to prospects in your geographic area, buying email lists and responding with email marketing messages, buying website ads, or paying for a banner ad along the bottom of your real estate magazine. Some will split the cost of online lead generation on Facebook ads and pay-per-click campaigns. Depending on the arrangement, the mortgage originator may pay for some or all of the costs involved.

>> **Mortgage originators can help convert leads.** Most agents make the mistake of getting the mortgage originator involved in a transaction too late. They wait until after they've secured the client relationship to introduce their loan partner. Make the introduction earlier in the lead-conversion process. Tandem lead conversion is a powerful strategic-partnering technique.

REMEMBER

The odds of lead conversion rise significantly when two strategic partners are working the same contact. When one of you achieves a face-to-face meeting, you both win, because either of you can cross-sell the services of the other.

>> **The mortgage originator can play the role of a prospect's professional advisor.** Although most prospects view agents as salespeople, their psychology toward mortgage originators is quite different. They tend to see and trust mortgage originators as consultants rather than as the salespeople they truly are. By forming strategic partnerships with your mortgage originator, you can put that psychology to work and secure more clients more quickly. I've seen agents increase their closed transactions by more than 25 percent through this simple tandem lead-conversion approach.

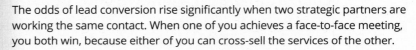
TIP

Also form a strategic partnership with your title company. Title representatives can help you conduct research and establish geographic mailing lists. They can also provide statistics that help you see what homes have sold and at what prices over past years, including which areas and neighborhoods have seen the highest number of sales.

Each state and province has different rules regarding how much information title representatives can share. Check with a title representative or your broker to find out the possibilities in your market area.

Chapter **3**

Mastering Any Marketplace

Each and every real estate marketplace brings its own unique challenges and opportunities. The agents and companies that recognize those unique opportunities before the competition can seize, get ahead, or gain a foothold or advantage in any market condition. All real estate marketplaces experience shifts and cycles — a cycle of strong appreciation in property values, then a cycle of flat appreciation, and then loss of appreciation for a cycle. A cycle could last a few years, 7 years, or 10 years. I have experienced four complete cycles of appreciation and correction in my almost 30 years in the industry.

Agents often wish for a shift in the present market condition. A few years ago, when we had lots of foreclosed properties, short sales, and challenges in getting homes sold, agents wished for less inventory and more buyers. The mantra was: *If only the market would change.* This is not a news flash, but . . . it did! We are now in a seller's market with low inventory, many buyers, and multiple-offer situations on highly sought-after properties and areas. My comment to agents then, and now, is: *The marketplace will shift. That is guaranteed. Our job is to not wish it were easier, but to make ourselves better.* Make yourself more skilled for any marketplace. Know the right steps, strategies, and skills that will ensure your success in any marketplace.

A Seller's Marketplace Seems Easy

For some reason, most agents wish for a seller's marketplace. The number of new real estate agents hits a peak in seller's markets. The stature and profile of real estate, because of media and public perception, rises in a seller's market, and the competition increases exponentially.

The National Association of Realtors (NAR) defines a *seller's market* as a marketplace where the inventory of active listings on the marketplace is less than 5–6 months. The lower inventory of homes, or absorption rate, the stronger the seller's market. For example: If you have 5,000 homes for sale in your marketplace, and 1,500 homes sell each month, to calculate absorption rate you take the 5,000 divided by 1,500 and you have 3.33 months' worth or inventory. That would be a strong seller's market.

In this market, homes will sell quickly if priced reasonably. If the trend continues long enough, some agents start to discount fees to try to attract listing inventory. Sellers become emboldened. They become more demanding in their prices for their homes, are less flexible on repairs, and can become more emotional because they know they are in the driver's seat.

The *residual value* of a listed property is reduced — the ability for the property when marketed to create leads for the listing agent. Real estate sales is an inventory business. When you have listing inventory, you have something to market to attract both buyers and sellers. When a seller's market occurs, the days on the market of your listings starts to shrink. Your time to market a property, and thereby yourself, may be slashed in half or more.

This can mean the number of leads that you create from a listing can be slashed in half or more. If the normal days on the market in your area is 60 days, in a seller's market it could drop to 27 days, and for really high-demand homes in a seller's market, it could be less than a week. The number of web visits and web leads will drop. The number of leads you will generate from Zillow, Trulia, and Realtor.com will be reduced. You might have properties that sell so quickly that they're sold before you even do an open house.

REMEMBER

We need listing inventory in real estate sales to create leverage and momentum. That is hardest to do in low listing inventory markets.

The seller's marketplace for agents, in my view, is the most challenging, hardest marketplace. For the skilled agents that have prospecting, lead follow-up, and overall sales skills, it is even more so because of the leverage lost due to homes that they list and then sell so quickly. These agents lose some of their overall advantage dramatically more in their listing inventory. The marginal agents who have buyers utilize the inventory to create income. If you have listings, you will attract buyers over time, but the minute a listing moves to pending status, its lead-creation value becomes nil.

The coming soon listing strategy

To combat this challenge, the "coming soon" listing strategy was invented. In a seller's market, you must employ a coming soon strategy with your listing inventory. I want to disclose up front that many agents become frustrated by this strategy. You can't listen to the naysayers. When you take a listing, you represent the interests of the seller. The best interests of the seller may run counter to what other agents might want in your marketplace and the buyers as well.

REMEMBER

In the coming soon strategy, you are working to extend marketing time, build urgency for your listing, and create exposure, all while not negatively effecting days on the market.

In our online, information-based world, the length of time any seller has been on the market is well known. It is known to every agent in the MLS — along with the history of the property, when it's been on and off the market, and at what price. The days on the market will either generate urgency or apathy on the part of buyers and other agents in the marketplace. The longer a property is on the market, the more apathy takes root. Days on the market are the mortal enemy of the seller.

The coming soon strategy starts with pre-marketing a property, which does not trigger the clock of days on the market. You want to put your regular real estate sign on the property, with a Coming Soon banner or sign rider. You can also use the Coming Soon section on Zillow. Some MLSes now have "coming soon" sections to market to agents through. Doing social media marketing, Facebook posts, ads, and even direct mail and door knocking are all options. All this happens without fully imputing the property into the MLS as an active listing. Your seller must approve of these steps, and you must disclose why.

TIP

When you go live on the market, delay showings for a few days to create urgency and a backlog of showings. This creates more showing activity in a shorter length of time. In the correct version of the coming soon strategy, neither you nor your company is allowed to show the property prior to other agents. That would be unfair and contrary to representing your seller in achieving the best possible buyer and price. This is where some agents make their mistakes.

The final piece of coming soon is delaying any offers to be presented for a few more days. This gives ample time for all agents to become aware of the property, show the property, and encourage their buyer to craft a competitive offer for your seller's review. Additionally, it will ensure that you have the opportunity to conduct a mega open house for your seller. This certainly benefits the seller in attracting buyers to the home.

The attraction of new competition

When a seller's market is in full swing, the volume of agents reactivating their licenses is dramatically increased. This increase in competition can dilute the number of listings any one agent can acquire through that larger number of licensed agents. Everyone has a friend or acquaintance who is a real estate agent in a seller's market. In these times, if you are stopped by the police they might ask you for your real estate license rather than your driver's license because more people would be likely to have a real estate license.

Sellers don't think they need you

The people who are considering selling see the apparent ease with which homes are selling. They see For Sale signs changing to Sold signs in a few weeks. They get the impression that all they need to do is put a sign in the ground, create an Internet listing, and get their home on Zillow, and it will sell easily. They start to say, "Any agent can sell our home in this market."

REMEMBER

The truth is, any agent might be able to attract a buyer, but that buyer might not be the *right* buyer. The buyer who might pay a premium — who is more creditworthy, more earnest, and able to perform — probably won't be found by a less-skilled listing agent. The creation of multiple offers, protection, proper counsel, and guidance can't be achieved by hiring any old agent. Those are the hallmarks that a highly skilled agent must sell as value to sellers who think selling the home will be easy or who feel they want to consider an agent who might be cheaper in cost.

You will also experience sellers who go it alone because they feel they can. When it appears easy due to a seller's market, the market sees a surge in For Sale By Owner properties. This creates an opportunity for an agent who is undaunted by the cavalier attitude of sellers doing it on their own. Some sellers will have success on their own. The vast majority will not. The increase in FSBO listings can be a wonderful income stream for an agent willing to patiently follow up and let the sellers discern that it might be more challenging than they thought.

Demonstrating your value to sellers

In a seller's market you have to demonstrate your value beyond just getting their home sold. Their mind-set is that finding a buyer is easy. You need to highlight your other services in other areas beside the marketing, finding a buyer, and making the sale. You could demonstrate your value through the coming soon strategy. If you track your numbers, you could prove that you create more multiple offers, a higher list-to-sales price on average, the security and protection from a properly crafted contract, or that you have a lower level of transaction fallout as examples of value.

Buyers in a seller's market are looking for some measure of leverage and negotiating power. They have very little, at least initially, with the seller. Their real opportunity is at contingency removal a few weeks down the road after a home inspection. At that time the seller has likely finalized their plans for moving. They have a home they want, have laid down the groundwork for the move, and have even spent many hours in preparation for the move. The buyer at that point can come back and work to secure more favorable terms or price. It doesn't always work out advantageous to the buyer who tries to negotiate at that point, but they do have more potential leverage than they had when the offer was first accepted.

REMEMBER

Even if the seller sells the property in a few days, if the transaction with the buyer falls apart, when the home goes back on the market in the MLS it will show two to three weeks on the market. That clearly is not to the seller's advantage. As an agent, the security and protection you provide to a seller to help them avoid this worst-case scenario is extremely valuable. These extra days and weeks on the market, in many cases, can cost the seller thousands of dollars.

TIP

The Big Three statistics demonstrate your overall value and results to a seller. You should know these three stats for yourself and the MLS:

>> Average list-to-sale price ratio

>> Average days on the market

>> Your listings-sold-to-listings-taken ratio

The list-to-sale price ratio, when compared to your market's average for all agents, can show that you sell homes for more money than other agents. If your average is 98 percent and the MLS average is 95 percent, you can express to a seller you create a 3 percent premium for your sellers. On their $300,000 home, that would equate to $9,000 more in their pocket in net dollars at closing.

Fewer days on the market would reduce the number of mortgage payments, tax payments, and maintenance costs on a home they no longer want to own. Fewer days on the market would also connect to heightened buyer urgency on their home — and the stronger negotiating power they would have with potential buyers and agents.

A higher listings-sold-to-listings-taken ratio percentage would indicate reduced risk on the part of a seller listing with you. They could have better peace of mind because of your skill and results. It also proves that whatever your marketing strategy is, it is working more effectively than that of the other agents that they might consider selecting in the marketplace to list their home.

Reducing the effect of discount brokers

In seller's markets some agents become desperate. That desperation equates to staying in business at all costs. Because they have limited value or can't sell their value well, their only option is to reduce their fees. They compete on cost because they can't on value. There is an age-old equation in sales:

Value = Benefits – Cost

In a seller's market, because the seller might perceive the value of a full-service agent to be reduced, they mentally move to the cost side of the equation. Agents who can't clearly define their benefits have to maneuver cost so value is more aligned.

Numerous "discount" or fee-flexible real estate companies enter real estate in seller's markets, Some offer rebate models. In the last few years, a number of them have raised venture capital money to launch and build up their market share while still losing money. It's unlikely that many will survive a market shift, due to their economic model. All you have to do is look up the history of discount real estate companies like Foxton's, Help U Sell, or Assist To Sell. Foxton's is out of business, and Help U Sell and Assist To Sell are shadows of their former selves. This is also true of agents and teams that run a discount model. The costs of the real estate business are substantial. There is a reasonable margin that must be maintained to be successful.

REMEMBER

By being clear on your value and what you can provide and how they benefit the seller, you can reduce the effects of agents, teams, and companies who sell cost savings exclusively. Be aware of whom you are up against in even listing presentations. You can't afford to get blindsided that they are considering a discount option. (If you want to become highly skilled at the listing presentation, turn to Chapter 12.)

Buyer's Market? No Problem

When a market has shifted to a buyer's marketplace, the mood can sour. Because a buyer's market lacks the energy and urgency of the seller's market, the attitude of everyone — sellers, buyers, and agents — can deteriorate precipitously. The additional shift can create momentum in the opposite direction for your success and career. Because attitude can influence actions and income, it's what you do when you recognize you are in a buyer's market.

You have to look at the positives and opportunities when gripped by a buyer's market. One clear opportunity is the investor niche of the market. When an investor sells their property, they have created liquidity and locked in their long-term gain that they achieved in the appreciation of their property. They have reduced the risk of further reduction on their gain and locked in their appreciation of that asset. In the early stages of a buyer's market, having an investor sell their property can save them from a 10, 20, or even 30 percent drop in value. For investors who have multiple properties or are in retirement or nearing retirement, selling even some of their assets can be the insurance against cataclysmal event like we had with the foreclosure and short sale meltdown of 2008–2012. Those years wiped out huge amounts of equity that took five years to recover.

Another option is an investor selling on a contract, where the buyer puts a substantial down payment down like 25–35 percent in cash. The seller then receives a steady income similar to when they owned the property and received rent. They eliminate the headaches of being a landlord and reduce their risk of the property depreciating. They also only pay the capital gains tax on the amount of funds they have collected thus far. This can reduce their overall tax liability or at least spread it over time rather than a one-time big payment. All while earning interest on the note and trust deed provided to the buyer. For some investors who want to avoid the risk of ownership in a buyer's market, this could be the perfect option.

As a teen and into my 20s, I watched my parents sell off most of their investment properties on a land sales contract. They structured the contracts so that the buyer couldn't pay off the contract until after 10 years of payments had been received. That stipulation guaranteed them 10 years of payments so they clearly could budget their expenditures in their retirement years. They spent years acquiring these properties, renting them to tenants, paying off the mortgages. They then spent years collecting the monthly contract payments from buyers who had put in substantial down payments — so my parents' income was assured. They removed the headaches of being landlords but still received a sizable income each month playing the role of the bank.

REMEMBER

Buyers have a larger sense of fear in a buyer's market. Agents have to deal with that fear head on. The truth is, buyers become frothy in a seller's market and fearful in a buyer's market. The correct approach to wealth is Warren Buffet's advice: "Be fearful when others are greedy, be greedy when others are fearful." Being a contrarian when it comes to real estate will serve you and your clients well. The challenge is the fear and dealing with it correctly.

To properly handle fear in buyers, or in sellers who want to sell to a buyer, you must discuss length of ownership. How long do they expect to own this home or investment property they are considering? If the property is a home they intend to raise their family in, and it's a ten-year property ownership timeframe, the "perfect timing" of hitting the very bottom or even the top of the market is less important. If you take any ten-year period of time in the history in most markets, real estate has appreciated. The peak of the market in pre-crash 2007 was the highest prices paid for homes in history. Then came the correction: 22 percent was lost in some markets; other markets lost 50 percent. Nationally, in 2017, based on the Case-Shiller index of home value in the 20 largest markets, the market is 4 percent above its 2007 peak. A person who held on during the correction would be fine today.

The vast majority of people buying real estate look brilliant after ten years. That period of time of ownership allows any negative cycle to be absorbed. I bought a commercial property in the summer of 2007. My timing could not have been worse. I watched the value go down for years, eventually dropping to 50 percent of what I paid for it. I decided to hold on to the property and just ride the value down with the expectation it would go back up.

I could have given the property back to the bank or done a short sale. Those were options at that time, and many people were taking advantage of them. But I knew my loss in value would be restored if I held it long enough. I also knew that by using a deed in lieu of foreclosure, or short selling the property, my personal credit and FICO score would be severely affected. I would lose hundreds of points on my FICO score and be unable to buy property for a while. (In *short selling* a property, you secure a buyer and then ask the bank to take less than what is owed on the mortgage. The bank takes the loss rather than the seller.) Given the then-current nature of the marketplace, with large inventories of houses, commercial buildings, and apartments selling for 40, 50, and 60 percent of previous value, I needed unblemished credit so I could acquire assets in the heavily discounted market. It proved to be the correct decision because I was able to secure numerous investment properties that more than made up for my poor timing on my summer of 2007 purchase.

I continued to make my payments, collect my rents, and pay my taxes. The rents also dropped so I had a net negative each month when that happened. When you fast forward almost ten years now, the value has been fully restored. My equity after ten years of paying a mortgage has improved. I have gotten strong tax advantages from depreciation of the building. I recently refinanced the building because of the increase in value and dropped my interest rate by 2 percent. I secured a 15-year mortgage that only changed my monthly payment by $6 over the previous long-term mortgage. I will now own the property free and clear in less than 14 years.

Do you even want sellers?

When it gets more challenging to sell properties due to a buyer's market, many agents shun listings. They feel listings are too difficult to sell so they stop pursuing them. That is one of the biggest mistakes ever.

REMEMBER

In any market condition, you want listings. You list to last in this business.

The shift that you make is that you only want listings from people who are motivated to sell. They have to sell and are willing to do what's necessary based on current market conditions to sell. The people who would *like* to sell or *want* to sell — you may not want them as listing clients. Their desire to sell might not be great enough.

You also want to monitor the different price points as well. For example, if you find that the upper end of the marketplace has too many listings and competition, you might tighten your requirements further. If the absorption rate jumps to 18 months or more in the upper end, you only take listings of sellers willing to price or accept offers below what the market value for their home is presently. That's because you are in a strong buyer's market and prices of homes are dropping. You always want sellers who are motivated and willing to do what the market dictates to sell.

Where to find leads when they're scarce

You can target investors from the seller or the buyer side. You can also target *move-down* buyers — those who have owned a home long-term, might have raised their family in the home, and need less space. Those homes tend to be higher in price. That type of a seller who sells in the early stages of a buyer's market will sell their larger home for a higher price today than they might in the future. Rather than exposing themselves to a future 10 percent reduction in value for their $600,000 home, they sell and downsize to a $300,000 home. If the market corrects 10 percent, their old $600,000 home will go down in value $60,000, but their new $300,000 home will only go down $30,000, saving them $30,000 in lost equity. That doesn't even account for the lower maintenance costs and tax savings the downsized home will provide.

TIP

Some of the best lead sources are expired, cancelled, withdrawn, and terminated listings of other agents. Because fewer homes will sell, more sellers are unsuccessful in selling. This lead opportunity is fantastic in a buyer's market. Look for the sellers who *have* to sell, not just want to sell. In a buyer's market, you can create the opportunity to make more money than even in a seller's market by working *expireds* (see Chapter 10 for more).

Convincing sellers — why sell now?

You must understand the seller's goals, objectives, and desires well enough to be able to persuade them of the advantages of selling in a buyer's market. The move-down seller is fairly easy because you can show them monetarily, as mentioned earlier. But there may not be a monetary advantage for the seller to sell in a buyer's market. They may just want to simplify, or have a lower hassle factor, more freedom, less maintenance issues of the home, a change in location or lifestyle. They may want to be closer to family, whether that is children or parents. You have to probe the reasons why they are even considering moving. What are they hoping the move will accomplish for them? What lifestyle do they desire later in life? You have to be willing to gain perspective on your seller to really help them.

Sometimes when you probe that deeply with caring and concern for your client, the best counsel and advice is for them not to move at this time. If that is the case, then you must state that emphatically to them as well. There are plenty of reasons to sell in any market, provided that is really what's best for your seller. If not, keep in touch, follow up, offer updates of the marketplace trends, and wait for the right timing. Your seller will respect that you were honest enough to put their needs above yours.

Once you recognize that the timing might not be right for them, you must determine the exact terms and conditions they need to sell. You will then want to put into your CRM solution a reminder every few months to check back in. You might sort them into sellers that need the marketplace to increase value by 5 percent, 10 percent, or 15 percent before they can sell. When, through your analysis that the market has shifted and appreciation has reached 5 percent, you call and announce the fact to the 5 percent group of potential sellers. You tell them it would make sense to have a second appointment to review their home value and the marketplace numbers.

Building urgency in buyers to act

Because urgency is not automatic in a buyer's market, agents need to create it to move buyers to action. One way to build urgency is to demonstrate to a buyer what a value a particular home might be that they are interested in. Doing a competitive market analysis (CMA) and showing them a seller who is actually undermarket, or a property that they might be able to secure undermarket, can build urgency. Buyers in a buyer's market are attracted to deals. Find deals and present them to your buyers to create more urgency. Show your buyers what the market is really like in the market segment. If they are looking for a home in the XYZ school district between $250,000 and $300,000, show them over the last quarter the number that have sold against the number that's available. By demonstrating the number of buyers that have bought, level of competition, and the average list price compared to sale price, you can potentially heat up their level of interest.

The urgency and desire of a buyer can be increased by getting them to craft an offer. When you get a buyer to take a run at a property that meets their needs, you can sometimes get a seller who really wants to sell to sharpen their pencil and take less money for the property, causing the buyer to get a really good deal . This can heat up the buyer because they start to get emotionally interested and invested in the home and may feel a little more urgent and more flexible about their terms and conditions.

If the buyer's market has been prevalent for a few years and price correction has happened, you can often use the previous value that the home will eventually appreciate back to as a motivator. You can quantify the discount the buyer is receiving from the previous high water mark in value. This can set the bar to a future value level in their mind. Real estate markets appreciate over time. A buyer needs to understand that the opportunity of a buyer's market is contained in the action of actually buying and closing a property.

Shift Happens

A shift in a real estate market is inevitable. That might sound like doom and gloom but it's the truth. *Any* market will shift or change over time. A shift in the market catches most companies and agents off-guard. Is it because it's never happened before? That's typically how agents react, but cycles have been happening in markets, from seller's markets to neutral markets to buyer's markets and back, since the beginning of time. Through observation and analysis, you can better prepare for a shift.

Recognizing early stages of a market shift

At its core, a shift occurs when supply and demand moves or adjusts. The law of supply and demand is exactly that — a *law*. A law creates certain and specific rules and parameters. The most important factor of a law is that it produces certain out-comes. In real estate sales, the law of supply and demand is absolute. A buyer's market will always create buyer hesitancy, fear, and apprehension in a large pool of buyers. The inventory of sellers who want to sell will increase until there are more sellers who want to sell than buyers who want to buy. A seller's market always produces the reverse. Fewer sellers than buyers produces higher pricing and value on properties. Where is your market now, based on the law of supply and demand? Where is it shifting to or trending toward? How is the law of supply and demand influencing the market in certain locations and price ranges in the marketplace?

Real estate markets tend to follow a seasonal pattern as well. The inventory of homes for sale tends to build for the spring/summer selling season. It starts to ebb in the other direction into fall, moving into the winter. We only hope in real estate that the pool of buyers increases in relation to the increase in listing inventory. Here's how I define the three kinds of markets:

>> Seller's market has less than six months of inventory.

>> Neutral market has six months of inventory.

>> Buyer's market has more than six months of inventory.

REMEMBER

Be aware that you could have a buyer's market and seller's market occurring at the same time depending on price range or location. In Bend, Oregon, where I live, in the upper end, which would be $750,000-and-above properties, we currently have 10.3 months of inventory. It's well entrenched into a buyer's market. But at the entry level, below $300,000, we have 1.7 months of inventory. A raging seller's market.

To recognize the shifts you must watch your absorption rate numbers, or months of inventory numbers. Based on the current sales per month, how many months would it take to sell off the inventory if no new homes came on the market? Is there a net gain or loss of inventory month-by-month?

TIP

A market, when shifting, will usually start in the opposite ends of the market-place. A marketplace that is shifting from a seller's market to a neutral one, and then to a buyer's market, will show indications of that in the upper and upper-middle price segments. It will happen in the more elite properties first. Conversely, a shift to a seller's market from a buyer's market will start at the lower end and low-middle of the market and work its way upward.

REMEMBER

You have to view the real estate market as the playing field of the game of real estate. We don't control the market — we control our attitude about the market. We control our mind-set, focus, and intensity toward what we do. We control our actions or "the plays" that we run. When a football team encounters a muddy playing field they don't forfeit the game. They change the plays to take advantage of the field conditions to improve their odds of winning. They might even change equipment to enable them to gain better footing. That is what I am suggesting you do as well in a shift.

Shift recognized — now what?

When the marketplace is shifting from seller's to a buyer's market, you need to get ahead of it. In my conversations with sellers at those times, it's imperative that I convince them to make their pricing beyond competitive to compelling. The value of their home must leap out of the MLS online and say, "You gotta buy me because I am such a deal!"

Your counsel must be to have them price toward where the market is trending to. To clearly express to them the danger of chasing the market down. Buyers turn into deal shoppers the longer a buyer's market progresses.

Because fewer of the sellers in the market will possess the level of motivation needed to sell in a buyer's market, you will require more seller leads than before. You will need to invest more time in finding motivated sellers. It's likely you will turn down listings due to that motivation level. Before, you might have listed 90 percent of the people you met with. The new sales ratio might be 65 percent or lower in a buyer's market. This means you will need more listing appointments to produce the same results as before.

The good news is, there will be more expired, withdrawn, and cancelled listings you can work. In an extreme shift, there will be more foreclosure properties, so cultivating relationships with bank executives and asset management companies can be effective ways to generate well-priced listing inventory. It's also likely that your sphere of influence may diminish, and past clients will have fewer referrals to give you. That source of business will take a hit as well. You will need to make more personal contacts and mobilize them more — even educate them about the state of the market and type of prospect they might be on the lookout for you.

In any marketplace, you will have a certain percentage of business of people that have to sell because of DDT. No, I'm not talking about the pesticide used in the 70s that decimated certain wildlife like the bald eagle population in the United States. I'm talking about *death, divorce,* and *transfer.* Setting up a strategy to market to family law/divorce attorneys, probate attorneys, and companies that transfer people in and out of your market can help any agent not only survive, but thrive in a buyer's marketplace. When the market is shifting from a buyer's market to a seller's, there are unique challenges and opportunities as well. When the days on the market starts to drop, as well as inventory of homes, you know the shift is on.

First, target the move-up seller market. If you market to production builder neighborhoods in established move-up prices ranges, you can generate more listings and sales. A *production builder* is one like DR Horton, KB Homes, or any builder that builds hundreds or even thousands of homes in your marketplace with an in-house sales staff. They typically sell a high percentage of their homes inhouse. Because of their constant open houses, special financing incentives, and required registration of buyers, they typically sell a large volume of homes direct to the buyers. An agent would typically need to register their buyer before that buyer walks into the model home on their own to be part of the transaction and get paid. That's why buyers are often unrepresented by real estate agents in buying production builder homes.

TIP

Targeting people who bought in production builder neighborhoods a few years ago and now have equity in their home is a must. Finding those who do not have a primary real estate relationship is fairly easy. If you develop a strategy to serve the neighborhood through your information, marketing, and presence, you can usually establish a fast hold as the real estate agent of choice for the neighborhood. You will have limited competition because onsite or in-house sales staff for the production builder are rarely allowed to represent other sellers in reselling their homes. The builder wants its team 100 percent focused on selling its new homes, not reselling homes.

Focus on motivation

When a market shifts, the motivation of buyers and sellers can often shift as well. Your job as the agent is to gauge the motivation level of the prospect, whether buyer or seller. Does the market change create urgency or apathy? With sellers, you must recognize that the higher the motivation, the lower the sale price they will be willing to take. Conversely, the lower the motivation, the higher the sale price they will want for their home.

Ask questions like: "What is your desire to sell? What is the ideal timeframe? When do you want this move to happen? Is there anything might cause you not to make this move?" Use a scaling system from 1–10: "On a scale of 1–10, with 10 being 'I have to sell no matter what' and 1 being 'I am holding out for a premium price on my home,' where do you fall?" Then follow up: "Can you share with me why you selected a ____?" People with higher levels of motivation have reasons why they are buying or selling, but they won't automatically come out and share them. You need to ask if you want to receive your payment for helping them. As an agent, you need to probe and ask questions to determine their desire to move. The higher the motivation, most likely, the higher your compensation will be.

OOPS — DESIRE, NOT MOTIVATION

Avoid using the word *motivation* with a buyer or seller. It's a word we use as salespeople to describe desire. We can use it with each other in the industry, but it's too salesy for public use. It makes the buyer or seller feel that we could be a slick-talking salesperson who only cares about the commission. Use the word *desire* with prospects instead.

2

Creating Leads in Our Online World

IN THIS PART . . .

Maximize the potential of your Facebook use, a major new resource for leads and much more.

Put IDX technology to use in your marketing by turning it into a lead-generating machine.

Leverage your blogging, CRM, and website efforts to supercharge your leads.

Find out how to use the Big Three — Zillow, Realtor.com, and Trulia — to your advantage.

Chapter 4

Facebook: An Online Lead Juggernaut

Social media has changed the real estate game. No one social media platform has changed real estate agents' marketing greater than Facebook. With Facebook, you can find and communicate with prospects, market yourself, your services, and your listed properties, and converse with your past clients and sphere of influence. Facebook is truly the thousand-pound gorilla in the social media arena, with more than 1.7 billion monthly active users, and more than a billion mobile daily active users on average.

WARNING

All of social media has greatly influenced real estate agents' time management. The overinvestment of time in social media can reduce revenue rather than increase sales. According to the National Association of Realtors (NAR), a recent study shows that prospects coming directly from social media account for less than 6 percent of sales. Although this figure was zero a few years ago, social media still doesn't directly account for a huge part of most agents' business. I do think that a good social media strategy, especially on Facebook, creates the opportunity to communicate and interact with your past clients and sphere of influence. If you ask most agents, they're likely to say that social media accounts for a much larger portion of their business than it actually does. For many agents, the time invested in social media can consume a large part of their day.

Although Facebook is no doubt an increasingly important lead-generation tool, allocating the right time, strategies, and communication systems helps you maintain the correct balance between traditional business strategies and new tech-savvy strategies.

Although real estate agents have many social-media options, including established sites like Twitter and LinkedIn, Facebook is the most commonly used social media tool in real estate. Even fast-growing social-media newcomers like Instagram and Pinterest trail Facebook in terms of power. Although Instagram is more popular with a young, hip audience, a big portion of that audience is still living at home with parents. My 15-year-old son, Wesley, and his friends are using Instagram much more than Facebook. That is true with the 20-something crowd as well. Many of them are saddled with college debt and have a limited opportunity to buy a home at this time. Many of those users aren't ready to purchase or sell homes. Other sites will come and go, and it's nearly impossible to use every social media tool without spending all day in front of your computer. That's not a recipe for success in a business where face-to-face interaction still matters.

Personal or Business? Using Facebook Effectively

Facebook is the most used social media tool in the world. Using Facebook in real estate can be a great way to build relationships and stay at the forefront of the technological world. But because real estate agents often use both their personal and business relationships to conduct business, the line between the two can become muddled. I personally believe you need to establish both types of uses for Facebook.

Establishing a personal profile enables you to post your personal history — your likes and dislikes, photos, stories, and so on. This is the most common experience on Facebook. This type of profile is a one-person profile that highlights your interests and connections with others.

From a business perspective, Facebook enables you to brand your product or service. (Just a hint . . . the product or service is still *you* until you grow a larger market presence and leverage yourself through other people or a team.) Facebook gives you numerous free methods to interact with prospects, clients, and people you know. This allows your company to connect and encourage people to "Like" the page so they receive valuable information and updates.

Using your personal page to create business

On your personal Facebook page, you need to achieve a balance between communicating your business interests and sharing personal updates. Your personal profile should be mainly personal with a sprinkling of business information. For the vast majority of agents, the personal page is what will drive your business to a greater extent than your business page. That's due to the relationship aspect of the real estate business.

TIP

Your photo is one of the most important first decisions. Facebook is a casual and informal media. Your profile and cover photos should reflect that. You don't need the glamour shot, professional headshot, or air-brushed portrait; in fact, it's probably better not to use those. This is your personal page, but you'll get crossover from personal contacts with whom you do business, so it's important to choose a photo that represents who you are in a casual setting, but that isn't too hobby driven or inappropriate. Remember that your profile photo will appear in most posts, communications, and connections. Choose one that shows you as both the warm, personal person next door and the professional. The mistake I see too frequently is a picture that makes one appear unapproachable.

Walk the fine line with business on your personal page

Too many agents cross the line. They post every new listing on their personal timeline. Most of your friends don't want an overload of property listings invading their newsfeed. The rule of thumb is four to five personal posts for every business post you make. Err on the side of caution. If you think you may have overdone the business posts this week, you probably have.

One option that is softer than an "in your face" listing announcement is a congratulations post to a new buyer who has closed. Creating a thank-you or congratulations post with a photo or video of the happy family is a powerful way to cross over to business from personal. Be sure to tag the happy buyers so all their friends are informed. This enables you to engage with a large, growing group of friends and followers. You can even send friend requests to the people who comment or post. This is a simple way to use your personal page to generate business and say thank you to clients.

TIP

To amp that up further, ask the client if you can tag them in your congratulations announcement. You don't want to tag them without their permission. If they agree, and most will, you will see their friends post and congratulate them on their new home. Be sure to review and watch each response. You can see people frequently say, "We want a new home too!" Or, "We would love to move to that area as well." Those are comments that create initial lead opportunities.

Watch for life changes

One of the best ways to use Facebook is not posting but listening. Just review your friends' posts to see what is happening and changing in their lives. The coolest part of Facebook is how quickly you can pick up on clues and cues of change. Be sure to engage, respond, or even just give them a thumbs-up.

Before Facebook, we often heard about job transfers, marriages, pregnancies, empty-nest situations, and many other life-changing events months after they happened. With Facebook, you can be front and center when life events happen to congratulate or commiserate with your friends, clients, and past clients.

TIP

The right message or comment can lead to a wealth of new business. Telling people how pleased you are about the announcement of a new child can lead them to mention that their home is now getting cramped. You generally won't have to say too much, because your warm greeting will jog their memory about your real estate business. If you need to lightly or casually remind them of your profession, do it after a few comments back and forth. You can also private message the person if you don't want to publicly seem like you're pouncing on a lead opportunity.

Instant messaging: A cool tool

I have become a big fan of Messenger, Facebook's instant messaging (IM) service. Although not everyone uses it, or has the app on their phone, it is growing in popularity. It's a perfect way to send a quick "hello" or "was just thinking of you" message to someone. The key, though, is *short* messages. It's much easier for someone to respond if they don't have to scroll in reading your message. Think of the window size on a standard sized smartphone screen when the Messenger window is open — and I'm not talking about a phablet-sized phone. Your message should be concise: "I was thinking about you. How are you?" Or "Saw your recent post on _____. Just thought I would reach out and wish you well." Or "Is there anything I can do for you?"

Some will respond quickly, which lets you know they are regular users of IM. For others, it will take days or weeks to respond to you. You then know these late responders are infrequent users and you will likely need to select another method of communication with them.

These clues can help you create a list of people for whom an IM check-in is an option to create dialogue. When you use of the voice-to-text feature on your smartphone, the speed at which you can create a personal touch is cut even further. You don't have to wear out your thumbs. I occasionally couple instant messages with my workout time. If I'm on the treadmill or out for a walk, I can be IM-ing away with a few people at once and getting my workout done.

WARNING

Because past conversations or greetings are easily accessible through scrolling back, don't get too scripted. You run the risk of sending the same message to someone again. Doing that makes you look sloppy or careless and can break the relationship and connection with your past client or friend you're trying to reach out to.

Getting people to share your posts, business or personal

No technique can make up for poor content. The first rule of getting more shares is to post something worth sharing. You can increase the sharing if you make the post visually stimulating as well as mentally stimulating. Use photos and videos as much as possible — the share numbers go through the roof when you do.

If you're going to use a photo, select an interesting shot that will catch the audience's attention. Creating a great headline is another way to increase shares. Many people only read the opening headline, but if it's provocative and engaging you can get them to share.

Anecdotal stories that align with what's happening in the real estate marketplace can be good shares. Also think about posting general marketplace updates, funny stories, announcements of big sales, and pictures of hot new listings.

When all else fails, ask. The adage *Ask and you shall receive* is still in play. Gently asking your followers to "help you out," "share if you would like to," or "feel free to share with your friends" can increase your shares, as well.

Post for pleasure (and business)

Keeping people up to date with both your personal life and business can be a chore. Here are a few tips on how to keep up with posting and creating variety for you and your friends:

>> **Share what's up:** Don't be afraid to share about your family and what's happening. This makes you approachable and shows that you're just like your friends, clients, and prospects. As your production grows and you become an elite producer, it's even more important to remain approachable. Share your likes and dislikes with your friends. If you ask questions that create interaction, you can improve your position in the newsfeed of others who answer and

comment. Post about places you're going and share pictures of your experiences, both professional and personal.

» **Don't share inappropriate or sensitive views:** Be careful not to post political views. This is especially true in election season. Many people are sensitive and can become highly charged at this time. Be careful with religious views, as well as perspectives on hot-button social issues. Any photo of you that doesn't align with your professional image is also a no-no. Avoid the revealing bathing suits, the giant margarita, or the less-than-flattering hangover picture.

» **Share your photos:** Most people prefer to see visuals rather than text. Your photos can be either personal or community photos. Create the reputation of being your community expert. Photos of local places and events create an image of you as "the man (or woman) about town."

» **Share interesting articles or links:** The key is sharing links to things your network will find interesting. They can be notices about local events and issues, or they can be real estate articles from respected sources such as *The Wall Street Journal*, *USA Today*, NAR, or other major brands in business or real estate. This demonstrates that you're well read, educated, and on top of the market trends.

» **Acknowledge others:** If you've received great service, or if someone in your network has achieved success by winning an award, opening a business, and so on, acknowledge that. You're spreading the wealth of who you know to aid others in achieving their dreams.

TIP

Use the check-in feature when you visit stores, restaurants, and travel destinations. Check-ins can create conversations or spur memories from others that will open dialogue between you and friends. The more interesting you seem in your check-ins and experiences, the wider the net you cast for posts from others.

Creating your business page

Facebook created business profiles to reduce the business promotion that was happening on personal pages. Although I believe real estate agents need both personal and business profiles because of the crossover of contacts in those two parts of life, the purpose of a business page is to engage with the people who Like your page, interact with the community where you live and do business, and, finally, share valuable information that relates to real estate investment and sales. The difference between the business page and your personal page is that the business page can be viewed by anyone. Most people set the privacy settings on their personal pages so that those pages can be viewed only by confirmed Facebook friends. But people don't have to Like your business page to see your posts there.

A Facebook business page should be part of your overall online marketing strategy. Agents try many different strategies for Facebook business pages. Some agents have one business page where they drive much of their online interaction. Others segment their business pages to align with different aspects of their business, such as short sales, foreclosures, buyers, or sellers. Starting out, this is probably more complex than you need to get.

The keys to a powerful Facebook business page are as follows:

» **Frequently updating the content of your pages:** The more you update and refresh the information, the more your Likes will grow and the more people will come back to see what's new. People who have Liked your page receive a notification when you post something. By posting regularly, you keep your face and message in front of your prospects, clients, sphere of influence, and past clients.

» **Creating posts that lead to interaction:** Using questions to foster interaction is also a way to create interactivity. When you create engaging content that gets people talking, reposting, and sharing, you know that you've been successful in expanding your reach.

» **Generating leads by creating posts that lead back to your website or main hub of information and marketing:** Because so many consumers start dreaming about home ownership online, you must always develop strategies that enable them to leave a trail online.

Figure out what to post on your business page

You should post quality content to entice new Likes and retain the current group of followers. Before you get all fired up to promote your page to the world, post good content and a reasonable amount of it. No one wants to Like a page that has limited information and value. You don't need a truckload of posts, but you need some value that can be seen and digested. Perhaps you want to ask a few close friends and family members to take a quick peek before you promote the page. The more powerful the content, the more it will be shared. Sharing is one of the most useful aspects of Facebook. It explodes your reach exponentially.

TIP

You may want to post market data, for example, to update your followers on the state of the marketplace. Share numbers for the inventory of homes for sale and sold properties. Also talk about what segments of the market are hot in terms of price range, geographic areas, key neighborhoods, and types of properties. Posts about staging, home improvement, decorating, and design also attract eyeballs.

Practice consistency

A key to posting is consistency and frequency. You need to post at least five times a week. When you post, use photos, videos, or links on a handful of those posts and you will see growth. You can't set the standard for yourself that every post is earth-shatteringly brilliant. The truth is that not every post will create the attention you want. Your job is to build a voice and build a habit. When it comes down to it, success comes to people who are consistent more than it comes to the brilliant.

Find the right mix

The right mix in your posts fosters community and connection. The focus of 40 percent of your posts should be to engage others in conversation and communication. Use 20 percent of your posts to link to other content that positions you as well informed and that has value to your followers. Another 20 percent can be general business or economic news that influences the greater real estate market. The final 20 percent can be real estate specific about trends nationally, regionally, or locally. Local trends should outweigh the regional and national.

You can post listings, but don't overdo it. What you want to do in posting listings is to tell a story. Don't just list general information, such as the number of bedrooms and bathrooms and the price . . . boring! Share something that makes the listing unique, desirable, or different. Maybe it has an interesting historic story: Did someone famous or infamous once live there? Does it have unique amenities, such as a rare type of hardwood floor or one-of-a-kind design features? Use those aspects to draw people in and they will most likely connect with you and respond.

Using Facebook Marketing Strategies

The marketing opportunities for Facebook in creating leads of buyers and sellers are really endless. Because Facebook possesses so much information and data on each of us — our use of it, our preferences, who and what we interact with online — Facebook is Big Brother even more than the federal government. Facebook knows where you live based on your IP address. It knows what you earn and buy. As an agent, using this information to target your market can be explosive to your pocketbook.

Targeting sellers

Any agent worth their salt wants more listings. Finding listings is harder than finding a buyer in today's marketplace. Frequently a buyer that you create needs to be a seller first. Always ask any buyer, whether they are a referral, an online lead, or even if they just walked into your open house, the following questions:

>> Do you currently own or are you renting?

>> Do you need to sell your present home before you can purchase a new home?

Agents can frequently miss the seller who is there by only focusing on the buying aspect because the lead came through a buyer channel.

Delivering value to draw sellers in

Posting content on your business page or personal page about the state of the market and trends can create engagement, dialogue, and interest. One of the best strategies is guiding the education of the seller who needs or wants to move up in either size of home or to a better location using the *rare moment in time* strategy. In most markets, we are at that "rare moment in time." The equity positions for a seller have been restored in the last few years. These equity positions now allow a seller to consider a home upgrade. Because of price appreciation, they are no longer underwater in equity or now have better equity to use to upgrade to a larger home.

REMEMBER

The rare moment in time also comes from the interest rates being still at very low levels compared to the past. Most people are mentally immune to the deleterious effects of rising interest rates. What negative effect will take place to their buying power or payment? We are oblivious to how low the rates are and have been in the last few years. The historic average mortgage interest rate over the last 40 years is 8.65 percent. That is much higher than where we actually are presently at the time of writing (around 4.25 percent in early 2017). The difference on a $300,000 mortgage in monthly payment between the two interest rates would be $863 a month. For a buyer who expects to be on their next home in ten years, the ten-year accumulation of extra interest payments would be $103,560 in payments.

Getting seller prospects to raise their hand

Using a *geographic* strategy with sellers is also effective. Posting your open houses and boosting those posts so they appear based on geographic ad settings inside Facebook can create more traffic to your open houses where you can meet the neighbors. You can offer a sneak peek, pre-marketing a listing before it goes live on the MLS. Post it to your Facebook page and boost the post with $15–$20 of Facebook ad space geographically, especially if it's a move-up home in a hot market or hot neighborhood. This strategy will create for you people who need to sell to buy. You might not sell this or that specific home, but you will create leads.

Creating "What is my home worth" campaigns

One of the more popular ways to create leads with sellers is to give them access to valuation services. You create an online landing page featuring a nice home image on it with a sign-in field for their address and other information. You will need a service relationship with an online valuation service like Bold Leads (www.boldleads.com), Prime Seller Leads (www.primesellerleads.com), Market Leader (www.marketleader.com), or Cloud CMA (www.cloudcma.com). These services connect to your site, and when the prospective seller inputs their address, they have enough data on the home to send them a simple home value.

TIP

I also recommend requiring the phone number and email of the prospective seller so you can follow up with a more comprehensive market evaluation for them if required. Most valuation services give a basic range number based on the analysis of the marketplace and tax records. If people abandon the inquiry after they put their address in because they don't want to give out their phone number or email, you still have the address and can research them using Cole Realty Resource (www.colerealtyresource.com). This company has phone numbers for about half of the people in most marketplaces by address. You can also secure some emails as well.

Targeting buyers

Targeting buyers is much easier than targeting sellers. Typical buyers want to look at homes. You can easily post to your Facebook page a message about buying opportunities — "Now is a great time to buy" — with a link to your IDX website so they can search real estate in your marketplace. For early-stage or just-starting-to-look buyers, searching for homes is what draws them in. The strategy of having a great URL in your Facebook post or boosted post is key. (For a deeper dive on using targeted sites and stealth sites, turn to Chapter 5.)

The value strategy for buyers

Any data, charts, market trends reports, or interest rate information conveys value to a buyer. Because most real estate markets currently have historic low inventory levels, buyers searching for a home are probably feeling frustrated by not finding what they want or when they inquire about a home, or that the home is already sold. This is where a *coming soon* strategy linked to a Facebook posting or marketing strategy can produce big results.

In the coming soon strategy, you pre-market a new listing that is about to hit the marketplace. You have taken quality pictures and put them on your website, or even on a property specific site with a property-specific URL. If the property address is 60766 Current Way, you buy the URL 60766CurrentWay.com from a service such as Go Daddy (www.godaddy.com) for very little cost — between $3 and $10 gets you a URL for a year. You then create a post for Facebook with a couple of pictures. Announce that this property will hit the market in a few days, and if someone wants to be a first-look buyer, they should contact you. Be sure to include the custom URL and your contact information as well. The scarcity, urgency, and exclusive access buyers feel will do the rest for you in the lead-generation category.

Using your company listings to create leads

As a newer agent, it's often hard to gain momentum because you lack the listing inventory that other, more experienced agents have. Your ability to gain permission to market company listings online and on Facebook will benefit you in a couple of areas.

The obvious way is that you will create some buyers from your postings and boosting your posts geographically as well as through psychographic segments you can target through Facebook. Targeting income levels, buying habits, and other data can create valid niche opportunities based on the property you are marketing. The other main benefit is that your Facebook friends will be seeing new home inventory and will assume that these are listings you've taken. It's okay to let them assume that. They will see you as a successful agent.

REMEMBER

When asked directly, in any situation, whether you are the listing agent by anyone, honesty is the best policy — tell them you're not the listing agent of the property if you're not. If you're posting new listings to your Facebook page, both business and personal, and boosting those posts periodically, you're building your brand as an up-and-coming success in the real estate business.

Using best buy lists to capture buyers

Everyone who is even mildly interested in real estate is attracted to a deal. That's human nature. Who wouldn't want to brag at the cocktail party what a rocking world-class deal they got on a home? Although foreclosure, bank-owned and short sales are seen as the best deals in the marketplace, that's not necessarily true — but perception is reality for some people. Foreclosure and short sale deals in most markets are actually few and far between. People still want them and are attracted to agents that project "insider" access to deals.

In a recent NAR study, about half the buyers said they would not consider a foreclosure property. That means about half *would* consider it. Few buyers will end up buying a foreclosure — nevertheless, they do equate foreclosure with deals and undermarket opportunities on properties.

Creating a list with the best values in certain price ranges, property types, or geographic areas is an effective way to attract buyer interest. When you connect that list to your Facebook post and link it to a sign-up page where people can get your list each week or each month, you are using Facebook's reach to build your marketing and email database. You can connect your social media with email marketing, which gives you a one-two punch.

Using the secret weapon of Facebook Lists

One of the least used but most important features of Facebook is the Friend Lists function. You can create Friend Lists of people and categorize them so it's easier to follow their posts. Use the Smart List suggestions in Facebook to separate some of your lists. These smart lists break your contact list down by city or high school, for example. Smart Lists are helpful, but setting up your own lists is even better.

As you build the number of friends you have in Facebook for your personal page, creating Friend Lists allows you to more easily see what your most important clients, past clients, and prospects are posting on Facebook. Once you put them in a list, you can filter your feed to display just that list, meaning you don't have to wade through your whole newsfeed for the day. You just go to your Friend Lists tab and see recent posts from your key people.

Creating your list categories

Set up specific categories or specific watch lists around the type of business you want to do. I recommend setting up Buyer Watch list and Seller Watch lists. Put in people who are high-level prospects with whom you interact and who have shown an interest in a different home-ownership situation. Others on your watch lists may be going through different life events. It's a good idea to set up relationship categories and client categories in lists too.

You can use different client categories, such as Past Clients, Sphere of Influence, or Business Referral Partners. It would be advisable to create a few lists based on your level of relationship with these people. If you have 30 people who send you 80 percent of the referrals you receive in business, then by all means create a Top 30 list on Facebook.

It's easy to create different lists. Facebook changes its interface all the time, but currently you click Home to go to your newsfeed and click Friend Lists on the left-hand side. From there you click Create List. You'll see a pop-up menu that requires you to name the list, and then you can select the friends you want to be part of the list. You can place people in multiple lists. There is no limit to the Friend List feature.

Selecting the people and prospects placed in your lists

The selection and strategy of your list names and categories are important. What most agents struggle with is who to put in what list. As mentioned earlier, you should have Buyer Watch and Seller Watch lists for people who you feel desire, want, or are going to buy or sell in the future.

Watch lists make it easier for you to monitor these peoples' posts. They still remain in your newsfeed, but they also appear in the list area on the left-hand side of your Facebook page. All you have to do is click your watch list, and the recent posts of all the people on that list appear on your screen. You might also create Move Up Buyers or Downsize Sellers lists. Lists let you monitor a smaller, more organized set of posts each day, which is much faster than scrolling through your whole newsfeed to see what people you deem to be viable prospects have posted today.

You can also choose to send your posts directly to the people on these lists, rather than to all your friends. For example, you can create a post that will appear in the newsfeeds of just those on your Buyer Watch list. Maybe you read a great newspaper article about rising interest rates and why people should buy now. You can post the article but target it to your Buyer Watch group. This way, you're sending information of value to the group that is most likely to use it.

Using lists helps you avoid over-posting business messages on your Facebook page. You can post business messages more frequently to your lists because you know they are already interested in what you're posting — so it doesn't seem as self-serving and self-promoting.

Communication your targeting message

Because your "list" people are your best prospects and relationships, you want to communicate a targeted message of your value, knowledge, expertise, and status of the market and interest rates. You need to be able to inform them about things like the state of the marketplace, where the market is trending to, what's happening with inventory and sales numbers in your marketplace, the rise and fall of interest rates and how they might affect buying power or payments.

Creating valuable content can be a challenge for even skilled agents. It takes time to do the research and maintain attractive graphics. The truth is, most agents don't have — or take — the time or energy to use Facebook to its fullest potential.

TIP

Keeping Current Matters (www.keepingcurrentmatters.com) is a wonderful resource. It's a service that produces great tools with graphics that can help deliver more value and targeted message to your lists.

Chapter **5**

Creating Leads with Online Search

The world of online leads is exploding and growing at an exponential pace. We have seen online leads go from 2.3 million just a few years ago to more than 70 million in 2016. Given that fact, the number of actual homes sold has held fairly steady at around 5–5.2 million for those same years. The net result, then, is a whole bunch of leads being created that don't buy or sell. This means agents are wasting time processing and working leads that have little chance in them earning a commission check. The good news with online leads is that the number of consumers who are using the Internet to find an agent is significantly up in the same span of time. Thirty-three percent of the buyers in 2016 found the agent they used through their online search for homes.

The birth of Interactive Data Exchange (IDX) has transformed how agents market themselves and their listings and has dramatically expanded the marketing reach of any agent. All MLS systems across the country have adopted IDX technology. IDX technology enables you to do more than just share your listings; it enables you to create registration opportunities for consumers — typically buyers searching for homes. You can allow them to search for homes through your website and then ask them to register so you can secure their email address, phone number, and other information useful in following up with them.

Because IDX has influenced the real estate industry so heavily, you need to dig deep into the opportunities it presents. IDX can level the playing field, putting you on more even footing with larger-producing or more-experienced agents. Because you can share all MLS listings on your website — and it looks like they're actually *your* listings — IDX helps you widen the information you offer to the public. You can feature homes that meet the needs of any prospective buyer who comes to your website. Before IDX, you could only showcase your own listings.

The ABCs of Online Leads

Creating online leads involves an ever-changing series of strategies and substrategies. The vast majority of these center around working to move a potential prospect out of the background of searching for properties and into a *revealed* position. Until they are revealed, the online property searcher can review a large volume of information without any agent knowing about their existence or level of interest.

This ability of the consumer to remain stealthy online makes the sales process and sales conversion more challenging. When you mix in all the site options — from company websites, to agent websites, to public MLS access through the Board of Realtors, and then add the Zillow, Trulia, and Realtor.com types of third-party real estate property and information sites — there is a wide variety of options for the prospective buyers or sellers to access information about real estate in your market.

Distinguishing two types of leads

In the world of online leads, the vast majority of leads are created through the buyer channel rather than the seller channel, although keep in mind that people searching for a new home as a buyer may also be a potential seller as well. They have just used searching for their dream home as their first step.

According to the National Association of Realtors (NAR), for 42 percent of the people searching online, the first step is to search for homes. It's *not* to contact a real estate agent. People only do that first 14 percent of the time. Going online and looking for a property on their own is the attraction. The younger age demographic contact a real estate agent an even smaller percentage of the time because they're even more tech-savvy.

On the other hand, I believe we are starting to see some of the younger demographic become more interested in real estate ownership. We are in the early stages of moving to a more normal historic pattern of 40 percent of all sales being in the first-time home buyer category. In recent years, that category bottomed out at 19 percent. By 2015 it had climbed to 31 percent. The result has been a larger portion of tech-savvy buyers. We have also seen the percentage of buyers whose first action is to read and gather information about the home-buying process climb to 13 percent.

With this shifting and changing, it's helpful to identify two basic lead types:

>> Online forced-registration leads

>> Direct-inquiry leads

In a *forced-registration* lead you are capturing information on a lead by triggering a registration on a web page. Typically, you require registration to be able to use your site to search for properties. This trigger can happen before they even see a property or it can happen after the Internet visitor has seen a few listings, and the forced registration comes up (usually in the form of a pop-up box) before they can look further.

You may be thinking, "Yes, I have gone to websites where they require me to give contact and other info to get what I want." You may go on to admit, "I don't like it so I don't fill out the form and go somewhere else." That's called a *bounce* — the prospect bounces off the site. You may not like forced registration when you're the consumer, but it has proven effective — in fact *more* effective than just letting everyone search for property and hoping they contact you when they're interested. Unfortunately, that's not very likely.

Direct-inquiry leads occur when a prospect inquires about a specific property to gain more information. They have an interest in the property or want to see it. This type of lead is often a little farther along in the home-search process. They may or may not already have an agent they're loyal to.

REMEMBER

Direct-inquiry leads are more likely than forced-registration leads to have an agent relationship. You also have to assume that, if they're inquiring about a property, it's likely that they've asked other agents about specific properties as well. You must be prepared for competition for this buyer prospect.

Dealing with the prospect brush-off

We frequently get sidetracked by a reflexive "no," called a *brush-off*. A typical brush-off can come from a prospect in either the forced-registration category or the direct-inquiry category. Here are some typical brush-offs:

>> I'm just looking.

>> I'm not ready for a real estate agent.

>> I'm just browsing.

>> I was just curious.

These are the responses you receive more than 70 percent of the time from an online lead you reach on the phone. Why are brush-offs so common? Let me put you in a scenario: You go to a department store to buy a new blouse. You arrive at, say, Nordstrom. You walk in the door, and the retail clerk greets you. "Welcome to Nordstrom. May I help you?" What is your instantaneous response? What do you say without even thinking? Almost all the time, you say, "No, I'm just looking." Am I correct?

The response you gave is one you've probably used thousands of times. Just like anyone else, you stick with what has worked. It's also what an online buyer does. They have the same shopping experience you have — and they know the script to get rid of a salesperson with ease. The online prospect is trying to disengage you or potentially even discourage you from ever calling back. They are trying to show a lower level of motivation so you move on to another prospect. Your objective in that case is to elongate the call so you get beyond the reflexive "no" and expand the conversation.

Let me give you two suggested scripts that work extremely well to move beyond the typical brush-offs.

Just looking

I certainly understand that you are probably in the information-gathering stage, would that be correct?

Let me ask you this: It seems like you are looking for a _____, _____, _____. If you found something you really liked, something that really spoke to you, at a great value, then what would happen? So, it might prompt you from just looking to move right into a more active buying mode? Is that what I am hearing?

Not ready for a Realtor

That's just fine that you are just looking. You might be interested to know, that's the stage that a good Realtor can add a lot of value.

If we could spend a few minutes together, I can save you some time and help you avoid some of the pitfalls that many people make in the "just looking stage." I can direct you to some resources and websites that will make the looking stage you are in more productive and fun.

These two scripts are highly effective with brush-off buyers. The first appeals to the human nature in us that wants a good deal: If you put a good deal in front of them, does it entice them? The second script involves getting them to understand that you can provide value even in their early searching process.

Converting the forced-registration lead

Because some registration leads are in the early stages of reviewing the market-place, using a softer approach is advisable. Using an opening statement like "I want you to know this is a customer service call, not a sales call" can lower the apprehension on the part of the prospect so you can have a more open, engaged, and honest conversation. In an *honest conversation*, they are more truthful with you about their timeline, desires, and expectations.

TIP

Don't assume just because the buyer is a forced-registration lead that it's a long-term, nurture type of lead. That's one of the big mistakes made by agents. They're not alone — many so-called Internet experts have come to that wrong philosophy as well. The truth is, you don't ever want to assume "no" until you know. You have to sell *value* to the forced-registration lead. You have to convince them that there is value to meeting you and considering your services, even in the market research stage. You have access to information that will make the information-gathering phase more valuable and informative for them, whether they purchase now or years into the future.

Converting the direct-inquiry lead

WARNING

This is the lead variety you really don't want to make mistakes with. These prospects have taken that additional action to request more information from you about a property. The first rule in lead conversion of this category of lead is *speed to lead*. Time's a-wasting with this lead category.

THE OBJECTIVE: A FACE-TO-FACE APPOINTMENT

When you're doing lead follow-up, no matter the method — phone call, text, or email — the objective is to *get an appointment face-to-face*. NAR has tracked the percentage of buyers who buy from the first agent they meet with. For years it's between 65–67 percent. What that means is you have a two-thirds chance of getting the commission check if there is one to be had. For safety reasons, you need to follow an appointment strategy of closing for a face-to-face at your office first. If you can't convince them of that, then you want a face-to-face at a neutral site. A coffee shop is an excellent option for a neutral site. If you can't get that, then a property showing. Chapter 21 discusses strategies to keep you safe when meeting strangers.

TIP

In a recent study, the online consumer has a low opinion of the agent if they don't respond within 20 minutes of a direct inquiry. By contrast, the registration lead doesn't really want a response or call back. A direct inquiry wants a response *now*. Your target zone to respond is within five minutes. An MIT study conducted on online-inquiry leads revealed 100 times greater reach rate if you call within 5 minutes as compared to even 30 minutes. Yes, you read that correctly: 100 times increase.

You also can't assume, even if you give them the information about the home, that you will gain an appointment and they will buy that home. In fact, you have to assume this *isn't* the right home for them. According to NAR, less than 5 percent of specific inquiries lead the prospect to buy that specific home. Let me put that in perspective. If you talk to 100 direct-inquiry leads, and they all buy a home (that's a big assumption), only 5 would buy the specific home that you talked with them about. Those odds actually stink, and you would be broke fast if you ignored them.

The best strategy is to quickly know a property, or even two, that you might flip them to or be able to discuss in further detail. What you don't want to say if you get stuck is "Let me look a few properties up for you." That makes you sound like every other agent they have ever talked with before. It announces to them you don't know the inventory in the marketplace — that you bring limited value to them, which is the opposite of what you want to convey.

DIY Mentality and Misconceptions

The typical online prospect has a do-it-yourself (DIY) mentality. They believe that they can see all the information they need on their own. They have the misconception that they have access to the same information that all agents do. The truth is, that is completely false. They don't know how far off they are. I have to tactfully show them the errors in their thinking. Most agents have never done the legwork and research required to tell online prospects what they're missing and how important what they *don't* have is.

Stop reading. Grab two of your devices — tablet, laptop, desktop, or phone. Sign in to your MLS access as an agent on one device. Select a property to review — any property you want. On the other device, access that same property through your website or even Zillow, Trulia, or Realtor.com as an online consumer, with no proprietary agent access.

With the devices side-by-side, compare the information available. Are the agent comments abbreviated or condensed for the consumer? Does the consumer see the number of days on the market? Certainly, not knowing days on the market can cause a consumer to think a property is a better deal than it might be. Can the consumer see a clear and full history of the property — when it's been on and off the market, all price reductions, and prices paid by previous and present owners? Use Table 5-1 to record what you see on the devices. Then when you talk with an online buyer, you can tell them what information they lack and why it's important — and why they should set an appointment with you to gain access to such information.

TABLE 5-1 ## Consumer Information Compared to Agent Information

Features	Agent Access	Consumer Access
Days on market		
Full history: All price reductions		
Full history: Past times on market		
Full history: Price		
Full history: Listing agent details		
Full history: Expired, withdrawn, canceled		
Complete agent comments		
Tax information		

Selling your value to the online shopper

By using a prospect's fear of lacking important information, you can establish the value you bring to the table as an agent. The best way to position and sell value is to do so separately from your role as designated door opener to a home. Here are some key services and values to sell an online prospect:

>> You can help them understand the marketplace better.

>> You get them better access to deals and undermarket opportunities.

>> You connect them to off-market properties or coming-soon listings.

>> You give them a higher level of service.

>> You can help them gain an advantage in negotiating.

>> You give them the representation they deserve.

Any of these is a valid reason for them to set a meeting with you face-to-face — which is your goal (see the nearby sidebar "The objective: A face-to-face appointment"). The following sections provide a few specific scripts you can use to sell a few your value more efficiently.

You help them understand the marketplace better

Few agents understand the effects of supply and demand on the marketplace. This age old law dictates a lot of what happens in the marketplace. To know the market, you need to track active listings in predetermined price ranges as well as the amount of homes sold monthly, percentage of list price to sales price. Also, if an agent is really doing their job, they will show you absorption rate or months' worth of inventory currently for sale. This gives you a tremendous snapshot of how competitive the marketplace is and how competitive you need to be. I provide this type of advantage for my buyer in the marketplace. Do you see how this creates an advantage for my clients? Should we book that appointment for Starbucks?

They get a higher level of service

One of my primary jobs is helping you to select the home that best suits your needs and budgetary considerations. I will counsel you on different options and features with each home. We will also discuss school districts, resale value, potential features that are functionally obsolete that could affect the future value of the home, area and neighborhood value trends, and anything else that would affect your short-term or long-term enjoyment and equity in the home you are considering. Are these the type of services you would like from an agent? I agree, why don't we meet? Do you have time later this week?

You give them an advantage in negotiating

Negotiating can take many hours. The marketplace, quality of the property, price of the property, demand of the property, and motivation of the seller all are factors in negotiation. They all influence the negotiating process in each transaction. I will evaluate each of these factors and we will discuss them at the time we decide to make an offer. These are fixed when based on the marketplace and the quality and price of the property that just securing the property as the buyer selected take primary position. Other times, negotiating the terms, meaning price, possession, and seller repairs, is more important than other parts of the agreement.

You can be assured that when we work together through negotiation, we will evaluate and execute on all these areas. Do you see how there are more factors than just the price?

You give them the representation they deserve

I believe that all buyers deserve to achieve quality representation. Unfortunately, because the average agent, according to the National Association of Realtors, represents fewer than six clients per year, that is not the case. That is why it's imperative to consider meeting and working together because we helped ____ clients secure high-demand homes just last year alone. It means we helped more families last year than most agents do in ____ years.

There Is No Substitute for Speed to Lead

Online leads have little margin for error when it comes to response time. You could have the greatest sales skills and sales scripts, but if you're too slow on the callback response, the prospect will bounce to another agent or property.

TIP

The five-minute callback rule is the gold standard. To insure faster response, set up your online leads to come straight to your phone as texts. Be sure your audio notification is turned on during work hours. Frequently agents have online leads sent to their email — where it mixes in with Viagra ads or offers of money from recently deceased Nigerian government clerks.

Designing your lead follow-up strategy

The correct lead follow-up strategy can mean the difference between a few transactions or a lot of transactions from online leads. The right strategy incorporates calls, voicemail messages, texts, emails, and video emails.

REMEMBER

In the first 24 hours of the lead, if it's a direct-inquiry lead, you should make four call attempts to reach the lead.

In the first, initial five minutes, the best strategy is to *not* leave a voicemail message. You want to trigger that 10–15 percent of people who will give you the "curiosity call back." Some people can't stand it when there was a missed call with no message. They can't help themselves and are compelled by their nature to hit the redial button on their phone. I would never leave a voicemail message on the first call attempt to an online lead.

TIP

You want to then call that lead again, inside of 15–20 minutes, and if you don't reach them, then you leave your first voicemail message. The best follow-up times where people answer their phone are 8–9 a.m. and 4–6 p.m. These two time slots have a 164 percent better reach rate than the worst time, which is 12–2 p.m. in the afternoon. The right strategy would be to make an additional call between the 4–6 p.m. time slot with no voicemail message. And then call between 8–9 a.m. the next day and leave your second message.

Are phone calls still effective?

I am a big believer in the value and efficiency of telephone communications in sales. In fact, I literally wrote the book on telephone sales — see *Telephone Sales For Dummies* (Wiley, 2007). That said, phone communication can be difficult and frustrating. People answer their phones less today than they used to, and the younger generation primarily uses their phones to text and instant message. But the fact remains: No one is more persuasive via text than in a live conversation. The phone allows for a more fluid back and forth communication. We are more persuasive on the phone because we can inject energy and emotion into the message. I can't build a heightened sense of urgency with a prospect effectively via texting, even it's a live text dialogue. Text messaging is only words. The prospect uses their own emotions at the present moment as a filter to communication.

Using text to connect with a prospect

You might draw the conclusion that I am anti-texting based on my love of the phone (see the preceding section). On the contrary, I believe texting is very effective when used in concert with the phone and email. As a stand-alone strategy, though, it falls short in the area of convincing a prospect of your value. It's hard to convey value in a short text. The most effective texts are short and are focused on opening dialogue or offering a specific call to action. For the online buyer targeted prospect, the text needs to center around their interest — which is a specific home, type of home, or price range.

Here's an example of a good text: "You inquired about the home at 61 Hidalgo Way. Would you like to see the home? I have time today between 3 p.m. and 5 p.m. or I am available after 2 p.m. tomorrow." This kind of service access statement followed by a choice receives a higher response rate.

To take the response rate even higher, use a dual text strategy. You send the first text out at about the 15–20 minute mark after the lead comes to you. You then wait another 15–20 minutes for a response. In that timeframe, you send another text that is *really* short: "Please let me know." This gives them a little reminder nudge. It also frames a low level of obligation in their mind. This doesn't work with everyone, but reasonable people and considerate prospects will text you back that those times either work or don't, or give you a short explanation of their situation and why it would be premature.

TIP

Any response you receive is the opening to a potential dialogue.

Video email: The secret sauce

I am truly in love with video email. The reason is, a good portion of leads, especially forced-registration leads, don't leave phone numbers. They also generally have an image of a salesperson as a used car salesperson, with a gold chain around their neck, in a leisure suit and loafers, complete with gold pinky ring. We are clearly at a disadvantage from the start.

A video email breaks through that image in their heads. It's you on video reframing that image. It's your short video expressing thanks, service, and value. They can see you left your leisure suit in the closet.

TIP

You don't need to be a videographer to deliver a good video message. In fact, a more personal, less scripted, less produced, more real video gets a better play rate and personal reaction from your prospect. Because most agents feel overwhelmed by video, I highly recommend checking out BombBomb (www.bombbomb.com). BombBomb makes it easy to send video emails. You can use a phone, webcam, or most devices to shoot your video. You can actually shoot video right from the BombBomb software. There is no downloading or rendering. You can create easy evergreen videos for online buyers and use the same ones over and over again. You just change a few things in your body of the email and send. Here is a link to get information and a special trial offer on BombBomb: www.bombbomb.com/REChampions.

Persistence pays off

If rule number one is *speed to lead,* as stated earlier in this chapter, rule number two is *there is no replacement for persistence.* It takes at least six impressions for a person to remember who you are. The vast majority of people in sales quit long before they reach even six attempts to reach a prospect. Salespeople give up too easily.

REMEMBER

Don't assume "no" until you know! This fact is true in attempts to reach a prospect, as well as when we encounter the roadblocks of "no" or "not yet." According to the National Sales Executive Counsel, the average salesperson makes 1.3 attempts to reach a prospect via phone. You need to make at least 7 attempts over a span of 10–14 days before you cease your active follow-up sequence. That's far more than most agents will make.

The WAV Group, a real estate brokerage consulting company, did a secret shopping study with 76 different real estate companies. They portrayed themselves as online buyers more than 7,700 times. They discovered that over 47 percent of online buyer leads were never responded to at all! Don't be like your agent competition. Most agents are more interested in setting someone up on an IDX feed or email drip. They are focused on sending people stuff and hoping their stuff is better than all the other agents sending them stuff. The need for *call persistence* has never been more necessary.

I love this quote from Calvin Coolidge, 30th president of the United States, on persistence:

> *Nothing in this world can take the place of persistence. Talent will not; nothing is more common than unsuccessful men with talent. Genius will not; unrewarded genius is almost a proverb. Education will not; the world is full of educated derelicts. Persistence and determination alone are omnipotent.*

Knowing the Psychology of an IDX Lead

Converting an IDX lead into a client is different than converting a traditional lead from an ad call, sign call, or open house. In those cases, you have a prospect who is reaching out to you in a more direct and fully revealed way. They know they're going to encounter a salesperson.

IDX leads often don't realize that a sales call or sales encounter is forthcoming. They're usually in the early information-gathering stage, so you're connecting with someone who is still formulating their ideas and actions. In contrast, a prospect at an open house is usually further along in the process. Many IDX leads want to remain anonymous in their search so they won't be "bothered" by a salesperson. When you reach them, especially via phone, they'll often try to give you the brush-off (discussed earlier).

REMEMBER

Although brush-offs like "I'm just looking" can be true statements, it's amazing how many of these people end up buying a home through another agent who managed to navigate the brush-off. To be successful with IDX leads, you must approach them from a customer-service angle rather than a sales angle. You need to get the prospect to open up and engage in dialogue with you; open-ended questions work best. For example:

>> What caught your eye about this particular home?

>> What amenities are you looking for in your next home?

WARNING

Don't make the mistake that most agents make of trying to pre-qualify the prospect. Asking the prospect financial questions too early can stop the flow of information. I can assure you that the prospect doesn't want to give away personal financial information to a stranger on the phone within a few minutes of saying hello.

This section provides insight on converting IDX leads into actual clients.

Be first in line

Although IDX systems are a terrific advancement for generating leads, you must still cross the bridge from email or phone contact to an actual personal meeting. The goal and objective must be to secure a face-to-face appointment, even if the prospect is months away from starting his search in earnest.

REMEMBER

According to NAR, 67 percent of buyers hire the first agent they meet. Your goal is to be that first meeting! Boiling that down, you have a two-in-three chance of securing a commission check if you beat the other agents to the face-to-face meeting. Many IDX prospects visit multiple websites and leave a trail for multiple agents and companies to follow. They're leaving breadcrumbs in more places than Hansel and Gretel. You must pick up the crumbs before your competition does.

Don't set it and forget it

Most enhanced systems and IDX support systems are sold as self-contained, low-effort systems. But you can't idly stand by and let the system do all the work. The highest conversion rates on IDX leads come from a salesperson's active participation in lead conversion. It's where you're calling, sending email drips, personalized emails, and video emails, leaving value-packed voicemail messages, and sending texts. If you can find IDX prospects on social media sites, send them private messages.

Additionally, you have to constantly manage and monitor the findings, such as the following:

>> What is your overall conversion rate?

>> Is there a stage in your process where prospects tend to unsubscribe because of too many contact attempts?

>> How long do buyers usually look on their own before engaging your services?

The real success in IDX is making adjustments to your strategies, systems, and scripts to increase your conversion rate. It's a constant process of monitoring, refinement, and change.

CUSTOMER SERVICE WORKS

A number of techniques are effective in getting prospects to open up. When you call them back, my favorite technique is what I call the *customer service call*. You approach them softly: "This is a customer service call to the person who recently called our real estate information line. Were you the person who called? How did you like the service? Did you get all the information you needed?" After you get through those early questions, just move into a standard buyer script to convert the lead and book a face-to-face appointment. I really like the customer service call approach. It is softer, and you produce fewer negative responses like "How the heck did you get my number?"

Show and tell

Although most IDX leads want to remain anonymous, their below-the-radar position doesn't lead to high conversion rates. It also causes them to miss out on marketplace information and opportunities.

Because they have access to the MLS, many IDX prospects falsely believe they have the same information a real estate agent does. As mentioned earlier in this chapter, that assumption is false. Every MLS system is different, but I don't know of one that shares *all* the information with the public. The listing agent's comments are often abbreviated or withheld, and recent listing or sales history about the property is often omitted. Real estate agents have access to a wealth of information that prospects can only get from them.

REMEMBER

Your job is to demonstrate your *value* to the IDX prospect. You can do that by demonstrating your knowledge base. You can also do it by sharing with prospects some of the information they lack. Tell them how important the information is and how you can get them access.

The final step in converting an IDX prospect is not giving up too soon. Just because a prospect hasn't responded to your inquiries, voicemails, and emails doesn't mean they're not viable. Remember, the average salesperson makes 1.3 attempts to reach a prospect via phone — pathetic. You can't expect to succeed if you only try 1.3 times to contact someone. Resolve to make a minimum of seven attempts for any lead you generate. The key to succeeding in real estate sales is the number of attempts you make to reach a prospect.

Ask them to engage

The Biblical adage *Ask and ye shall receive* is true about sales as well. You won't receive if you don't ask. This is true whether you're asking an IDX prospect to meet you for coffee or showing a buyer the perfect home for their needs. You need to ask them to buy it.

REMEMBER

You must ask the prospect to engage your services. Show the value you can provide so they have the desire to engage. They need to see something from you that is unique or different. Maybe you offer a list of properties that are foreclosures or good values. Maybe you provide a market trends report that gives prospects a better understanding of the current and emerging market conditions. The deliberate act of asking for engagement in your emails, phone calls, and voicemail messages creates a higher conversion rate and better return on your IDX systems and strategies.

Making the Most of Your IDX System

IDX allows agents to project the image that they have more listings than they actually do. The technology enables agents to create branded prospect communications, highlighting all MLS properties, rather than just their own listings and those of their company. If you're a newer agent with fewer listings, the IDX can level the playing field with agents who have heavy listing inventories.

Your IDX technology should be integrated on your website home page, blogs, and other points of contact with prospects and clients. The IDX gives consumers access to all listings available in your MLS system. Most off-the-shelf IDX solutions, such as those provided by your Board of Realtors or MLS system, come without squeeze-page technology. To be truly effective in generating leads with IDX, you must use squeeze-page strategies.

A *squeeze page* is a web page that is designed to extract (squeeze) information from prospects in exchange for something of value (typically, access to listings). Prospects are required to input information, such as their name, email address, and phone number. The page may also include a question or two about where prospects are in the buying process. These help the agent determine the time-frame and motivation of the prospect. Squeeze pages usually pop up after a prospect views a certain number of homes or hits a time limit, prompting prospects to register their information.

TIP

Most MLS-provided systems don't have built-in squeeze pages, so you need to upgrade through a programmer or add-on service.

Many studies of online marketing have determined that a squeeze page needs to pop up after the prospect has used or developed some attachment to your site. For example, if you require prospects to enter all that information before they're allowed to even view their first property, most will skip your registration process and bounce to another site. But if you let them view three or four properties before your squeeze page pops us, the number of people who actually provide valid information grows exponentially.

WARNING

Some people are determined not to reveal themselves, and they'll get around your squeeze page by entering John Doe or Ima Buyer as the name or putting their phone number as 123-456-7890. You have to understand that some people just don't want to reveal themselves yet; move on to better prospects.

Combining your property search system with other strategies

The beauty of IDX is that you can find so many ways to expand its reach. By allowing IDX to join forces with pay-per-click campaigns, Facebook postings, and enhanced lead-generation systems, you can amp up your ability to collect prospect information. With stealth sites, you can also use marketing strategies integrated with IDX to target specific groups of prospects, such as investors, foreclosure buyers, or first-time buyers.

Working with pay-per-click campaigns

An effective pay-per-click campaign starts with research. You have to know what terms buyers and sellers are using to search for homes. If you live in Seattle, Washington, for example, what are the most-used search terms? Is it "Seattle Washington real estate," "Seattle Washington homes," or "Seattle Washington homes for sale"? In other words, what are people typing into their search engines?

TIP

You may also want to research the niche markets in your area. How many prospects are searching for real estate in the cities of Bellevue, Bothell, Kent, or any of the other bedroom communities near Seattle? You can also narrow your niche focus by researching what buyers are looking for, such as foreclosures, bank-owned homes, short sales, townhomes, condos, or homes with acreage. You can find keyword rankings by going to the Google support area or using independent experts like www.seocentro.com and www.seobook.com. Many resources enable you to access rank positioning for search terms in your marketplace. Also look at pay-per-click ad rates. Those rates are set based on what someone is willing to pay for the key ad positions. The higher the volume of people searching, the higher the cost per click.

If you're focusing on submarkets, start with smaller bedroom communities in your area. Check out the search traffic for these submarkets. How does it compare to the larger nearby city? You may be able to create a strong position more easily and quickly in a submarket. The real trick is knowing the *search volume* (how many people search for homes in these submarkets) for a host of possible markets and submarkets.

Also look at the competition in the organic search area. *Organic* search results are the non-pay-per-click rankings — the first three sites that show up in search results. Studies show that more people go to the first organic site because they know that site has achieved that ranking from offering valuable information.

You want to know who occupies these key organic spots. These sites likely have strong, relevant information that is updated frequently, and many other websites probably link to these sites. Any good businessperson should know what the competition is doing, so scope out these top-ranked sites and see what your competition is doing right.

Most search engines have both pay-per-click and organic listings. In the organic listings, websites show up at the top of the list for free because algorithms in the search engine deem them to be high-value sites. It's difficult to grab the organic top spots away from those who already hold these positions. It can be done, but it takes time and dollars. But in pay-per-click listings, you can claim a space in the top three or at the top of the sidebar by outbidding your competition for clicks. If you want to enter the bidding, simply go to any search engine and look at the current bids. Increase the bid, and it's yours. These search engines don't play favorites.

The key to effective pay-per-click marketing is twofold:

>> **Have a powerful URL.** When you're trying to create clicks and website traffic, the right URL can make a difference. A good URL often includes your geographic area, such as www.besthomedealsdenver.com, www.seattlebankownedhomes.com, or www.liveinportland.com. You can create URLs based on the type of property, geographic area, and submarket. You can have multiple URLs that redirect to the same site but cast a wider net. Don't exclusively drive pay-per-click visitors to your general website. You can build smaller sites that target a specific niche of buyers or sellers. When they land on the site, they can really feel at home because it contains exactly what they're looking for rather than an overload of links and information they don't want.

>> **Create strong wording in the description box.** You only get a few lines of text in the pay-per-click ad, and the description must be compelling and speak to the prospect you're trying to attract. It must stand out from the other ads and organic search results.

For example, if you want to create a pay-per-click ad focused on foreclosures, you can say: "Best deals on bank-owned homes. Save big money on your next home."

Using enhanced lead-generation systems

Many different lead-generation systems can support and expand on your IDX system. These systems can also connect with your Facebook ads, pay-per-click campaigns, and other forms of marketing. Many of these systems help with search-engine placement, but the biggest benefit is conversion of the leads you generate. Systems like BoomTown (http://boomtownroi.com), TigerLead (www.tigerlead.com), **Kunversion** (http://insiderealestate.com), **Realty Generator** (www.marketleader.com), **Zurple** (http://zurple.com), **Real Geeks** (www.realgeeks.com), and others like them can help you better manage and convert your leads.

These systems also provide better service to your clients and prospects than most basic MLS IDX systems. They enable consumers to track, monitor, and save properties they mark as favorites. As with a standard MLS IDX, they enable online prospects to set up specific search parameters that notify them instantly when a new property matching their criteria comes on the market.

Most of these services, unlike the basic MLS IDX systems, offer a *smart-drip* campaign that sends targeted messages to prospects at intervals based on their level of activity on the site and on what they're searching for. As an agent, you have all that information compiled in your dashboard, so you can view all the prospect's actions and favorite properties.

The final component of most systems is a customer relationship management (CRM) solution. This creates a closed-loop system to manage both your lead generation and lead conversion.

Building stealth sites

One good strategy is to develop *stealth sites* where your personal branding isn't so prominently displayed. Most states require your name, your company name, and your contact information to be displayed on the site, but if users have to scroll all the way down to see it . . . they probably won't. This gives the website the appearance of a free service. This strategy creates the perception of a "salesperson-free site." It makes prospects more comfortable and less hesitant to register when asked to. This can increase your lead volume and conversion rates.

You can build multiple stealth landing pages inexpensively to deliver your IDX offer. For each page, get a URL that will be powerful in both search engine optimization (see Chapter 12) and pay-per-click campaigns. For example, you can target Seattle buyers interested in foreclosed properties with a landing page like www.SeattlesBestForeclosureDeals.com. Any URL that speaks to a target audience can drive traffic.

Chapter **6**

Creating a Larger Online Presence

Because 92 percent of buyers and sellers use the Internet to search for real estate, with 81 percent being frequent property searchers, your online presence is more important today than ever before. For an agent who wants to grow the level of listing and sales, your online image, presence, lead creation, and lead-capture system must have a strong online focus.

The sellers of today are aware that buyers and real estate information has gone online. They don't expect as much print or direct-mail type of marketing for their properties. They are, however, less knowledgeable about the inner workings of the online world compared to the print world. It was easier for them to see what their agent was doing to get their home sold when they opened up the newspaper and saw their ad or received the direct mail piece, as their neighbors did, about their home.

Building a Quality Website for Long-Term Success

As a newer agent or one who is working to ramp your business up to the next level, being able to make the investment in a quality website is necessary to growth. The cost of websites can run from a few hundred dollars (plus hosting) to tens of thousands of dollars for an elaborate custom website.

WARNING

If you are in the early stages of your career, a template website with a few bells and whistles might be good enough for the short run. IDX integration is a must-have, though. Your site *must* be able to aggregate properties from the MLS onto pages on your site, even if you have zero listings. Your listings versus the MLS listings should not be easy to distinguish on the site. If your site has an area called My Listings, for example, and you have none at the time, a buyer or seller sees that you have zero listings and will draw the conclusion you are new or do little production.

TIP

You *do* want to highlight your personal listings in a separate or first-to-see area, but it should say Featured Listings or something similar. The IDX functionality is essential for capturing prospects and creating the right image. Buyers are most interested in homes and the ability to search for homes.

Knowing your website's purpose

The purposes of a real estate agent's website are as follows:

>> To tell your story in more depth

>> To allow people to connect with you

>> To produce leads for your sales efforts

The challenge with many template websites, especially the very basic versions provided by brokerage companies at no cost, is that they are essentially electronic business cards. They have limited information, limited custom-messaging opportunities, and little if any lead-generation capacity.

REMEMBER

The primary goal of a website — in my view, having been in sales for 30 years — is to create leads. The lead-generation aspect of any website in creating leads is more challenging today than in years past. That's because the level of competition for lead creation is fiercer. This is especially true online, where we have large companies with venture capital funds trying to make inroads in the real estate sector.

Creating leads through your site

There are two basic options in lead generation for your website when it comes to prospects searching for properties:

>> Organic search

>> Pay-per-click

Organic search is what you normally think of when you think of what search engines do. A buyer or seller goes to Google, Bing, Yahoo!, or any other search engine and types in a search term like "Bend Oregon Real Estate" or "Homes for sale in Bend Oregon." The search engine then grabs the best sites based on their algorithm and serves those links up to the searcher.

The challenge with organic search in most marketplaces is that Zillow, Trulia, Realtor.com, or large real estate companies already have the top search positions for most markets and search terms. They have big budgets to invest in their websites to keep being ranked. It's unlikely that you will organically be ranked at a high level in the near future.

The other option is *pay-per-click,* or PPC. It's where you buy search engine ad space in the ad blocks for specific real estate terms in your marketplace. Your ads come appear above the organic results or over to the side of the page of organic results when someone does a search for real estate terms in your area. With PPC, you are buying specific terms and phrases, so you need to understand through research how many people per month are using certain terms to help them find real estate in your area.

The PPC strategy for lead generation can be very effective in creating leads and opportunities if your site has value for the searcher and you have a capture mechanism on your site. The most common capture mechanism is their ability to search properties easily. That IDX technology is foundational for lead creation. Once the buyer has seen a few properties, a squeeze page or squeeze pop-up box comes up requiring them to register. This is how forced registration leads are typically created in real estate sales. Refer to Chapter 5 for detailed information on forced registration leads.

Delivering value online

The longer a visitor to your site stays, the higher the odds you can create a relationship, create a lead, or transfer value. But for visitors to spend their valuable time lingering on your site, your site must have value. Some options for providing value would be articles and information about the home-buying process.

Twenty-seven percent of first-time home buyers go online first to read and learn about the home-buying process.

TIP

If you have a lot of high-value content on buying a home, and if it's specifically written about how to do it in your marketplace, that can increase traffic and leads. You also might be able to get a higher organic ranking for those individual articles on your site. Additionally, you could drive PPC campaigns for first-time buyers for those specific pages of your site rather than just the main website URL, which can improve your targeting.

Consider providing free reports, infographics, and content on the following topics:

>> Selling a home

>> Buying a home

>> Staging a home for sale

>> Getting top dollar for your home

>> The state of the marketplace

>> Avoiding the typical errors buyers or sellers make

>> Saving money when you buy a home

>> Negotiating with a seller to get the best deal

TIP

One of the best sources for content for agents to use on websites, blogs, and social media is Keeping Current Matters (www.keepingcurrentmatters.com). It does an outstanding job of analyzing the national and regional marketplaces. It creates high-quality infographics, articles, and tools that you can rebrand and use as your value to clients and prospects. Check it out.

Understanding Real Estate Blogging

Blogging today is sort of what newsletters were ten years ago. The biggest difference is the interactivity you can create with a blog. Although many agents agonize over what to write in their blogs, the basic rule is the same as for any other social media platform: Consistency is key. If you're going to blog, you must do a couple of blog posts each week — not once a week or once a month.

Nothing is worse than going to a blog that hasn't had any new posts in a while. It shows a lack of attention on the part of the agent. I certainly know how hard it is to come up with something meaningful to write about a few times a week. But you don't have to have written a number of books to be effective at blogging.

In fact, you don't have to write much at all. You could do a video blog, for example. And no, you don't have to be a videographer. A simple HD webcam on your computer, smartphone, or tablet can even do the trick in creating simple but effective video blog communications.

Creating the look and feel of a professional blog

Blogging is much easier today than ever before because of the wealth of programs, apps, and software that can incorporate a blog into your website. A simple Word-Press site with a template layout is easy, quick, and worth checking out. I recommend WordPress (www.wordpress.com) because it's easy to use. Many web designers use it as well, and it really is the best option for agents. Blogs are effective in helping you climb up the search-engine rankings because search engines like the new content that a blog provides.

Add street cred to your blog: Feature a guest blogger each week. You very likely have access to a number of guest bloggers, such as your mortgage originator, home inspector, insurance agent, home stager, interior decorator, attorney, accountant, title officer, contractor, and remodeler.

Setting up your writing and posting schedule

Setting up your blogging schedule or "theme days" is one of the most important first steps to having a successful blog. Many professional bloggers post multiple times a day or post on multiple blogs a day. Doing it at least a couple of times a week is the minimum if you want to enhance your readership. Also, posting at the same time each week helps create anticipation for your posts. Decide on a schedule to post — but also to write. If you don't carve out a set time to create new content, you'll always be doing it at the last minute. The quality will suffer, and the pressure you feel will explode.

You can set up different segments or even different days that you post about certain topics. You can do a "photo Friday" theme. You can blog about your community, using photos to illustrate your topic. You can highlight restaurants, businesses, and new attractions in your community on a certain day. You can regularly deal with zoning or planning issues that affect your community. You can feature a real estate column each week where you share rate alerts, give tips on home values, talk about the current state of the marketplace, give the pros and cons of home-ownership versus renting, or discuss your keys to your marketing plan.

Always be ready to gather observations in your daily life. Don't go anywhere without your digital camera. Your smartphone can take pictures, but most digital cameras are far better. Post what you observe and craft a blog from it — a wild paint job on a home, a pink above-ground oil tank, a new park, a horrendous traffic jam, and so on. Be a gatherer of experiences and photos for later use as well; file them away on your computer, tablet, or smartphone.

TIP

Try an app like Evernote (www.evernote.com) to store photos with your brief observations so you can reconstruct your feelings, thoughts, and ideas at a later date when you want to incorporate the photos into your blog.

Positioning yourself as the marketplace expert

The vast majority of consumers think they know more than real estate agents. It's why we typically score so low in the annual Harris Interactive poll of trusted professionals. We must change that. The best method is to demonstrate market knowledge, and a blog is an effective way to continually demonstrate and flex your knowledge muscles. Use market data from your MLS. Share list-to-sale price ratios, days-on-the-market numbers, and real estate trends.

Real estate values and market activity are controlled by supply and demand. When either of those changes, you'll see a corresponding reaction in the real estate market. If supply goes up and stays up, prices will usually moderate, flatten, or start to move downward. If the demand increases because the number of buyers increases, you may see the opposite results. By regularly commenting on these trends, you establish yourself as an expert.

REMEMBER

Your market data and trend projections should explain, educate, and forecast what the law of supply and demand is reflecting in your real estate market. Using your blog a handful of times a month for this targeted purpose can inform your readers and position you as the expert.

TIP

Don't forget to include a *call to action* (CTA) with these types of blog posts. A good CTA is "If you're looking to move into the upper end, it's a buyer's market, so call me right away" or "A large volume of foreclosures just hit the market, so if you're looking for a great deal, call me or text me now." You want to move people out of reading mode and into action — calling and reaching out because they see a clear opportunity or feel a heightened fear of loss.

Integrating a Customer Relationship Management (CRM) Solution

The real estate sales business, like all other businesses in the world, is in a techno-revolution. New technologies have created tremendous changes and growth in our industry. Agents and companies are dramatically changing the way they do business to take advantage of this vast new frontier. And technology is moving at a faster rate every day. As an agent, you must prepare and learn to capitalize on this revolution. The days where you could do your business out of a shoebox with 3 x 5 note cards is gone. The power of the online age has made many of the things we did years ago obsolete. Agents need to set up their business to run like a true corporation to be successful. With these changes, there are a few specific areas we need to evaluate.

Contact management and customer service software systems have become more imperative for agents. Agents need to have tremendous amounts of information about their clients and potential clients to stay competitive. This information will enable them to become a valuable resource to their clients and, in turn, sell more to their clients. In addition, these agents will receive more referral business because their service level has increased. To join these successful agents, you need to be able to keep in contact with your clients quickly, and more frequently, if you hope to create winning sales situations.

I firmly believe, based on socioeconomic trends, rising interest rates, and the recent market correction, that in the future people will not move so frequently. The average years that people spend in a home will increase. A few factors are contributing to this trend. The first is the desire of Americans to simplify their lives. The second key reason is that the largest segment of the population has only one move left. The Baby Boomers are now seeking to retire while they are still active and are starting to evaluate where to move next. They have more selection in the types and variety of housing than all preceding generations. I think this will be one of the most viable sections of the marketplace.

These factors will create the need for agents to control data and be able to access that data better and more efficiently of prospects and past clients. We have to know preference, family sizes, life stages, and experiences. Even tracking the potential equity and interest rates of the mortgages can help you add value and predict real estate interest. You have to be able to gather the data, control the data, search the data, and communicate with your database more efficiently in email, text, and social media. That's why the need for a CRM has never been more important.

Using a CRM as your electronic brain

Customer relationship management (CRM) software lets you house your business contacts, leads, clients, and prospects in one place. It enables you to organize all correspondence via email and input call notes into client records that are searchable. More advanced CRMs have internal texting and social media features where your texts are also recorded in a client record.

A quality CRM will help remind you when to call, text, message or mail both clients and prospects — all while reminding you of your appointments and commitments. Just think of it like an automated business assistant. You must have a command of your CRM. This software is the lifeblood of your business. It will enable you to create sales. There are many good software packages out there, including the following:

>> Top Producer (www.topproducer.com)

>> RealtyJuggler (www.realtyjuggler.com)

>> Wise Agent (www.wiseagent.com)

>> Follow Up Boss (www.followupboss.com)

>> Realvolve (www.realvolve.com)

Each has its own particular strengths and weaknesses. Do your homework and carefully check out each one.

WARNING

When you purchase CRM software, you must evaluate the training that each one offers. If you can't get good, solid training, don't buy that software. Some of the value of the software is learning it quickly and efficiently. If you are going to have to teach yourself while trying to run your business, you will never fully utilize the software. You must be able to use the full power of the software to be able to bring the most success to your business.

TIP

Make sure your CRM software is online in the cloud rather than just on your hard drive. I would advise you not to purchase software that is not in the cloud. You want to be able to access your data from anywhere on any device. If you expand your business beyond yourself, you will need the capabilities to have other people to access it as well.

Many of the larger real estate brokerage companies provide CRM solutions to you as an agent. Even though that might be tempting, because it is free, do the same due diligence that you would if you had to pay for the software yourself:

- » Is it easy and functional?

- » Is the software intuitive and pleasant to work in all day? Software that makes you want to pull your hair out will be used infrequently.

- » Are automatic follow-up procedures and timing built in for leads, current clients, pending transactions, past clients, and sphere of influence?

- » Are these action plans easy to apply to a new client or prospect record?

- » Do the action plans include triggers for specific emails, texts, and calls?

Property search system + CRM = money

TIP

One of the most powerful combinations is using a property search website system with a CRM. These two, when combined, enable you to create leads online through social media and PPC campaigns that then drop into your CRM solution, or have a CRM solution with them. Here are a few:

- » Real Geeks (www.realgeeks.com)

- » Boomtown (www.boomtownroi.com)

- » Commissions Inc (www.commissionsinc.com)

- » TigerLead (www.tigerlead.com)

They create online buyer leads as well as track buyer information: How many times they have come back to view properties, what properties they have viewed, what properties they have saved or favorited, and how long they used your site on service, for example. You can also set up custom searches or refined searches for these prospects. Send email, text, or make calls right out of the software. Set the prospects on automatic drip campaigns of emails and communication so automation will support your sales attempts and efforts. This is the highest level in CRM lead generation and lead conversion systems.

WHY CAN'T I JUST USE OUTLOOK?

The most common software people use in real estate sales — thinking it is CRM software — is Outlook. The main reason? It's probably free, because you likely already have it on your laptop or tablet. The problem is, even when Outlook is used at its full capacity, it's merely a reminder and scheduler. Outlook is not a true CRM. If your goal is to earn a few hundred thousand dollars a year in income, you will quickly outgrow Outlook as a viable option.

Chapter 7

Creating Leads with Third-Party Websites

The real estate industry has historically been in control of real estate information and access to that information. That all changed as the online presence of real estate grew. When local multiple listing services began to sell access to that information to third parties, the new age of real estate information access was born for buyers and sellers.

This big change has created both opportunities and challenges for real estate companies and agents. Because we don't control the information and its access, our value proposition needs to be different than in the past. The consumer was forced to rely on an agent previously to understand what properties might be for sale, background information on those homes, what the sellers paid for them, even what the taxes are on the properties. Now the consumer can get all that information without an agent. The monopoly of information is gone and agents must sell their value based on experience, knowledge, expertise, negotiating prowess, and more.

Some companies are trying to gain back control of yesteryear by not allowing the MLS a direct syndication of their listings to third-party websites. Though I understand their frustration with the current state of third-party sites using the companies' listing inventory to create leads of buyers and sellers — and those leads then in effect being sold back to the company and agents through monthly service fees, zip code exclusivity per lead costs, and referral fees — I personally believe the time for protective strategies is long over. That train left the station years ago.

Any agent or company that doesn't allow open access and syndication of their listings is not doing what is best for their client, the seller. I personally believe the third-party companies are just too powerful, with too many eyeballs using them to search for homes online. Our job as agents is to expose our listings to the widest group of buyers and agents. This increases the odds for our seller that their home will sell, and for market value or higher.

The Elephant in the Room: Third-Party Real Estate Sites

There is clear frustration with companies like Zillow (www.zillow.com), Trulia (www.trulia.com), and Realtor.com (www.realtor.com). The latter was actually owned at one time by the real estate community. The term *Realtor* is a registered trademark by the National Association of Realtors. NAR was instrumental in the establishment of the trademark but no longer has ownership of the Realtor.com company.

The traffic growth of these three heavyweights continues to explode. In 2016, the term "Zillow" was searched on Google more than the search term "real estate." The power that comes from "ZTR" — Zillow, Trulia, and Realtor.com, with more than 231,000,000 million combined visitors a month — is undeniable. Zillow alone has more than 124 million monthly visitors, Trulia has 57 million, and Realtor.com has more than 50 million at last reporting. Zillow Group is reporting that it has 62 percent of all real estate online searches. Think about that in context: Apple has 32 percent of the cell phone market, and Apple is the most valuable company in the world.

The love-hate relationship with Zillow, Trulia, and Realtor.com

If you review online forums and Facebook groups frequented by real estate agents, there is little ambivalence toward ZTR. The views posted by agents are strongly held and run the gamut. There are plenty that have vitriol for these third-party companies. The frustration agents share about the lack of control, high costs of leads through those companies, low conversion rates, and lack of momentum expressed by Internet home searchers is splashed all over these forums. The agents who do use ZTR effectively and make money from their usage and association with these companies are a small minority. Whether that's because few agents are having success, or they don't want to share their success rates with others, or they're just too busy with the leads created by ZTR and making money, I'll let you be the judge, but the malcontent crowd is loud and proud.

TIP

My advice is to treat it all as white noise. There is an opportunity here, as with any marketing strategy or service. The questions are: Does it fit you, your goals, and the type of business you are building? It is a good business strategy for you and your sellers to create exposure and leads with these companies? Can you create a return on your marketing dollars, time, effort, and energy sufficient to create a profit?

Results can vary by marketplace

The truth is, each of the major online search platforms in Zillow, Trulia, and Realtor.com have their pluses and minuses, like anything. Each has its own system, strategy, and terminology for agents to consider and use. Because your marketplace has unique buyers, sellers, economic conditions, marketplace conditions, and technology usage, among a host of other factors, you might achieve different results with each one, or different results than another agent in a different marketplace.

Bend, Oregon, where I live, is a smaller town of 90,000 people. It's a resort town with a high concentration of second homes and a high percentage of more affluent buyers who have relocated from other places. The strategies agents use with the third-party sites are more effective when they mirror strategies used in other ski and golf resort markets than they are when they use strategies common in, say, Portland, which is three hours away.

As an agent, you must be able to track and monitor the results you're getting from each online lead company. How many leads are you getting from Zillow each month? What is the conversion rate for the leads you receive from Trulia from lead to appointment? How much did you earn in pending and closed commissions from your Realtor.com leads? As a business owner, you have to look at each of these individually and ask each of these questions.

You're not looking for a one-to-one ratio. In other words, if I spend $1 with Realtor.com, I am not looking for a $1 in return in revenue. That is a sure way to lose money as a business owner. Too frequently agents view an expenditure in terms of "I only need one transaction to pay for this marketing." That doesn't factor in your time, overhead, and a profit margin. Any business that is going to have longevity needs to create profits. When you're investing in marketing and lead generation, you need, at a minimum, four to five times return, in my view, to achieve a good profit margin.

The only way to determine that is to monitor and track numbers and to try something for a reasonable period of time. Especially with third-party online lead-generation strategies, it will be six months before you will know if you are going to be profitable. Because of the delay in income, with online buyers having a longer sales cycle due to transactions needing to close, at the six-month mark you will have to look at both closed dollars and pending dollars based on your ZTR leads. You might even look at the people you are actually showing houses to from Zillow, Trulia, and Realtor.com and determine the odds of their likely buying and closing in the next few months. As agents, using sound business evaluation skills is your only option.

Zillow, the White Whale of Real Estate

Zillow has more unique visitors than both Trulia and Realtor.com combined. If you're thinking of wading into the waters of third-party sites for lead generation, you must take a serious look at Zillow. You will notice that I devote a lot more space here to Zillow than to Trulia and Realtor.com. I do that for a couple of reasons. The first reason is that it is the largest and most powerful of the three. To me, Zillow has earned the lion's share of the discussion because of its power. The second reason is that the three have practices in common. They all work to innovate new ways to create leads, capture online searchers, agents, and companies, and they copy each other's ideas and strategies. Because of that, some of what I say about Zillow also applies to the other two. It would be redundant to write as much about Realtor.com and Trulia.

Also, Zillow owns Trulia now. It bought Trulia in February 2015 for $2.5 billion in stock. Because of its strength and the Trulia acquisition, Zillow is the strongest outside player in the real estate game. It has morphed a lot of Zillow technology, systems, and strategy into Trulia. There are more than two million real estate profiles for real estate agents on Zillow. The National Association of Realtors has about 1.3 million members, so Zillow has 54 percent more real estate agent profiles than NAR members.

Pay to play as a featured agent on listings

If you search homes for Zillow, and I would suggest that you do, you will typically see about four agents listed on each property. Zillow is trying to give the consumer options regarding agents they might select to get information on the property, or on other properties. It is rewarding consumers with choice and power.

The top agent in the list of four agents is the listing agent — or their company has purchased featured agent status. Not all companies pay for their agents' listings to be at the featured agent status. You or your company must buy that status for your listings. You might be thinking, "Why is that important?"

Many online buyers want to get information from the listing agent directly. They feel the listing agent is the one most knowledgeable about that home. That usually is a correct assumption. They also feel that, because there would be only one agent involved in the sale, that they might be able to receive a rebate on commission or negotiate a lower sales price on the home. Although that is possible for some agents, it's not with others — but perception is reality to some online searchers.

If there is low inventory in your marketplace with multiple offers happening, online buyers tend to believe that by going with the listing agent, their odds of being the buyer and beating out the other buyers who want the home improves because the listing agent could earn more money due to the full commission going to them, or at least the listing agent knows all the offers that are being made on the property. They might gain insider information that can help them create a better offer. I am not saying any of this is correct thinking or is ethical on the part of the listing agent. I am just giving you a window into the thinking of some prospects.

Some companies also pay for *exclusive* agent status. They pay Zillow to be the only agent listed on all their company listings. In researching Zillow to understand its system and strategy, if you see a few listings with only one agent, you know the company has a very tight relationship with Zillow and pays dearly for it. At a minimum, you need to pay the money to be a featured agent and be marketed as the listing agent.

TIP

Many agents don't realize or don't want to spend the money with Zillow, whether because of principles or cost. That is, quite frankly, foolish thinking. The cost to be a featured agent is typically $25 or less per listing. It's a small amount of money to pay to receive leads from your listing on a site that has 124 million unique views a month.

TIP

If you are competing with an agent whose company does not syndicate its listings to Zillow, or does not a least pay for featured agent status on Zillow, you owe it to the seller to point out that difference in marketing. You can easily pull up one of the competing agent's listings and one of yours and show how different it looks. How the leads will go to other agents rather than the agent they are entrusting the job of selling their home to. That can be extremely impactful to a seller needing to sell.

Using premier agent status even when a new agent

Premier agent status with Zillow is the next level up from featured agent. It is where you pay for a portion of a zip code or area of listings to create leads. You will be one of those other three agents attached to a listing that a buyer is viewing. You could be right below the listing agent or be the first one listed if the listing agent has not paid for featured agent status. You could be number four out of the four agents listed. The order and which listing your profile is connected to are based on Zillow's algorithms and your investment with Zillow.

REMEMBER

As an agent, you are typically buying a percentage of the number of leads created in a specific zip code or a specific minimum number of leads you will receive each month. As an agent paying for a certain number of leads, you must monitor whether you receive the set amount agreed to. To guess or estimate at the end of the month is not sufficiently accurate in your tracking to determine whether paying premier agent status is worth the investment.

You could spend tens of thousands a month in large market areas controlling the lion's share of the leads in one zip code. You have to properly balance your need for leads against what is a reasonable number of leads you can actually work per month well. I find that most agents can't work more than 40–60 online leads a month well. When they create more than that number, they go to waste. Because of an overabundance of online leads, the number of calls, texts, and emails directed toward each lead drops, and so does the conversion rate.

It's possible to pay equivalent to, in competitive markets, $80 or more per lead from Zillow. This might seem like a lot, and it is a sizable amount per lead. If you are converting 5 percent of your leads to closings, then you would be paying $1,600 in lead-generation costs for every transaction you get from Zillow. If your average commission check is $4,000 this would not be profitable by the time you factor your time, effort, energy, and company split. For this to be a worthwhile investment you would need to either raise your conversion rate or average sales price, which would raise your average commission check.

Another option is to have your lender or other vendors that share in your success contribute to the costs of your lead generation and premier agent leads you purchase. You can do that through a joint marketing service agreement. A general rule of thumb is a lender can pay up to 50 percent of your marketing cost. A lender certainly benefits by you increasing your buyer business through your recommendations to your client base of buyers.

It's about the reviews

The typical buyer searching properties on Zillow determines which of the four agents they contact to get more information or schedule a showing first based on the placement of those four agents. The largest portion of them click the top name to inquire about the property. That's why featured agent status and owning your own listings are so important.

They next look to the reviews for the agent on the Zillow site. They can clearly see that you have been reviewed, how many times you have been reviewed, and the number of stars you have achieved. Too many agents appear as the listing agent or premier agent that have zero or very few reviews. That can dramatically affect the volume of leads you create. Few online buyers want to be a pioneer in selecting someone with no reviews based on someone they don't know. Your friends, acquaintance, and referrals might want to help you as a newer agent, but not an online prospect.

TIP

Gaining reviews in your Zillow profile is the process of first asking your clients and past clients to review you. You will need to take the risk to ask. Just sending out a request for a review is not enough. You will need to call and ask for their help. Let them know an email with the link is coming. Ask them to complete it in a specific timeframe and follow up to remind them if they haven't done it yet.

Some Zillow searchers look no further than the sheer number of reviews you have on your profile. They feel safer that way and select the person who has the most, or nearly the most. At a minimum, you have to get in the ballpark with other premier agents as fast as possible. You might be thinking, "Okay, how many do I need to have to be competitive?" That can depend on your marketplace. I see marketplaces where agents have hundreds of reviews and others where 20 reviews is a lot. You must study and react to your marketplace. If you are evaluating a zip code to buy where an agent or team has hundreds of reviews, you might want to select a different area until you can climb closer to that number.

The online buyer moves from sheer numbers to number of stars and may even read the most recent reviews. You might want to help the people you are asking to review you by listing some of the highlights or key phrases that sum up the unique service you provided for them.

WARNING

Make sure your reviews don't sound too similar with the same phrases repeated throughout individual reviews. That can taint your reviews to a reader. They then discount the objectivity of the reviews and move on to another agent to consider.

When the importance of reviews was realized a few years ago, a lot of agents got on the review bandwagon to increase their reviews. In most agents' profiles, you can see the spike in their reviews over a few months' period of time. This is where they went back to past clients to have them review them. Many of these agents have had a limited numbers of reviews since. The need for fresh and current reviews is important as well. Zillow lists the recent reviews as a tally. By not having any reviews in the last six months to a year, the Zillow user knows that your reviews and service lack the credibility they desire.

Any agent doing a decent amount of business will have the odd bad online review to deal with. You won't ever make everyone happy. We deal with one of the largest, most emotional decisions in one's lifetime. You must first accept that less than favorable reviews will happen. It's not if, it's when.

When that bad review happens, you need to take action. I would contact the reviewer first to see how you might correct the issue. If the issue that caused the poor review was out of your control, or can't be corrected, then craft a response to the review. You want to express your concern for the dissatisfaction and state that you contacted the reviewer to resolve the issue. If there were any extenuating circumstances, insert those but in short form. Never attack the reviewer, even if that reviewer was wrong.

As with any online review mechanism, there will be trolls. There will be people who review you that you never represented nor ever met. The buyer that you refused to show a property to because it didn't feel right, or they hadn't been pre-qualified or pre-approved yet. It's easy to flame an agent today with a negative review because of the cloak of invisibility. Harry Potter is not the only one who can be stealthy in our online world.

If the troll review gives the wrong impression of your service or you didn't actually serve this online offender, contact Zillow to see if you can have the review removed. If that is unsuccessful, then your only option is to quickly respond and get additional reviews so you can bury this review a couple of pages down so it gets rarely seen. Most buyers are not going to page through all your reviews.

Check your production

Zillow also has added a production display in the last few years, based on the number of sales reported overall and in the specific area that the buyer is looking in. Zillow also displays what you have accomplished in the last 12 months in sales in both categories. You must constantly check the accuracy of these. Zillow can only report information that is relayed to it directly or through syndication through your MLS. You need to make sure that every listing and sale is awarded to you properly.

Consumers want someone who is highly knowledgeable and a specialist in the marketplace they want to list or buy in. Zillow can tell them what is for sale and what Zillow thinks the home is worth in Zillow's "zestimate." A zestimate is a value Zillow bases on a proprietary algorithm for your market. Zillow doesn't calculate actual listings and sales, nor does it do a comparative market analysis. Frequently the zestimate can be significantly off from the actual value of the home. Zillow even admits the zestimate estimated national error rate is 6 percent. That means on a $300,000 home, on average the zestimate is off by $18,000. Most consumers would not be pleased with an agent who was that far afield in their CMA.

REMEMBER

The rule in dealing with zestimates: If the zestimate is higher than value, the sellers think it's gospel, and the buyer thinks it's a trashy romance novel.

Realtor.com: It's Not Ours Anymore

The acquisition of Realtor.com by Move (www.move.com) has brought another major player with very deep financial pockets into the real estate field. The people at Move make for a worthy competitor to the dominance that Zillow has carved out in the online real estate space. Some have characterized these two companies as clear opponents engaged in an epic battle for market share, consumer users, and agent users. The real estate community are spectators in the stands watching the tennis match where the ball is hit back and forth between these grand slam champions. Although I don't feel we are merely spectators, I do recognize that the amount of money and eyeballs Realtor.com commands can't be ignored or denied. Our job is to learn how to generate leads and create our brand and service differentiation to attract business.

Lead-generation options with Realtor.com

By outward appearances, Realtor.com has a more exclusive strategy than Zillow. When consumers are searching Realtor.com for properties, they are not given several agents to choose from. They do see the office that has the listing. It shows that this property is "brokered by XYZ." The vast majority of consumers may not know what "brokered" means, but the office is listed there.

The big difference between Zillow and Realtor.com begins once you have selected a property to investigate as a consumer. In Zillow, you choose among four recommended agents if you want more information. As a consumer, you can see their number of reviews and star ratings. You can see their recent sales production. You can then further investigate all four agents through their agent pages, read their biographies and reviews, and see their other listings and sales.

On Realtor.com the listing agent's information, headshot, and company are at the top of the property information page. Numerous buttons down the page prompt the consumer to contact the agent, request a private showing, ask the neighborhood expert, ask to get comps through "Want to get comps?" and "Tell me more about this property." Realtor.com has created numerous opportunities and places for the searcher to click a button so that the pop-up to harvest information appears.

The consumer's mentality, when they fill out their information, is that the listing agent will be contacting them. In most cases that will not be true. Realtor.com, like Zillow and Trulia, distributes the leads to agents who have paid for a percentage of the leads produced in a zip code.

If you decide to invest some dollars in marketing with Realtor.com, the most important first step on the call is to *never state that you are not the listing agent.* There are a number of buyers who, once that is known but they don't know you yet, will look at the masthead of who has the listing and then call them or email them directly. This advice is true of all Internet leads, but especially for Realtor.com leads due to the perceived exclusive promotion of one agent.

If you make statements like "Let me check with the listing agent" or "Let me call XYZ Real Estate to get you that information" or anything like that, it could give away that you are not the listing agent. Instead, use a statement like "I have never been asked that before on this property, let me do a little research." Or: "I will need to check with the seller before I can confirm that." Or: "That's a great question, it may take me a little bit to track down the information from the seller. When would be a good time to reach you back this afternoon with an answer?"

Obviously, I'm not advocating you call the seller directly to get the information on another agent's listing. That would be against the code of ethics. You would always call, email, or text the listing agent to secure the information the prospect might need. If the online lead wants a showing, set a tentative time and say you will need to confirm that with the seller. Your objective is to get the appointment.

Realtor.com has an option called *turbo boost* for your listing. By paying additional money, you can become the exclusive agent to receive all leads from your listing. That additional amount varies by marketplace and even by whether your company has a national relationship with Realtor.com. Some national companies like RE/MAX, Coldwell Banker, and Keller Williams have paid online companies like Realtor.com and Zillow to enhance their agents' opportunity at online leads being exclusive.

Avoiding some of the pitfalls

Realtor.com's numbers are less than half of Zillow's monthly search traffic. However, the pricing, costs, and fees for Realtor.com are not half the cost of Zillow's. Realtor.com (because of the money backing it from parent company News Corp., which owns Move) can and probably will start to close the gap.

One of the back-end issues of Realtor.com is you will need a CRM to manage the communication of the lead. Realtor.com doesn't even have a rudimentary CRM solution with its system. With all leads you create, you have to drop them into an IDX feed system through which you can control and monitor the prospect. As an agent, for Realtor.com, as with all lead generators, you will need to track your numbers. You will need to track total leads and separate the leads with email versus ones with valid phone numbers. Those convert at different levels. Then track appointments and converted clients, and finally, closed transactions and revenue.

TIP

You will also want to calculate the actual cost per lead as well. What did you spend versus how many leads were produced? Cost per lead is an important metric to review. Zillow has come out recently with an agent dashboard where agents can review their cost per lead, lead volume, and number of leads. That can save a lot of time in monitoring your return on investment.

Trulia: The Third Spoke in the Wheel

Trulia was founded in 2004 in San Francisco, near Silicon Valley. In its first ten years in the third-party real estate lead-generation game, it became a legitimate source of buyers for the agent community. In early 2015, Zillow brought Trulia and has given it a new look and feel that is similar to Zillow.

Trulia runs the four-agent model where a consumer can see four agents recommended as premier agents. It highlights the listing agent at the top, provided that listing agent is paying for the featured agent status to be promoted. At a minimum, with all the big three online lead-generation systems, you will need to at least invest the marketing dollars to be noted as the listing agent. You want to check every time you are in competition with other agents for a listing to see whether they are doing that on all of the big three platforms. If you find out they are not willing to invest the small amount in receiving their own leads, it tells you a lot about their business practice.

I've noted a trend in my research where companies are creating company profiles on Trulia and buying premier agent status. They are then using multiple agents' production that feed under their company's premier agent heading. What they are doing is creating a team out of company production. Then each agent who is part of the "team" has their own profile and bio page. Because it is acting as a team, all reviews and sales also aggregate to the large company team profile.

Because the cost for online leads in any system can be quite expensive, this strategy can help new agents or agents who are ramping up their business brand together to get into the online-lead game at a lower cost. They can quickly achieve online credibility in sales numbers and reviews because the numbers of numerous agents are combined.

The Trulia platform has been transformed to resemble Zillow. There are a few differences in how the properties are displayed and the location of buttons and information, but the strategies, opportunities, terminology, and lead-generation systems are a match. The competition is lower on Trulia because the online users are less than half of what Zillow is producing.

TIP

As an agent, you might invest where fewer agents are buying leads to gain a foothold in the third-party online world. Your cost per lead would likely be less. As you cut your teeth on learning the ropes of converting online leads and perfecting your system of lead follow-up, Trulia might be a good option to take the plunge into third-party lead generation.

3

Creating Leads through Timeless Channels

Unlock the secrets of client development and discover how, when, and why to prospect and market for business.

Know the advantages of referrals and create a winning referral-based strategy.

Get the goods on how to win business from expired and FSBO listings.

Discover how to plan the perfect open house and how to use open houses as the ultimate prospecting approach.

Chapter **8**

Sales Prospecting to Generate Listings and Sales

Prospecting is one of the easiest but most misunderstood concepts in the field of sales. This is especially true with the explosion of online lead generation, reduced phone communication, and increased texting and instant messaging. Attempting to balance prospecting and marketing has never been harder.

Sales trainers constantly try to sell their "prospecting-free systems" on worldwide speaking circuits, basically saying, "You'll never have to prospect again if you use my system." And because salespeople secretly don't want to prospect, they readily buy into the too-good-to-be-true no-prospecting philosophy. But both marketing and prospecting have a place in your business. The correct positioning for today's technology world is to be prospecting focused and marketing enhanced.

As a salesperson, if you buy into the myth of a prospecting-free or marketing-only system, you're failing to master sound prospecting approaches, and you're abandoning the need to continually develop new leads. You're risking your very livelihood in the real estate business.

As a new real estate agent, I joined an office full of experienced agents who were doing well. I knew that to succeed I needed to prospect. I didn't know much more than that, but I understood the value of prospecting based on the results I'd experienced in my previous sales jobs.

I'd come into the office at 7 a.m., and by 8 I'd be talking to expired listings, FSBOs, people within my sphere of influence — whoever I could reach on the phone. The snickering from the other offices didn't escape my notice, nor did it redirect my efforts. The laughing died down within six months when my listings and sales put me on top-performing lists — and it stopped altogether when I made over six figures in my first year in the business. I became the number-one agent in that office after my third year in the business, and my commitment to prospecting never stopped.

TIP

Prospecting is the pathway to sales success.

Knowing Why Prospecting Still Works

The purpose of *prospecting* is to develop prospective clients for your business. The prospecting method, even in today's world where people text more than answer the phone, still has merit and success attached.

Figure 8-1 shows a hierarchy of pyramid of sales and communication. This pyramid shows the power of persuasion is increased, as well as the impact, the higher you move on the pyramid.

As Figure 8-1 shows, informational marketing strategies are the lowest level of communication and influence. The direct mail and advertising we do, for example, through billboards or other advertising mediums, require a lot of impressions because of the limited persuasion they contain. Incorporating some type of social proof or validation can increase the effectiveness, but they are at the bottom of the information zone.

When we move up into email, social media, text communication, and video email, we are still in the information zone. We are transferring information — creating a connection but not selling. Let me give you an example. I will agree that I will achieve a higher response rate to a Millennial prospect if I send a text. Millennials use texting to communicate. Response rate is part of selling. It's an important part of selling . . . but it's not the only part of selling. I have to persuade, handle concerns, and change thinking in order to make a sale.

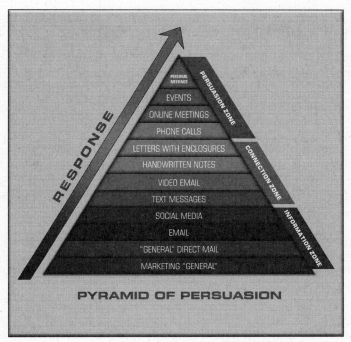

PYRAMID OF PERSUASION

RESPONSE

PERSUASION ZONE
- PERSONAL MEETINGS
- EVENTS
- ONLINE MEETINGS
- PHONE CALLS

CONNECTION ZONE
- LETTERS WITH ENCLOSURES
- HANDWRITTEN NOTES
- VIDEO EMAIL

INFORMATION ZONE
- TEXT MESSAGES
- SOCIAL MEDIA
- EMAIL
- "GENERAL" DIRECT MAIL
- MARKETING "GENERAL"

FIGURE 8-1:
Pyramid of
persuasion.

REMEMBER

There is no evidence, in fact, that I can do that better via text than via phone or face-to-face conversation. All evidence is that the conversion rates are better in face-to-face and phone-to-phone voice communication than in electronic communication.

All the electronic options are part of an effective sales strategy. I need to build effective social media messaging. That messaging needs to create engagement and a relationship. The text messaging needs to be short and effective and have a solid call to action (CTA). The missing element in most text communication is the CTA.

All electronic communication is in the information zone of communication. Because of the image and public perception of salespeople, especially real estate salespeople, the more we can break through that consumer mind-set of agents that know little, earn a lot, don't do much, and are out for their self-interest, the more effective we will be in establishing trust and credibility.

I need to smash that mental image of a salesperson that they have. This is especially true for online leads, whether that is pay-per-click, organic, Craigslist, Facebook ads, or other forms.

Video email

TIP

That is why I feel that video email is one of the most effective methods of communicating with prospects. You explode their mental image of the "sleazy salesperson," that embedded image they want to hold onto to protect themselves from sleazy salespeople.

Use video that has a warm, connective opening and that's easy for them to use. I am not talking about sending a link they must click that redirects them to a different landing page. The image of your smiling face with a Play button right there in their email for them to click is easy to use. The video plays quickly and effectively, no matter what type of device they are on, from laptop to tablet to mobile.

Your video message needs to be connective, conversational, natural (meaning it doesn't feel staged). If it delivers value or positions you as the marketplace expert, it's a home run! The creation of video email makes communication so much easier than most agents think.

So, how do you do it? Software programs can have you up and running with your video emails in minutes. For example, a program like BombBomb (`www.bombbomb.com`) can truly change the way you handle lead conversion. BombBomb is a total game changer because of its ease of use. All you need is a phone or webcam. You record the video right through the BombBomb program. A few clicks, a few minutes to record, and you are sending out personalized video email en masse or to one individual person. Go to `http://www.bombbomb.com/rechampions` for a free trial and special pricing.

Handwritten notes

As you move up the pyramid in Figure 8-1, your eyes are probably pausing at the *Handwritten Notes* in the center section. You might be thinking, "How old-school." I understand that may seem outdated in today's instant technology world. The ability to communicate quickly, efficiently, and electronically is so tempting we've abandoned the personal touch of a note. This section discusses why I think you must seriously consider incorporating handwritten notes into your lead conversion and communication strategy.

No one does it

The truth is, few people wrote handwritten notes even back when snail mail and phone were the only strategies for sales communication, before the advent of the fax machine. Today even fewer people still use handwritten notes to communicate, say thank you, appreciate, and connect. I would venture that most people go a whole year without sending or receiving a handwritten note.

I remember my mother requiring me as a child to sit down and send a handwritten thank-you note for each gift I received. That's not done today by many parents. That is what makes this form of communication so powerful. I send out my fair share of handwritten notes. I send them to people I work with in a speaking, coaching, or training capacity. My objective is to communicate appreciation, encouragement, and life impact.

In the last few years, I have been surprised at the reaction and value in the social media world that handwritten notes create. That's not why I ever started the habit of doing them, but probably one in ten that I send out get posted to Facebook. The receiver is so taken by the extra effort that they post, tag, and introduce me and my brand to their friends. Again, that was never my intent, strategy, or expectation in sending a note and it never will be. It's just a wonderful bonus for doing the fundamentals of communication well.

TIP

There is a principle of success that aligns with a handwritten note strategy: Do things others don't! If you follow the herd, you will receive or manifest what most people have in life — you manifest their level of success, happiness, and wealth.

Your mailbox isn't overflowing

What *is* overflowing is your email inbox. You are trying to compete for attention in our electronic communication. You may get hundreds of emails a day. You must separate, file, delete, and unsubscribe to countless email correspondence. The truth is, an overabundance of email in your inbox is worse than direct mail marketing ever was in the 1970s and 80s. It is hard to get noticed through email in this noisy electronic world.

Notes create a personal touch

The electronic world can seem impersonal. In social media, you need to be working to create a relationship. The relationship naturally happens faster when you use media others don't, the media that are unique and special.

Creating a connection can come from a simple thank-you note. It could come from just a "thinking of you" note. The best, in my view, is an encouraging note. Most of us, especially in business and national sales, receive a few knocks each week as we climb the ladder of success. If you are connecting with others or helping others by encouraging them on their pathway to success, the reward of just personal satisfaction of knowing you invested in the life and well-being of another is priceless.

Receiver's perception of time investment and value

The handwritten note says, "I care about you enough to invest my personal time to communicate with you." It says, "I value you so much that I was willing to invest the cost of a stamp, notecard, and most importantly, time in a relationship." The note takes the level of trust and connection to a new level.

Phone and face-to-face communication

Creating effective communication and persuasion on the phone is more complex than most salespeople think. Because they've used verbal phone communication since they were in diapers and Grandma was fawning at their first words, most people think they're automatically effective in phone communication. Although the method of phone contact is higher up in the persuasion zone, your skills might need improvement.

The advantage of phone connection is you can inject more of your emotions and tonality and use broader word selection and even a kind of body language when you communicate. When persuading someone, you need to transfer your energy, enthusiasm, and expertise to them. The lower forms of communication farther down the pyramid don't have the capacity to communicate energy and enthusiasm as effectively or persuasively as a phone call does. Sure, you can use a few emoticons to spice up your social media communication, but those fall far short because of the wide latitude of interpretation of them by the receiver. The voice-to-voice communication of phone calls will not be replaced or go out of style.

The most effective is the top of the pyramid in being face-to-face (or F2F, as the kids say). This is where you can connect and persuade at the high level of efficiency and effectiveness.

REMEMBER

The objective with any prospect in the real estate industry is to gain that face-to-face meeting as quickly as possible.

Once you're face-to-face you can, as the salesperson, position yourself as the expert, build trust with the prospect, determine their wants, needs, and desires more completely, and determine service expectations and outcome expectations. The sales ratios of success for one prospect or client rises exponentially, and the odds of you securing compensation for the time, effort, and energy you will invest moves heavily in your favor.

The true problem area or choke point for most salespeople is the phone connection. You may have forgotten some of the skills, scripts, and strategies of successful phone-to-phone voice persuasion. Or worse, you never learned and perfected them in the first place. You may have thought phone calling was dead — or you may hope that's the case because you would rather text, email, and do social media, which carry less personal rejection.

No one likes personal rejection. You wouldn't be normal if you weren't affected by personal rejection. The rejection you might experience by a non-response to an email or a "get lost, not interested" response via email is much lower than a phone-to-phone rejection. Phone and face-to-face rejections connect with our personal self-worth and value.

The skill level has fallen off in the personal selling arena. The skillful use of the phone to engage a prospect and persuade them to meet has been to some extent lost. The ability of real estate agents to persuade through market knowledge, client benefits, and competitive points of difference or unique value propositions has fallen through the floor.

The real estate prospecting process involves two steps.

1. **Identify and create leads** by establishing contact with potential clients who are interested in what you're offering. Prospecting means connecting with friends and past clients and asking for referrals. The key is the last part, specifically *asking for referrals*.

2. **Secure a face-to-face appointment** for a future pre-determined time.

Real estate agents seek two categories of clients: sellers, who become listing clients, and buyers, who become real estate purchasers. The following sections provide tips on how to prospect for clients in each group.

Prospecting for seller leads

Listing leads come from past clients, those in your sphere of influence, expired listings, FSBO conversions, open houses, notices of default, non-owner-occupied homes, lead cultivation, and door knocking — but they rarely come without some effort. The tendency when people are sending you referrals is to send you prospective buyers. The public's perception is that real estate agents sell houses: that we put people in our cars and drive them around and find them a home to buy. If you evaluate thousands of agents' businesses, as I have, you'll see that most referrals are buyers.

To find sellers, you have to do some active prospecting and lead generation:

>> Seller referrals don't come naturally. Specifically ask those within your sphere of influence, your circle of past clients, and your referral groups to share the names of people who need or want to sell real estate.

>> To achieve a greater listing inventory and develop a specialty as a listing agent, cultivate listing prospects by working expired and FSBO listings.

>> To prioritize your efforts, see the sidebar "The prospecting hierarchy of value" later in this chapter for help assessing which sources of listing leads are the most productive for your business.

Prospecting for buyer leads

Prospecting for buyers is easier than prospecting for sellers, in part because referrals arrive more naturally and in part because open houses attract prospective buyers and provide you with such a great prospecting platform. Additionally, buyers are more naturally created from your marketing efforts. Because you have listings, buyers will find you. You are marketing what they want — a home or a good deal. Most agents will have far more buyer opportunities than seller opportunities or leads.

TIP

If you're short on buyer prospects, increase the frequency of your open houses. The real estate industry has shifted to a more do-it-yourself buyer. According to NAR, 65 percent of prospective buyers have walked through a home they first viewed online. The vast majority utilize open houses because they don't have to reveal themselves as buyers and register their contact information. They get to remain stealthy.

The types of houses you hold open determine the kinds of prospects you generate. Higher-priced, more-exclusive properties draw more-discerning buyer prospects, and lower-priced properties attract less-affluent prospects.

To build your business quickly, work to generate leads from more first-time home buyers by planning more open houses in the low range of your marketplace. The benefits of developing first-time buyer prospects include

>> First-time buyers can be sold into homes quickly because they aren't burdened with the need to sell in order to make purchases possible.

>> They lack experience with other real estate agents. They don't have current agent affiliations, nor do they approach a new real estate agent relationship with baggage that may have been acquired from a less-than-stellar past experience.

>> They acquire strong loyalty when good service is rendered, allowing you to establish a long-term relationship that may span 10 to 15 years and multiple home sales and purchases during that period.

>> They provide you with an opportunity to establish relationships with their friends who are also considering first-time purchases.

Understanding the Four Pillars
of Prospecting

Most salespeople suffer from some form of sales aversion or apprehension. They mentally play in their heads, "People don't answer a call anymore." Or: "This won't work." Or: "I have other things I need to do." You must push through that negativity. For long-term prospecting success, apply the four disciplines discussed in this section that are common to agents who consistently achieve their revenue and quality-of-life goals.

1. Set a daily time and place for prospecting

You can't work your prospecting around your day. You have to work your day around your prospecting. You have to establish the habit and engage in the discipline of prospecting on a daily basis and from a controlled environment where your prospecting tools are available and readily accessible. To paraphrase from the hit 1960s *Batman* TV series, prospecting success is all about "same bat time, same bat channel."

I often ask agents who are just starting or have renewed their focus for prospecting, "When does prospecting happen during your day?" I can see they made their contacts, but what I really want to know is did the contacts happen during a scheduled prospecting time, or did they just "gut it out" — just do it because of sheer desire, commitment, discipline, or will? That's better than not completing the prospecting, but it's not sustainable in the long run. Somewhere along your ride to success, the will to do it will have to be replaced with the habit of doing it.

In my private office, I set up a prospecting station that included a stand-up area, a computer, and a telephone with a headset. Tacked on one wall were scripts for use when contacting expired-listing and FSBO prospects, past clients, those in my sphere of influence, and those whom I reached via cold calls. On another wall I posted all my objection-handling scripts, including a few options for each objection. This kept me prepared for any dialogue or direction the conversation took and helped me avoid fumbles.

Knowing that body language makes up 55 percent of the power of communication, even when communicating by phone, I kept my intensity and focus high by standing up. The headset — an absolutely essential prospecting tool — enabled me to keep my hands free so I could gesture or accentuate points as if I were speaking directly to my prospect in person.

When making an investment in a headset, don't get the cheapest one you can find. Spend a few hundred dollars to get one of high quality. Otherwise, you'll end up with such poor sound quality that your prospect won't be able to hear you clearly — hardly a formula for prospecting success.

2. Fight off distractions

The truth is, most agents welcome distractions that take them away from prospecting obligations. An inbound phone call, a text message, a social-media message or post, a problem transaction, a home-inspection question, an incoming email, an agent who wants to talk, a broken nail — anything will do. It's called creative avoidance, and agents generally excel at the art.

Whether you're just starting out or are a top agent, distractions never just go away. Real estate pros face more distractions than ever because of the access and technology driving the real estate industry. In fact, the best agents have even more potential for distraction because of the volume of business, the number of staff people, the size of client transactions, and the scope of responsibilities they juggle. The difference between prospecting avoidance and prospecting success comes down to the question, what do you do when the distractions hit? Do you postpone prospecting while you put out a fire? Do you decide to make just a few calls to settle the pending issue? Do you justify not starting your prospecting at the appointed time? If you said "yes" to any of those questions, you're practicing creative avoidance.

To fight off distractions, you have to bar their access:

>> Turn off your email, so the "you've got mail" icon doesn't tempt you.

>> Ask the receptionist to take messages for inbound calls during your prospecting session.

>> Turn off notification messages on your cell phone and mute the speaker.

>> Close down social networking sites.

>> Put a sign on the door: "Don't bother me; I'm prospecting."

>> Tell anyone who asks for a meeting during your prospecting period that you already have an appointment — working to find a potential prospect.

3. Follow the plan

Success boils down to taking the right steps in the proper order.

To get your prospecting steps and order correct, you must follow a prospecting plan. Know who you're going to call and for what reason. The best approach is to set up each day's prospecting plan a day in advance.

WARNING

If you wait to put your prospecting plan together at the beginning of your prospecting session, chances are too high that you'll talk yourself out of more calls than you make. Your mental process will get in the way of action, causing you to think things like "This person will think I'm calling back too soon . . ." or "This person won't buy or sell right now . . ." If you establish a plan in advance, you'll be ready for action instead of second-guessing. Follow these steps:

1. Do your research; establish your plan and set up for the next day's prospecting a day in advance. Before you leave your office for the day, determine the prospecting calls you're going to make the next day. Assemble everything you'll need for the calls and put it on your desk so it's ready for your attention as soon as you walk in the door.

2. In the morning, quickly review your calls and daily goals. Don't take too long! You could be setting yourself up for creative avoidance. The longer the span of time between when you start your day and when you start prospecting, the lower the odds you will start at all.

3. Spend 20 minutes practicing scripts, dialogues, and objection-handling techniques. Establish a pre-call routine and create a pattern or plan that you repeat over and over again before each prospecting session or call.

   As an analogy, think of how other professionals warm up before performances. You expect musicians, actors, and athletes to be fully prepared and ready to go when their concerts, plays, or games begin. Follow the same rule. Warm up in advance so that by the time you pick up the phone, practice is over and you're ready for the real thing.

4. Review a few affirmations, such as "I'm a great prospector," "When I prospect, people love to talk with me and set appointments with me," and "I will generate leads and appointments before I'm through today."

You're now ready to pick up the phone with focus, intensity, and an expectation of success.

4. Be faithful to yourself and finish what you start

Stay faithful to your daily objectives by completing all your prospecting contacts down to the very last one. When you're running a race, you have to run the whole way. No one remembers who was ahead at the 80-meter mark of the men's

100-meter race at the Olympics. The winner has to complete the full circuit before he can claim his medal.

Don't drop out early; finish what you start.

Building Momentum in Your Prospecting

You can work harder. Or you can work smarter.

Most successful agents don't go into a secluded room, pick up the phone, and toil away making hundreds of random calls over a nonstop eight-hour period. Few people would even consider that approach. I know I wouldn't, and I doubt you would. Instead, those who win at prospecting begin by targeting who they will call and why. They don't waste their time or effort calling iffy contacts who may or may not even be in the real estate market.

Prospecting is only effective if it generates a lead from a truly qualified prospect — someone who is interested in what you offer, needs the service you provide, and has the ability and authority to become a client of your business, or to refer you to someone who could.

And that's where targeting comes to your rescue.

Targeting the right prospects

Let me give you an example of the power of targeting. I work with an agent in New York. She's an ace when it comes to monitoring her marketplace, and as a result she wasn't surprised when she saw her market's housing inventory change quickly in a short period. For months she'd watched the momentum of the marketplace start to increase. During a coaching call she said, "The shift is in full swing." What she was saying was that the housing recovery was happening. Inventory was going down and prices were rebounding.

In the face of those changes, I asked her, "Based on this market change, who should become your new target for prospecting?" After a few minutes of discussion, she aimed her focus on her next prospects: non-owner-occupied properties. More specifically, she targeted a subset I call reluctant investors — millions of people who wanted to sell their homes but were forced to keep and rent out the homes because of lack of equity. Because of the market change, some of these previously underwater owners were no longer underwater. They didn't really want to be landlords and preferred to sell.

This agent correctly determined that when reluctant investors became aware of the changing tide, they were likely to want to sell and create the freedom they had desired a few years ago.

My client made a decision to call these listing prospects. She shared the market evaluation, inventory, and absorption rates. Then she asked if they wanted to take a more in-depth look at their particular situation. As part of her script, she asked owners whether, with the potential to sell and come out "whole," they felt the hassles of repairs and rental management were worth the benefits of continued ownership.

Almost immediately, my client launched her new prospecting plan. Within 90 days of our call, she had listed 10 reluctant-investor properties, with another 50 leads that she expected to list in the next 12 months. Her success was based largely on focused target-based marketing. She went after the right people at the right time and achieved tremendous results.

Setting and achieving prospecting goals

In setting prospecting goals, focus on four core areas:

- ❯❯ Number of contacts you should make each day and week
- ❯❯ Length of time on the phone
- ❯❯ Number of leads you should develop
- ❯❯ Number of personal appointments you should set

REMEMBER

Start with easily attainable numbers so you can build up your energy, intensity, focus, and discipline slowly and steadily. You wouldn't run a marathon without working up your daily and weekly mileage over time, and the same premise applies when establishing and meeting prospecting goals.

Number of contacts made

A contact is a personal conversation with a decision maker who can make a purchase or sale or refer you to someone who can. A contact is not a conversation with the babysitter, a 10-year-old neighbor, a friendly teenager, or an answering machine.

When I take on a new coaching client, I almost always start them with a goal of five contacts a day, and I suggest the same for you. Make a goal of 5 contacts a day without fail, resulting in the completion of 25 contacts a week.

It will take three to four weeks for contact with five prospects a day to become a habit. After you achieve the goal for three consecutive weeks without missing a single workday, you can raise your goal to seven or ten.

Length of time on the phone

The length of time on the phone indicates a few key things about you and your business. Your ability to be on the phone 60, 70, or even 90 minutes at one time leads to discipline, focus, and sales. If you can work with high intensity, making one call after the next, and get into a flow and rhythm, you are showing the skill of a quality salesperson.

The length of time on the phone equates to "talk time" for the day and each call. *Talk time* is measured by how long you are on the phone. Most sales calls end fairly quickly — inside a minute. Typically, the prospect delivers a "brush-off" response to get rid of the salesperson. The salesperson either handles it well and elongates the call or the call ends.

TIP

On initial sales calls you want to elongate the call into the 7–10-minute range, which is the money zone. This magic zone ensures that you have enough of a conversation to get information about the prospect and multiple opportunities to close for an appointment. See Figure 8-2.

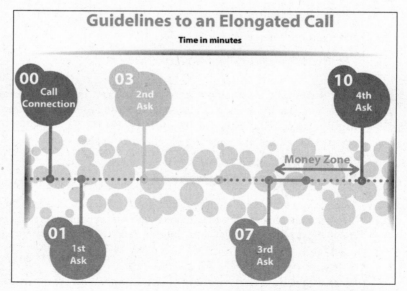

FIGURE 8-2: Guidelines for an elongated call.

© Real Estate Champions. Used with permission.

The talk time for each individual call and daily total talk time are indications of success as a salesperson.

Number of leads established

Leads are contacts that have demonstrated through their dialogues that they possess the basic motivation and desire to make a change in their living arrangements. In prospecting, we have to make some assumptions until we either pre-qualify a client ourselves or they secure an appointment with a lender that determines they have the financial capacity to make a purchase.

To advance your business, aim to develop at least one lead per day and five leads per week.

Number of appointments secured

An appointment is a face-to-face meeting with prospects, during which you discuss their needs and wants, share how you work, and aim to gain their commitment to work with you in an exclusive relationship to sell their home or find them a home to purchase. An appointment is the launch of the agent-client relationship. It's *not* a meeting during which you show a property.

Like your lead-generation goal, your appointment goal should be set at a reasonable level: One appointment a week is a solid start. If you acquire two appointments, terrific, but make sure that you're able to secure at least one.

If you're thinking, "Hmm, five leads and only one appointment a week from all those calls . . . ," realize that these are starting goals. It's far better to begin with aims you can actually achieve rather than ones that overwhelm you from the onset. As you gain consistency and skill in prospecting, both your numbers and your ratios will improve.

Even if you only maintain the starting goals, you'll have a good year as a newer agent. At the end of the year, you will have made 1,250 contacts and created 250 leads. You also will have set and conducted 50 appointments and gotten two weeks off with your family to boot.

Even if only half of the appointments turn into listings or sales, you'll have 25 deals in your first year. In most companies, that will make you rookie of the year. You'll also earn in excess of $125,000 in gross commission income. I don't know too many people in real estate or in any other profession who make that type of money in their first year.

THE PROSPECTING HIERARCHY OF VALUE

Some approaches involve a shorter contact-to-contract cycle than others, therefore delivering a greater return on your time investment and a higher value for your business. In order, here are the factors that most influence the value of your prospecting approaches.

1. **Past clients:** The highest-value form of prospecting is calling past clients and those in your direct sphere of influence. These people have either used your services in the past or know you and your character. Asking them to do business with you again is described as canvassing. Asking them to refer their friends is described as prospecting for referrals.

   These calls are the easiest to make because they reach those with whom you have established relationships. Typically, real estate agents experience less resistance when placing calls to this group than to any other. They also make the calls with high expectations that their efforts will generate leads. How long it takes to acquire leads with this approach varies greatly. You can secure a lead on your very first call or on your 100th call, so the ratio of leads generated to time invested is difficult to anticipate.

2. **Expired listings:** I can make a case for this being the number-one highest-value prospecting approach, as well, because of the ease of locating expired listings and the relatively quick contact-to-contract cycle. Expired listings come up in the MLS daily, along with all the information you need to make the contact. Many go back on the market with another agent within a week, so the sales cycle is short, which is a key reason that expired listings offer such a high rate of return for the effort.

   Few agents engage in calling expired listings, largely because the sellers, who haven't experienced success with their last agents, can be hostile toward new agents, as well. Many agents feel it's "beneath them" to contact these prospects — which further contributes to the opportunity for the ones who do.

3. **FSBOs:** Converting sale-by-owner contracts requires more work than securing expired listings. You have to seek out these sellers through newspaper ads or FSBO subscription services like The RedX (`www.theredx.com/signup/dirkzeller.html`). After you target a FSBO property, figuring out whom to call takes another round of effort, which is why FSBOs are farther down the value hierarchy.

   The sales cycle for FSBOs is four to five weeks on average. FSBO sellers generally try to sell by themselves for that timeframe before engaging a real estate agent. During that period, you must follow up weekly to secure an appointment four to five weeks away.

4. **Open houses and door knocking:** These face-to-face techniques require more time investment than phone contacts because you can't see as many people face to

face as you can speak with on the phone — but it's harder for people to reject you face to face.

5. **Cold calling:** This technique, tried and true since the advent of the phone, has lost effectiveness over the years because of the preponderance of busy two-income families and the onset of do-not-call registries. If you are calling around about homes that have recently been listed or sold, it will generate business. Other people put their homes on the market after a neighbor lists or sells. Using a service like Cole Directory (www.coleinformation.com) to secure phone numbers in neighborhoods is effective. They also provide cell phone numbers, which is highly effective.

Using technology to your advantage

The key to increasing your effectiveness and efficiency is leverage: putting yourself at an advantage above others. Leverage in prospecting is the ability to shorten the time spent doing research and increase the actual talk time or number of contacts you make in a day. Two types of technologies come into play when you need something to do the research for you.

Data service technology

If you use data-service technologies, such as RedX, in working expired listings, you can cut large amounts of research from your schedule. RedX downloads the data for expired listings, compares and pulls out only the still-expired prospects, scrubs them for National Do Not Call Registry compliance, and grabs cell-phone numbers for a large percentage of prospects. The time one would spend researching all this can be done in moments . . . cha ching!

Auto dialers

Using an auto dialer to make phone dials explodes your number of contacts per hour. The auto dialer, depending on the number of lines you use, can triple the number of contacts you make in an hour, automatically increasing your production. One of the best auto dialers is by Mojo Dialer. It has one-line and three-line systems. Imagine having your computer dial three numbers at a time and leaving a message with a click of your mouse, without recording a new message each time.

If you're using a three-line dialing system and you have two prospects pick up at the same time, the system selects one and stops dialing while you're on the phone. The other person is hung up on, unfortunately, but that option is better than playing a recording like those political ads that bombard phone lines during campaign season.

Shattering the myths

You've heard at least some of the reasons agents give to avoid adopting sound prospecting techniques. "My market is different" or "You don't understand how we do things here in Mayberry" are among the many. The truth is, the techniques in this chapter work in every market area, everywhere in the world, at any point in time. So bury the myths, starting with the ones that follow.

Try this magic pill . . .

Real estate success is built on a series of fundamentals. One of those fundamentals is prospecting.

Plenty of people are working to sell agents on some magic pill they can take to avoid the fundamental need to prospect. They are greeted by a willing market because many agents secretly hope for a prospecting-free existence, just as we secretly hope those guys on the late-night infomercials are right that we can buy a home for no money down at below market prices or eat whatever we want and not have to work out and still lose weight.

Dream on. You'll never find a magic mailing program, social-media ad campaign, Craigslist posting, calendar, magnet, marketing piece, or website that will make up for the fundamental need to pick up the phone and start prospecting for new clients.

Here's an approach that's too good to be true . . .

Agents are quick to share with you how they got where they are today, passionately describing their techniques, people who helped them, or products that made the difference.

While a few of these agents can tell you the cause-and-effect link between their actions or techniques and their sales and revenue, more than 95 percent truly have no idea or can't quantify their success for you.

Your job is to pull the curtain back. In the movie *The Wizard of Oz*, Dorothy, the Tin Woodman, the Scarecrow, and the Cowardly Lion are all mesmerized by and scared of the great and powerful Oz. It takes a dog, Toto, to reveal that Oz is just a little man pulling levers and using a sound system to produce the semblance of greatness and power.

In the future, when someone approaches you with great and powerful business-generating techniques, pull back the curtain with these questions:

>> How many transactions does this technique generate for you annually?

>> How much time do you need to invest personally to set this up and maintain it?

>> What does it cost you to use this marketing service to generate leads?

>> What is the conversion ratio on this technique?

>> What percentage of your business comes from this activity?

>> How many buyers did you get from this approach?

>> How many sellers did you get?

>> What is your net profit from this activity after all costs are subtracted?

>> Have you included the value of your time in that equation?

Most people (other agents, your broker, other trainers, or sales gurus) can't answer most of these questions. However, they're all positive that what they're advocating is the cat's meow for you and your business. I recently received a marketing piece from an agent touting his approaches to business. He had sold 60 homes in his third year in the business — a respectable number. Based on his personal success, he was promoting his lead-generation model as better than prospecting because he did 60 deals and generated more than 1,200 leads a month. The average agent would be frothing at the mouth to achieve those numbers.

I immediately grabbed my calculator and did the math. He generates more than 14,400 leads a year, which means his 60 transactions represent a lead-conversion rate of .004167 — less than half of 1 percent. Put differently, he has converted only one person for every 240 leads generated through his so-called "prospecting technique." I see only two logical conclusions here: Either the leads he's generating are marginal at best, or he's really poor at securing face-to-face meetings and subsequent deals. I'll leave you to draw your own conclusion.

REMEMBER

If it seems too good to be true, it probably is too good to be true.

Top producers don't prospect . . .

This myth is based on some truth. Many top-performing agents *don't* prospect after they've "made it" as agents. But you'll be hard pressed to find top producers who got where they are without prospecting at earlier stages in their careers. And you'll be even harder pressed to find top producers who can weather the swings and changes of the marketplace without going back into prospecting mode at least on an occasional basis.

To become a top producer, you must prospect. And to remain at the top of your game, you must continue to prospect. Don't quit prospecting ever! As you become more and more successful at real estate sales, you may even do more prospecting, in part because prospecting becomes more natural and easier than ever. As you acquire name recognition and market presence, the people you contact are increasingly honored and pleasantly surprised to receive your calls. They know you're busy and successful, and they respond not only with their own business but also with many referrals.

My clients and friends don't want to be bothered . . .

Agents who use this excuse are focusing almost exclusively on the canvassing or referral portion of the call, rather than on the connection the call allows with a long-established associate. Wouldn't you be delighted to get a call from your accountant, doctor, dentist, or insurance agent, asking how you and your family are, thanking you for your business, and seeing if there is anything they can do for you? I bet you can count on one hand the number of calls like that which you've received in the last 20 years. You'd probably be stunned and appreciative. Your sphere of influence, past clients, and other associates will feel the same.

Every time I work with a new client, I hear the same excuse: They don't want to bother anyone. Then they make calls for a week, and when I talk with them again, they always say the same thing: "I was amazed how easy it was. My clients were really happy to talk with me. I couldn't get them off the phone. It was great to catch up."

Knowing the Numbers and Ratios

Sales is a numbers game. Prospecting is a numbers game as well. The problem is, too few agents actually know their numbers and how to track them. The following sections help you understand and set objectives for your ratios of contacts to leads, leads to closings, appointments to contracts, and contracts to closings. Knowing this information moves you almost immediately into the league of our industry's most productive agents.

The law of accumulation

The law of accumulation basically says that achievement is the result of ongoing and constant effort. Everything in life, whether positive or negative, compounds itself over time. An illustration of this is money. If you want to be a millionaire, all you have to do is save a little on a consistent basis, and the law of accumulation will take over. If you put away $2.74 a day from age 20 until 65 and receive an average rate of return of 9 percent over those years, you'll be a millionaire. You've saved about $45,000 over those 45 years; the law of accumulation does the rest. If you ask most people whether they'd trade $45,000 for $1 million, they'll say yes, but few actually make the effort.

You can expect an equally uneven return when you invest in prospecting. The tricky part is that the reward for your miniscule investment of prospecting effort doesn't happen overnight. You have to prospect for 90 days before the law of accumulation does its thing. As my good friend, the late Zig Ziglar said, "Life is like a cafeteria. First you pay, and then you get to eat."

The power of consistency

Marginally successful agents take a binge approach to prospecting. Highly successful agents are far, far more consistent in their efforts.

I can't think of an agent who better exemplifies the power of consistency than a man I met a number of years ago named Rich Purvis. Rich had entered the field of real estate after 25 years in a fire-fighting career. His goal was to earn $100,000 a year, and when I met him in March his income was a disappointing $2,500. I told him, "If you call ten contacts within your sphere of influence each day, you'll get your $100,000 before year's end."

I can count on one hand the number of times he failed to make the ten contacts. He blew by his goal of $100,000 in less than nine months and ended up earning more than $120,000 that year. The next year he crossed the $200,000 mark. It was all the result of his extraordinary consistency.

The never-ending prospecting cycle

Agents can easily find time to prospect when they have no listings, no pending transactions, and no buyers to work with. The secret is to continue to prospect even when you're busy with all the other activities.

Look at a typical agent's annual income stream and you'll see that it goes up and down like a yo-yo. Most agents have four to six good income months per year. The rest of the time — bupkis. If you overlay their revenue streams with their prospecting numbers, you'll see that revenue decreases when prospecting tapers off, leading directly to the business void that follows.

Your job as a salesperson is to fill a pipeline of leads so you always have new prospects to work with. And the only way to keep a healthy pipeline or conveyer belt of leads is to prospect consistently.

The importance of tracking results

Any business in sales can be broken down to a series of repeatable numbers that, over time, produce a pre-determined result. When you establish goals and track your performance over a few months, you can determine the activities you need to earn the income you desire.

When I was selling real estate, I decided that I needed one appointment per day in order to reach my income goal. I knew through tracking my numbers that I needed three leads to create one appointment. What's more, I knew I needed to make twelve contacts to generate one high-quality lead because, through monitoring my numbers, I knew that two of every three leads would be "tire kickers" — contacts who didn't have the desire, need, ability, or authority to either list or buy in the reasonably near future. Based on that knowledge, I determined I needed to make 36 contacts a day: 12 each for the three leads I needed to result in one appointment. Miraculous!

Use Figure 8-3 to establish and track your prospecting numbers.

DAILY PROSPECTING GOALS AND RESULTS

ACTIVITY:	GOALS:	RESULTS:
Prospecting contacts made		
Leads obtained		
Listing appointments scheduled		
Qualified listing presentations made		
Buyer interview appointments scheduled		
Buyer interview appointments made		
Qualified offers written		

Total "real working hours" invested

Prospecting hours		
Listing hours		
Showing hours		
Offers hours		

Rate your day (1 - 10) _____   Comments:

© John Wiley & Sons, Inc.

FIGURE 8-3: Use a tracking sheet like this to monitor and evaluate your prospecting efforts.

The law of averages evens out your numbers over time. Don't evaluate yourself on a single day's achievements. Even a week is too short a period for evaluation. I've had days when I didn't set a single appointment. I probably had weeks that I got skunked. During a three-month period, however, I was always within a 5 percent margin of error on my number.

The challenge of managing contacts

To store your prospecting information and assure prompt and ongoing follow-up, employ contact-management software such as GoldMine, ACT, or Salesforce. Also, look into real estate-specific software packages such as Top Producer, Wise Agent, or RealtyJuggler, which are designed to help you with your sales functions and also with business management, including creating market reports, generating correspondence, and tracking your closings.

Regardless of the system you select, you must be able to access your contact database with reliability and ease.

This isn't the place to apply a shoestring budget. Minimally you want to invest in a computer (preferably a laptop) and all the software necessary to build and run your business, including contact management, MLS access, and agency management.

WHILE YOU'RE BUDGETING . . .

Budget for ongoing self-improvement.

Start with a budget for a wardrobe that presents you as a successful agent. Some people will make assumptions about you based on the way you dress. Dress for success. Just as important, budget to attend every business seminar you can make time to attend. Your personal education and skills-based training is fundamental to your climb up the ladder of success.

In between, buy books and tapes, download podcasts, and get your hands, eyes, or ears on every piece of media that can help you develop sales skills, mental focus, leadership, discipline, and motivation. The most significant asset in your business right now is you. Ten years from now, the most significant asset in your business will still be you. Don't fail to invest in yourself.

Staying in Touch

Use your contact-management system to trigger the next call to a prospect and make staying in touch automatic and easy.

» Each time you end a prospecting call, determine when the next call will take place. Find your prospect's timeframe and when you should speak again. Then schedule the contact right then and there.

» When talking to a past client or sphere member, schedule the next call without even asking. Then, the next time you call, they'll be pleasantly surprised to hear from you.

» In addition to making calls, send emails to thank contacts for their time and to reiterate your service offer.

» Get permission to add contacts to your blog or email newsletter mailing.

» Follow up first-time contacts with a copy of your agency brochure or marketing piece. Or send a "Just listed" or "Just sold" card to demonstrate your success as an agent.

» Craft a personalized business letter, perfectly typed onto your letterhead and sent out in your matching envelope.

TIP

But wait! Great as all the aforementioned suggestions are for your business, none of them beats the all-time winning touch of a handwritten thank-you note that says to the receiver, "You were so important that I took the time to pen this in my own hand instead of touching a few buttons on my computer or spitting out a pre-planned, standard-issue, regurgitated letter that I've sent to 1,000 other people just like you."

Most of us get hundreds of emails a day, most of which we don't even want. We receive hundreds of pieces of junk mail a month, mostly from credit-card and mortgage-refinance companies.

The handwritten thank-you note breaks through the clutter. It looks like an invitation to something special. It enhances the personal relationship and keeps it active until you talk again in a few days. It's still the best way to keep in touch in our technology-driven world.

Chapter **9**

Generating Referrals, Recommendations, and Introductions

Salespeople love referrals. They're the sincerest form of compliment and a remarkably cost-effective route to new business.

The objective of generating a large portion of your business from the referrals, recommendations, and leads of your friends, contacts, past clients, and current client leads to a good business. *Referral* is the way business is done, especially in business-to-consumer sales like real estate, financial services, and insurance.

As a newer agent, your scripts and strategy have to be more refined because your experience level in doing transactions has yet to be fully developed. You will rely more on the relationship connection, so you will need to ask for referrals in a more polished delivery.

Knowing the Referral Truths and Consequences

WARNING

Before you turn even a moment of effort away from prospecting activities and before you put all your hopes into winning business through a full-tilt referral-generation program, be aware that in addition to all the benefits that come with referrals, a 100 percent referral-based business has some downsides. Proceed with awareness of these ironclad truths:

>> **Truth #1:** Especially for newer agents, over-reliance on referrals results in slow growth simply because a newer agent doesn't have a large enough database of existing clients and contacts to draw upon.

>> **Truth #2:** Relying entirely on referrals for client development is a narrow, exclusive, unbalanced approach. For one thing, if incoming referrals decline, you won't have other lead-generation systems in place to bail your business out of trouble. What's more, when referrals do come in, more will be for buyer prospects rather than seller prospects. Most people view real estate agents as people that drive people around and show homes. Referrals result in more buyer sales than seller sales. You are developing to be a buyers' agent — although sellers' agents are the ones who experience the greatest success and build the strongest long-term real estate sales businesses.

>> **Truth #3:** The percentage of referral-based business is on a downward trend over the last few years. According to NAR, consumers are shifting to the Internet and other social forums to find a real estate agent. The percentage of referral-based business for buyers has dropped 7 percent over the last five years. Although referrals should always be the most important part of your lead-generation and business strategy, the trend away from referrals shows that maintaining a deep well of other lead-generation strategies is vital to success.

Building Your Referral Base

A referral-based business is one that generates most of its leads as a result of contacts provided by friends, family, clients, colleagues, and other associates. Sounds great, doesn't it? It *is* great, if — and here's a big if — you have a large sphere of influence and enough patience to wait out a lag time of at least 90 days, and often longer, between when you begin to cultivate referrals and when referrals begin to generate revenue for your business.

REMEMBER

Building a referral-based clientele is a long-term strategy rather than a quick-fix tactic. If you're looking for near-term results (and what newer agent isn't?), in addition to referrals, you must be developing clients through additional lead-generation systems as well.

Defining referrals

At its core, a referral is a recommendation.

In its best form, a referral is a high-quality lead and a high-probability prospect who is introduced to you by someone both you and the prospect regard highly.

Finding sources of referrals

Most referrals come from family members, friends, current clients, past clients, people you've met through networking situations, and people you know through social or business dealings. It's people you either have a personal contact and connection with or know through online and social-media platforms.

TIP

When working with referral sources, make it your objective to secure names, addresses, home phone numbers, cell-phone numbers, work phone numbers, and email addresses for those in the market to sell or buy. Also, make connection on your social media platforms like Facebook, Instagram, Twitter, and LinkedIn. Once established on even a few of these, you can reach out to pursue the leads. Ask the referral sources to make a personal contact on your behalf — meeting with or phoning the prospect in advance of your call to share your name and a little bit about the success you helped them achieve. Some people are uncomfortable turning over contact information for a potential prospect to a real estate salesperson, or any salesperson for that matter. They're afraid the salesperson will turn into a pest. The following script works well to put the referring individual more at ease:

> "Bob, I appreciate the referral opportunity and you offering to give your friend Suzi my business card, but I will tell you it's rare when a referral actually calls the agent. My real concern is that in our marketplace more than 65 percent of the agents have been in the business less than a handful of years. The average agent, according to NAR, does 3.5 transactions a year. The probability is that your friend is going to get an agent who doesn't understand the marketplace and may not be as skilled. I'm sure that's not what you want to have happen. Would there be a way we could design that would allow you to be comfortable with giving her number to me so that I can make a soft introductory call?"

The key phrase is at the end of the script. You are asking them to see if they would be willing to give the number to you instead. That way you control your destiny, not someone else. The upcoming sections provide information for working with different groups of potential referral contacts.

Current clients

Current clients are people you're actively representing, right now, in real estate transactions. Current clients are a rich pool of referral opportunity mainly because, more than any other group, they have real estate on their minds. They're in the midst of deals that they're constantly talking about with their friends, associates, family members, and neighbors. They're posting pictures of their dream home or their new home on Instagram and Facebook. They're pinning real estate pictures on Pinterest boards. Their online and offline conversations revolve around their real estate wants and needs, their moving plans, real estate trends, and market activity. They're churning the waters for your next prospect with every post, tweet, and pin.

REMEMBER

If you don't ask your current clients to recommend you to their friends or to refer their friends to you, you're really missing out on a huge opportunity to reach potential prospects. You can bet that your name comes up in your clients' conversations, even if it's just to say that they have an appointment or that they're awaiting information from you. Putting in a few good words on your behalf is a natural and easy thing for them to do. You just have to ask. You talk to your clients regularly to communicate about selling their home, finding a home, monitoring their transaction progress, or working toward closing. During the course of those conversations, ask for referrals.

Figure 9-1 shows a timeline for real estate agent referrals, and Figure 9-2 illustrates a winning strategy for the referral ask.

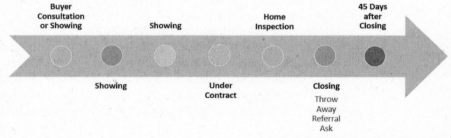

FIGURE 9-1:
Typical real estate agent referral ask timeline.

© Real Estate Champions. Used with permission.

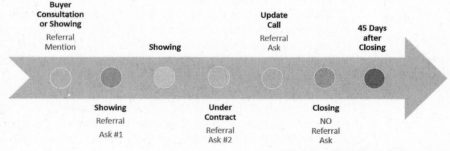

FIGURE 9-2:
Winning strategy for referral ask timeline.

© Real Estate Champions. Used with permission.

TIP

Don't forget to have your clients include you in their social-media world. Getting your clients to post about their experiences and tag you on their Facebook pages brings you into their circle of friends. It opens the door to them liking your business page and forming a service relationship. Be sure to engage in posting and include your clients in your posts.

Past clients

These are the people you've helped through real estate transactions in the past. They have first-hand knowledge of the quality of service you provide. You need to tell them that you want to provide the same level of excellent service to their friends and family members by requesting their referrals.

Clients you've recently served provide the most fertile opportunity, both because their experiences are fresh in their minds and because they're still buzzing about their recent move to everyone they know. The new social-media environment makes this group a gold mine — it's on fire with posts, tweets, and pins of their new home.

I've always believed that in real estate, "birds of a feather flock together." Groups of friends and colleagues often move or buy in bulk. Because Bob and Susie just moved, more of their friends are seriously considering moving. They're thinking: "Bob and Susie did it, so why can't we?"

Social media increases the speed of the news, widens the scope of people who know about it, makes the news easier to share, and makes the news more visual through pictures and videos.

Networking contacts

In sales, *networking* means building business contacts into referral alliances.

REMEMBER

The objective of networking is to meet success-oriented people with whom you can exchange referrals, advice, counsel, contacts, and even wisdom. Ideally, networking results in professional relationships with others who are committed not only to their success but to your success, as well.

WARNING

The truth is, most salespeople talk about networking more than they actually do it. They attend a chamber of commerce, BNI, or Rotary Club meeting, have an enjoyable lunch, visit with a few friends, and chalk the time up to "networking" even though no new alliances were formed, no existing alliances were deepened, and no referral resources were generated. In other words, no networking took place.

To make networking work for you, follow these tips:

TIP

>> **Network with the right mind-set.** When you network, make up your mind to develop prospect recommendations, not just the names of leads. Many referral alliances are established with the single objective of generating leads. Attendees learn the names of new businesses, new managers, newly arrived residents, or others who are possibilities for your future contact. Now a lead from a referral alliance is better than no lead at all, but it's a long cry from the name of a prospect provided by a networking associate who shares extensive background and then offers to put in a few good words on your behalf.

>> **Acquire warm referrals.** A warm referral begins when a networking associate makes contact on your behalf with a person who is in the market for your services. Warm referrals involve calls or correspondence that convey your qualifications, the quality of your service, and reasons why prospects should at least interview you for the opportunity to represent their interests in real estate transactions.

When establishing networking relationships or referral alliances, work to gain a mutual agreement that those in the network will engage in the practice of exchanging warm leads.

Business and social contacts

Many people you meet socially or through business dealings will never become clients. They may have previously established agent relationships, or they may not be in the market for a real estate transaction. Nonetheless, they're important to your business because they're in a position to give and receive referrals.

REMEMBER

Notice the words *give and receive* in the previous sentence. The law of reciprocity is alive and well in 21st century business circles. It's the old tenet of "I'll scratch your back if you scratch mine."

In his book *The Seven Habits of Highly Effective People,* Stephen Covey talks about emotional bank accounts into which successful people must make deposits before making withdrawals. Apply that wisdom as you build your referral network. Start by sharing business referrals, counsel, help, and wisdom with others, and before long the recipients of your kindness will repay you with like efforts. Help your friends, family members, and associates build their businesses; in time, they'll help you build yours.

To be successful at generating leads from networking, you have to master the primary questions you will get asked when at a business event, cocktail party, or even in the grocery store line when wearing your name badge. These are door openers like "How's the market?" and "What do you think interest rates will do?"

and "Do you think now is a good time to buy or sell?" and "What do you do?" All these questions are asked commonly by people in social and business settings. These are questions we must be prepared for:

» How's the market?

"There has been a dramatic shift in the market . . . there are still a lot of good opportunities even today."

"Where there are not as many incredible deals as we saw a few years ago, there are still some very solid values in today's market."

"The market has really shifted and continues to improve significantly. The trends point to some real opportunity for . . ."

One of the keys is to segue the conversation back to them in a targeting question about real estate:

- Are you looking to buy or sell?

- Do you invest in real estate?

- Do you have real estate holdings?

- Do you have an interest in the real estate market?

- Are you considering a move?

You have to have a soft delivery on these questions so it doesn't seem like the Spanish Inquisition. Have a curious, sincere tone in your voice.

Whether they ask how the market is doing or about interest rates or whether now is good timing, you will always want to link in the question at the end. You want to hit the ball back over the net in conversation.

» What do you think the interest rates will do?

"Because we are closer to historic low levels than the typical interest rates, the trend for interest rates will be upward."

"Most expert economists are projecting interest rates to (increase/decrease) about __ over the next __ months."

"According to the economic experts at (National Association of Realtors, Zillow, Trulia, the Wall Street Journal), they are forecasting interest rates to (increase/decrease) to __ within (6 months, by year end)."

"We have seen rates move __ in the last few months. This has already added to the monthly housing cost for all buyers."

If you really want to set yourself apart as an expert, talk about increase of interest rate in terms of *basis points* rather than percentage points.

There are two reasons to do this:

1. **You sound more like an expert.** You are more exact about what you are talking about. One percent of interest rate is equal to 100 basis points. So, a quarter-percent increase is 25 basis points. The loans are not really priced in interest rates but basis points. That is true for all parts of the loan, from origination to servicing of the loan. There are very few agents who talk in basis points.

2. **The perception is larger, which builds urgency.** Twenty-five basis points sounds larger than one-quarter percent. Fifty basis points sounds larger than one-half percent. The ability to build urgency and project urgency can cause some prospects to consider their options sooner, faster, or more deeply.

>> **Do you think now is a good time to buy or sell? Do you think now is a good time to move up?**

There are a number of derivatives of these types of questions. The first step is to make sure you are answering what their specific needs might be. If they ask you the "or" type of question, you might need to probe their specific circumstances to better respond to them:

"Are you more interested in buying or selling?"

"Are you leaning to one or the other?"

"Are you considering upgrading/downsizing?"

"I am convinced that most people should at least research their options because of the market improvement we have seen in the last ___."

"Based on the market adjustment we have seen in the last ___, it certainly makes sense to review the options and opportunities people have today."

"We have shifted to a ___ marketplace in the last ___. That shift has removed much of the uncertainty of the marketplace. There are some low-risk opportunities in today's market for ___."

"Buyers in today's marketplace might not get the rock bottom deals of ___. They are getting opportunities to buy properties well below the high-water mark of ___."

"Sellers are doing much better in sales price than just a few years ago, in today's marketplace."

>> **What do you do?**

You also have to be able to describe what you do. This might not come up directly in conversation with your sphere or past clients. It is part of personally promoting yourself when an opening comes about.

The "Here's what I do" statement has a couple of key components:

1. **It's short in length.**

   It can be as short as 15 seconds for a social type of interaction where someone says, "What do you do?" You could have a longer version (about a minute long) for a more in-depth view of your area of specialization.

2. **It intrigues, creates interest, or engages the listener.**

   You want to create an opening to have a more detailed conversation later.

3. **A good one has structure.**

   It's not off-the-cuff. It's planned and has a direction to it that frames you.

4. **It can have a close.**

   "I aid people in finding and acquiring rare opportunities in real estate properties, whether that is a family home that creates wonderful family memories or investment property that creates wealth for my clients."

   "I educate and guide people through the challenges of the real estate market. My specialty is evaluating clients' needs, analyzing the marketplace and finding the opportunities of the real estate marketplace in ___. Then crafting and executing a plan that helps them use the selected piece of property as a building block for their family memories and financial present and future."

TIP When dealing with your referral sources, make it your goal to provide service and value in excess of expectations and to keep your accounts with others in the black, rather than the red.

Constructing a referral database

One of the best ways to start generating referrals is to construct a referral database composed of all the people who are likely to help you by referring your services.

TIP If you're like most agents, your first list of business and social contacts will look embarrassingly short. That's because few people dig deep enough to think of all the people with whom they have business and social ties. To jog your memory, use the worksheet in Figure 9-3. Then list the names of people in each category who know and respect you and may be willing to refer prospects your way.

Following the three golden rules

To win referrals, you have to follow three important rules. Close isn't enough. Follow just two of the three, and the growth of your referral-based business will be stunted. Follow all three, and you'll open the floodgates to success.

Referral Database Worksheet

Create a list of contacts in each category who may be willing to refer prospects your way.

Accountant	Colleges	Investments	Printing
Advertising	Computer	Jewelry	Property Mgmt.
Aerobics	Construction	Laundries	Rental Agencies
Airline	Consulting	Lawn Care	Resorts
Alarm Systems	Contractors	Libraries	Restaurants
Animal Health/Vet	Cosmetics	Limousines	Roofing
Apartments	Country Clubs	Loans	Satellites
Appraisers	Credit Union	Management	School
Architects	Day Care	Manufacturing	Secretaries
Art	Delivery	Mechanics	Shoe Repair
Athletics	Dentists	Medical	Siding
Attorney	Dermatologists	Mortgages	Signs
Automobile	Doctors	Motels	Skating
Baby-sitters	Dry Wall	Museums	Skiing
Banking	Electrician	Music	Skydiving
Barber	Engineering	Mutual Funds	Soccer
Bartender	Firemen	Newspapers	Softball
Baseball	Fishing	Nurses	Software
Beauty Salon	Florist	Nutrition	Spas
Beeper Service	Furniture	Office Machines	Sporting Goods
Bible School	Gardens	Office Furniture	Surgeons
Boats	Golfing	Optometrist	Tailors
Bonds/Stocks	Groceries	Orthodontist	Teachers
Bookkeeping	Gymnastics	Pediatricians	Telecommunications
Bowling	Hair Care	Pedicures	Tennis
Brokers	Handicapped	Pensions	Theaters
Builders	Handyman	Pest Control	Title Company
Cable TV	Hardware	Pets	Training
Camping	Health Club	Pharmacies	Typesetting
Carpet Cleaning	Health Insurance	Phones	Universities
Cellular Phones	Horses	Physician	Video
CPAs	Hospitals	Plumbing	Waste
Chiropractors	Hotels	Podiatrist	Weddings
Church	Hunting	Pools	Wine
Cleaners	Insurance	Preschools	

FIGURE 9-3: List the names of contacts in as many of these social- and business-contact categories as possible to form your referral database.

1. Be referable

You can't generate large numbers of quality referrals unless you're referable. Being a pleasant person isn't enough. To attract referrals, follow these tips:

> **Do what you say you'll do, and do it with excellence.** People known for mediocre results never win the kind of accolades that lead to recommendations.

> **Know your clients' expectations.** The only way you can know what your clients expect from you is to ask. The typical agent thinks a client simply wants

to get a home sold or find a home to buy, when in fact that end result tells you nothing about the client's service expectations. Ask your clients these questions:

- What do you expect from the agent you choose to work with?

- What are the top three services I could provide that would add value when working with you?

- If you've worked with other agents in the past, what did you like best and least about the experience?

>> **Deliver exemplary service that exceeds expectations.** Meet and exceed the service expectations of your clients and they'll become ATMs for referrals. Chapter 17 is full of tips for using service and follow-through to win clients, and their praise, for life. Also, follow these steps:

- Survey your clients on a regular basis to find out whether their needs are being met and how you can serve them better. Sending a survey is so easy today. The advent of online survey systems such as SurveyMonkey makes it fast and inexpensive. For as little as a few hundred dollars a year, you can create surveys for current buyers and sellers, clients who just moved, past clients, people who used your website and IDX service, and a host of other options.

- Become a recognized real estate expert and share your expertise by calling clients regularly with reports on market trends, equity growth, and investment opportunities.

- Continue to serve your clients after the sale closes.

- Get to know your clients beyond their real estate needs.

>> **Say thank you.** This step is so simple, yet in our what's-in-it-for-me world, most service providers overlook the power it possesses. When was the last time you were thanked by your attorney, accountant, or banker for your business? When was the last time the person who pumps your gas, handles your dry cleaning, or bags your groceries thanked you for continuously directing your service dollars into their paychecks?

Extend your thanks verbally. Put your thanks into handwritten notes. Find simple and creative ways to express your appreciation to the people who put food on your table, gas in your car, dollars in your retirement account, and tuition dollars into the education accounts for your children. Your thanks will be rewarded with referrals.

>> **Admit and correct mistakes.** Should your service fall short, admit it, apologize, and make amends . . . fast!

Sometimes, the most loyal past clients — and the strongest referral alliances — result from perfectly corrected mistakes. When things go awry, too many people

TIP

put more effort into covering their tracks than righting the wrong and helping the client. Follow these steps instead:

- Find out what the problem is and solve it quickly.

- When the problem has been identified, admit it was your fault. Diffuse frustration or anger by saying, "You're right; I blew it, and I'm sorry."

- Tell them how you'll make amends. When they know you're committed to their satisfaction, the healing of the relationship can begin.

- Follow up to see if the problem is resolved to the client's satisfaction and to see if there is anything else you can do.

2. Mine your contacts

The first step toward mining — or extracting value from — your referral contacts is to segment your database into manageable subgroups.

WARNING

To use your resources effectively, you have to put most of your effort toward contacts with the highest referral potential. Contrary to popular opinion, you can't afford to treat all referral sources with equal attention. Unless you establish priorities, you won't have the time or energy to devote to the contacts who will benefit your business most.

» **Start by creating a top-level or platinum group of contacts.** This category includes clients who were a delight to work with, people who are in key strategic positions, and friends and associates who are strongly likely to refer business your way. Go through your complete database looking for those with the following traits:

- People who understand your need for business referrals

- People who really like you and want to help you

- People who did business with you in the past and were highly satisfied by your service

- People who previously sent referrals to you, even if the referrals never resulted in a commission check

This is your best group of referring partners or referral alliances, and you must treat them accordingly. They deserve personal attention and personal interaction from you on a regular schedule.

TIP

You might even create a top-20 or top-50 list within this group. This superelite list merits your highest level of attention. Send them special and personal correspondence a couple of times a year, and see them on a face-to-face basis a few times a year as well. Invite them to special client-appreciation events — or invite them in very small groups to attend functions or special activities with you — to further crank up the referral machine.

» **Create a second-tier or gold level of contacts** that you want to cultivate into platinum affiliates.

This group includes influential people who are likely to refer you if you meet a few conditions. You may have to ask them consistently over a period of time before their referrals come through. Or you may have to achieve greater familiarity or top-of-mind consciousness before they're comfortable with the idea of sending business your way.

To develop this group, take time to establish your credentials and competitive position. By proving how you save clients money, sell more quickly, and handle smoother and better transactions, in time you'll develop advocates who will serve you with referrals for years to come.

» **Create a silver level of contacts** for future cultivation.

This group includes contacts who *may* refer someday, but the jury is still out regarding when and if. Still, because you know them and they know you, they deserve your attention and follow up.

The people in this group are in a position to refer business, but they may not be overly excited about you or, in some cases, any service provider. Include in this group people you've only recently met, people with limited social circles, and people who are tremendously analytical or demanding and whose need for proof and perfection may put the brake on their willingness to share referrals with others.

Anyone who doesn't fit into the platinum, gold, or silver category has limited referral value to your business. Some trainers advocate purging iffy contacts out of your database, but I don't share that view. After all, how hard is it to include the extra names when you distribute your email newsletter monthly, at absolutely no extra cost? How hard is it to interact with them on your Facebook or Instagram account? When the data is collected and contact permission is obtained, the hard work is over. All you have to do is hit "send" or post and engage on a regular basis, backed by an occasional snail mail.

TIP

Consider creating a bronze category just to keep remote possibilities in your contact circle. Especially when your overall database is small, you want to wring potential out of every hope. Inexpensive, regular contacts are a step in the right direction toward engaging the interest of these contacts and developing them into future referral sources.

3. Leverage your relationships

In your everyday dealings, you come into frequent contact with people who, with a little effort, you can lead up your relationship ladder and cultivate into referral sources.

For many newer agents, these daily encounters are centered on the lives of children — through meetings with teachers, participation in school events, visits with other parents, sideline conversations at soccer and T-ball practices, and the list goes on and on. Beyond that are all the people you meet in church groups, golf or athletic clubs, neighborhood associations, and other social outlets. Cast your net carefully and you'll bring many of these people into your referral circle. Use the networking tips and strategies from earlier in the chapter.

Be aware, these sources don't develop into referrals automatically. Far from it. It's your obligation to let people know what you do, why you're the best, and how you deliver successful outcomes.

As you leverage personal relationships, start by setting a high expectation for the quality of communication and service you'll deliver. At the same time, set moderate to low expectations for quick referral results. Cultivating acquaintances into referral affiliates takes time, patience, and persistence.

What's Up? Referral Strategy

To develop referrals, start with a referral mind-set.

>> A referral mind-set exists when every prospecting, marketing, and customer-service action is accompanied by the realization that the contact could lead not only to new business but also to positive word-of-mouth advertising and the recommendation of your service to others.

>> A referral mind-set exists when you create, believe in, and implement strategies that purposefully generate referrals as a regular part of your business-development activities.

>> A referral mind-set exists when you know that prospecting is a key route to referral success. In the same way (and often at the same time) that you prospect for client leads, you need to prospect for referrals. Chapter 8 is jam-packed with advice on how to proceed.

Generating referrals is among the easiest, most cost-effective ways to gain new business leads, but success doesn't happen overnight. Even your platinum-level referral sources need to be constantly contacted and reminded to send business your direction. The upcoming sections help you set your objectives and develop a system that first delivers the kind of service that wins recommendations and then transfers that value, through ongoing communication, into new business opportunities.

Defining the type of referrals you seek

Before you launch a referral-generating effort, know what you're looking for. You need to be able to focus your referral sources on an idea of what your ideal real estate prospect looks like. Include the following information:

TIP

 Moments when people become great prospects: Help your referral sources notice the signs that indicate friends are in the "thinking about moving" stage. This is the point at which you most want to enter the game, before the transaction is already underway. Universal signs to watch for include pregnancy or adoption, promotion or job transfer, trouble with aging parents, a recent empty nest, and trouble in a marriage or relationship.

WARNING

Left to their own good intentions, people will call to tip you off about people they've just learned are in the buying or selling process. By the time a mutual friend hears that people are actively looking to buy or are in the midst of selling, it's too late. By then, the prospects probably already have an agent relationship.

Your interest in helping people sell their homes: The standard consumer view of real estate agents is that they put people into their cars, drive them around, and sell them houses. If you don't expand this initial impression, most of your referrals will be for people seeking to buy rather than sell homes. Buyers are great clients and important sources of revenue, but the best agents build their businesses through listings. By cultivating referrals for those thinking about selling their homes, you'll put your business on a faster growth track.

Your real estate niche: If you're particularly effective serving a specific niche of real estate clients, such as investors, seniors, younger-generation buyers, or first-time buyers, let people know. Likewise, if you want to gain more of a certain kind of buyer, you need to inform your referral sources about your expertise in the desired segment and what prospects in that area look like.

When communicating your market niche interests, start by sharing your overall competitive market advantage and inviting all referrals. Then explain how you've developed a particular niche market expertise that you want them to know about so that they'll think of you when they learn that their contacts have interest in your specialty area.

WARNING

Your point isn't to get referral sources to screen leads for you. You still want them to recommend the name of anyone with interest to buy or sell property. The more the better.

Setting and achieving your referral goals

In a really effective referral-development program, you may aim to achieve two referrals a year, on average, from each of your platinum-level sources, one a year from those in your gold group, and one every other year from those in the silver category. Referrals from sources at the bronze level are too hard to project, but for all other categories, you need to give yourself an annual goal to aim at. In the beginning, you may just pluck your goal from thin air, but after you establish your first-year expectations (or hopes), you'll have a good benchmark against which to measure progress and set your future aim.

As you set goals and track progress, consider these tips:

>> The number of referrals you aim to generate from platinum-level sources should be double what you expect from gold-level sources, and your expectations from gold-level sources should be double what you expect from silver-level sources.

>> Whenever you receive a referral, note whether the source is listed in your platinum, gold, silver, or bronze categories. This helps you track whether those in each category are performing at the projected levels. If not, you'll know to enhance communications and referral-generation efforts.

>> As you qualify and work with referrals, note which of your database groups — platinum, gold, silver, and bronze — are delivering referrals that lead to business. If you notice that some categories are generating referrals that are dramatically more or less qualified than other categories, study your own communications to see how your messages to those in various groups may be contributing to good or weak leads.

Approaching your referral sources without begging

Marketing for referrals can still be done effectively through traditional channels — mailers, calendars, recipe cards, and other outreach and appreciation efforts — but it is nowhere near as effective as prospecting for referrals by making personal calls and requests. Creating a regular communication pattern through social media channels is needed as well. The key is consistency of communication with people online and offline.

The hard truth is that most consumers stand a far better chance of finding a poor agent than a great one. When you can personally convince them that you're among the best in the field, referrals follow.

REMEMBER

When cultivating referral sources, realize that most people who send referrals your way do so for a variety of reasons, but above all they recommend you for the following two reasons:

>> **People want to promote friendship and trust.** People like to help people they like and believe in. Take time to get to know those in the platinum and gold levels of your database and to let them get to know you. Share the vision you hold for your business. Let them catch your enthusiasm and buy into your dream. The result is a vested interest in your success and the desire to help you achieve your goal.

>> **People want to be champions.** Each time you deliver superb service and an excellent outcome, you create clients who are willing to champion your business. And based on your exemplary performance, you create clients who know firsthand that by recommending you to others, they'll become champions in the minds of their friends and family members.

It's never too early to begin building referral relationships. You can start during the first meeting or call with any prospect, using a script such as this:

"Fred, I build my business primarily based on referrals from clients. The benefit to you is that my focus will always be to give you the best service possible. The reason is that I want to earn the honor to talk with you in the future about who you know that would benefit from my service. The only way I deserve to have that conversation is based on the job I do for you. I know that if you're delighted with my service, you'll want to help me and your friends out."

REMEMBER

The consistency of your communication with potential referral sources is key. Be in front of referral sources and at the top of mind at all times. Be consistent in calls, mailings, and social-media interactions. You can't go dark or quiet for extended periods of time.

TIP

One of the new advances in communication that is highly effective and personalized is video email. I personally feel that video email is a game changer in relationship building. I use video email to keep in contact with our vast list of current, past, and future clients. You can communicate in a personal but leveraged way to key groups. Another advantage is the ability for people to share and post your video. I truly believe that using a video email service like BombBomb can up your referral game. Go to www.bombbomb.com/rechampions to see what it can do.

When approaching referral sources, keep a couple of important rules in mind:

WARNING

TIP

>> **Rule #1: Respect the referral process.** When you're asking for referrals, you're entering the hallowed territory of another person's treasured relationships. In ancient times, people would go through extensive purification ceremonies before stepping onto holy ground. Asking for referrals is almost that special.

Don't ask for referrals by adding a throwaway line onto the end of another conversation, saying, "Oh, by the way," before you ask for a business referral. That tactic minimizes the importance of the referral, instead of raising it to the high level of honor and respect it deserves.

A quality referral request should take at least five minutes; ten may be even better.

My friend Bill Cates, the Referral Coach and author of the book *Beyond Referrals* (McGraw-Hill Education, 2013), advises that you advance your referral request with the statement "I have an important question to ask you." This forces a pause, builds anticipation, and sets the tone for a meaningful conversation.

>> **Rule #2: Ask for help.** If you're soliciting referrals, you are, in fact, asking for help. So say so. The trouble is that egos get in the way and won't let the words out of most agents' mouths. "I need your help" or "I value your help" are powerful keys for opening the referral floodgate.

>> **Rule #3: Ask permission.** In particular, ask permission to explore your client's contact database — not by rifling through computer files but by becoming aware of and gaining access to associates you may be able to serve. When asking for permission, use a script like this one:

"I'm delighted that I've been able to serve you. I was wondering about others you might know in your life who would also benefit from my service. Could we explore for a few moments who else we might be able to serve?"

The final question in the script is an important one. Too many agents ask for referrals and then leave all the burden of thinking up names on the shoulders of their clients. The truth is, your referral sources don't want to work that hard. They'll work that hard *with* you, but not alone.

>> **Rule #4: Get specific.** Don't just make a general request for referrals and leave it at that. Saying "Do you have anyone you might like to refer to my business?" is sort of like a department store clerk who asks, "May I help you?" The automatic response, 90 percent of the time or more, is "No, just looking."

Sharpen the focus of your request by leading clients into areas or niches in their lives where they have day-to-day relationships. Ask them about potential referrals among the families in their church, people they know through their children's soccer team, and prospects they've met through school affiliations. If they're members of associations or groups, pull out the member roster and spend a few minutes talking about the names.

Asking the right questions at the right time

After they've asked for and received a referral, most salespeople stop and wait for the magic to happen. In fact, this is when Phase 2 of the referral–generation process kicks in. Follow these steps:

1. Thank your referral source, immediately! Say thank you the moment the referral comes through, and say thank you again when you follow up with a handwritten note.

2. Determine the nature of the referral. To increase the probability of a successful first call, you need to determine the level of the lead you're dealing with. Slot the referral into one of four referral tiers:

   C Level: This is a cold referral. Your referral source has provided you with the name and phone number of a potential prospect but doesn't want you to use his or her name to create an opening.

   B Level: This referral is lukewarm. You have the prospect's name and phone number and permission to use the name of your referral source to open the door, and from there you're on your own.

   A Level: This is a warm referral. You have the prospect's name and number. You have permission to use the name of your referral source as a door opener. Plus, your source has given you time to ask questions about the lead that will improve your odds of connecting with the prospect on the first call.

   AA Level: This is the whale in the referral fishing game. With an AA-level referral, you have all the resources of the A level, plus the insider's edge because your referral source contacts the prospect before your call to introduce you. This advance contact paves the way for a welcomed first call. It can also lead to a lunch or face-to-face meeting where you, your referral source, and your new lead get together to transfer the relationship into your hands.

To significantly increase your conversion odds, spend a few minutes with your referral sources finding out answers to these questions:

- How do you know this person?

- How would you describe your relationship?

- What type of a personality will I encounter?

- What are a few of this person's personal interests?

- What organizations does this person belong to?

- Is there anything that you can see that we have in common?

REMEMBER

Get more than the prospect's name and number. Ask questions and go the extra mile to move the referral lead up to a higher probability of conversion.

3. Thank your referral source again, offering your assurance that you'll provide the same level of quality service that your referral source has received from you in the past.

Honoring the referrals you receive

Not all referrals turn into transactions. In fact, not all referrals possess the necessary desire, need, authority, and ability to qualify as likely prospects for your business. That doesn't mean every referral isn't important to your business; it just means that not every referral demands the same follow-up.

When handling referrals, take these steps:

1. **Qualify the lead** and determine the odds that your investment of time and resources will result in a commission check. Turn to Chapter 10 for help with qualifying prospects.

WARNING

2. **Develop only qualified referrals into client prospects.** When working with referrals, agents often feel compelled to work with every lead, regardless of the person's qualifications or willingness to commit to an exclusive agency relationship. I believe this is an error. Ask yourself: If this person came from an ad call, sign call, open house, or any other lead-generation system, would I pursue the business given the person's qualifications and commitment? Don't change your standards, expectations, or code of conduct because the lead was referred to you.

TIP

3. **Thank and reward your referral sources for every single lead.** Too many agents reward referral sources only when the leads they provide produce a return in the form of a commission check. That's a huge mistake. If you train friends and associates to think that you only value referrals that result in closed deals, you run the risk that they'll start trying to prescreen leads, passing along only the ones they think will result in sales. Reward and acknowledge every referral you receive.

4. **Keep your referral sources informed of the lead's progress.** Especially if you're faced with the need to drop a prospect, let your referral source know what's happening. Explain that although this time the match didn't work out, you sincerely appreciate the recommendation and are honored by the referral. Try to avoid the gory details as you walk the tightrope, sparing yourself from wasted time while preserving the strength of your established referral relationship.

Developing and Expanding Referral Relationships

After you've received a referral, gathered information, and ranked the lead, it's time to pick up the phone. The advice and scripts in the upcoming sections help you with each step of the lead-conversion process.

Making first-time contact

The first call is the hardest one. Until you make first contact, you don't really know the quality of the lead. It can turn out to be a huge business opportunity — or nothing at all. You have to hope for the best; the referral lead could result in years of business and an important new referral alliance. Or it could go into the trash 60 seconds after you make the call. As you initiate contact with a new referral, heed the following advice.

Know the two objectives of your first call or visit

The primary objective of your first contact, like the objective of any other first sales call to a new prospect, is to book an appointment. The first appointment may take the form of an exploratory session aimed at determining the wants, needs, and desires of the lead, or it may be an appointment to conduct a buyer consultation or listing presentation.

The secondary objective of your first contact is to open the door, establish trust and respect, demonstrate your knowledge, and establish your position as a reliable resource.

REMEMBER

In your first contact, you're not trying to make a sale; you're just trying to achieve a face-to-face meeting.

Use the name of your referral source to open doors

The best way to get beyond your prospect's defenses is to share the name of your referral source. By presenting the name of your mutual associate, you establish immediate rapport and credibility. In your opening statement, include a reference to your referral source by using a script such as this:

> *"Hello, Mr. Smith, this is Dirk Zeller with Real Estate Champions. The reason for my call is that your name came up in a conversation yesterday with Bob Jones with the Acme Delivery Company."*

Then continue by using a linking statement such as:

> *"He said you're neighbors" or "He said you used to work together" or "He said your sons play soccer on the same team."*

> *"Well, Bob Jones is a very valuable client. Bob knows I primarily work with referrals; he suggested I give you a call. He thought it would be worth a few minutes of our mutual time to see if we should meet."*

You can also use a variation like:

> *"Bob was pleased with the service I provided to him and his family. He thought you'd like to evaluate how I might be able to assist you in the future."*

Converting referrals into clients and referral sources

After you establish a solid opening connection, it's time to ask probing questions that help you determine the wants, needs, desires, and expectations of the lead. Depending on your findings, the lead may result in a qualified prospect whom you convert into a client. Or, you may determine that although the lead isn't ready to buy, sell, or commit to an exclusive agent relationship, the person is a valuable resource to be added to your referral database.

Use the techniques I share in Chapter 4 to assess the lead's business potential and gather the information you need.

Personal visits and calls

Leads generated through referrals come with a higher client-conversion probability than leads received from ad calls, sign calls, or any other cold sources. Because of that fact, consider investing some additional time as you launch the relationship. Instead of or in addition to a personal call, consider stopping by to personally meet your new leads in their home. After they attach a face and voice to your name, they'll find it more difficult to reject you or select someone else to represent their interests.

TIP

If a personal visit isn't possible, aim to enhance the sense of personal connection through an increased number and frequency of calls. It takes, on average, four to six calls for you to leave a lasting impression.

Written notes, email messages, and mailers

Between calls and personal visits, build a bridge with personal notes and email messages. Written communications will never replace the personal touch of phone calls or face-to-face visits, but in between live contact, they do a great job of keeping the connection alive.

Send market updates, testimonials, letters from other satisfied clients, information on your current listed properties, and news about key awards or recognitions you've received.

Beyond that, treat referral leads as if they're already clients by adding them to your newsletter list and to insider mailings that share news from your office.

Chapter **10**

Expired and FSBO Success in Any Marketplace

Certainly technology plays a big role in a real estate agent's success. Throughout the chapters in Part 2, you can find numerous ways to leverage and use technology. However, going "old school" and using traditional methods of generating business is still effective. When you blend these traditional lead-generation strategies with new technological tactics such as social media, IDX, and your website, you have a powerful force. The main reason you want to evaluate and implement traditional strategies is that two tried-and-true methods lead to new listings: expired listings and for-sale-by-owner listings (FSBOs). The value of a listing can't be overstated in building your business. Whoever has the most listings usually wins the game.

REMEMBER

Although both expired listings and FSBOs are great sources for generating listings, these can't be the only revenue streams you spend time generating. You must have at least three sources from which you create leads, revenue, and listing opportunities. Expired listings and FSBOs can be time consuming if done correctly, but they're certainly worth it. You have to find a mix that works well with the amount of time, effort, and energy you plan to spend working these and other areas of business generation. The truth is that you can't attack ten different lead generation models at once. You have to select the best handful to use to generate your listing business.

If you like the idea of being a successful agent who works these areas, read on. This chapter reveals why and when to pursue expired and FSBO listings and how to convert others' real estate sales failures into your success stories.

Three Reasons to Work Expired and FSBO Listings

If you've been in the real estate business for any time at all, you've probably already sensed that many agents have a preconceived negative impression of expired listings and FSBOs. These agents act as if these listings represent secondhand goods that aren't worthy of their interests and abilities. These same agents may also look down on fellow agents who work expired or FSBO listings. As a result, they turn their backs on tremendous revenue potential and literally thousands of annual listings. And that's great news for agents like you who can reap great success by converting expired and FSBO listings to new listings for your business.

I honestly believe that agents who work, or have worked, expired and FSBO listings with successful outcomes are the best salespeople in the real estate industry. They prove they're skillful in sales, time management, prospecting, lead follow-up, presentations, objection handling, and closing. They know how to put their sales skills to work to book appointments, make presentations, and persuade potential customers to become clients. As a result, they make more money and have more listings.

A new agent with aspirations to climb to the top tier of success in residential real estate should work expired and FSBO listings for three reasons:

>> **They're easy to find.** You don't even have to ask the owners if they're considering selling. All you have to do is notice the "For Sale by Owner" ads and signs or go online to sites like Zillow (www.zillow.com). Zillow even has a section for people in the very early stage of FSBO in a searchable section called Make Me Move. These are people who would move at a certain price. You can also scan the MLS files for *expireds* — property listings that expire without buyer offers. It's not rocket science.

TIP

Use a technology service like RedX (www.theredx.com) or Vulcan 7 (www.vulcan7.com) to help you compile data in an organized and efficient manner. With a few clicks, you can have the service monitor expired listings and FSBOs for you. Gone are the days when you had to review newspapers, drive through neighborhoods, and watch the MLS. Software now manages and tracks all such information sources. You can also use a customer relationship management (CRM) system to help you organize the information your tracking service uncovers.

>> **They exist in any kind of market conditions.** You read that correctly. If you're skilled at converting expired and FSBO listings, market conditions will have little bearing on your income and overall success. Here's why: In a market that's experiencing sluggish sales, buyers are in control and listings move slowly, if at all. As a result, a large number of listings expire each day, week, month, and year, providing you with a near-endless supply of conversion opportunities. On the flip side, when the marketplace is robust and listings are moving briskly, sellers enjoy quick sales, high list-to-sold ratios, and multiple offers. In this environment, more FSBOs sprout up. Consumers think selling a home is easy, so they devalue the services of agents and try to sell on their own.

TIP

Agents who work expired and FSBO listings can bulletproof their businesses by shifting their listing emphasis to fit market trends — focusing on expireds in sluggish markets and on FSBOs in brisk markets.

>> **Working expired and FSBO listings provides the best training an agent can get.** No question about it, if you're going to convert four, five, or even six expired or FSBO listings a month, you're going to become a great salesperson. I'm not going to whitewash the truth: You'll work hard getting there. But the rewards — in terms of self-discipline, time management, sales skills, personal confidence, and, last but certainly not least, a whole lot of money — make the effort well worth the investment.

The ABCs of Expired Listings

When a homeowner and agent agree to work together to sell a property, they sign a listing agreement that is valid for a specific length of time. Unless the home sells and closes within the specified time period, or unless the owner and agent agree in writing to extend the time period, the listing expires. Many agents don't even try to win listing extensions because they're embarrassed to ask for them. They didn't get the home sold during the term of the listing, so they assume the owner won't grant them additional time to sell the property. To avoid the owner's rejection, they avoid the conversation altogether. Their reluctance leads to the opportunity for the assertive agent to move in and convert the expired listing to a new piece of business.

REMEMBER

Securing an expired listing is a simple process that many agents make more complicated than necessary. All you have to do is text, make a series of phone calls, make personal visits, send marketing pieces, or connect via private messages on social media. I tend to focus on a more direct and basic approach of phone calls, texts, and personal visits. Direct mail can also be effective. The direct mail that some agents send can be cute, clever, and even corny packages, postcards, and letters. Some agents create envelopes that look like express deliveries. I've even seen agent-created mailers shaped to resemble firecrackers that, when opened, reveal the message "Bang! Your listing is dead." And we wonder why it's called junk mail.

Agents who rely exclusively on direct mail to win expired listings come in a distant second behind those who call and text directly or use a call and mail combination. A homeowner with a ready-to-expire listing is flooded with direct mailers from real estate agents, all competing to grab the owner's interest. However, it's personal contact that really grabs attention.

Expireds are high-probability prospects

With the seller's information in hand, you're ready to proceed with what I call a *high-probability lead*. Leads come from many sources: Internet inquiries, pay-per-click campaigns, social media, ad calls, sign calls, referrals, open houses, direct mail, and even cold calls. Some deliver possible leads; others deliver probable leads. The difference lies in the likelihood that the leads will convert to business. *Possible* leads convert less than half the time. *Probable* leads convert far more often.

REMEMBER

Working probable leads is much more efficient, and it's difficult to find a more probable lead than the owner of a home with an expired listing. The owner has demonstrated the desire or need to sell and shows the existence of a problem you can help solve. The problem, of course, is that after waiting out the entire listing period, the owner's home didn't sell. However, the problem in most owners' eyes is that the previous agent didn't perform well. In more than 80 percent of cases, though, the real reason the home didn't sell is that it was overpriced. More than half of the time, these homes go right back on the market with a different agent — why not you?

Engaging conversations

Working expired listings is an all-or-nothing game, but it shouldn't be the only way you generate leads. Instead, make expired listings just one of your pillars of business. You can't proceed in a half-hearted, here-today-gone-tomorrow fashion. Either you work expired listings — every day and consistently — or you don't. You can't try to work them for a few days when you're low on listings and then quit, only to return to the effort weeks later. You won't find a business card stating that an agent is "kind of" in the business of working expired listings. To capitalize by converting expired listings, be ready to make working expired listings your way of business life.

TIP

You don't have to work your whole marketplace in expireds. You're better working a smaller geographic area, but do it consistently rather than a larger area inconsistently. You can tighten up your geographic range or price range to throttle back your opportunities and better meet your time constraints. The most common mistake is working too many prospects and spreading yourself too thin. You're better off doing fewer listings well rather than many poorly.

TIP

As a new agent, my work life revolved around expired listings. I realized that in any given month most listing expirations occurred over the course of a few days, and that is still the case today in many markets. Up to two-thirds of all the listings that expire occur during the last few days of the month and the first day of the new month. If you're going to work expired listings, get ready to make those days very long work days. I followed this routine:

>> **I arrived at the office around 6 a.m. and printed out the expired listings.** Some days I ended up with more than 100 listings on my desk.

>> **At 6:30 a.m. a staff member came in to start researching phone numbers not listed on the MLS printout.** We searched four different sources for missing numbers: We first searched the Coles directory. Then we moved on to the MLS Metro-scan search. If we still didn't have the phone number, we searched through Yahoo! People Search. Finally, we packaged the rest up for the title company to search the tax records. We asked the title company to have those back to us before 9 a.m. At times, I also called the previous agent to ask for the seller's phone number. I often offered the agent some of the commission if he or she gave it to me. I did this because if I got the number and few other agents in the market had it, I had a higher probability of securing the listing.

>> **Based on gut instinct, market knowledge, and the information contained in the MLS printout, I sorted the properties by quickly determining why each one didn't sell and putting the ones that offered the highest probability of listing conversion and sale on top.** Also, I moved to the top of the list promising properties located in areas where I really wanted listings.

>> **I then practiced my scripts and dialogues, taking time to anticipate the objections I might hear from the seller and practicing how I'd overcome the barrier.** I knew before placing a call to the owner that my objective was to move beyond any objections and secure an appointment.

>> **After 30 minutes of practice, by 7:45 a.m., I was on the phone, aiming to reach people before they went to work and before other agents began making contact later in the morning.** I would list 80–90 listings a year from expired listings each year once I got my consistency and system in place. Today with programs like RedX, all that researching and cross-checking has

been eliminated. RedX and other similar computer programs can eliminate the research time, compiling phone numbers, scrubbing the lists for no-call compliance, and checking to see if properties have been relisted. To get more information on RedX, visit www.theredx.com/signup/dirkzeller.html.

WARNING

Today, your schedule is dictated by limitations stipulated by state and national do-not-call registries. For more information, see the sidebar "Keep it legal! The National Do Not Call Registry." If you can't secure the phone number because of the Do Not Call Registry, or if you simply can't find the number, go directly to the homeowner's front door and use the scripts, dialogues, and surveys in this chapter (respecting, of course, any No Solicitation signs). You'll reach fewer people, but you'll be more effective because you're face to face (many people prefer talking face to face).

» **My goal was to be the first agent to get through to the owner of every expired listing, but obviously that isn't always possible, especially on a day when the pile of listing printouts reaches a hundred or more.** After I made contact, scheduled an appointment, and established a good connection and sense of trust, I warned the homeowners about the number of calls they'd receive in the next 24 to 48 hours. I suggested that to avoid interruptions they could unplug their phone for the day. I knew that if the owner could dodge the calls during the first day or two following the listing expiration, most agents would quit trying to get through. See the section "Calling the seller: What to say" for more info about contacting owners of expired listings.

REMEMBER

The key to success with expired listings is to work them consistently and with commitment. Most agents who claim to work expired listings do so only at the end of the month and, even then, only sporadically. I never took a vacation at the end of the month because I didn't want to miss the flood of expired listings when they came through. And, in between, I also watched for the three, four, or five listings that expired on a daily basis. Only a small group of agents work expired listings as a way of life, but I can vouch for the fact that those who do build great businesses.

Qualifying expired listings

When working expired listings, get ready to work with owners who are frustrated that their homes didn't sell and who, in most cases, blame their agent and, by association, all agents in their real estate market. Many also blame the marketing strategy, the marketplace, and the lack of effort put forth by the real estate community. They're not happy campers.

KEEP IT LEGAL! THE NATIONAL DO NOT CALL REGISTRY

Many agents cheered when the National Do Not Call Registry took effect in 2004. With the stroke of a political pen, they were handed an excuse for not picking up the phone. When real estate company executives asked me what the law meant to our industry, I answered truthfully: The effect would be negligible; 97 percent of agents don't prospect anyway, so the new restrictions affected only a miniscule segment of agents. Consumers are delighted with the registry, but most salespeople are even happier with the built-in excuse.

Today, with more than 200 million phone numbers on the no-call list, it's here to stay. The only salespeople who aren't affected are charities, fundraising organizations, consumer research groups, and politicians. Imagine that! Politicians created a loophole for themselves. Within the law, you can still prospect. You just have to follow the rules:

- **You can turn your call into a survey.** You can collect information on home-buying trends, real estate services, consumer expectations of real estate agents, or a million other aspects of the industry.

- **You can gain advance permission, preferably in writing, to place calls.** For example, at the bottom of your open house sign-in sheet, buyer interview data form, or email newsletter subscriber form, include a permission statement. By signing, prospects grant you permission to call them with updates on market activity and their equity position. With this signed statement in hand, you have carte blanche permission to call the prospects until they tell you to stop, at which time you must stop immediately.

- **You can call within the boundaries of the law's inquiry provision.** This provision allows a salesperson to make follow-up calls for 90 days after the initial contact. Use this 90-day period to make the sale or prove your value so that the prospect grants you written permission to become a regular contact.

- **You can call within the law's 18-month after-the-sale provision.** This provision allows a salesperson to make contact during the 18-month period that follows the last purchase, payment, or delivery of services. In some cases, this provision creates a never-ending prospecting opportunity. For instance, every month you make a credit-card payment, you essentially give your credit-card company permission to contact you for another 18 months — permission that won't expire until 18 months after you finally make your last payment.

Every three months, obtain from your broker a current list of all contacts that your company has permission to call with a sales script. As a real estate agent, it's essential that you work inside the parameters of the law. The fine for each offense is up to $11,000.

In most cases, the blame is misplaced. The real culprit is usually the price the owners expected to reap from their property sale. If you help them dive back into the market with the same unrealistic price expectations, you'll set yourself up for another unhappy ending. Your ability to gauge the owner's level of motivation to sell at this time, along with the market conditions, will determine your likelihood of receiving a commission check. To help qualify your clients, find out the following:

>> Are they determined to acquire a buyer at their inflated sale price?

>> Which is more important: to obtain their desired price or secure a sale?

>> Are they open to discussing the true market value of their home?

What you're trying to find out with these questions is whether the owners *have* to sell or just *want* to. Someone who's forced to sell is a higher-grade prospect and is more likely to result in a sale — and a commission check — than someone who's testing the market. Sellers who are being transferred out of town, going through financial difficulties, expecting a child and living in a home that is too small, or going through a divorce usually have to sell. While some of these situations are uncomfortable and unfortunate, they create opportunity for an agent who can help them come to a successful conclusion.

Take time to ask questions and probe the answers to find out the prospect's situation. Many prospects are reluctant to reveal the reasons behind their decision to sell. Some feel an agent may try to take advantage of them — and unfortunately in a few cases, they may be right. The vast majority of agents I've ever met, however, want to help people achieve their dreams and desires.

TIP

The best way to extract the information you need from prospects is to keep asking questions. If you don't get the answers but you feel that the prospect has motivation, ask for a quick appointment to preview the home. By getting in the door and meeting face to face with a seller, you have a better chance to get your questions answered while also having a look around the property.

Calling the seller: What to say

When you call the owner of a home with an expired listing, you have one objective: to secure an appointment for a face-to-face meeting. Ideally that is for a listing presentation, but if you can gain only the opportunity to preview the home, take it. Remember, the owners will likely be contacted by other agents, so you need to move quickly and skillfully by following this advice:

>> **Address their situation.** Quickly convince the owners that if they choose to work with you, the outcome will be different than the last time. Explain why

working with you provides them a higher probability of sales success than they'll receive by working with any other agent.

REMEMBER

» **Be proactive.** The most serious sellers will re-list their home within a couple of days of a listing expiration. To land the listing, you can't be low key with your dialogue and delivery. These owners are ready for action. You must convey power, conviction, and belief in your ability to achieve success.

WARNING

» **Leave yourself wiggle room.** At this stage in the game, you may not be aware of all the factors. You don't know the condition of the home, the neighborhood layout, the level of access the owners are granting to potential buyers, the price and timeframe they're trying to achieve, the probability that their expectations can be met, or what the previous agent really did over the course of the listing term.

Because so much is up in the air, you have to leave yourself a little wiggle room by not overcommitting to what you can and can't do for the client. You also don't want to commit to what you will charge in terms of commission. You need to be flexible, depending on the market and motivation of the prospect.

» **Turn the most frequently asked questions to your advantage.** Be ready to answer the questions, "What will you do differently?" and "Why did my home not sell?" by saying that you don't have enough information to give an accurate answer. You can say something like, "Are you asking me to guess, or do you really want to know for sure?" When they say, "I want to know for sure," you book an appointment to see the house and have a friendly discussion. With that helpful move, you get your foot in the door.

» **Gain information.** The owners need to understand clearly that, without first-hand knowledge of their situation, you can't determine which approaches will achieve their desired outcome. You need to see their home in order to review its features, benefits, condition, and curb appeal.

You also need to figure out the previous agent's marketing strategy. Ask the seller what the other agent did to market the property. If you can, get the previous agent's fliers, ads, and brochures. Taking a look at the previous agent's website may also help. Finally, you need to gain an understanding of the owners' expectations regarding timeframe, listing price, sale price, and access for showings, as well as their interest in your evaluation of the competition they face in the current marketplace.

» **Differentiate yourself.** Use your track record (or your firm's if you're new in the business) to gain credibility with the owners. As you present your success story, do so with the caveat that your success is based on your outcome with clients who sought your counsel, accepted your recommendations, and implemented your advice. Tell the owners that you want to contribute to a similarly successful outcome on their behalf. You may even want to supply references of satisfied clients — especially those whose listings were also expired before you worked with them.

>> **Provide the option of an easy exit.** The seller with an expired listing most likely wanted to fire the agent long before the listing term was up but, in most cases, was bound by the contract terms to wait out the agreement. Acknowledge that the owners feel cautious about tying their home up for another long period of time. To put them at ease, offer them an easy-exit listing agreement or include a 100 percent satisfaction-guaranteed clause. Either approach allows the owner to sever the agreement any time before it expires, which greatly reduces the perception of risk they may have about committing to another agent.

Sales skills

Winning expired listings is the result of superb sales skills, including:

>> Daily prospecting

>> Focused dialogue

>> Strong delivery

>> Solid ability to handle objections

>> Compelling description of the unique benefits you offer

>> Ability to win appointments that end in listing agreements

As you initiate contact after the previous listing has expired, your first objective isn't to convince the owners to re-list with you. Instead, your initial aim is to pique their interest and make a compelling argument regarding why they should take the time to see your presentation. The sample scripts in the following section can help you plan your approach.

Sample scripts

Following are some sample scripts that you can build on when making initial contact with the owner of an expired listing. No matter which script you follow, remember this: Don't get sidetracked. Stay focused on your single objective, which is to secure an appointment with the owner.

Script for an expired listing:

Hi, I'm looking for ___. This is ___ with ___.

Is your home still available?

OR

When do you plan to meet with agents about the job of selling your home?

OR

I noticed that your home was no longer on the MLS. I was calling to see if you still wanted to sell?

1. When you sell this home, where are you hoping to move to?

2. Do you have a timeframe to get there?

3. What do you think caused your home not to sell?

4. How did you select your previous agent?

5. What are your expectations of the next agent you choose?

6. Has anyone shared with you the real reason your home failed to sell?

7. Homes fail to sell for only a few reasons: lack of exposure, changes in market competition, and price. One you control, one the agent controls, and one no one controls. Which do you think it is?

8. Let me ask you . . . do you want to know which one for sure?

9. All we need to do is meet for 15 to 20 minutes and take a look at your home. Would __ or __ be better for you this week?

Response to the objection that all agents are alike:

Boy, I can sure understand where you get that impression and feeling. And I know the kind of frustration you feel because I've felt it myself when I've taken over listings like yours only to find poorly written and prepared offers. Mr. and Mrs. Seller, there really is a difference in agents. If there weren't, we would all be doing the same level of business in terms of listings, sales, time on the market, and list-to-sale price. And we'd all have the same level of client satisfaction. Wouldn't you agree?

So the real question is what's the difference, right? I would be delighted to spend just a few minutes with you to help you understand the differences. Would __ or __ be better for you this week?

Response to the question "Why are you calling me now?":

It sure seems like a lot of people are calling, doesn't it? Your home's listing came up as expired, so I'm calling to see if I can be of service. In order for me to accurately assess my ability to help, I need just a few minutes of your time and to see your home. Would __ or __ be better for you this week?

Response to the question "Where were you when my home was listed?":

That's a great question, and I'm sure this is a source of frustration for you right now. I can assure you that I personally take the responsibility of selling someone's home very seriously. In many cases, my clients have entrusted their largest asset to me.

Because of that trust, I work almost exclusively to ensure their sale. With a 98 percent success rate against the market average of 68 percent, I must be doing something right. Wouldn't you agree? When would be the best time for us to meet to evaluate your situation? Would __ or __ be better for you this week?

Using technology to leverage your expired efforts

Several major technological advancements in the past few years have made it easier to work expired listings. The first is data service technologies like RedX, which reduce your research time and increase efficiency. The second is auto dialers. The use of an auto-dialer can increase the number of people you contact by at least 100 percent. Most companies that provide technology data, like RedX or Vulcan 7, can also build an auto-dialer into their system.

TIP

Don't forget about using social media to garner expired listings. It's a valid and oft-overlooked way to contact sellers. You can find some prospects on Facebook, Twitter, and LinkedIn. Instead of posting on someone's wall, I recommend using the private-message function to ask whether you can reach out to them via phone. If you can only reach them through a private social-media message, you may be the only agent who reaches them.

WARNING

The caveat is that this only works for less-common names. I'm not going to invest my time looking for a John Smith with an expired listing in Portland, Oregon . . . there are too many. I would, however, look for a Dirk Zeller in Portland, Oregon. You also must realize that, because you're not Facebook friends, your message goes to a secondary message area. They might not see it for a few days or weeks.

For-Sale-by-Owners Think Selling Is Easy

Converting FSBO listings involves a process that in a number of ways is similar to working with expired listings. However, the key differences between the two areas are:

>> **Timing:** If you contact the owners of a FSBO, you can usually expect them to take at least a few weeks to try to sell on their own before they commit the listing to you. According to the National Association of Realtors' research, five weeks seems to be the "give-it-the-old-college-try" timeframe.

>> **Sales approach:** When working to convert an expired listing, you need to take control in order to prevail over a bunch of other unknown agents who are vying for the same listing. The owners of the expired listing rarely have an

agent preference at this point. Their "first-choice" agent was the one whose sign just came down. This isn't always the case with FSBO owners, who sometimes have an agent in the wings just in case they don't have success on their own. For this reason, you need to take a lower-key approach and work to build a relationship in order to win over the FSBO listing.

Understanding why to pursue FSBO listings

When the marketplace is active and everything in sight seems to be selling, as has been the case during the writing of this edition of the book, FSBO listings abound and FSBO sellers achieve a reasonable sales success rate without the services of an agent. So, you may be wondering why an agent would even spend time trying to convert FSBOs to agent–represented listings. Here are just a few good reasons:

REMEMBER

>> **FSBOs are simply too tempting and attractive a market segment not to work.** You know who these owners are because they're actively marketing their presence in the marketplace. You also know they have motivation or they wouldn't be spending the money to advertise their home for sale. It doesn't make sense to ignore this great market segment, though most agents do.

>> **Owners of FSBOs are viable, qualified client targets.** Unlike other prospective clients, you don't have to wonder whether they own their home, whether they're serious about selling it, or whether they have the authority and ability to conduct the deal.

TIP

>> **Owners of FSBOs are easy to find and reach.** One of the most difficult steps in the sales process is locating prospects in need of your service. With FSBOs, like expired listings, you know who your prospects are, and you know how to get in touch with them. Reaching FSBOs is easier than reaching expired listings because FSBO sellers want to be found.

>> **The vast majority of FSBOs fail to sell without an agent.** Even in a robust market, fewer than 30 percent of FSBOs sell themselves. This means that more than 70 percent of the owners, if they want to sell, eventually enlist the services of a real estate agent.

>> **FSBO sellers often net lower prices than those achieved by agent-represented sellers.** Among the 30 percent of FSBO homes that result in a sale, most are priced right at or below fair market value. In fact, to FSBO sellers, price is the primary marketing ammunition. The only reason buyers take the additional risk of working with a FSBO is that they're trying to buy a home for less money than they'd spend on a traditional transaction. The problem is that low price is exactly the opposite of what the homeowner is trying to achieve.

More than eight out of ten serious FSBOs end up as agent listings within a reasonable period of time — usually four to five weeks. According to NAR, 63 percent of the FSBO sellers who sell do so in four weeks or less. Originally, owners set out to sell their own homes for one reason: They want to save money by not paying the agent commission. They view the real estate commission that an agent earns as too much pay for such an easy job. They think that money would be better spent when put toward an additional down payment or a get-out-of-debt plan. They ask themselves, "How hard can it be?" as they pound the FSBO sign into their front yard and post their home on Craigslist, FSBO.com, Zillow, and other websites. In the back of their minds, many think, "Let's give it a go. We'll probably meet a few agents along the way, so we can always change our minds." And most do. After a month of the hassle, time, energy, emotion, and stress of trying to sell their own home — after running ads, fielding phone calls, holding open houses, and showing parades of people through their home — 90 percent of homeowners rethink their situation. Fortunately for agents, selling a home isn't all that easy.

Using technology to find FSBO listings and opportunities

Because FSBO owners want to be found, you don't have to look far:

>> **Subscribe to RedX.** This company compiles information from FSBO newspaper ads, FSBO websites, and other real estate sources to provide you with a complete list of FSBO opportunities in your area. For a low monthly fee, it delivers daily email lists of the most recent FSBOs right to your desktop. With a subscription, you also get full access to a searchable six-month FSBO history. You can't beat the service. It enables you to redirect the hours of time you spend on research into time spent calling FSBO contacts and winning over new listings. As a bonus, the company offers a special package of discounts to readers of this book that it doesn't offer to the general public. Visit www. theredx.com/signup/dirkzeller.html.

>> **Check the aggregator sites.** Check sites such as www.fsbo.com and www. byowner.com, which help FSBO sellers increase their home's exposure. The websites also make it easy for you to find homeowners and contact them. Some sellers don't put their phone numbers on the sites. They want prospective buyers to contact them via private message. This gives you a less direct way to reach them. If you don't have a phone number, you can reach sellers by personally making a visit to their home.

Some FSBO sellers also post their homes on Craigslist. If you just monitor the activity on Craigslist, you can garner some of the active FSBOs. They place their home on Zillow in the For Sale By Owner section. The thing to remember is that many FSBOs use one or two methods of exposure. According to NAR, more than 38 percent of FSBOs don't actively market their home. Only 33 percent of FSBOs put their home on the Internet . . . a staggering statistic considering that almost 90 percent of buyers are searching the Internet for homes.

Zillow's "Make Me Move" sellers

Zillow's website feature called Make Me Move can create a lot of opportunity for an agent. A potential seller prospect creates a description of the home, uploads pictures of their home, and sets a price that would cause them to sell their home. Many of these sellers are pre-stage sellers. They're not ready to put their home on the market actively; they are merely testing the waters. This is especially true for their price. Most are quite a ways off from the real market value of their home.

Many of these people will follow a process of being a Make Me Move, to them trying to FSBO, and then to listing with an agent. Make Me Move creates an organized list of pre-stage seller prospects. You can see how long they have been attempting to sell, how many people have viewed the listing, and what they paid for the home in the past. There is a large volume of information you have a Make Me Move prospect.

A small percentage of these prospects understand the right marketing strategy for their home. In reviewing Make Me Move listings posted on Zillow, over 43 percent of them had five photos or less. Many of those had only one photo a buyer could look at. Another 19 percent had between 5 and 10 photos, and only 17 percent had more than 20 photos to view on their home.

Some of the Make Me Move prospects put their phone number in their listing. Most use Zillow as their primary communication messenger. You will need to fill out an online form and submit to get more information. Using Cole Realty Resource (www.colerealtyresource.com) based on their address to access phone data is an option as well, so you can more directly connect with them.

The sales cycle is longer for these types of leads. Over time, they do list and sell their homes. Because they want to try, test, or are in no hurry, your follow-up, constant communication, and the value you transfer are important.

WARNING

You want to discover early in your interaction with them whether they feel like they are committed or have an obligation to another agent. You don't want to spend months following up on a Make Me Move prospect to find out their brother-in-law is a real estate agent and they feel obligated to him.

Converting FSBO opportunities to listings

Plan to take a patient approach to FSBOs. Realize that you can't do or say anything — short of offering to give your services away — that will rush the owners' decisions to abandon the idea of selling their own homes. Basically, you're playing a waiting game that you can't win in a hurry, but that you can quickly lose if you're pushy or confrontational.

WARNING

Agents who are filled with hyperbole about themselves and their service, or who try to tell owners that FSBOs fail to sell themselves, use the wrong tactic. Owners don't want overly confident agents making them feel like idiots for trying to sell on their own — even if they are!

The best approach is to dial back your sales pitch and enhance your emphasis on service. Focus on helping the owners in their effort. Always encourage them and wish them success, but don't give away all your valuable services without a signed contract.

Organizing your plan of attack

Confine your efforts to a concise geographic area that enables you to stop by the FSBOs and see the owners as regularly as every two weeks. When it comes time for them to convert to an agent listing, they'll find it harder to reject you or not interview you if they've met you and know you personally.

TIP

If you work a large geographic area and are unable to whittle it down to a more concise area, expect to encounter a great many FSBOs. The easiest way to organize the opportunities is to track each home by the owners' phone numbers. Owners will change their ads and their asking prices, but they'll rarely change their phone numbers. Organizing each home under its phone number eliminates the risk of duplication.

REMEMBER

All you're trying to do is gain a commitment that if the owners decide to turn the selling of their home over to an agent, they'll interview you for the job.

Targeting your prospects

In targeting FSBOs for conversion, use the following selection criteria:

>> Clear motivation to sell

>> A short selling timeframe

>> A specific place they need to be by a certain date

>> The capacity to sell at fair market value with a commission

>> A high-demand home in a high-demand neighborhood

>> Owners who don't have a best friend or relative who is a real estate agent

You need to ask owners these questions to understand how they fit into your criteria. By asking, you know which prospects to invest your time in.

TIP

The best approach to target FSBOs for conversion is to create a Top 10, Top 20, or even Top 30 list. If you try to work much beyond 30 FSBOs, excellent service becomes a difficult proposition. If you pursue the best 30 FSBOs, knowing that 80 percent — or 24 of the 30 — are likely to list in the next 60 days, you have 24 solid prospects, or about 12 a month.

If you provide solid advice, counsel, service, and care, you can get 30 percent to 50 percent of those 12 FSBOs to interview with you. Depending on your skill in the interview, you may convert two to five prospects into listings each month. Think about it: A business source that generates five listings a month is a great source of business. And even if it delivers only two a month, that's still 24 listings a year. Not bad!

Making the initial contact

Making initial contact with owners of FSBO homes is the toughest step for most agents, so I recommend that you make calls as soon as you see a FSBO come onto the market. By doing this, you can call owners of new listings to have a professional conversation before the onslaught of calls from other agents begins to come through.

REMEMBER

If you're the first agent to place a call or attend a FSBO open house, you'll find some owners more open to dialogue. You'll also find it easier to distinguish yourself when you're the first to get through, rather than after 50 other agents have already done so. Some FSBOs are "die-hard" and will be dismissive in needing your assistance. This attitude may come from a previous negative experience or from overconfidence. Don't be bothered by this because most of these FSBOs will soften over time.

Another benefit to calling FSBO owners early on Saturday or Sunday is that you leave your afternoons free to drop in on some FSBO open houses. Meeting owners face to face in their own homes presents an effective way to establish contact. The owners are sure to be home, they're expecting visitors, and they're ready to make contact and discuss the sale of their home.

Putting the mail carrier to work

Because of the four-to-five week sales cycle involved in converting FSBOs to listings, you can use mailers more effectively with them than you can when dealing with expired listings. By mailing helpful items once or twice a week, you give yourself a reason to make follow-up phone calls on a regular basis.

After every face-to-face or phone contact, follow up with a handwritten thank-you note. The owners are getting mail from many other real estate agents, so to avoid the round file (also known as the trash can), personalize your notes with handwritten exterior addresses.

Also, use your mailers to send useful information that sellers may need. Too often, agents act like the adversaries of FSBO sellers. Take a different and better approach by helping them out. Most have no idea what they really need to do to complete the sale. For example, if they receive helpful advice from you every five days, when it comes time to sign their home over to a listing agent, they're more likely to think favorably of your interview invitation.

To use mailers effectively, follow these suggestions:

>> Send the owners a property disclosure form and information on disclosure laws, including how the law affects the value and sale of their home. Buyers can back out even at the last minute if the owners don't handle this detail properly.

>> Send a sample purchase and sale contract and maybe a counteroffer form, along with the explanation that nothing ever gets agreed upon in the first contract.

>> Send owners of older homes a lead-based paint disclosure form to give to the buyer of the home, if appropriate.

>> Ask your lender to prepare a financing sheet that the owners can give to the buyer.

>> Send numerous other items to service FSBO sellers and create a connection, including the following:

- Sample net revenue sheets

- Sample walk-through inspection forms

- Updated market analysis reports of comparable properties

- Sample brochures or photos of the owners' home

- Guest registers for use at showings

- Lead tracking forms to log information on people who call about the home

- Lists of homes that would meet the owners' needs if they're looking to purchase a new home in the area

- Free reports about selling their home

Free reports are an effective device because they enable owners to educate themselves and increase their likelihood of success, while simultaneously positioning you as the expert. By sending these reports, you establish yourself as a strong resource to help them succeed. Then, when they don't succeed, you'll be there to pick up the pieces and list and sell their home.

Dialing for dollars

As you work your high-priority FSBO homeowners, make phone or in-person contact at least once a week. Use these communications to see how sales activity has been, whether a weekend open house is scheduled, whether they got your latest mailing, and, most important, whether they sold the home.

REMEMBER

A portion of FSBOs sell on their own, but a big difference lies between getting a purchase offer and closing the deal. The fact that the owners achieved a sale doesn't mean that they'll get their money. The quality of buyers who shop FSBOs is lower than that of those who shop homes listed in the MLS. For this reason, when FSBO sellers report that they've sold their home, keep following up. A large number of these sales fall apart before closing. When that happens, sellers who thought they were on the downhill slope wave a white flag and call in a real estate agent. Make sure that you're still in touch when that moment of frustration arrives.

Overcoming rejection and staying resilient

FSBO sellers will reject you because they prefer not to use your services. But if you maintain a steady, professional relationship, offering help and staying in contact for four to five weeks, you'll usually be able to win an interview. From there, if you have excellent presentation skills, a listing follows. Increase your odds of success by taking these two precautions:

>> **Limit the number of FSBOs you cultivate.** Focus only on the best potential clients, as described in the section "Targeting your prospects," earlier in this chapter.

>> **Avoid prospects with low motivation or unrealistically high price expectations.** These sellers are usually the most toxic, and too often they'll try to take their frustrations out on you.

Mastering the game of lead follow-up

REMEMBER

Working FSBOs fundamentally turns into a game of lead follow-up. You need to personally and regularly contact your FSBO leads to discover their motivation and qualifications, book face-to-face meetings, disqualify prospects as necessary, provide regular service and communication, and schedule presentation appointments. Then you need to repeat the service and communication steps several times weekly until the listing is in hand.

Coming face to face

To make personal contact, begin by asking the FSBO seller if you can come by and see the home. You can explain that you want to stay informed of the regional housing inventory, or that you're working with buyers who may be interested. You can present yourself as a potential investor, or, when you can, use the *reverse-no technique*. The idea is to get the prospect to say no, which you end up reversing into a yes for business. For example, you can ask: "Would you be offended if I came by to take a look at your home?" No is what she really wants to say, but you end up turning her no into a yes to your real request to see the home. Following are sample scripts for each approach.

Script for keeping up with the inventory:

> *Mr. Seller, your home is located in my core area of sales. Because it is, I'd like to come by and preview your home. Would there be a time on __ or __ to do that this week?*

Script for working with a prospective buyer:

> *Ms. Seller, I understand you're selling your home on your own. Let me ask you this: Are you cooperating with real estate agents? What I mean is, if a real estate agent brought you a qualified buyer at an agreeable price to you, would you be willing to pay a partial commission?*

> *We're working with a few buyers for your area that we haven't been able to place yet. May I come by on __ or __ later this week to see your home?*

When you use the script for the prospective buyer approach, understand that you're not interested in reducing your commission. What you're really trying to do is achieve a face-to-face appointment to collect more information on motivation to determine the probability of securing a listing in the future.

Script for a potential investor:

> *Mr. Seller, your home is located in a solid area for real estate investment. I was wondering if I could come by to see your home as a possible investment purchase, to see if it's a property that would meet my investment needs. Would __ or __ be better for you?*

In using this approach, realize that the key phrase is "investment needs." You'll rarely find a FSBO that meets your investment needs. My personal investment need is a home that can be acquired at a 70 percent discount below fair market value, whereas most FSBOs are trying to sell their homes at 110 percent of fair market value. However, this technique gets you in the door to see the home and talk with the sellers.

Script for a reverse-no:

> *Ms. Seller, would you be offended if I came by to take a quick look at your home?*

TIP

The reverse-no technique can be used with any script. It capitalizes on the normal reflexive human reaction of "no" in order to achieve a positive response. It opens the door and allows you to then set an appointment.

FSBO survey script:

> Hi, this is __ from __. I'm looking for the owner of the home for sale.
>
> Your home is in my core area. I'm doing a quick survey of the FSBOs in this area. May I take a few minutes to ask you some questions?
>
> The ad in the paper said that you had __ bedrooms and __ bathrooms.
>
> Do you have a two-level or one-level home?
>
> Are all the bedrooms on the same floor?
>
> Are they good-sized rooms?
>
> How is the condition of the kitchen?
>
> Are the bathrooms in good condition?
>
> Can you describe your yard for me?
>
> Is there anything else you feel I should know?
>
> It sounds like you have a great home; how long have you lived there?
>
> Why are you selling at this time?
>
> Where are you hoping to move to now?
>
> What is your timeframe to get there?
>
> How did you happen to select that area to move to?
>
> How did you determine your initial asking price for the home?
>
> What techniques are you using for exposure and marketing of your home?
>
> Are you aware that more than 86 percent of home buyers begin their search on the Internet now?
>
> If there was a clear advantage for you in using me to market and expose your home, and it cost you very little, would you consider it?
>
> Let's simplify. Set a time to get together for 15 to 20 minutes, so I can see your home and understand your objectives. I have time available __, or would __ be better for you?

Building relationships

FSBO relationships are built over time. By introducing yourself to the owners the first weekend their FSBO is announced, before the masses start calling on Monday, you create a good connection. By sending tools, educational materials, free reports, and forms, you become an ally. By taking a personal interest in their situation, you create a solid connection that often pays off when they decide to go with an agent they know and trust — preferably you.

FSBO owners unwittingly let buyers basically steal the "saved" commission through underpriced offers. People don't shop FSBOs because it's the cool thing to do. They do so because they know they can secure a low price and a high initial equity position.

REMEMBER

By building a relationship over time, you demonstrate your value to the FSBO seller. Whether you're working with FSBOs or expired listings, your goal is simply to be one of the two, three, or four agents whom the owner will interview when the time comes. You just want the opportunity to compete and make your presentation.

Using stats to make the case

For most agents, the missing ingredient when talking to any buyer or seller is stats — the use of numbers and facts to move the discussion beyond opinion to what the facts are of the marketplace. This is very true when trying to encourage a FSBO to give you an opportunity to help them. FSBO sellers are less successful in accomplishing their desired outcome today than in the past. In 2005, 13 percent of all sales were FSBO sales. That has dropped to 8 percent. FSBOs are at a disadvantage in today's technology-driven world.

For FSBOs that are successful in selling their home on their own, over 38 percent knew the person they sold their home to. It's a friend, family member, or neighbor. A very large portion of FSBOs are not really marketing their property to find a buyer. They already have someone to sell the home to! Additionally, for the more-than 73 percent who sold to someone they know, the sale happened in less than four weeks.

Looking at the NAR stats on FSBOs creates a clear picture of what is happening with FSBOs. Let's look at some of these numbers for FSBOs where they didn't know the buyer and needed to produce one. According to NAR, 45 percent of FSBOs that successfully sell do so within two weeks of coming on the market. That is a huge percentage. That means the longer they are on the market, the lower the odds of achieving success. By eight weeks on the market, 68 percent of FSBOs who are going to sell have sold. The median number of weeks for successful FSBOs is four weeks. In trying to educate a FSBO and differentiate you as an agent, you want to show and share with them these stats. You don't want to say they can't do it. You do want to indicate to them that their best opportunity is in that first four weeks and that their marketing strategy needs to be designed to create a sale in that period.

NAR produces a Profile of Home Buyers and Sellers Report every year (www.realtor.org), packed with stats and analysis. There's a complete chapter of stats and analysis of FSBOs. Few agents review this data and are missing out on easily accessible information to position themselves as experts.

Chapter **11**

Open Houses: New Agents' Bread and Butter

I f you're one of the many real estate agents who think open houses are only good for selling the home being shown — or if you judge success by the number of sales you generate as a result of your open houses — expect this chapter to redirect your thinking.

REMEMBER

Real estate agents may view open houses as ancient marketing methods. But the truth is that open houses still have value for producing sales and, especially, prospects. Even though today's buyer does much of his upfront shopping via the Internet, open houses continue to draw do-it-yourselfers and provide a valuable avenue to get face to face with these buyer types.

Well-documented research shows that fewer than 5 percent of buyers purchase a home they visit during an open house. This proves the open house to be, at best, a pretty ineffective sales approach for that actual home.

Despite this statistic, open houses are an important tool in an agent's business arsenal for a very good reason: Open houses give you a setting to show your audience what a great agent you are, ultimately providing a terrific opportunity to generate prospects. And all savvy agents know that prospects are the lifeblood of real estate business success. You can also demonstrate firsthand your market knowledge and command of technology because of the portability of an agent's office in today's world.

Count on this chapter to help you plan, stage, and host open houses that generate buyer prospects, listing prospects, and — if the stars align just right — perhaps even a buyer for the home you're showing.

Online Buyers Have Helped Open Houses

Open houses aren't the best vehicles for selling homes. So why do real estate agents bother with them? Because open houses are a great means for prospecting.

REMEMBER

An open house provides a real estate agent with a neighborhood storefront from which to do business for a day. Each time you host an open house, you set up shop in a client home and open the doors to the opportunity to meet prospects, establish relationships, and expand your real estate clientele.

If your real estate business could benefit from an influx of buyer or seller prospects, start staging more open houses. You can hardly find a more effective way to generate leads face to face. And, as a bonus, occasionally your efforts will net a sale. Not a bad bonus for a solid prospecting tool.

Think of the open house as the real estate agent's equivalent to the retailer's *loss leader*, which is something that creates the initial opening for a sale. In the same way that a grocery store manager offers milk at a discounted price to draw shoppers into the store, a real estate agent invests time and money in an open house to build traffic, attract prospects, hand out business cards, and cultivate sales of other products.

Buyers often want to search for homes on their own before committing to a real estate agent. Many prefer to not reveal their phone numbers, email addresses, or intentions at the onset of their search. They feel that by attending an open house, they may get to view a home they're interested in without having to commit to an agent.

According to the National Association of Realtors (NAR), 38 percent of Internet home searchers drive by a home they're interested in. NAR's findings show that buyers take action when they're interested in a home. They check out the neighborhood, the condition of the home, and the curb appeal. For 65 percent of buyers, the next step is walking through the home that caught their eye online. The largest portion of this group accesses the home during an open house — where they can remain anonymous. Doing an open house helps you tap into the do-it-yourself mentality of today's buyer.

A chance to meet potential clients face to face

The explosion of online real estate marketing and shopping has led to a dramatic drop in the number of phone-to-phone and face-to-face meetings between real estate agents and their prospects. The open house is a proven way to gain clear and easy real-time access to prospects who are ready to buy or sell homes.

REMEMBER

In addition to giving you the opportunity to meet home shoppers who drop in, an open house gives you the opportunity to meet the neighbors and friends of the sellers — all of whom may end up in the real estate buyer or seller market in the future. Take time to figure out the needs, wants, timeframes, and motivations behind each person's home-shopping experience. Form a connection with the shoppers. After they meet and visit with you, home shoppers find rejecting you as "just a salesperson" much more difficult.

A means of catering to the do-it-yourselfer's home-buying needs

As inventory levels have dropped in most marketplaces, the competition for high-demand homes has increased. Consumers are starting to believe that finding a good home for sale is a tough task and that when a good home comes on the market it won't last long. In some markets, frustrated buyers are taking matters into their own hands by actively searching listings online, spending their weekends doing home-shopping "legwork," and attending open houses in droves.

TIP

When do-it-yourself home shoppers drop into your open house, you're safe to bet on two things:

>> They're serious about finding a home for sale.

>> They usually aren't represented by an agent.

In other words, they're great buyer prospects.

A high-touch opportunity in a high-tech world

One of the big challenges facing real estate agents in today's wired world is discovering the identities of their prospective clients. Buyers cruise and click their way around hundreds of real estate websites, requesting information via email from scores of agents without ever revealing more than an email address.

WARNING

As an agent, you can respond with an email that provides the requested information, but it hardly allows you the chance to provide your professional counsel and to establish a professional relationship. For one thing, it's almost impossible to distinguish yourself from other agents via email. Also, while email enables you to communicate promptly, it doesn't enable you to easily determine the desire, need, ability, and buying authority of the prospect. Communicating via email also stops you from determining the prospect's motivation and timeframe and from customizing your advice to the prospect's unique situation.

REMEMBER

That's where open houses come to your rescue. Open houses cut through the electronic interface and put you right in front of prospective buyers and sellers. From there, you can distinguish yourself, define your prospect's interests, and begin the professional relationship that leads to real estate success.

HOW MANY OPEN HOUSES SHOULD I HOST?

Real estate agents always seek a magic formula that defines how many open houses to host and when to host them. I hate to disappoint you, but I haven't found a pat answer. However, here are a few good guidelines to follow:

- **If you're a new agent** trying to build a clientele and get your business off the ground, host open houses weekly, or at least frequently. Volunteer to hold open houses for the listings of other agents in your company.

- **If you're an established agent** working to increase your business and win market share (see Chapter 14 for more on the topic of market share), add up how many open houses you've hosted during recent months and aim to increase that figure at least proportionately to the amount you're working to increase your business.

- **If open houses are fundamental to your lead-generation strategy,** you should hold an event at least several times each month.

Setting Your Prospecting Objectives

REMEMBER

The main purpose of an open house is to attract solid buyer and seller prospects. So, when setting your objectives for each open house, shift your focus away from selling the featured home and toward acquiring prospects.

Before each open house, set your prospecting objectives, including the following:

TIP

>> **Number of contacts from whom you hope to collect information** for use in future mailings and other forms of follow-up. Not everyone is willing to share personal contact information, but with skill and effort you can expect to gather lead information from at least 50 percent of guests. For success, follow these tips:

   • Have a sign-in sheet and tell guests that you've been asked by the seller to track the attendees from the open house, and ask if they would please help you keep that commitment to the seller. Don't pounce on them when they enter the door. Instead, wait until they settle in for a moment.

   At the bottom of the sign-in sheet, be sure to state that by signing this sheet they're agreeing to allow you to contact them in the future with real estate information. This helps you stay legal with the National Do Not Call Registry.

   • Have your business card ready to hand to people who walk in. As you hand it to them, ask for theirs at the same time. Often without thinking, they'll dig into their purse or wallet and automatically hand you their contact information.

>> **Number of buyer interviews you hope to schedule.** Again, no single magic figure exists, but my recommendation is that you aim to achieve interviews from at least 25 percent of the guests who provide you with follow-up contact information. To achieve interviews, consider these steps:

   • Ask for the opportunity to meet. You may use a script like this:

   "Bob and Mary, in order for you to maximize your initial equity position and minimize your upfront costs in securing a new home for your family, we simply need to meet. Would ___ or ___ be better for you this week?"

   • Most people at open houses are also sellers. They need to sell their current homes in order to make a new home purchase possible. Ask to come by and take a look at their home. Use a script such as:

   "Bob and Mary, would you be offended if I came by to take a look at your home? Would ___ or ___ be better for you this week?"

- If you can't secure a face-to-face appointment, aim to at least set a specific time that you can contact attendees by phone. Then you can work to acquire an over-the-phone appointment for a specific day and specific time to speak next. Simply agreeing to call them later in the week is not good enough.

Check out the upcoming section, "Being the Host with the Most: Effectively Managing the Open House," for help planning the strategy to achieve your attendance, lead-generation, and prospecting objectives.

Planning Your Open Houses to Gain Maximum Exposure for You

REMEMBER

To achieve success with an open house, follow four clear rules to ensure the greatest return on your investment of time, money, and resources. If one of your current listings doesn't meet the following four criteria, consider skipping the open house for that listing.

>> **Rule 1:** Feature an attractive home in a high-demand area.

>> **Rule 2:** Choose a home with great curb appeal.

>> **Rule 3:** Market to the neighbors.

>> **Rule 4:** Lead prospects to the home with easy-to-follow signage.

The following sections provide advice on how to achieve each of these four success factors.

Featuring a high-demand home

Here's a hard truth to swallow: No one comes to an open house to meet the agent. They come to see an appealing home, and your role as the hosting agent is to make that house shine. Your reward is the list of prospects you amass, and, 1 out of 20 times, a home sale to boot.

TIP

As you prepare for an open house, think of the home you're featuring as the headliner of the show. Choose a home with star power by following these points:

>> **Select a home in a high-demand, low-inventory area.** Scarcity is a well-proven marketing strategy. People line up to get into crowded restaurants. They respond enthusiastically when told they're limited to "one per customer." And they'll show up at your open house in flocks if the home you're showing is one of only a few for sale in a well-regarded neighborhood.

>> **Do your homework before making your selection final.** Study the inventory levels in the neighborhood you're considering for your open house. Obtain the prices of recent sales to be sure that your home is within the acceptable range. Research the number of days that recent sales and current listings have been on the market. Then compare your findings with research on nearby neighborhoods to be sure that the home you're considering competes well.

The statistics you compile provide you with information you should be tracking anyway, so even if you rule out the home you're studying, the time you spend on the effort is worthwhile.

WARNING

Open house selection isn't a time for guesswork. Use your market knowledge to choose a home with high appeal and demand. Rely on gut instinct only when you're deciding between two homes with equal market appeal.

Looking good: Leveraging the power of curb appeal

All agents have seen it happen: A prospect pulls up alongside an open house, touches the brakes, takes a careful look, and then drives off without ever going inside. Nine times out of ten, the house failed the drive-by test. It lacked curb appeal.

It's your job as an agent to counsel the sellers to turn the house exterior into a perfect ten.

TIP

In preparation for an open house, work with the sellers on at least the two areas that most significantly affect the home shopper's first impression: landscaping and paint color and quality. (For complete information on getting the house ready for showing, flip to Chapter 13.)

Marketing to the neighbors

Many agents achieve greater open house results from neighborhood marketing efforts than from general public exposure. As you plan your open house announcement strategy, pay special attention to your nearest prospects by marketing to those who live right around the house you're showing. Follow these steps:

TIP

>> **Consider a neighborhood "sneak preview."** Invite neighbors into the house an hour before the home opens to the general public.

>> **Send at least 25 invitations to generate an adequate neighborhood response.** Better yet, hand-deliver 25 invitations. Before you allow yourself to assume that door-to-door delivery is too time consuming, realize that this simple touch will increase your invitation response rate dramatically.

>> **Use neighborhood events to gain access to prospects in restricted-access neighborhoods.** Restricted-access neighborhoods include gated communities or condo complexes that require the public — including real estate agents — to gain permission before entering. This entry barrier makes prospecting in these areas difficult at best. So whenever you achieve a listing in a restricted-access neighborhood, leverage the opportunity to stage an open house neighborhood preview that enables you to meet and establish relationships with surrounding homeowners.

Guiding prospects to the open house

Open house advertising is important, but it pales in comparison to the importance of a well-selected open house site and a signage strategy that leads prospects to your open house front door.

In choosing your open house site, make sure that you do the following:

WARNING

>> **Select a home near a well-traveled street to gain exposure from the traffic volume.**

Be careful that the home isn't too close to the traffic or you'll get traffic *by* the home but not *to* the home. Remember that buyers are reluctant to live too close to a thoroughfare or busy street.

>> **Hold your open house in a home that is no more than three directional signs away from a well-traveled street.** Otherwise you'll lose prospects as they try to navigate what feels like a maze.

The New Strategy of Mega Open Houses

In the past five years, open house strategy has changed and expanded with the birth of *mega open houses*. The purpose of a mega open house is to increase the number of attendees and create an event-like atmosphere. These open houses follow some of the basic rules and principles from earlier in the chapter. The mega open house puts these strategies on steroids to dramatically increase the traffic of buyers and your name recognition.

Creating a neighborhood event

In creating a neighborhood event, you are trying to attract both buyers and sellers to come to your open house. There are a number of ways to increase neighborhood traffic. The uniqueness of the property can create an attraction. If you're holding a home open that is a curiosity or even an oddball type of property, a number of the neighbors could be attracted to come to that open house. You could use language like "Never been seen," "First-time open house," and "Only public viewing" to build the sense of exclusivity and urgency in the neighborhood.

TIP

The pre-marketing of your open house to create a neighborhood event must be a big part of your strategy. You could use a neighborhood-exclusive time slot. For example, the public open house starts at 1:00 p.m., but the neighborhood exclusive starts at noon. You position this "sneak peek" as something proprietary to the neighbors. You offer the extra exclusive hour so the neighbors can see the home and bring their friends who want to live in the neighborhood. If they are a Mrs. Kravitz type of neighbor, they will usually show up. These people tend to know everyone's business in the neighborhood, so connecting with them can often create leads on who is thinking about buying or selling. It also gives you someone to keep in touch with to keep your finger on the pulse of the neighborhood.

To create a neighborhood event, you want to direct mail the homes in the neighborhood about the open house. You could post flyers and information at the community mailbox area, if there is one. Another option would be to hire some local kids to deliver door hangers in the neighborhood for your open house. You could also door knock the neighborhood to talk with the neighbors and personally invite them to your open house. The combination of a number of these strategies will ensure you the greatest level of foot traffic on open house day.

Facebook-targeted marketing

Facebook is a new powerhouse tool when it comes to open houses. Mark Zuckerberg and company have a lot of data on all of us: what we look at online, where we live, what we earn, what we buy. As a real estate agent, you can use Facebook to target eyeballs that would be likely be interested in your open house. This type of in-their-face, every-day-seen marketing can be very effective for open houses.

TIP

At a minimum, set up a sponsored post or ad on any open house that targets thousands of people living within a few miles of your open house. When they review their news feed, your open house ad comes up for a few days. Your best strategy is to run a campaign for about three days in length. You don't want a weeklong open house Facebook campaign — that's too long. Your best results will happen in a few days and start to trail off after those initial few days. The investment is small: In most markets, you will spend $15–$50 to reach a large number of geographically targeted people.

Another option is to target income level if the property requires a higher income than normal. You can appeal to higher income earners and remove some of the people who might not be able to afford the property you are holding open. Facebook has many ways to target your message. Posting to your personal and business pages can drive traffic as well. Don't forget to create a new post the day of your open house to tell your friends to come by.

REMEMBER

Don't miss the extra bonus of building your brand and image that happens with your Facebook open house campaigns. If you have a geographic area where you have strong production, increasing your investment in Facebook marketing can create the response from people. "I see your name and signs everywhere." You can create a celebrity status for yourself by doing a mega open house strategy on all your listings in your core area.

Three signs and a cloud of dust

The days when an agent put out a few signs for their open house are gone, in my view. In a mega open house strategy, you want 15, 20, or even 25 open house signs. The adage *more is better* comes to mind.

Use lots of signage

The typical agent uses a few open house signs. The open house creates an opportunity to carpet bomb an area with you and your brand. As a new agent, if you put out 20–25 open house signs, it looks like you have a much larger market share and presence than you actually do.

Your objective should be to place 20–25 signs in high-traffic locations as far out as a couple of miles away from your open house. You'll have to invest some money in signs, but it's worth getting more people and exposure to your open houses.

You may be thinking, "That's a lot of time to invest for an open house." You're right. It will take you 45 minutes to an hour on each end of your open house to put up and take down that many signs. But these signs are sales tools that will increase your business.

Choose different signs for diverse buyers

TIP

You need to announce and offer different types of opportunities for different prospects. Your signage to direct people to your open house should offer "free list of homes" or highlight if they're bank-owned or foreclosed homes. Don't just use the same generic signs in all locations. Why use signs for bank-owned and foreclosed homes as a sign strategy? Most people want a deal. They equate deals in real estate to banks owning homes. They know the bank is eager to unload the house from its portfolio, so they see the opportunity for a bargain.

According to NAR, 63 percent of buyers are interested in buying a bank-owned property. The interesting stat is that only 4 percent actually buy one. Although buyers turn out in droves to look at bank-owned homes, they rarely buy them because of factors such as the poor condition of the home, paperwork hassles, undesirable locations, and so on.

Even if you're not holding an open house of a bank repo, your sign will create interest. You may also have a sign with a free list of bank-owned homes in the area. Remember, you're trying to increase traffic and attendance at your open house. You can also combine all "offers" on a few signs as well.

More is better because it looks like you have the whole world for sale. You want to create an image of lots of listings, activity, and success. By placing open house signs, even miles away on major streets, you direct traffic in from miles away. People are mobile and out and about in their cars. If thousands of people see your signs a few miles away, a few will stop by to see the home or check it out. You only need a few from each sign to turn an ordinary open house into a mega open house.

TIP

If you get even just one person who saw each of your signs and decided to just check it out, by placing 20 signs rather than 3, that's 17 more people who come to your open house. If only 10 percent of those 17 people have an interest or are been thinking about the potential of buying or selling, that's 1.7 prospects. If you do those extra signs on 30 open houses a year, that's 510 extra open house attendees and 51 extra prospects who have an interest in buying or selling. If you only converted 20 percent of those 51 to actual sales, that's an extra 10 sales. In most markets that would be at least $50,000 in extra income — all from buying another 20 signs and putting them up and taking them down 30 times. How's that for return on investment?

Don't discount the other people who continue to see your signs out week after week but are not ready yet. They see you as successful, prosperous, and willing to work hard just by seeing more of your signs. You are building an image and brand that will get calls and inquiries "out of the blue."

Banners and flags and blowups, oh my!

Once you have a strategy to drive them to your mega open house, you need to position the exterior of the home on open house day as a party or event. For a big party, you usually have at least banners and balloons. The same should be true for an open house.

You want colored balloons with your branding colors. Invest in large feather flags and banners that can be seen down the street to announce your event. The feather flags are highly effective with neighbors because they create attention. A neighbor may have received your marketing piece or seen your Facebook ad and thought about going to the open house, but then it slipped their mind. The feather flag that says "Open House" reminds them as they drive down the street and they stop.

You're trying to catch people's attention and compel them to stop and come in the door. Focus your attention on drawing people to the open house rather than on yourself. The house at this point is the main attraction. You are using it as your storefront for the day. You want as many people as possible to cross the threshold.

Being the Host with the Most: Effectively Managing the Open House

A successful open house requires a well-chosen and presentable home, a well-organized host, and an impeccable follow-up plan so that no prospect gets lost in the post-event period. Use the following information to guide your planning.

TIP

In addition, you may want to use the worksheet featured in Figure 11-1 to be sure that you cover all the planning bases and arrive ready to open the doors to a successful event.

OPEN HOUSE PLANNING WORKSHEET		
Planning Step		Notes

ADVANCE PLANNING
Select the right property/Factors to consider
    High-demand area
    Attractiveness of home
    Curb appeal
    Proximity to major street
Set open house objectives
    Number of visitors
    Number of leads
    Number of buyer interviews
Set the open house hours
Plan neighborhood events, including:
    Sneak peak event
        Establish date/time
        Determine number of invitations
        Decide whether to mail or hand deliver
    Other neighborhood events
Plan directional sign strategy; choose sign locations
Plan advertising and write ads
Assess curb appeal; advise seller re: suggested improvements		

DAYS BEFORE THE OPEN HOUSE Place open house ads Prepare and produce flyers or home feature sheets Research up to six similar properties to share with prospects Advise seller of hour to depart prior to open house		
OPEN HOUSE DAY Prepare house by opening blinds, turning on lights, and arranging music, candles, and so on. Place guest book or sign-in sheet and pen in entry area Put out flyers or home feature sheets Put out and carry a supply of business cards		
FOLLOWING THE OPEN HOUSE Send hand-written note to each attendee Send requested or promised material to prospects Make phone calls to set appointments		

FIGURE 11-1: Use this worksheet to standardize your open house planning.

© *Real Estate Champions. Used with permission.*

Setting up for success before prospects arrive

TIP

Before you swing open the doors to open house guests, be sure that the home is clean, bright, and welcoming — and be sure that you're ready to present not only the home you're showing but also other homes that may better fit the interests of your prospects.

Presenting the home you're featuring

Arrive at the open house with fliers or feature sheets presenting the property you're showing. Bring enough copies to provide one to each visitor as a way of reminding the prospect of the home and, especially, of you. A few tips:

>> Keep the feature sheets simple.

>> Include a picture of the home and information about bedrooms, bathrooms, square footage, and amenities.

>> Include your picture and contact information.

REMEMBER

Research proves that most guests won't buy the home you're showing, but they may very well buy into the idea of working with you on their future home sale or purchase. The feature sheet provides prospects with information on how to contact you.

Discussing other available properties

Before the open house, arm yourself with information on about a half dozen other homes that are similar in price, amenities, neighborhood status, and geography to the one you're showing. Then when an open house guest indicates a lack of interest in the home you're showing, you're prepared to quickly and easily shift the discussion to another possibility. Load the listings onto your tablet so you can quickly access them to show buyer prospects. You can also prepare and preview properties in a price range just below and just above the price range of the home you're in and have that information loaded as well. Come armed with your tablet and prepared to show your market knowledge and expert command of the inventory.

TIP

The best research approach is to personally tour each home so that you fully understand and can quickly describe its attributes and how it differs from the home you're showing. At a minimum, take a few minutes to review the pictures and virtual tours of each home that is similar to your open house. Then if a prospect expresses to you that the open house home won't work because the backyard is too small, for example, you have firsthand knowledge with which to describe the large yard of another home you can recommend.

Shooing the homeowners out the door

Having the seller underfoot during an open house only causes barriers between you and the potential prospects. You must make arrangements for the seller to be away during open house hours, and here's why:

- >> Without intending to do so, the owner may convey to the prospect a strong desire to move, causing the prospect to believe that the owner is anxious to sell, which may prompt a lower initial offer.

- >> The seller may say something that raises a red flag about the condition of the property.

- >> The seller may describe his or her favorite things about the house. If these features are ones the buyer dislikes and is thinking about changing, the seller's input may simply shut down interest in the home.

REMEMBER

Most sellers want to help you sell their homes, and, the truth is, the best help they can provide is being absent during the open house.

Setting the mood with last-minute touches

Right before opening the doors to your open house, take a moment to enhance the warm, welcoming feeling attendees want to experience upon arrival.

- >> Throw open blinds to expose nice views.

- >> Turn on lights to brighten corners.

- >> Burn candles and plug in air fresheners to scent the air.

- >> Play soft music.

- >> Set out simple but tasteful refreshments to encourage attendees to linger.

- >> Place a guest book or sign-in sheet, along with a pen, in the entryway or at a point where guests gather.

- >> Keep a stack of business cards and house flyers in a visible location.

Wallflower or social butterfly: Meeting and greeting during the open house

REMEMBER

Your objective during the open house is to meet guests and sell guests on meeting with you. Your measurement for success is how many appointments you book for after-the-open-house buyer interviews, which are meetings during which you determine the prospect's motivation, timeframe, wants, and needs, and the prospect learns how you work and what services you provide.

Successful buyer interviews conclude with a prospect commitment, which takes the form of a signed *buyer-agency agreement*. This agreement is a contract to exclusively represent the buyer. At its core, the buyer-agency agreement is like a listing agreement where your compensation is guaranteed if the buyer buys. If the buyer buys any home (either an MLS listing or a FSBO), you're compensated for your time, effort, and energy. The single best way to obtain a buyer interview is to convince the prospect when you're face to face at the open house that you're the best real estate resource based on

>> Your superb knowledge of the marketplace.

>> Your high level of professional service.

>> Your ability to deliver a buyer advantage in the marketplace.

>> Your ability to facilitate the best lender arrangements and the smoothest closing transaction.

>> Your experience saving buyers money in the short run via lower sale prices or initial down payments, or in the long run via reduced payments.

>> Your commitment to delivering the quality representation that the prospect truly deserves.

REMEMBER

Most agents who host open houses are too interested in obtaining contact information so they can initiate rounds of mailings and follow-up activity. Don't let your objective get off-track. Your aim is to get an appointment (not just contact info) so that you can make a personal presentation.

The big difference between highly and marginally successful agents can be measured by the number of appointments they schedule and conduct daily, weekly, monthly, and annually. When you host an open house, keep your eye on the prize, which is the chance to sit down following the event in a quality one-to-one appointment with the most valuable asset your business can acquire: a quality prospect.

TIP

As you work to develop prospects, consider these tips:

>> **Invite attendees to sign the open house guest book or sign-in sheet.** Many guests may be reluctant, at first, to provide you with the information you want and need — which includes their names; addresses; email addresses; and work, home, and cell-phone numbers. However, the longer you visit with the guests and the more they see that you can provide them with valuable information, the more willing they are to provide the information.

>> **Present your business card to introduce yourself and create a professional impression.** Use the simple act of transferring your card to open the dialogue door with the prospect. Then, after you get a conversation going, begin getting the information that you can use as you convert the guest to a buyer or seller prospect. Use these tips:

- **Ask the prospect a timeframe question.** How long have you been looking? Have you seen anything you've liked? How soon are you hoping to be into a new home? The answers tell you not only about the prospect's timeframe but also about her motivation. If a couple says that they've been looking for six months, you know that they're not very motivated buyers or that they're slow to make a decision. Either one is not a good answer.

- **Ask the prospect a dream question.** What are you looking for in your new home over your present home? What features do you want in your new home? Describe your perfect new home for me. By getting the prospects to share what they want, you open up the dialogue. You also show that you care and are there to help them.

- **Don't be a tree.** In other words, don't be rooted in the kitchen or family room. Wander the house and stay close to the prospects without hovering around them. You have a secondary responsibility to protect the home and the property of the seller. If the open house guests are in the master bedroom and you're in the kitchen, they could be in the jewelry box and you wouldn't even know it. Make sure you're in the general area of your guests at all times. If the bedrooms are at one end, meander down the hallway and ask a question, checking on the whereabouts and interests of your guests.

- **Ask the prospect to buy.** Before open house guests leave, ask them to buy the home. If you've not yet secured their information, you have nothing to lose. If they're not interested, ask them what about the home causes them to feel it's not right for them. Doing so opens up the opportunity for sharing information on other listings.

Winning follow-up systems and strategies

TIP

Promptly after the open house, send handwritten thank-you notes to every single person who provided you with contact information. In today's world of email and computer-generated correspondence, the power of a handwritten note is multiplied many times over.

When following up, don't assume that your event was the only open house your prospect attended. I guarantee you that this isn't the case. Realize that you're in competition with other agents, and one way to prevail is to prove that you're the one most skilled at lead follow-up. After your handwritten note is received by your prospects, take the following steps:

>> **If the prospect requested additional information or you offered to provide specific information, send it promptly.** But send it separately from and following your handwritten note.

>> **On the afternoon or evening of the day your handwritten note is expected to arrive in the mail, place a phone call to the prospect.** If the open house was on a Sunday, your handwritten note should be in the mail on Monday, and you should make your phone call the next day, usually on Tuesday. The objective of the call is to book a buyer presentation appointment in your office. If the note hasn't arrived when you call, don't sweat it. Proceed with your questioning and appointment-setting focus. Your note will arrive the next day to the surprise of the prospect.

>> **Later that same week, probably on Thursday or Friday, phone again.** This time, tell the prospect that you've found a property that is similar to what he or she is looking for in a home. Explain that you want to meet to evaluate its suitability. Aim to have the meeting take place in your office. Remember, you're in competition with other agents. Whoever gets the prospect into their office first dramatically improves the odds of acquiring a commission check.

>> **Repeat the previous step weekly for a few weeks.** If you're unable to get the prospect into your office within a few weeks, the quality of the prospect is probably lower than first thought. It's probably time to cut the prospect loose and move on to more motivated buyers.

REMEMBER

When you prospect at open houses, among the leads you acquire are people who hope to move but never will. I call these *hope-to prospects* rather than *have-to prospects*, and it's your job as an agent to determine which prospects fall into which category. That way you can turn your time, attention, and talent to the needs of the more motivated prospect group.

4

Winning the Business and Getting Paid

» **Perfecting your presentation and delivery skills**

» **Overcoming objections**

» **Bringing presentations to a successful close**

Chapter **12**

Making Your Listing Presentation a Masterpiece

P rospects are potential clients who are interested in considering the service options you provide. That's the good news. The not-so-good news is that prospects seem to assume that all agents are cut from the same mold — that all agents do the same things in the same ways. This is especially true with tech-savvy consumers who are empowered by broader access to information about real estate. That access is as close as the smartphone or tablet. Young consumers are so immersed in technology that you have to drive home your value and difference to them. The technology accentuates the sameness of real estate agents. Most agents have a website and online persona that is larger than life . . . even if they sell only one home a year. With technologies like IDX systems and Zillow's Premier Agent status, agents with no listings seem like agents with lots of listings. You can hide your lack of sales skills, experience, and knowledge behind the flash of technology.

Few consumers realize that when a property comes on the market and they see it online through Zillow, Realtor.com, or Trulia, the agent (or agents) they see named next to the property had to purchase that ad position, and usually they are not the listing agent of that home. Most online buyers probably assume they are the listing agent. Consumers are truly unaware of the different skills, systems, and philosophies various agents bring to the job — and the huge difference in results they achieve.

Too many consumers view agents with a commodity mind-set. A commodity is an interchangeable, difficult-to-differentiate offering selected primarily based on price. Want an example? I was pushing a grocery cart through the produce section of the grocery store a few days ago. I had my son, Wesley, with me. He loves bananas, so we put some in the cart. They were $0.79 a pound. In the next aisle I saw a different brand of bananas for $0.39 a pound. Guess what happened? I took the original bananas out of my cart and put the cheaper bananas in. Wesley isn't brand sensitive when it comes to $0.40 a pound. That is a commodity mind-set!

Too often, real estate agents are viewed as a bunch of bananas. Most listing presentations sound about the same, so it's no big surprise that prospects frequently make their selection based on highest listing price and lowest commission rate. This chapter helps you set yourself apart. It provides the steps to follow as you convey your differences, distinctions, and competitive advantages in presentations that are planned, practiced, rehearsed, and perfected. No more winging it! You're about to move into the league of the best, most preferred real estate agents.

Qualifying Your Listing Prospects

The success of a listing presentation is determined by what you do before you even walk through the door. Most agents enter the meeting flying blind, ill prepared and oblivious to the needs, wants, desires, and expectations of the prospect.

REMEMBER

Make this pledge to yourself right now: Before you enter another listing presentation, ask your prospects quality questions in advance.

Using questions effectively before your listing presentation

Ask questions that enable you to obtain important information about the customer's desires, timeframe, motivation level, experience, and expectations of outcome and service. Without this information, you can't possibly serve the client well. You won't be able to sell your value as well either.

Many salespeople, especially in real estate sales, think they'll offend the customer if they ask questions. Here's an analogy that should put your mind at ease. Imagine you're sick and schedule a doctor's appointment. You arrive, the doctor enters the exam room, and you look up and say, "Guess what sickness I have today?" From across the room, the doctor is supposed to assess your symptoms, diagnose your ailment, and prescribe a cure without checking your ears or throat, listening to your lungs and heart, or, most importantly, asking you questions about what's wrong and how you feel. It sounds ridiculous, yet it's what real estate agents do when they try to serve clients without first asking questions to determine their wants, needs, and expectations.

Without good client information, a listing presentation becomes an explanation of your services and service delivery system. But what if the prospect sitting in front of you wants to be served differently? Then what?

The customer ultimately determines whether your service is outstanding, fair, or poor. Because the customer judges the quality of service received, the only way to start the service process is to learn what customers want, rather than trying to guess their desires and expectations. Additionally, your level of service satisfaction determines the level of referral volume you receive from that client in the future.

Knowing why and how to question listing prospects

Question prospects for two main reasons:

>> **Question listing prospects to safeguard your time.** By questioning prospects before you meet with them, you assess their motivation, desire, need to take action, ability to act, and authority to make selling decisions. You also assess the odds that the prospect will result in income-producing activity. The questioning process increases your probability of sales success by determining which prospects are likely to result in commission revenue and which are likely to consume hours without results.

>> **Question listing prospects to determine their service expectations.** What kind of service do they expect? What selling approach do they follow? Is there a match between your philosophy and theirs? If not, can you convince them that your approach is better than their preconceived notion of what and how you should represent their interests? If not, are you willing to turn down the business? The only way to address these issues is to learn what your prospects are thinking before you make your presentation.

Before you enter a listing presentation, diagnose the situation you're entering and the opportunity it presents by learning the prospect's answers to key questions. I recommend that you acquire this base of knowledge over the phone when you're scheduling the presentation appointment. If you wait until you're face to face with the prospect, it may be too late. By then you want to be offering a tailored presentation, not acquiring baseline information.

Focus your pre-appointment questions around the following four topics:

1. **Motivation and timeframe:** Ask questions that reveal how badly the prospect wants to buy or sell, and in what timeframe. Sample questions include:

- Where are you hoping to move?

- How soon do you need to be there?

- Tell me about your perfect timeframe. When do you want this move to happen?

- Is there anything that would cause you not to make this move?

2. **Experience:** A prospect's view of the real estate profession is filtered through personal experience and experiences related by friends and family members. The following questions help you gauge your prospect's real estate background and preconceptions:

- How many properties have you sold in the past?

- When was your last sales experience?

- What was your experience with that sale?

- How did you select the agent you worked with?

- What did you like best and least about what that agent did?

3. **Pricing:** The following questions help you gauge the prospect's motivation or desire to sell. They'll also help you determine whether the prospect is realistic about current real estate values.

REMEMBER

Let me share an old real estate sales truth: The higher the list price, the lower the motivation; the lower the list price, the higher the motivation.

Listen carefully to the answers to the following three questions. They'll reveal whether your prospect is ready to sell or just fishing for a price:

- How much do you want to list your home for tonight?

- How did you arrive at that value for your home?

- If a buyer came in today, what would you consider to be an acceptable offer for your home?

If you want to approach the seller with a softer series of questions in the pricing area, you might try these:

- Most people do a little investigation on real estate values before they sell their home. What have you found?

- Most people have a general idea of what they want for their home. What's yours?

4. **Service expectation:** Learning your prospect's service expectation is absolutely essential to a good working relationship, but I caution you that when you begin to ask the service-related questions, you'll likely hear silence on the phone. Likely your prospect has never met a service provider concerned enough to ask what he wants, values, and expects. As a result, you may have to probe and ask follow-up questions to help the prospect open up and enter a dialogue.

- What do you expect from the real estate agent you choose to work with?

- What are the top three things you're looking for from an agent?

- What will it take for you to be confident that my service will meet your requirements?

Following your phone interview, use the answers to questions in each of the four categories as you compile a qualifying questionnaire on the prospect. Figure 12-1 provides a good format to follow.

Deciding on a one-step or two-step listing presentation

When I say one-step or two-step, I'm not talking about dancing, although many agents feel that is what they're doing with some sellers. My goal has always been to help agents fill their dance cards. The real problems arise when you're doing the cha-cha and the seller wants to waltz.

What I'm referring to is whether you meet once or twice with a seller before you secure agreement or commitment. This decision of whether to pursue a one-step or two-step presentation is important.

LISTING PROSPECT PRE-LISTING QUESTIONNAIRE

1. How is the prospect going to make the decision?

_____

2. When is the prospect going to make the decision?

_____

3. Does the prospect have the financial capacity to move forward?

_____

4. What, specifically, does the prospect want to achieve?

_____

5. What, specifically, does the prospect need from you?

_____

6. How do you assess the prospect's ability to move forward with a decision?

_____

7. Does the prospect have enough motivation or desire to complete a sale or purchase?

_____

8. How will the prospect judge your performance?

_____

9. Who else is the prospect considering?

_____

10. Who else will influence the prospect's decision?

_____

FIGURE 12-1: Complete a qualifying questionnaire as you prepare for each listing presentation.

© *John Wiley & Sons, Inc.*

One-step presentations

A one-step presentation requires you to ask questions in advance of meeting with the seller. You can do that when you set the appointment or about 24 hours in advance when confirming your appointment. The one-step means you need to craft a solid competitive market analysis, or CMA, without seeing the home in advance. This can be done if your market knowledge is up to date and properties in the seller's area are homogeneous. If the seller owns a home in a production or high-volume builder neighborhood with a small selection of floor plans, it's much easier to value homes because of the uniformity of size and amenities.

Two-step presentations

If you feel you must see the home before you can complete your CMA accurately and express the value of the home confidently, you'll need to do a two-step process. In the two-step, you conduct two appointments:

>> **The first appointment:** You ask the pre-listing questions at the first appointment with the seller; it's more of a meet-and-greet type of appointment. You don't share what you know about the value of the home, what you'll do to sell it, how successful you've been, or why the prospect should do business with you. The purpose of the first appointment is to see the home layout, the condition of the home, the amenities of the property, and the feel of the neighborhood and to build a connection with the seller and ask your pre-listing questions.

>> **The second appointment:** This appointment doesn't need to take place at the seller's home. In fact, I advise that you work to secure the second appointment at your office. Key reasons to consider this strategy include:

- **You have greater control at your office.** Distractions are minimized, and it's a professional environment. Prospects come more ready to do business. It's normal to meet professionals like doctors, attorneys, and accountants at their offices — and you want the prospect to see you as a professional.

- **Your time investment is reduced.** Rather than driving to and from the prospect's home, you can save that 30 minutes or hour and invest it to secure more leads or business.

- **Prospects can experience your business.** It's helpful for prospects to see the physical space where you work, the high-traffic location of your office, and the comfortable and professional feel of the office. Prospects can also see and experience the tools, technology, and systems you use to expose their home, connect leads to buyers, and provide great customer service.

  If you have a team of real estate professionals, prospects can meet the members of the team, which increases the personal connection between prospective sellers and the people who will be serving them.

The biggest mistake agents make in two-step listing presentations is what I call the one-and-a-half-step presentation. This happens when, either because your presentation structure isn't set or the seller leads you, you start to give information about what you'll do or the value of the prospect's home in step one of the two-step.

The second step of the two-step presentation should really be about explaining why the prospect should hire you, determining the value of the home, and securing agreement to proceed. If any of these topics slip into step one, you've done a one-and-a-half-step presentation. The problem is that this approach can diminish the most important presentation, which is the second one. It throws off the key points, trial closes, and flow of your step-two presentation. It also gives sellers the impression that they've already gotten all the information they need . . . giving them an excuse to cancel the second presentation before you give it.

Checking your prospect's "DNA"

Based on your qualifying efforts, determine the likelihood that your prospect will convert into a good client for your business by conducting a DNA analysis. This involves measuring the prospect's level of desire, need to take action, and ability and authority to make a purchase or selling decision.

D for Desire

Desire or motivation is the strongest indicator of a successful business outcome. A prospect's burning desire can overcome all other deficiencies, including a lack of financial capacity. If they want something badly enough, most sellers will make the adjustments they need to create the sale.

The summer before my junior year in college, I painted houses to earn money for my tuition, books, and room and board. When I started work on the last house of the summer, I learned that the owner was selling a 1976 BMW 2002. I wanted that car, even though buying it would take all my summer earnings and college savings. My parents tried to counsel me away from this foolish idea. My ability to buy was limited because of money, but my desire was greater than my lack of ability. I ended up borrowing the money for the car and still covering my college costs. This creative ingenuity didn't please my parents at all. Looking back, it wasn't one of the smarter decisions I've made in the past 35 years. But it did teach me a lesson about the power of desire or motivation to compensate for other shortcomings.

WARNING

One word of caution: Desire isn't the same as interest. Anyone can have interest. Interest doesn't reflect intent, and it doesn't indicate a high probability of action. If a prospect says "I have an interest in selling," probe deeper to see whether the prospect has real desire to sell, or just interest.

I've found that many "interested" shoppers are looking for something that doesn't exist. Truly, I've heard interested prospects say, basically, "If you can get me $50,000 above market value for my house and find one I can buy at $75,000 below market value, I'll list my home with you."

Get real! The truth is, if I find a property for $75,000 below market value, I won't sell it to him; I'll buy it myself, and so should you!

N for Need

A need is a specific and identifiable problem that your service can help a prospect overcome.

Many prospect needs stem from lifestyle changes that prompt environment changes. A family expecting another child needs a larger home. Empty nesters tired of yard work and home upkeep want to move to a maintenance-free condo. A divorce requires one household to become two households, forcing a home sale and several purchases in the aftermath. The need to buy or sell based on environmental changes such as these prompts the majority of real estate transactions each year.

One of the reasons I worked expired listings was that the owners' level of need was so apparent. After sitting with an unsold home for months or longer, the sellers' need to find an agent who could solve the problem was pretty clear. My job was merely to convince them that by working with me their problem would be solved — that I would deliver a different and more-positive outcome.

A for Ability and Authority

Clients need both ability and authority to conduct a real estate transaction.

Ability relates to the financial capacity of your prospects. Do they have the financial wherewithal to sell their current home and buy the one of their dreams? Do they have enough equity in their current home? If not, can they borrow a larger sum to buy the one they want, or do they have access to additional funds to achieve their goal?

If they're in financial distress and have no equity to sell, are they willing to do a short sale? Are they willing to take the hit to their credit to get out from under the home with negative equity? Further, you need to evaluate whether the bank is likely to accept a short sale from this seller. Is the seller really a hardship seller, or is he just doing a strategic type of short sale?

Authority means the prospect has the power to make the decision — to say yes or no to the deal. Find out: Are you working with the ultimate decision-maker or decision-makers, or is someone else also involved? Will the prospects decide autonomously, or will they seek the guidance or advice of others as they make their decision?

WARNING

Agents make a huge mistake when they make listing presentations without both spouses or significant others in attendance. Whether both names are on the title matters little. In our family, we own properties that show only my wife's name on the title, and others that show only mine. This is purely an estate-planning move on our part. If we decide to sell, I guarantee that our input will be equal in decisions about pricing and who should represent our interest in the sale.

Presenting to Qualified Prospects

A quality listing presentation involves considerable advance planning, careful research and analysis, and highly developed presentation and sales skills. These enable you to derive maximum impact from the minimal time you have to present yourself and your recommendations, close the deal, and obtain signatures on a listing agreement.

Your advance planning takes two forms: First you need to ask pre-listing questions of your prospects, determining not only their desires and expectations but also their ability to make the buying or selling decision and complete the transaction. The previous portion of this chapter provides prospect-qualifying advice. The other essential ingredient in a listing presentation is a competitive market analysis, or CMA.

The following section guides you as you prepare a presentation that displays the full complement of your sales skills and abilities and helps you win your prospects' confidence and secure their listing.

Knowing the purpose of your presentation

REMEMBER

Be crystal clear on this point: The objective of a listing presentation is to secure a signed listing agreement before the meeting ends. If you've decided the two-step is the right approach, then in that second step you're securing the signature before you part company. You're not paving the way for a "be-back" listing, where you plan to return at a later date to handle paperwork and secure final prospect approval. Your purpose is to make your case, close the deal, and get ink on the paper right then and there while you're face to face with your prospects. If you don't, the odds of securing the listing start to swing away from you.

WARNING

If you let even a few days or a week slip by, your prospects will have a hard time separating your presentation from the presentations of other agents they meet in the meantime. And the moment they lose sight of your distinguishing attributes, they'll revert to a commodity mind-set, focusing on price and selecting an agent based on who offered the lowest commission or highest list price.

I've personally made more than a thousand listing presentations, and I've coached and listened to the presentations of hundreds of other agents. I'm totally convinced that a quality listing presentation can and must result in a signed contract at the presentation.

These are two reasons you need to get the listing agreement signed during the presentation:

1. The moment you leave the appointment, anything can happen. A buyer can appear out of nowhere, knocking on your prospects' door with a direct offer. An agent who interviewed your prospects a few days ago may be desperate enough to call with an offer to cut her fee by another percent. At Rotary, church, or a chamber of commerce meeting, your prospects may meet another agent. Or they may begin to confuse you for a different agent whose presentation they didn't like at all. The list goes on and on. The only thing you know for sure is that when you don't get the signed listing agreement at the appointment, you leave it up for grabs.

2. You need to feel the win. The win in the listing game is when the contract is signed. Don't underestimate the power of that personal victory. Selling involves the risk of rejection. If it didn't, it would be called order taking, and you wouldn't be paid so well because it would be so easy. A listing presentation gives you the chance to go for the win, perfect your close, and attain the victory. Give yourself the satisfaction and adrenaline rush of walking out of the home with a signed contract. Your drive home will be the shortest ever known. If you don't get the contract signed, however, it will be the longest few minutes you've ever known.

I have an incredible coaching client named Rita Tsoukaris who sells homes on Long Island. She's a listing machine in her market area. She takes more than 125 listings a year. Yet a while back when we tracked the number of contracts she was getting signed on the night of the appointment, we found that her close rate was less than 40 percent.

This finding got her focused on the uncompensated time she was spending on second meetings with listing prospects. It also made her think about how many listings were lost following the first meeting. A month later, her closing figures had changed dramatically. With a new resolve to get the contract closed on the night of the appointment, she skyrocketed her closing rate to more than 70 percent.

Delivering a compelling presentation

A quality presentation follows these four steps: You begin by building trust, move into a demonstration of the benefits and advantages that you bring to the prospects, present your pricing recommendation and rationale, and move to close the deal by presenting a listing agreement and getting the prospects to sign on the proverbial dotted line.

The appointment itself takes under an hour. The preparation involves a good deal more. The upcoming sections guide you through the preparations that go into each segment of the presentation.

Getting off to a good start

Paving the way for a good listing presentation involves only three steps, but you can't afford to skip a single one:

REMEMBER

1. **The first step, which is more like an overarching rule, is to be sure all decision-makers are present.** If one can't attend because an emergency arises, reschedule for another time. If a decision-maker is absent, you'll have to rely on the other party to relay your presentation, complete with paraphrasing, misinterpretations, abbreviated points, and omissions. Not a good option for you.

2. **Based on your pre-appointment interview, enter the meeting with a presentation that incorporates your prospects' needs, desires, and expectations.** The next section in this chapter guides you through the steps to follow.

3. **Open the presentation by building trust with your prospects.** Forget about finding common ground or seeking to establish rapport by talking about your common interest in fishing, hunting, water-skiing, or horses. Prospects see right through this disingenuous effort to establish a pseudo-friendship. They're looking for business associates. Get to the point.

   To build trust, summarize what the prospects have told you about their values, their goals for this move, the motivations behind the move, and what they hope to accomplish. Refer to your pre-listing questions and confirm the answers they shared with you. Confirm that you got their input right and communicate that what is important to them is also important to you.

This introductory and trust-building segment should take 10 to 15 minutes, max, at the beginning of your presentation.

The success or failure of your presentation can usually be traced back to this initial segment. If prospects don't feel that you understand and relate to their needs, wants, and desires, they'll tune you out after just the first few minutes, long before you get to the part where you tell them how great you and your company are and how you can get their home sold.

Setting yourself apart from the real estate agent pack

In this part of the presentation, you demonstrate the benefits and advantages prospects can count on when they're with you.

Most agents make a big mistake by either omitting this segment or using it to present features of their business rather than benefits derived by clients. There's a big difference between the two. An example of a feature is air conditioning in a home, or anti-lock brakes on a car. The benefits of air conditioning include comfort, coolness, and ease of sleep at night. The benefits of anti-lock brakes are safety, protection, and faster stopping.

SELLING BENEFITS, NOT FEATURES

The vast majority of salespeople, and especially real estate agents, sell features. Look at image ads for agents or listen to listing presentations, and all you'll see and hear are features:

>> I sold 150 homes last year.

>> I've been in the business for 20 years.

>> I work for the #1 company in the marketplace.

>> I'm a member of the million-dollar club.

>> I put my clients first.

>> I'm honest and have integrity.

>> Blah, blah, blah!

In these feature-dump presentations, prospects don't hear anything about what's in it for them — what advantages they reap as a result of the agent's attributes. As a result, they tune out a good deal of the presentation, and the rest sounds just like what they hear from other agents. No wonder clients tend to make decisions based on list price and commission.

TIP

If you want prospects to listen and care, don't talk about *you*; talk about what you offer to *them*. Turn every feature of your business into a benefit for the customer. For example, "I sold 150 homes last year" might become "I sold 150 homes last year, and what really matters to you is that nearly 80 percent were on the market for far fewer days than the regional average." See the difference?

PROVING YOUR COMPETITIVE EDGE

TIP

Compare your performance against regional averages to prove your competitive position. By citing industry averages, you clearly position yourself. You also give yourself the opportunity to demonstrate your superb market knowledge, which indirectly builds your reputation and directly benefits your clients. As you prepare to present your distinct edge, ask yourself:

>> What makes you different?

>> Why should someone hire you?

>> What are your strengths?

>> How do your distinct attributes result in unique client benefits?

Also take time to assess weaknesses in your service and ways to compensate for your shortcomings. For instance, if your stats are weak, present the benefits your client derives from your company's strong performance record. Or, if your time in the real estate field is short, present how experience gained in your pre-real estate career benefits your clients. For an idea of how it works, look at these sample scripts:

> *"One of your needs as a seller is an agent who understands how to create a successful transaction and satisfied client. Although I don't have ten years of experience in the real estate business, I'm not new to our mutual goal — your satisfaction. One of the reasons I chose to work with XYZ real estate company is its long and widely recognized success helping families like yours to achieve their goals and dreams. Our firm has led the region in successful transactions for XX years, and we bring that capability to your transaction."*

> *"One of your needs as a seller is an agent who understands how to create a successful transaction and satisfied client. Although I don't have ten years of experience in the real estate business, I'm very accomplished at achieving our mutual goal — your satisfaction. In my previous career, I served more than XX clients with a customer satisfaction rating of well over XX percent."*

USING THE POWER OF YOUR STRONGEST STATISTICS

To set myself apart, during every presentation I pulled out the power of my Big 3 — three key statistics that demonstrated my and my company's success in the marketplace. Here's the approach I use:

>> **Start by acknowledging what the prospect already knows: that agents all provide a similar service.** I'd say, "Every agent will put your home into the MLS." (In today's environment I might say, "All agents advertise your home on their own and their company websites.") Then I'd add, "If those tactics were all it took to achieve success, then every agent would sell hundreds of homes and more than 98 percent of listings would turn into closed deals, rather than the board average of 68 percent." With this introduction, I admitted that agents all do basically the same thing, yet they achieve vastly different results.

>> **Then set yourself apart.** I'd say something like, "Do you want to hear what really creates the difference for my sellers compared to clients of other agents? It's the power of the Big 3: sales skills, conversion ability, and conversion of leads to clients." Because my performance in those three areas was significantly better than the board's average, I knew I was creating a sustainable competitive advantage.

>> **Share a success story that shows the benefits your Big 3 advantages deliver.** In my case, I'd share that the average agent converts fewer than 2 percent of leads into clients. I'd then present the volume of leads my business and company generated and the corresponding conversion rates we achieved. *But,* I never quit at that point, as all it did was present a feature of our service. I had to show the prospects how this feature benefitted them.

>> **Show how your success story translates to client benefits.** I'd show prospects how more leads resulted in greater exposure for each client's home. I'd explain that because my team and I converted leads at 16 percent as opposed to the 2 percent average, my clients had a higher probability of selling their home. I proved the point by showing that I sold 150 homes a year and the average agent sold 4, largely because the average agent develops far fewer clients to work with. Although the average agent sells 9 percent of her own listings, we sold more than 32 percent of our own listings. That one number validated that what we do works better than what other agents do.

All of this resulted in a higher probability of sale, higher sale prices, and less hassle for the sellers working with me.

To underscore the point, I'd present this logic:

- Increased clients = Increased showings

- Increased showings = Increased competition for the sellers' home

- Increased competition = Higher probability of sale, higher sale price, or both

As a newer agent, you may not be able to show your own strong numbers, but you can present your company's Big 3 instead. For instance, you can focus on the fact that your company sells more units than its competitors do, that your company has more agents to help create more exposure, and that your company has high market share, which leads to increased buyer leads. Then present this logic:

- Increased exposure for your client = Increased number and quality of leads

- Increased number and quality of leads = Increased showings

- Increased showings = Higher probability of sale, higher sale price, or both

Listing presentations have become the dumping ground for technology in the past ten years. The typical agent goes on about his website; how many places it appears; how many sites it's linked to; his web traffic; his web hits; his number of unique visitors; and how the website integrates with Realtor.com, Trulia, or Zillow.

These are merely features of the service you and your company provide. The question is still: What's the benefit to the client? Because of the broader range of technology systems and solutions used in the real estate industry today as compared to even just five years ago, it's harder to stand out from other agents. To be successful, you must show the benefits you offer.

Gaining confirmation

After you've conveyed your benefits to the sellers, pause to confirm that they understand and agree with the points you've made. Do this through a *confirmation close* or *trial close*, using the following scripts as a guide:

> *"Do you see how our company delivers the benefit of greater exposure and higher probability of sale for our clients? Is that what you want?"*

> *"Do you see why we have such a large market share, and does it make sense how our market dominance benefits you? Do you want that type of edge in the marketplace?"*

> *"Do you see the advantages our sellers have in today's market because of the increased exposure we provide through our technology platform?"*

Presenting prices

The moment you receive confirmation that the prospect understands the unique benefits you deliver, move into the value segment of your presentation, during which you share your findings regarding the value of the prospect's property.

This portion of the presentation should take only about 20 percent of the meeting time. You make your clear recommendation; present the strong, concise rationale behind it; and seek the prospect's agreement. Keep it short by following this advice:

TIP

>> Don't use too many comps! Keep it simple while you tell the truth about the value of the home.

I'm a firm advocate for telling the prospects a single price or a very small range of difference. If you're a little unsure, give a range but keep it a very tight range, not a $50,000 variance.

>> After presenting your recommendation of value, ask the prospects if they understand why their home is worth the amount you've recommended. Asking this question is the surest way to learn whether your prospects agree with your number.

An alternate tack is to prepare a full net proceeds sheet, which shows the list price minus all closing costs. Walk them through each cost of closing based on the price you suggest. Then, when you get to the bottom line — the estimate of how many dollars will go into their pockets — ask, "Is this enough to get you where you want to go?"

>> Proceed to the close based on the answer you receive. Sometimes prospects agree with your recommendation, sometimes they don't, and sometimes they want to negotiate the number.

If they agree, the gate is open for you to go for the close and get their signatures on the listing agreement.

If they say no or want to negotiate, you have to find out how far apart you are. Ask them what they'll do if they can't get the extra money they're hoping for. Why do they feel your number falls short? Is their price goal based on the down payment requirement on the next home they're buying, or on their desire to obtain an 80 percent loan-to-value mortgage to avoid mortgage insurance? You can only work on solutions if you know your prospects' frame of reference, their financial objectives, and the reasons behind their pricing needs.

WARNING

>> If you don't gain agreement on value, you have an appointment challenge you need to overcome. Your job is to come to a meeting of the minds. There's no point in going further until you can arrive at agreement on the value.

There is a difference between value and price. What you are doing is determining the value of the home based on today's market conditions. That's why you don't go into the discussion of price until you agree on value.

You want to separate those two areas: value and price. If I am going to talk about the price, we might start at pricing strategies, until we have agreement on value. They might say to you, "Well, I want to start at a higher price." You can say to them, "We can discuss that option in a few minutes. Right now, we have to be clear on what the marketplace is saying to you on the value of your home."

Going for the close

As soon as you have agreement on value, go for the close and get a signed contract.

You may be thinking, "When do I tell them about the marketing plan?" You weave that into the discussion of why they should hire you. Most agents spend too long going over the marketing of the home. The days of "I do this and this and this" are long over. You can integrate your marketing info and connect prospects to the related benefits, but just doing 15 minutes on your marketing plan is ineffective.

The listing presentation is about the results you achieve. If your key statistics and the distinguishing benefits of doing business with you aren't strong enough, no marketing plan will fill the gap.

Prove that you and your company are the best. Convince the sellers of their home's value. Know their expectations of service and results and guarantee that you'll meet and exceed them. Then close the contract.

REMEMBER

Closing is the natural ending to a great presentation.

Making your presentation useful, interesting, and engaging

Most agent presentations put sellers to sleep, mainly because most presentations lack interest, usefulness, and structure.

The presentation advice in the preceding section provides all you need to know to overcome the structure and usefulness issues. To increase the interest quotient, follow this advice:

>> **Use presentation technology.** Put your presentation on a slide deck. That means PowerPoint, Keynote, or something else that has a visual component. You need to engage the seller in a selling experience that's not exclusively dependent on your words. The slides should be graphically appealing and contain more than just words. You need images, too. For example, if you're using testimonials from former clients, use an image of them in their new

home. Or better yet, take a video of them expressing how well you performed and play it during your presentation. The former clients will connect with your prospect. The seller will think, "Hey, we're just like them." The testimonial video will sell you better than you can sell yourself.

>> **Share market knowledge.** Become a student of the local marketplace and share meaningful statistics. Also track trends in the national marketplace, both to enlighten your prospects and distinguish yourself as a well-read, well-connected, and well-informed agent.

>> **Ask questions.** Listen in on typical listing presentations, and you'll hear the agent talking 80 percent of the time, with the prospect hardly getting a word in edgewise. I guarantee you that the seller finds that monologue uninteresting.

>> **Watch the clock.** Don't let your presentation run too long, and don't save the information the seller most wants to receive until the very end. If you put your price recommendation at the very end of a 90-minute presentation during which you did 80 percent of the talking, you can pretty well predict that your seller will be tuned out.

What the prospect has to say is more important than what you have to say. Great salespeople do less than 25 percent of the talking. You already know all that you need to know about what you're thinking. You need to learn what your prospects think, know, and desire so you can match your service to their wants and needs.

Keeping your presentation focused and targeted

Let's get to the point: A 90-minute presentation is neither short nor sweet. What in the world an agent finds to talk about for 90 minutes I have no idea. But I do know that sellers don't want to sit through a 90-minute appointment, and they most certainly don't want to listen to an agent for that long.

Within the first few minutes of the appointment, inform your sellers that your listing presentation will take no more than 45 minutes. Based on my own experience, I can tell you that more than half of the sellers will thank you when you tell them that your presentation will be brief. Many times, I've had clients thank me again when I was walking out the door with the signed contract, sharing their appreciation that I wasn't there all night!

A good, brief presentation results from a proper structure, a clear presentation plan, and a knowledge of what to say and how to convey it.

Many agents translate the terms *structure* and *plan* to mean "canned presentation." They say, "I don't want to sound mechanical and scripted." People sound mechanical and scripted for lack of practice, not because they have a pattern or process to follow. In fact, most companies require professional service providers to follow plans. For example, when I board a plane later this week, you can bet that I want the pilot to follow a "canned" preflight checklist, landing checklist, flight plan, and so on. I want the attorney who defends me to have well-constructed or planned legal briefs, questions, and arguments.

I'm not working to "can" anyone, but planning your presentation is essential. You need to have a framework that you're comfortable with, that allows you to deliver key facts, findings, and segments, using key phrases and dialogues, every time you present. I'd rather an agent err on the side of "canned" than just "wing it."

TIP

The previous section provides the structure to follow as you prepare a great presentation. Additionally, follow this advice:

>> **Know your prospects.** If you aren't completely clear on your prospects' interests and needs, flip back to the first pages of this chapter. One of the reasons I constructed the opening section on qualifying prospects so meticulously is that acquiring prospect knowledge is truly the key to a good presentation. You absolutely have to secure the right information before going into the appointment.

>> **Set a goal to keep your presentation to 45 minutes or less.** Look at every piece of sales material you present. Does it demonstrate clear benefits to the seller? Does it need to be used? Does the seller understand it? Does it create differentiation between you and other agents? As the saying goes, "When in doubt, leave it out."

>> **Be sure that your PowerPoint or Keynote slides convey a clear and powerful message.** An abundance of slides can eat up your presentation time and your chance to dialogue with the sellers. Typically, each slide in your presentation represents two to four minutes of presentation time by the time you advance it, talk about it, emphasize key points, and ask for questions to confirm your prospect's understanding. Do the math: 30 slides eat up at least an hour, putting you well over your time limit before you even get to the contract.

>> **Create some sizzle.** Your presentation needs to be exciting, interesting, and different. You also want to get them involved in the presentation. One way to do that is using a text-back feature like Dotsignal (www.dotsignal.com). Using a text-back feature can show that you are cutting edge in the technology area. According to the National Association of Realtors (NAR), 38 percent of buyers who see a home they like online get in their car and drive by it. You want to capture those drive-by buyers. This is where text-back comes into play.

By having a text-back sign rider on your real estate signs, you can provide access for consumers to text the number on the sign to receive more detailed information on the home, more pictures, floor plans, and virtual tours. The options of what you can offer are countless, and it's all delivered in a moment to their cell phone via text. What you receive is their cell number to call or text them to follow up.

You should have a demonstration account that you can use at a listing presentation. In the presentation, you have the seller use their phone to text to a number with a code. Instantly they get an example home with pictures sent to their smartphone. Then your cell phone will ding to announce that you just created a hot lead. This system creates a powerful example of how you can create more leads and respond to them faster than other agents in the marketplace.

The four components of a great presentation

WARNING

One study after another has shown that your body language and tonality account for more than 90 percent of your presentation's effectiveness. What you actually say accounts for less than 10 percent of the delivery. If you're scrambling to find the right words, as most salespeople are, you're spending your energy in inverse proportion to what impacts your effectiveness.

The solution is to plan what you're going to say beforehand, so that during the presentation you can focus on language, tonality, and the following four steps to a great delivery.

Conviction

Webster defines conviction as a fixed or firm belief. I'd add that there is nothing more compelling than conviction.

Your belief that you can get the job done draws clients to you. Your belief in the value of their home or how their home should be sold earns their trust. Your firm belief about where the marketplace is headed, backed by statistics that prove your point, sells you and your recommendations.

TIP

Before you go face to face with sellers, determine three things that you're going to express with absolute conviction. If your sellers share your views (you'll know based on your pre-listing questions), that's a bonus. If their views are opposite yours, be doubly persuasive and resolute in order to win them over to your point of view. Then, confirm that their view has in fact shifted. It's easy to forget this important step.

Enthusiasm

Enthusiasm sells in spades. People want to work with those who are enthusiastic about their home and the market. If the market is tough, you have to be frank and honest; you can't just hide market realities. But you can still be enthusiastic and show that you're excited about the opportunity to "beat the odds" of the marketplace.

Your listing presentation is more interesting if you're enthusiastic about your career, your business, the home, and the sellers. As the old sales adage says, "Enthusiasm is to selling as yeast is to bread. It makes the dough rise!"

Confidence

I believe that early in my sales career, confidence was my secret edge. Even when I was new to the game, I was confident that I was the best agent for the seller — the result of a deeply grooved expectation of victory that came from athletics.

Where have you experienced victories? Tap into those experiences as you pump up your confidence in preparation for prospect presentations.

If you lack confidence, determine what you need to do to increase your belief in yourself and your ability to achieve success. What activities may help increase your confidence? What skills do you need to master to dramatically affect your confidence? What one thing, if you do it with excellence, will change your self-confidence?

Webster defines confidence as "a belief in one's powers or abilities." The great motivator Napoleon Hill says, "What the mind can conceive and believe, it can achieve." I saw evidence of this truth a few years ago while working with a great agent in North Carolina. She didn't have confidence in herself, nor did she think she was a great agent. Even when she closed 100 units a year, she was still self-sabotaging her success.

I asked her to write out her standard of a great agent. She did so with great and specific clarity. Six months later she had met the standard but was still in self-sabotage mode. Fortunately, I'd saved her written document and could re-present it to her as proof of her success. She has never looked back.

ASSERTIVENESS

Agents don't want to come off as pushy or aggressive in their sales approach, and by mistake they shy away from assertiveness as well.

My definition of a great salesperson is "a person who convinces someone to do something that is beneficial to them or convinces them to do it faster."

Going for the close or asking for the order isn't pushy. It's assertive. As a real estate agent, your job is to persuade prospects that you have the best service, the best value, and the highest probability of success. You must convince them to sign up for the benefits you provide, now!

One of the easiest ways to exert your assertiveness is to tell the prospect it's coming. Early in the presentation, explain, "At the end of my presentation tonight, provided we're all in agreement, we'll finalize the paperwork so I can begin to work for you right away." This bit of foreshadowing may prove useful should you encounter resistance at the time of the close, at which time you can use one of these scripts:

> *"This should be no surprise. I told you I would ask for your business. You want me to follow through on what I commit to you, don't you?"*
>
> *"I'm proving to you right now that I follow through, right?"*
>
> *"Listen, Mr. and Mrs. Seller, homes are sold, not bought. Conversion of leads is so low because many agents lack assertiveness with the buyer. So my question is, do you want an agent who you know for sure will ask every buyer to buy, or do you want an agent you just hope will do that? Which gives you more comfort?"*

Being assertive in selling is a good thing.

Staying in control

Agents lose control of the listing presentation when they allow the sellers' agenda to take over the discussion. I've listened to agents who've lost control to the seller in the first five minutes. The problem for most agents is that if they lose control, they don't have the skill to wrestle it back.

The sellers' agenda is simple. They want to know what their home is worth. They want to know what you do to sell it and what you charge for your service. And for sure they want to know what they'll put in their pockets when the deal is done. If the sellers cause you to orient your presentation to the order of their interests, you won't walk out with the listing.

If you talk about the listing price of the home and your fee structure before you've built trust, credibility, and value for your service, you'll lose every time. Don't ever follow the seller's agenda!

Setting the agenda early on

The most powerful technique is to have an actual order or agenda you follow. I further suggest that you create it following the presentation guidelines earlier in this chapter. Then type it out to hand to the seller, saying:

> *"Mr. and Mrs. Seller, I've found this presentation order to be most effective for my clients like you. It allows me to present to you the important facts, marketplace strategies, and benefits you receive as my clients. In addition, we'll have plenty of time to answer all your questions so you're completely comfortable with your decision. Would it be all right with you if we follow this agenda for our meeting?"*

You can put your agenda on one of the first slides in your slide deck. I suggest also having it printed on high-quality paper. This enables you to hand it to the sellers, as well. It gives them something tactile to hold. When you ask them to approve it . . . it's in their hands.

The agenda also tells them clearly:

1. You are organized and professional.
2. You have thought this through.
3. You aren't making it up as you go.
4. You have a plan.

Keeping on track

When the seller brings up a point that may cause you to abandon your presentation plan, pick up the agenda sheet and ask:

> *"Would it be all right to discuss that when we get to this point in the presentation?"*

Your agenda may look like this:

i. Review agenda for the meeting.
ii. Do visual inspection of the property.
iii. Discuss clients' goals, needs, and expectations of me.
iv. Discuss my professional credentials.
v. Determine the value of your home.
vi. Select the initial list price.
vii. Complete the paperwork so I can begin serving you.

REMEMBER

The last item needs to be on your agenda. It alerts the clients in advance that you're going to close. In fact, etch all seven items in stone; don't move them or rearrange them. You have to build trust, credibility, and value in that order, or you lose.

Dealing with Sales Objections

Sales objections are part of selling. For most people in sales, they present an immovable object in the road to your success. Real estate agents often freeze when presented with a sales objection. They don't know what to do or say in the face of this perceived danger.

Consider this radical concept: Sales objections are actually good. Now that I've blown your circuits, let me explain. You can't sell anything significant without sales objections. Sales objections indicate an elevated level of interest, desire, or motivation to buy what you're offering. Think of them as requests for more information.

The prospect is saying, "I need more information. If I like the information you give me, I'll do business with you." What could be better than that?

Delaying or deferring objections

One of the best ways to delay objections is to refer to your approved agenda, saying:

> *"Mr. and Mrs. Seller, would it be all right if I answered your question when we get to item number five on our agenda? That's where we discuss ____."*

Better than 40 percent of the time, the sellers won't bring up the sales objection again. You handle the sales objection by delaying its arrival.

WARNING

Using your agenda to delay objections is particularly important when the concern deals with the recommended list price or the cost of your service. Don't ever respond to pricing concerns until you've determined the sellers' wants, needs, and expectations and established the value of your service.

Handling objections in four easy steps

Objections are inevitable, so be ready to deal with them following this four-step system.

Pausing

When an objection arises, hear the client out completely. Then pause to collect your thoughts and, for many salespeople, to lower what may feel like rising blood pressure. Pause to ensure that you heard the objection completely. Don't try to cut the person off. I've watched salespeople interrupt, as if they're hoping to stuff the words back into the client's mouth before they're even out. This is the biggest mistake you can make. It demonstrates rudeness and insensitivity.

Acknowledging concerns

After hearing the objection and pausing to consider it, acknowledge the concern. This confirms that you understand what the client said, and it also gives you a few moments to consider and prepare your response.

Notice, nothing in the previous paragraph advises you to agree with the client. You can acknowledge the concern and thank the client for bringing it up without saying that it's right.

You can acknowledge by using any of these phrases:

> *"I understand your concern in this area."*
>
> *"That's a really terrific question. I'm glad you asked it."*
>
> *"I can see where that might cause you concern."*

One of my favorite techniques is to follow acknowledgement of a concern with a question or comment that probes for more information. The following responses give you an opportunity to learn more while also buying a few moments to develop a response:

> *"I understand your concern in this area. Why do you feel that way?"*
>
> *"I can see where that might cause you concern. Tell me more."*

Isolating concerns

By now you may be ready to pounce on the objection with your best answers. Hold off, if you can, while you isolate the concern. Isolation at its fundamental level, asks: "If it weren't for this concern, we'd be working together, right?"

By isolating, you cause the prospects to lay all their concerns on the table. Through this one step you learn everything that is standing between you and a signed listing contract.

Use any of these isolation scripts as you help sellers get their concerns out into the open:

"Is that the only concern that holds you back from moving forward with me?"

"Suppose we could find a satisfactory solution to this important concern of yours. Would you give me the go-ahead?"

"If this problem didn't exist, would you be ready to proceed right now?"

By isolating the concern, you learn exactly what you're up against. You may surface another objection in the process — which is why many agents shrink away from this step — but you would have heard it later anyway.

Responding with confidence

By now you've heard the objection, paused, acknowledged, and isolated. Now is the time to respond.

The most commonly stated objections center around the agent's commission, the recommended list price of the home, the length of the listing term, and the need for extra time to make the listing decision. More than 80 percent of the objections you'll hear over the course of your career stem from these key concerns. Prepare yourself by outlining and mastering responses that convince sellers you're able to handle the concern more effectively than other agents.

TIP

Ask your broker for scripts the company recommends for handling sales objections. If the company doesn't have them, make an investment in your career and buy them from an expert.

Asking for the Business

After you've overcome seller concerns or objections, ask for the order. In sales terms, this means asking the prospects to do business with you.

At the end of a presentation, a typical salesperson's close is something like, "Well, what do you think?" It's obvious to me why the typical salesperson sells very little. Winding up with a question like "What do you think?" is hardly asking for the order or closing.

Closing is making a definitive statement about your conviction that you're the right person for the job and that the sellers should take action now. A good closing statement goes like this:

"Mr. and Mrs. Seller, based on your goals, needs, and expectations, I'm confident that I'm the right person to handle the sale for you. Let's get started now!"

TIP

As you say, "Let's get started," slide the listing agreement in front of them. Hand them a pen and smile. Most importantly, shut up! Don't utter a word.

Bringing the Presentation to a Natural Conclusion

Following any major sales transaction, people feel a bit of uncertainty, a feeling of "What did I just do?" Preempt that fear by addressing and controlling your clients' concerns.

Before you leave the meeting, recap what steps will happen next and what you'll be doing for your clients in the next 24 to 48 hours. Then reassure them that they made a great decision, that you look forward to serving them and working with them, that the goals they set will be achieved, and that they selected the right agent for the job.

Chapter **13**

Getting the House Ready for Showing

Getting a home ready for the big show is necessary to achieve a sale. The more competitively the home is priced and prepared, the sooner the rigor of showing will end. And the sooner the sale takes place, the sooner your clients can return to their normal routines — except for that little challenge of packing and moving. This chapter helps you guide clients as they transform their homes from how they look most of the time to how they need to look to win attention and positive decisions from prospective buyers.

Getting the Home Ready for Pictures and Virtual Tours First

Most home tours occur online before they occur in person. More than 90 percent of all buyers use the Internet to search and review homes, with more than 82 percent using it frequently to access real estate properties and information, so visual information is essential to selling homes. According to the National Association of Realtors, 42 percent of buyers find their home online and then contact the listing agent or their own agent. That figure was a mere 8 percent a decade and a half ago. We've seen a 425 percent increase in buyers finding their next home through independent Internet searches.

Today's consumers want to understand a home's amenities, feeling and experiencing the home online before they take time to drive by or tour the home. For a fair number, 38 percent, the next step is to gather the family in the car and drive by the home. Potential buyers frequently check out the neighborhood, curb appeal, and condition of the property before contacting an agent.

The essential image online

The first rule of online property marketing is pictures, pictures, pictures. A recent study comparing the average number of pictures per listing found that the average listing has fewer than five photos. The typical Multiple Listing Service allows agents to upload more than 25 images for a listing. This means that most agents use less than 20 percent of the visual impression power that is available. When buyers encounter property listings with few photos, they reach one of several conclusions:

They don't want to waste their time

If potential buyers can't align their wants and needs with the visual images of the property, they quickly cross it off the list for lack of information. Many buyers think properties are like buses; another one will be along in a few minutes or days. "I'll wait," they say.

The property barks at cars

In other words, the property is a dog! If the property was a quality one, buyers think, the agent would have taken more pictures of it. Their mind-set is that something must be wrong. Even if you overcome that hurdle and secure a showing, you now have buyers on your hands who are focused on finding something wrong with the property. You've dug yourself into a hole.

The agent is unskilled

Many buyers who search the Internet are just beginning their research. They're researching properties for sale while formulating ideas for their move. They may start the search process six months, one year, or even two years before they actually move. A large number must sell a home to buy their next home, and they will need an agent. But you've demonstrated to them a lack of basic marketing skills. Their thinking is that if they can't easily get a basic understanding of this property, everyone else who finds this home online will have the same issues. You have little chance of securing their business in the future.

Unlocking secrets to perfect property pics

You don't have to use a professional photographer for all your listings; however, some listings benefit from the expertise that a professional can offer. I personally would always use a professional photographer because of the importance of pictures. Especially if you list a luxury property, professional photography is essential. Other properties that warrant an investment include those with unique architectural attributes, enhanced amenities, objectionable characteristics, or challenging furnishings. A professional can capture just the right image of a positive feature and downplay something that might turn off a buyer in an online search. Remember, buyers are likely to be looking for ways to cross a property off a list rather than adding it to their list.

When you're tackling the role of photographer, the right props can really enhance a shot. The goal is to make whatever space you're photographing warm and inviting to the viewer. Placing wine and cheese in a kitchen, for example, can say to the buyer, "Welcome; come relax." Avoid props like magazines, fruit, and towels that give the home the "lived in" look. Your photographs need to be more like *Architectural Digest* than *Reader's Digest*.

The laws of lighting

In most cases, the more light, whether natural or artificial, the better. The only exception is light that creates a glare in your lens. Turn on the lights and, if you have dark or shadowy areas and angles, fill in with work lights. Because lighting is different in each room, consider shooting different rooms at different times throughout the day. This takes extra work, time, and effort, but it can improve the pictures and balance the lighting. In my own home, the back gets more light than the front in the morning. The opposite is true later in the day.

Think about lighting when taking exterior pictures, as well. Most exterior shots of homes look better from an angle rather than dead on. Additionally, you don't want the home to be backlit because of glare in the lens. Ideally, the sun should be behind you, shining on the home. If the entry is shaded, you can take the shot on an overcast day to reduce the shade in the shot.

The right angles

Your goal is to create interesting and inviting shots and angles. Try to avoid shooting more than two walls in a given room. If you shoot three walls, you create a box. When photographing an empty home or room, be sure to combine rooms in a shot or capture the spaciousness of the environment. Because you don't have furniture, you're selling the size and openness of the space. Shoot at chest level or even on a stepping stool to show less ceiling in the shot.

Creating the right images is an art, not a science. You have to play with the shots on each home you list. Thanks to digital photography, you can take countless photos and easily disregard the ones you don't like. You can never have too many to choose from.

Counseling Clients on Home Improvements

Before you counsel owners about home improvements, remember these two rules:

WARNING

>> **First and foremost, never counsel before you're hired.** Counseling happens after a client relationship is established. Attorneys don't offer legal advice before their services have been officially retained. Doctors don't diagnose without assurance of compensation. Real estate agents should follow suit. Wait until the listing agreement is signed. After it's signed, begin giving counsel regarding how the owner can achieve a quicker sale or higher price by making recommended home improvements and implementing staging advice.

Too frequently, agents give away their expert counsel during listing presentations in hopes of proving their ability and expertise to sellers. More often than not, though, the sellers simply take the counsel with them when they link up with an agent who is less skillful but promises a cheaper fee.

>> **Second, tell the truth.** If the sellers need to clean the home, tell them. If they're smokers and the house reeks from cigarettes, or if their pets are causing odor problems, tell them.

Likewise, appearances can kill buyer interest. If the home is crowded with too much stuff, say so. If the pink exterior color may cause people to click next on their browser or drive right on by, speak up. Holding your tongue only delays the day of reckoning. What's more, it's easier to be totally frank when you first notice the problem — though only after the listing contract is signed. If you counsel before you gain commitment, your advice may offend the sellers and cost you the listing. This is another reason to follow Rule #1 and get a signature before giving counsel.

Improvements that contribute to the sale price

REMEMBER

When it comes to preparing a home for sale, worthwhile and necessary improvements fall into three categories:

>> Improvements that bring a home back to standard

>> Improvements that correct defects

>> Improvements that enhance curb appeal or first impressions

The following sections provide guidelines for each area.

Bringing a home back to standard

Before you present a home with horribly dated décor, counsel the sellers to modernize the interior look to align it with the expectations of current buyers. Sellers don't have to go overboard; they just need to use a reasonable color scheme and provide enough of an update so that new owners feel they can move in without having to undertake an immediate face-lift. Share the following advice with sellers:

REMEMBER

>> **Keep improvements simple.** A total redecoration isn't necessary or even advisable. The objective is to arrive at a widely acceptable and reasonably current color scheme with paint, counters, and floor coverings. The color palette tends to shift, so picking something too trendy can be problematic if you're on the tail end of the latest trend . . . think avocado appliances in the '70s or black glass in the '90s. Advise your clients to create a warm, blank canvas that any prospective buyer can work with.

>> **Don't aim to create a design showpiece.** Realize that after the purchase, buyers often change a home significantly to make it their own. The sellers' objective is to allow prospective buyers to feel that their changes can happen over the next few years — that they're not glaringly and immediately necessary.

>> **Focus on the big stuff.** If the interior of a home looks current and the landscaping, yard, decks, and patios are well kept and serviceable, the buyers' need to make significant, immediate changes lowers greatly. As a result, they'll be more likely to buy the home. They may also make a more competitive initial offer than would be the case if the home presented obvious exterior or interior color or repair issues. If buyers have to make changes to a home, they have to pay for them with their own personal funds, not with money they borrow. Many buyers consider this fact when deciding which home they should buy.

>> **A little paint makes a huge difference.** Repainting is one of the most cost-effective ways to freshen the look of a home. It can even disguise design shortcomings.

Correcting defects

If a home has defects, the seller has two choices: Fix them or provide equal monetary compensation to the buyers, plus an additional discount for the hassle of updating. Few buyers will pay a retail price less repair costs to correct defects. They logically will want compensation for their inconvenience.

For example, if a roof needs repair or replacement, the improvement will be expected by both the bank and the buyer. The seller can offer one of the following two remedies:

>> **Handle and pay for the repair or replacement.**

>> **Provide the buyers with sufficient compensation to cover the cost and hassle of correcting the defect themselves.** *Hassle compensation* is money above what it costs to professionally correct the problem. The amount extended for hassle compensation differs by task and buyer. It comes in the form of a reduction in the sale price. Typically lenders don't create an allowance for this. In most cases, if buyers have to collect and decide between contractor bids, arrange for repairs, and check the work of the contractor, they'll want some compensation for their time and effort.

Other items that may need to be addressed are excessively worn carpet or windows whose seals are broken, especially when condensation has built up between the panes.

Enhancing first impressions

Any cost-effective improvement that adds curb appeal or enhances first impressions can increase the sale price. Here are a few improvements the seller can do:

>> Counsel sellers to create dimension on the exterior of the home by adding shutters or fish scale over a garage gable, select a better color palette, and, certainly, spend a few hundred dollars to plant annuals to brighten the exterior walkways. The effect will increase the probability of a sale and positively influence the sale price.

>> Inside the house, after improving the home's color scheme, advise sellers to assess the quality of the home's surfaces, including carpet, tile, vinyl, and countertops. Replacing surfaces is often far less costly than buyers anticipate. Many choices look expensive but aren't. A seller doesn't have to put slab granite on the kitchen counters. Simply updating old tile and cracked or chipped Formica will deliver a great improvement and pay off when it comes to price negotiation. Remember that choosing a light surface can create the feeling of a larger, brighter room. Just remember, when replacing surfaces like floors and countertops, be sure you aren't simply replacing a dated look with a less dated look.

TIP

>> When working with a limited budget (as most sellers do), counsel the sellers to improve surfaces in core areas first. Focus on the areas most used by buyers, which include the kitchen, family room, bathroom (especially the master bath), and master bedroom.

Improvements to skip

As a general rule, I advise sellers to skip any improvement that isn't simple and doesn't create value. Focus on improvements that will improve the pictures of the home. That will at least get buyers in the door.

TIP

When sellers ask about replacing cabinets, remodeling rooms, building book-shelves, replacing siding, adding decks, and even finishing basements, share the following facts:

>> According to *Remodeling* magazine and the National Association of Realtors, the average major investment update on a home recoups 81 percent at resale, or only four out of five dollars spent.

>> The highest average rate of return results from a minor kitchen remodel, which yields 93 percent of the costs incurred.

>> The lowest average rate of return comes from finishing a basement, which yields a 76 percent return. See the sidebar titled "The myth of the bargain in the basement" for more details on the risks of finishing a basement.

>> The more money spent, the higher the risk for the seller and the lower the chance of making a return or even breaking even.

THE MYTH OF THE BARGAIN IN THE BASEMENT

Advise sellers who want to increase home value by finishing their basements to proceed with caution for the following reasons:

- Any remodel returns only a portion of its cost at the time of sale, and historically basement remodels yield the lowest return of all.

- Even if the home is on a sloping lot that allows for a really nice walk-out or daylight basement, in many areas of the U.S. the value of the basement square footage is half that of ground-level or above-ground-level square footage.

- Too many sellers calculate home price or value on a square-foot basis, and there-fore they see an unfinished basement as a kind of lotto ticket. This is especially true for Mr. Fix-It and gung-ho personality types, who see the unfinished basement as an easy route to a higher home price.

Use these facts to help your sellers understand that their finished basement is likely not going to return the dollars they put into the remodel, and that the resulting additional square footage will almost certainly be worth less than they envision.

Passing the Curb Appeal Test

As a listing agent, one of the first rules of real estate you need to remember is that you have to get prospective buyers and other agents into the house that is for sale. They won't buy it — or advise others to buy it — if they don't step inside to see it. The technological world we live in makes this even tougher. With 76 percent of buyers first driving by a home they saw online, you won't get a showing if the home doesn't pass the online evaluation and the curb-appeal test.

Curb appeal is more important than ever

I believe curb appeal is more important today because so many buyers are do-it-yourself types in their home-search process. This means you won't be there to give them ideas on how to improve curb appeal. They've already said, "Next!" Real estate investors are the only exception to this rule: They'll often buy a house without ever looking at it. However, most sellers don't want to settle for the price a shrewd investor will pay. To get top dollar, you must win the curb-appeal game.

REMEMBER

As an agent, nothing is more discouraging than giving up your Saturday or Sunday afternoon to host an open house, only to watch cars drive by all afternoon without stopping. The culprit is almost always a lack of curb appeal — or first-glance pizzazz. The second most common reason is that the home is in a less-than-desirable neighborhood.

Few people have the gift to see what a home *could* look like. My wife, Joan, has that gift. She can look at a listing that I know isn't quite right and tell me exactly what to suggest to the seller. The following sections provide similar advice for you to follow.

Landscaping your way to success

Landscaping recommendations depend largely on the age of the home you're getting ready to show. Newer homes are frequently so under-landscaped that they look remarkably like the surface of the moon. Meanwhile, older homes are surrounded by such overgrown trees and bushes that they look like the jungles of Brazil.

TIP

Know the age of the home you're listing and more often than not you'll immediately know what kind of tool your sellers need to use to ready their property for showing: a machete or a shovel.

The most frequent curb–appeal obstacle comes from overgrown landscaping, which needs to be attacked with the following steps:

>> **Trim trees to create openness in the yard area.** Large fir or evergreen trees can make a yard look smaller than its actual size, particularly if expansive branches hang close to the ground. Advise the seller to remove some of the limbs of larger trees so there's a 12–15 foot space off the ground.

>> **Use the space opened by tree trimming to plant colorful annuals, which will brighten up the yard. You should also use annuals to brighten the sidewalks and paths to and around the front door.**

>> **If the seller's yard features grass, make sure it's healthy and green.** Recommend that sellers put down extra seed or replace sod in trouble spots if necessary. You want to achieve a look that's more like a golf course than a motocross course.

>> **Add landscape dimension to otherwise flat lots with plants, berms, or rocks.** Don't overdo it, but do add a little height and depth to break what otherwise might look like a dull lot.

>> **Create dimension through color.** The landscaping can look pretty mono-chromatic if you're presenting a home in a season other than spring. Colorful plants go a long way toward adding visual interest and strengthening curb appeal.

Exterior paint condition and color

In a split second, the color and condition of a home's exterior paint can either attract or repel a prospective buyer.

>> **Paint color:** Recommend that sellers think long and hard about pastel colors like robin's egg blue or baby pink, or color schemes that match the uniforms of their college teams. Just as with hard surfaces on the inside, the exterior of a home for sale should be painted in classic, muted tones, such as taupe or beige, with a soft accent color that is slightly darker than the body of the home.

The architecture of the home can contribute to the decision regarding what colors are appropriate. For example, white paint on a colonial-style home can enhance the property's visual impression from the curb, evoking images of great, stately homes such as the White House or George Washington's Mt. Vernon. However, the same white paint on a 1950s ranch home may result in a house that looks like a plain little box with no character.

>> **Paint condition:** Buyers are quick to cross homes in need of new paint off their lists, whether the chipped paint is on the body or trim of the home or on fences or railings.

The worst outcome is when a prospective buyer drives by but doesn't stop. However, even if he decides to stop and look at the house, trouble still lurks. If the exterior paint condition is poor and buyers consider the home anyway, you may wish they hadn't, and here's why: When buyers notice that paint is peeling, cracking, chipping, or stripped down to bare wood, they go into high-scrutiny mode and begin to pick the home apart. Rather than looking for wonderful things about the home, they fixate on what they think is wrong. They assume that because something as obvious as the paint is in poor condition, other aspects of the home have also been neglected. A buyer determined to find faults will succeed. No home can withstand a microscopic faultfinding inspection.

Even if the home passes the inaugural buyer examination, the sellers aren't out of the woods. If the buyer decides to make an offer, almost certainly it will be accompanied by an extensive repair list and the request that every minor offense be rectified before the closing. Then a home inspector will enter the picture, providing a more extensive report and the chance for the buyer to hit the seller up all over again. All this happens because of a little chipping paint that could (and should) have been fixed before buyers ever drove by to view the home in the first place.

Prepping the Interior of the Home

After prospective buyers are through the door, you need them to be greeted by a good first impression. Help sellers achieve the lightest, brightest, and largest interior possible by taking the following advice to heart.

In preparation for this chapter, I put myself in the seller's shoes and looked around our own home, asking myself what we'd need to do if we wanted to sell. Big surprise: We'd need to clear each room of tons of belongings, decorations, and furniture. We all have too much stuff. We have kids whose toys are broken or aren't played with anymore. We have clothes that hang in closets for years while we await the miracle weight–loss drug. One of the reasons homes have grown in size over the years is that we need more and more room to put our stuff.

To help sellers prepare their home interiors for showing, have them take two initial steps:

>> **Get them to rent a drop box or dumpster and throw away or donate anything they haven't used in a while.** In fact, you may benefit by doing the same thing in your own home. You'd be amazed at how invigorating it is to have that drop box in the driveway for a weekend. It's almost like a game to see how far and how fast you can fill it to the top. For most people who've lived in the same home for a while, it won't take long.

>> **Convince the sellers to rent a storage unit.** After filling a dumpster to the gills, they may still have things that should be moved out of the house — if not out of their lives. A storage unit provides an inexpensive, readily available solution.

After these initial steps are taken, you and the sellers can focus on other ways to make the home more appealing to potential buyers.

Staging a home

The term *staging* describes the process of rearranging and decorating a home's interior in an effort to downplay deficiencies and accent strengths. In its simplest form, staging involves adding specialty accessories like towels, candles, throw rugs, bedding, pillows, dishes, napkins, and stemware. Staging at its most extensive level involves rearranging or replacing furniture or even adding specialty furniture pieces to create a feeling of comfort and livability.

TIP

Before you advise clients on the staging process, gain knowledge about basic staging techniques and outcomes by visiting newly developed neighborhoods with model homes. Invest the time to see how new homes are being shown. Notice how the most appealing homes present master baths. Take a close look at desirable kitchens to see what is and isn't on the countertops. Note how towels, dishes, and glassware are displayed. Most of all, study how furniture is arranged in variously shaped rooms to create an environment that is open, warm, and comfortable.

If you're really challenged by staging and design, turn to pros for help. In most real estate markets you'll find people who specialize in staging homes for sale. Many interior decorators offer hourly consultations. Others offer, for a fee, full-service staging, where they work up a design plan, bring in the furniture and accessories, handle the installation, and dismantle it all after the sale.

TIP

Find out the names and experience levels of staging or interior design specialists in your market area. Then be ready to convince your sellers that it's in their best interest to invest in their home's interior look. Remind them that well-staged homes attract not only buyer prospects but also agents, who want to show attractive homes. In many cases, the investment pays off in two ways: a faster sale and a higher price.

Clearing the clutter

When buyers are house shopping, they're given the challenge of mentally removing the seller's stuff before deciding whether they actually want to move in. This type of mental gymnastics helps buyers assess how well the home they're viewing will accommodate their own possessions. (Later in this chapter, I offer tips to help buyers with these mental gymnastics.)

Some sellers' homes are so full of garage-sale and flea-market finds that the buyers honestly can't see the home through the clutter. They can't "move in" because they can't see anywhere for their own things to go.

TIP

If you're working with sellers who are surrounded by clutter, do the following:

>> **Advise them to remove excessive amounts of accessories and knick-knacks.** Whether they get rid of them altogether or pack them up in preparation for their anticipated move, get them out of sight. The result can do wonders for a home's interior appearance.

>> **Dismantle the "shrine wall."** A wall of pictures of children, grandchildren, nieces, nephews, friends, acquaintances, and snapshots of every experience the owners fondly remember adds clutter with little to no buyer appeal.

>> **Follow the design rule "When in doubt, take it out."** Advise sellers to keep clutter, wall décor, and placement of figurines and mementos to a bare minimum.

Knowing what to keep and what to remove

The point of showing a home is to allow prospective buyers to mentally move in and assess how well the home fits with their lives and possessions. Real estate agents know to listen and watch for buying signals, and one of the clearest and best signs is when buyers discuss how their own belongings may fit in various rooms.

REMEMBER

Buyers can hardly think about where their piano, china cabinet, or most-treasured family heirloom will go when they can't get their eyes past the visual onslaught of the furnishings, accessories, and clutter of the current owners. Use the following information to guide your recommendations regarding what sellers should leave in place and what they should move out prior to the home presentation.

>> **Pictures:** Suggest that the owners pack up all but a few of the personal photos in the home. If they have a wall covered with pictures, advise them to pare down to just a few.

>> **Appliances:** Except the ones that get used daily, store all small kitchen appliances. Leave the coffeemaker on the counter, but lose the blender and maybe even the toaster.

>> **Vanity items:** Remove most of what is on the bathroom vanity, including decorations and toiletries. A collection of items draws attention to a small vanity size.

>> **Closets:** Thin clothes out of closets to create the illusion of greater space. Even a good-sized closet that is crammed with clothes looks undersized and inadequate.

>> **The garage:** Too often, what gets removed from the home goes into the garage. Don't let your sellers make this mistake. Ask them to move household items into a rented storage unit instead. While they're at it, they can move garage items — from extra sets of tires to out-of-season recreation equipment — to the storage unit. Then advise them to organize what's left. Suggest that they hang bicycles from the ceiling and install a few inexpensive pre-made cabinets to hold paint cans, tape, shop rags, toolboxes, and the rest of the amazing collection of stuff that ends up in most garages. The objective is to end up with a clean, spacious garage that adds openness and perceived square footage to the home — and dollars to the final sale price.

TIP

If you encounter seller resistance, remind your clients that they're going to have to pack their stuff up anyway. By preparing their home for presentation, they eliminate visual clutter and get a leap on the packing process at the same time.

Simplifying traffic flow

The design rule "When in doubt, take it out" applies to furniture as well. Rooms that feel cramped and hard to move through usually have too much furniture in too little space.

TIP

To make a diagnosis and suggest recommendations, do the following:

>> **Walk through the home to find the spots that feel cramped.** Where do transition areas from room to room, or from one part of a room to another, feel restricted?

>> **Make recommendations to improve traffic flow.** The sellers can't move walls (without great expense), but they can move furniture that restricts movement.

>> **Evaluate the number of pieces of furniture in each room and note the sizes of each piece.** Ask yourself the following questions:

  • Are too many pieces of furniture crowded into one room?

  • Are furnishings too large and beefy for the room?

  • Does the furniture arrangement work in terms of space and flow?

>> **Be on the lookout for small, decorative pieces of furniture.** These pieces are often the biggest culprits when it comes to restricting walkways and creating a crowded feeling.

Most people have too much furniture in too small of a space. Be ready to recommend that the sellers remove furniture to create more open spaces, which makes the home appear larger and more comfortable.

WARNING

Your furniture-removal recommendations will most likely be met by owner resistance. Sellers will resist because they think that there won't be any place for people to sit. Stick to your story: Tell them a home with too little furniture almost always shows better than a home with too much.

Toning it down

Themed bedrooms — those with wallpaper, wallpaper borders, sheets, pillows, comforters, and wall hangings that all match — are very popular for children today. The problem is that buyers walk in and can't see an alternate use for the room. And if they *can* actually see an alternate use, they may also see the considerable expense and effort it will take to get the room from where it is to where they'd like it to be in terms of decoration and usability. As a result, the buyers will likely offer a lower price, if they make an offer at all, in order to cover the costs they anticipate when replacing the theme with a more neutral design.

TIP

Be on the lookout for the following red flags:

>> Loud or outlandish paint colors or wall coverings.

>> Immediately visible and highly personalized themes. For example, a vibrant pink bedroom with lots of stuffed animals may be off-putting to empty nesters or a family that has only boys.

Explain to the sellers that some buyers may be design-challenged and may have little sense of how to redecorate or of how much it costs to paint or wallpaper a room. Tell them that a more neutral design will attract more buyer interest and command a higher price.

Making a clean-up checklist

REMEMBER

Don't assume that sellers understand what needs to be done before a showing, even if they've bought and sold a home before. Take a proactive stance by providing a detailed step-by-step checklist of the steps they need to take before the first buyer presentation. Figure 13-1 is a good sample to follow as you provide your clients with valuable counsel and help them ready their home for presentation.

House Clean-Up and Presentation Preparation Checklist		
Task		Recommendation
Cleaning	☐	Hire professional cleaners to eliminate odors from pets or smoking, clean carpets, polish wood floors
	☐	Other:
Interior Walls	☐	Repaint to achieve a neutral, broadly accepted, contemporary color scheme; tone down bold colors
	☐	Repaper or repaint to eliminate themed rooms that limit usability
	☐	Other:
Interior Hard Surfaces	☐	Replace dated carpets
	☐	Replace dated counters with light, bright surfaces, focusing efforts on key areas in which owners spend the most time
	☐	Other:
Exterior Paint	☐	Repaint to eliminate chipping, blistering, or peeling and to achieve a neutral, contemporary color scheme
	☐	Repaint fences and railings if necessary
	☐	Other:
Landscaping	☐	Thin or limb large trees on mature lots
	☐	Plant annuals to add spot color
	☐	Reseed or resod lawn
	☐	Add dimension to flat lots with berms, plants, and rocks
	☐	Other:
Clutter Removal	☐	Rent chop box or dumpster
	☐	Rent storage unit
	☐	Clear out old, unused, outdated belongings
	☐	Pack up and store accessories and knick knacks
	☐	Dismantle walls of photos, leaving only a few good-quality framed pictures as decoration
	☐	Remove most small appliances from countertops, leaving only ones you use on a daily basis
	☐	Remove items from bathroom vanity
	☐	Remove items to open space in closets
	☐	Other:

FIGURE 13-1:
House clean-up and presentation preparation checklist.

(continued)

Traffic Flow	☐	Remove small pieces of furniture that restrict walkways
	☐	Remove large pieces of furniture that crowd spaces
	☐	Other:
Home Defects	☐	Repair defects or be prepared to provide compensation to buyers
Garage	☐	Move storage and out-of-season items to a storage facility
	☐	Hang bikes and other equipment from walls or ceiling
	☐	Install storage cabinets

© John Wiley & Sons, Inc.

FIGURE 13-1: continued

Making a Great First Impression: Final Ways

For most buyers, selecting a home isn't a logical undertaking. Instead, it's more of an emotional upheaval. Most buyers are swayed by the initial emotions they feel when they first walk through the door of a potential new home. Almost instantly, the home either feels right or feels wrong.

Rarely do people warm up to a home. After buyers receive a first impression, they soon figure out whether a home is "the one." That first impression can be the beginning of a sales success, or it can be a prohibitive factor that will be difficult to overcome.

I remember hearing my mother tell the story of helping my grandmother find a home to buy. They had looked at many homes before they walked into one that my grandmother actually liked. In fact, within two minutes she was dancing around the house saying, "This is the one I'm going to buy. I want this house now." All logic went out the window the moment she found the comfort, warmth, and space for her large dining-room furniture. It didn't matter that the home was next door to a car wash with loud air blowers (fortunately, my grandmother was hard of hearing). It also didn't matter that it was about 100 feet from a major street with heavy traffic. It felt right to her, and she bought it that day.

Good first impressions, feelings, and emotions control the sale, and logic takes a distant second place in the decision process. For this reason, you want to ensure that your home makes a good first impression with potential buyers. In the following sections, I share a few finishing touches that can make all the difference.

Enhancing the first glance

A home has ten seconds to make a good first impression. All the senses are in play, and a home either passes or fails the initial test.

Use this advice to positively engage all the senses in the first moments of the buying experience:

>> **Scent:** Fill the home with smells that invoke feelings of comfort, warmth, and calmness. Suggest that the sellers bake cookies, bread, or something that fills the home with a warm, honey-like aroma prior to presentations. If your clients aren't quite Martha Stewart types, suggest that they put a few drops of vanilla on some aluminum foil in a warm oven. Or, create a positive aroma with potpourri or candles.

WARNING

Don't overdo it with the scents. A scent that is too strong can drive buyers out of the home before they even get a good look.

>> **Sound:** Play soft, soothing music that is universally acceptable, such as classical pieces with limited instruments or even just piano music. Gangster rap or loud rock is inadvisable.

TIP

If the home has a sound system wired throughout each room, your music selections also give you an opportunity to demonstrate this feature of the home.

>> **Ambiance:** Ask the sellers to create a visually inviting environment by preparing a nicely set dining room table. Suggest that they place small flower arrangements in various rooms. You may even recommend that they build a fire in the fireplace if the home is for sale during the fall or winter months.

>> **Brightness:** Open all the blinds and draperies to let in natural light and make the home appear larger. Also turn on lights in corner areas to pull the eye to the perimeter of the room and provide a sense of expanded space.

Helping the buyer "move in"

When showing a property to buyers, your job is to help clients imagine living in the home. The more quickly you can get them thinking about actually moving into the house, the more quickly you'll help them make their decision.

TIP

The way to help the buyer mentally move in is to ask questions like these:

>> Susan, would you arrange your furniture this way?

>> Which of these bedrooms would be best for Bobby?

>> Where would you place the swing set?

>> How would your oval nook table fit in this nook area?

>> Where in the garage would you put your workbench?

>> Where do you think the big-screen TV could go?

>> What do you feel is the best location for your piano?

Any question that engages the buyer's imagination is a good question. If the answers convey negative feedback, the home is probably not the right one for the buyer. After you realize this fact, you can cross if off the list and move on to another home.

WARNING

I've watched too many agents walk buyers through a home making absurd comments like, "This is the family room," as if the clients may have mistaken it for a kitchen. Assume, quite safely, that buyers know which rooms are living rooms, kitchens, and bedrooms. They don't need an agent to tell them what's what. But, they do need you to help them trigger their imaginations so they can decide if the rooms are right for them.

Chapter **14**

Marketing Yourself and Your Properties

arketing is the topic that gets all agents to stop and listen. It's a big field that takes time, money, and a bewildering number of decisions. Marketing, as it should be, is high on the to-do list of anyone trying to make a sale.

I'm willing to bet that most agents spend more time wondering and worrying about how to market than they spend actually marketing. And the confusion is well-founded. The choices you face as an agent are practically without limit, and you have to compete with every other company that markets to consumers on a daily basis. Hundreds of times each day consumers are inundated with television and radio commercials, newspaper and magazine advertisements, direct-mail marketing, online marketing (too much of it in the form of spam), Facebook sponsored ads, outdoor signs, social-media communication, and countless other marketing messages.

The solution is to *focus.* Focus on what you want to accomplish, what you want to communicate, and who you want to reach with your message.

REMEMBER

At its core, real estate marketing is a matter of communicating a message about what you have to an audience that may or may not want what you're offering. If that sounds like a simple definition, it's because marketing real estate services and products is really not all that complex, as long as you take a focused approach. In this chapter, I share some advice on how to proceed.

Shifting from Print to Online

The biggest shift in real estate marketing in the past ten years has been from print marketing to online marketing — both for listed properties and for agent services in general.

A recent National Association of Realtors (NAR) study revealed a dramatic drop in the effectiveness of print advertising. Less than ten years ago, 9 percent of buyers found the homes they eventually bought in classified newspaper ads, display ads, and home magazines. At that time, only 8 percent of buyers found their homes online.

Fast forward ten years. Print-media options account for under 1 percent! That is a large drop, from 9 percent to almost zero. At the same time, the percentage of buyers who find their homes online has risen to 42 percent. Where do you think you need to invest your dollars?

Setting up a monitoring system

Before you invest a single dollar, set up a system to monitor returns or results. It makes little sense to throw money at a lead-shortage issue without being able to measure and monitor whether the new strategy is creating real dollars in your pocket.

What many agents fail to understand is that sellers are hiring them to generate buyer leads for their property. They are also hiring them to reach other agents who have ready buyers. If you do these well, you increase the odds of closing the deal. You also benefit from the many new leads you create when you discover that some buyers don't want this seller's home but need help finding something else. The marketing you do for a property can generate a broader lead opportunity.

Some of your listed properties are just great lead generators. These are properties you will list in your career that you won't sell. Your marketing must be compelling enough to create buyers that you can expose, show, and sell other properties to.

TIP

Set up a spreadsheet to monitor lead sources from all your marketing efforts, both online and offline. If your marketing has a strong call to action that asks prospects to text or call in a response, using a call-in system like Google Voice for each of your major marketing efforts is advisable. Here's how the system works: For example, if you send out a direct-mail piece to homeowners who are delinquent on their mortgage to offer help in selling their home, you can set up a Google Voice number for that specific marketing piece and have it forwarded to your cell phone. When you look at your phone and see the number, you know a distressed homeowner is calling for help (because that particular Google Voice number was assigned to that particular marketing piece). Track these calls as they come in to monitor the effectiveness of each marketing piece — in general, the more calls you get, the more effective the piece.

Before you start throwing money at different marketing tools, set up a monitoring system to maximize your results and decrease response-rate times.

Focusing your marketing dollars online

As a new agent, the first, second, and third place to invest your marketing dollars is online.

The two main issues you face with the Internet are quality and quantity. You want to drive visitors to your site so you can increase the odds of generating leads from it. You also want to increase the quality of the prospects so you can separate the really good buyers and sellers from all the rest. You want to achieve a reasonable conversion rate, preferably much higher than the 0.5 to 1 percent many agents now experience with web leads.

You have to do a delicate balancing act in terms of quality and quantity. If you had to choose one, which would you choose to do first — quality or quantity? Before you select, let me tell you the truth of the Internet. The volume of traffic is important. At the end of the day, the one who has the most visitors usually wins. You may build a beautiful website, but you have to drive traffic to make money with the Internet.

When you get the traffic, you have to convince people to stay and leave a trail of contact information. You need them to at least leave bread crumbs: their first name and email address. You can bring a couple of thousand people to your site monthly and end up with two or three prospects. I'm not talking about clients; I'm talking only about prospects. You now have to do the work of moving them up the loyalty ladder to becoming a client by converting them from web visitors to buyers or sellers.

You can do this by offering a free report, a market trends report, best values list, a newsletter, or something that a potential buyer or seller deems valuable enough to give you at least their first name and email address (see the later section "Converting ad interest to action" for more details on tracking prospects). You need to walk them up each step of the conversion track. With each level or step they take, your probability of earning a commission check grows. The object is to move the visitors to prospects, prospects to clients, and clients to referral sources. (See Figure 14-1.)

Conversion Track
(Relationship/Commitment Growth)

Suspects (Strangers) **Prospects** (Acquaintences) **Customers/Clients** (Friends) **Evangelists** (Family)

Re-Purchases

Referrals

FIGURE 14-1:
This conversion
chart illustrates
how prospects
can turn into
referral sources.

The more complete the contact information you can get people to leave, the higher the probability you can move them up to the client stage. More information increases the opportunity to move them to a fundamental sales channel of send > call > see.

The balance in this approach is you will have a higher bounce rate. A *bounce* happens when the online consumer bounces off your site or landing page because you have asked for too much information. Rather than filling out your form with their information, they leave your site.

Getting prospects to reveal their full contact information when they make their inquiries is paramount. For example, too many Internet leads come in without phone numbers. Getting a prospect's phone number enables you to text them or call them back — these raise the conversion ratio substantially. Additionally, you have that 90-day window of opportunity for future phone contact within the confines of the National Do Not Call Registry.

Most agents are chasing a lot of low-probability prospects through the Internet. They have an email address and are sending property-match searches daily. They even put prospects into a drip sequence. A *drip* is a series of emails over time that you send. They also have the prospects on an electronic newsletter list. These agents start the prospecting process but often let it stall at this stage. All those methods are automated, so agents invest limited time — but also reap limited rewards.

The Importance of Photographic Images

Most consumers searching online or in other marketing methods tend to hyper-focus on the pictures provided. They feel that they have the same information a real estate agent has access to. The choke point is created because the consumer is looking at virtual tours and images of listings instead of going out to experience the properties first-hand. They are relying on the images provided to tell the whole story. Pictures are the consumer's first impression of a property. Make sure yours are great.

Consumers are reviewing properties with a mind-set of "Hey, a picture is worth a thousand words." Many are thinking, "Because these pictures don't make my heart rate go up when I view them, this home is crossed off my list." Which means they bypass the listing. Essentially, they are judging a book by its cover. They don't get connected with it emotionally because the listing agent was a lousy photographer. Many agents are not well versed in lighting, photo angles, framing aesthetics, or capturing warmth, space, and emotion that can be achieved with the right photographs.

Putting pictures to work for your listing

Thank goodness for digital technology that enables you to email pictures of homes to prospects far and wide with the simple click of a mouse. The right picture can heighten interest, prompt purchase decisions, and deliver thousands of dollars in commission income. For that reason, your phone or a digital camera and photography expertise are necessary in your business.

I highly recommend using professional photography, but if you feel you don't have the budget, the next sections offer a few tips. If your phone lacks the quality, you need to buy a digital camera for your business.

Choosing your camera

Use a digital camera for taking pictures inside and outside the homes you're representing. If you're on a tight budget, you can find a solid camera for around $200. Just be sure it includes the following features:

>> **Point and shoot:** Cameras with this function focus and adjust for available lighting. They're easy to use, and therefore you're likely to use them often.

>> **A reasonable number of megapixels:** *Megapixels* determine photo resolution, which equals image quality. The bad news is that the more megapixels you get, the more money you'll spend. The good news is that you don't want to go overboard because, with megapixels, you can actually have too much of a good thing. They use storage space in your camera and your computer and also result in larger files that take longer to email. Besides, at a certain point, you can't even see any extra quality.

>> **Easy transfer and storage capability:** Select a camera with an easy-to-use function for transferring and uploading photos. You can also select one that automatically uploads photos to your cloud storage.

Taking digital photos

REMEMBER

The key to success in taking digital pictures is to take a lot of them. With digital cameras, you're not spending money on film and development, so each photo is basically free. When you're at a property, snap freely and often. You can always edit, resize, crop, rotate, and enhance your photos with special effects when you're back at your computer.

Capturing the best images

For exterior photos:

>> **Photograph when natural light is abundant.** If you live in a climate with long, dreary winters, you may have to take a first round of photos on a gray day just to capture an image to use when you announce the listing. Plan to go back on a brighter day (as soon as possible) to take a second shot that will replace the original one.

WARNING

>> **Position yourself so that the sun is directly behind, or at an angle behind, your back.** Otherwise, your photo will have a glare that you may have to remove during editing.

For interior photos:

>> **Create shots that give the illusion of spaciousness.** Do so by incorporating transitional areas, such as hallways or entryways, in with rooms in the same photo.

>> **Take lots and lots of shots.** Don't edit on the spot or be paralyzed by second-guessing. Don't use the camera's screen to evaluate the pictures at length. Capture as many images as possible and then wait until you transfer them to your computer to analyze, cull, select, and edit.

Choosing the best shots

The whole point of featuring photos is to entice prospects to come see the real thing. So select and use only those images that convey comfort, warmth, and unique quality, and that are capable of evoking a "wow" response.

TIP

If a photo shows a unique aspect of a bedroom, such as an angled nook or architecturally unique wall, use it. If the master bath — always a selling feature — is well beyond plain Jane in its look, show it. When selecting shots, choose quality over quantity.

Creating and organizing photo files

Set up a system so you can store and access the images you may need in the future. Following each photo shoot, first delete the pictures you don't want to use and then store the rest. When storing your pictures, your camera automatically suggests a filename. Rename each picture by choosing a name that describes the home or its address. Then move the images into folders that are labeled by property address.

Choosing Internet Strategies That Work

The first step to finding an Internet strategy that works for you is to establish which strategies you have at your disposal. At the moment, I believe agents have three viable strategies, which I discuss in this section. I also make note of using persuasive strategies via the Internet. With any strategy you need to monitor and measure the results. This helps you discover which strategies are most effective and which need more work.

Company websites

An easy way to make your presence known on the Internet is through your real estate company's website. It can be the most cost-effective way, as well. Most companies set up basic agent web pages within their site, so make sure you keep yours current. If a prospect comes to the company website, clicks on your tab, and sees just a blank template, you lose credibility.

You can have a website up and running within days or even minutes for the cost of a nice dinner, and it gives you all kinds of data about your visitors. Basic requirements for this type of site are a professional look, your company logo, professional photos of agents, bios of agents, and several means of contact for the visitor. The main purpose of this type of website is to make it easy to reach you. Visitors to this site will likely be people who have your marketing pieces and want to contact you.

BRANDING ISN'T FOR EVERYONE

Branding is a fairly standard term to marketers of all types. It basically means that you want to establish a memorable professional identity for your potential prospects and customers. Ideally, you want all the people in your market to think about you when they think about buying or selling a home.

However, a few factors associated with branding don't make it the best solution for 99.99 percent of real estate agents. First of all, it's *very* expensive. Second, it takes a very, *very* long time to establish a brand. Finally, it's almost impossible to quantify the effectiveness of branding. All three of these difficulties are contrary to what most people think the Internet is all about — and rightly so. On several fronts, therefore, branding isn't a very good choice for real estate agents.

Property information websites

These sites are focused solely on one property and can be very effective in systematizing the sales process of individual properties. You can purchase these sites for as little as $35 per month for 25 individual addresses, or you can spend up to $50 per month per address. You must treat these sites as part of a sales and marketing process.

Let's say you have a house listed at 123 Main Street. You fire up one of these sites, and it enables you to include a virtual tour of the home, all the particulars about the home, all of your contact information, and many more details. The site, by itself, really has no value, but if you run a marketing campaign or a Facebook ad talking about the home and include the URL, now you've gotten somewhere. You could link it to a direct mail campaign out to the neighborhood to generate leads.

WARNING

The problem with these sites is that prospects may make negative decisions based on a bad photo on the virtual tour or a paint color they don't like. You can't answer a prospect's objections, and you may never have the opportunity to even know his or her name.

So, these sites can be a valuable way for you to gain exposure for your properties, but the lead volume will likely be small — although the leads will likely be good ones. Use this type of site as *part* of your arsenal, to gain exposure for specific properties. Also, if you're trying to establish yourself in an area, these can be used.

Lead-generation websites

One of the biggest problems with the activities we find ourselves involved in as real estate agents is that we often forget why we're doing them. If I had only one choice for what a website would do for me, it would be to generate leads — not some leads, but a ton of them; not just any leads, but very qualified (ready-to-do-business-with-me) leads.

This brings me to my favorite kind of website, the lead-generation website. The sole purpose of this site is to generate a large volume of a specific type of lead, whether for buyers or sellers. This website is designed for a very targeted audience. This may be buyers or sellers of homes in Anytown, USA, or it may just be buyers or sellers in general. The narrower your focus, the more targeted your niche, the better.

For example, if you decide to target only buyers, you need to have the site loaded with content that is valuable to your target prospects. Let's say your site is geared toward buyers in Anytown, USA. The website must be focused solely on topics that (1) are valuable to buyers in your market area, including specific school districts or neighborhoods, and (2) help buyers accomplish their objective, which is to buy a home in the area.

You may want to include a section of community events and a list of key community facts and dates. Consider providing market statistics and featuring listings for prospective buyers to view. Also valuable is information about mortgages and home-design trends. You have endless options to create value for your prospects.

Another type of lead-generation site is connected to a back-end IDX search system. You are marketing for potential buyers to fill out basic information on bedrooms, bathrooms, location, and price range. These sites are connected to the MLS information so they can review properties based on their desired search criteria.

These sites work best when you do two specific things. The first is to keep your brand and yourself low key. You don't want large pictures of yourself and have your company brand everywhere. Being understated is best. The consumer will be less likely to leave their information for a salesperson because of their fear of being pestered. The second is using a URL that isn't your name or company.com. You have to think like a buyer. What are the search terms a buyer might use? A URL like www.SanDiegoHomeFinder.com tells the buyer that this site is for them. You could have subdomains with bedroom communities in the San Diego market to drive even more traffic.

This type of a URL also helps you with search engine optimization. Google views this type of URL as a valuable site. When you couple that with valuable information on the site, you will climb the search engine's search results ranking toward higher placement. If you run pay-per-click campaigns to the site in addition, the buyer who sees your ad will feel more comfortable that the site is a valuable site for their needs based on your URL.

TIP

There is often a big debate on forced registration versus non-forced registration landing pages on these types of sites. You may prefer to offer a site that does not force someone to register, but the truth is, forced registration is the only option. If you don't force someone to register, they likely won't. You can reduce the bounce by letting them see a few properties before the forced registration page comes up on the screen. The forced registration option is the only way you will know this online buyer exists. Some buyers will put in bogus information because you forced them to enter something. When that happens, laugh at the creativity of these people. You will likely be one of the first people to know that Mickey Mouse is considering a move out of Disneyland.

The Art of Persuasion: Getting Prospects to Buy into You

Your online marketing must include an element of persuasion. Having high-value content for a targeted audience isn't enough by itself. You must, through persuasive sales copy, persuade the folks who visit your website to become prospects.

TIP

I recommend that you contract with a good copywriter — preferably one who has website experience. You can find them online at such websites as Upwork (www. upwork.com) or any other contract-labor source. The key is to find someone who is good at persuasive copywriting for the Internet. I also look for someone who has an eye for quality design . . . although you may need to hire two different people to get both skills. A great copywriter can earn you hundreds or thousands of dollars for every dollar you spend. I know; I have one of the best on my staff.

The next sections discuss persuasive ways to get prospects to buy into you.

Get the customer to interact

The goal of a website is to interact with visitors and have them leave a trail. You also want them to come back again and again. They become more valuable with each visit and are more likely to leave a recognizable trail.

Here are three ways to interact via your website with potential customers:

>> **Offer free reports.** Get potential clients to take information that is valuable by offering free reports. Offer access to information (for example, "The 10 Mistakes Sellers Make When Selling a Home"). Such a report lists both mistakes and solutions. Someone who pulls that type of report is at least considering a sale. Another report (for example, "How to Guarantee You Get

Your Home Sold and for the Highest Price Possible") can lead seller prospects through the steps to ensure the sale at a top-dollar sale price. You can develop similar reports for buyers.

At this point, you're trying to generate a volume of leads. Free reports are a good first point of contact. Thousands of reports have already been produced, so don't sit down to write one. You can search the web for reports of this type that are free or practically so.

>> **Offer free newsletters and blogs.** Free newsletters and blogs are also an effective means of communication. Having an email or blog list of people who read your material regularly is immensely powerful. Your job is to provide value in that newsletter or blog. I encourage you to do a newsletter monthly and a blog post a couple of times a week. Start with a generic or template version and then move on to a more customized approach when you get a feel for what prospects are looking for.

>> **Offer a consistent message.** The ability to consistently communicate with an audience is extremely valuable. Some of my marketing results come from the consistency of the message delivery, as well as the message that's delivered. It's easier for an agent to be consistent if he or she starts with a template newsletter. Test it: Evaluate how much or how little work it is, and see whether your contacts like it and read it. Then work up to a hybrid or combination newsletter, in which some material is your own and some is from a template. If that goes well, create your own newsletter. One of the keys to marketing is consistency.

Expand your reach in cyberspace

One strategy is to link to other sites and sources to increase your search-engine ranking. However, there is a difference between quality and quantity. Search engines give weight to the relevancy of a link. If you go out and link to anyone and everyone, your search-engine ranking probably won't improve that much. Instead, your links should be focused on real estate and/or your specific market area.

Here are two ways to gain presence on the web:

>> **Search engine optimization (SEO):** The goal for every agent should be to have a website that is optimized for search engines. The value of being ranked highly in search engines continues to grow. SEO means that your website, because of its design, keywords, and links, comes up higher on the list when someone does a search for real estate in your area. Because you have higher positioning, you're more likely to create traffic to your site and, in turn, leads.

Major search engines like Google, Yahoo!, and Bing represent about 90 percent of all Internet search traffic. If you aren't ranked with them, you won't be found *organically* (without paying them). You will have to invest marketing dollars on Facebook or pay-per-click campaigns. Most people don't go beyond the first page when they type in a particular search. If you're number one on a search engine, you can expect about 40 percent of searchers to click your link. If you're number two through number five, you can expect to share the next 40 percent. The rest go to the remainder of the first page. It pays to be number one. The next four ranked sites have to share the same traffic that the top-ranked site gets.

WARNING

A word of caution — before you run out and hire someone to implement SEO strategy for your website, be careful! SEO strategy is a tricky business. You need to make sure you're working with a reputable firm that stands behind its work. You also can't have the philosophy of once and done. Effective SEO strategy is never-ending. Everyone is fighting for that front-page position. It changes each day, so you have to work to maintain your ranking.

>> **Pay-per-click, not pay-per-prospect:** More and more agents are getting into pay-per-click advertising as an answer to their online marketing. Pay-per-click advertising on search engines and other sites can be effective, or it can be a bust. Most search engines feature pay-per-click areas on the right-hand side or top of the main organic search results. People bid for the spots on a pay-per-click basis, which can range from a few cents to a few dollars each. The truth is, only about 10 percent of searchers go to the pay-per-click section. The vast majority of people use a search engine to search a specific phrase and then select the top-ranked organic sites to click on.

REMEMBER

You're not paying per prospect but *per click.* A click doesn't mean you're going to get anything. Pay-per-click can be used effectively if you know the conversion numbers of your website, meaning you know how many people take a free report, sign up for your newsletter, ask for more information, identify themselves as a lead, or book an appointment with you after they get to the website. You have to watch the analytics of your site. Only use website hosting services that let you review your traffic. To make pay-per-click advertising profitable, you need to know your numbers, both online and through your standard sales process. Until then, you're only guessing whether it works and is profitable.

Using Technology to Market Yourself and Your Properties

The technology of marketing and lead generation is changing rapidly. Mixing old and new technologies to "get your name out there" is a solid choice. "I want to get my name out there" is code for "I want to build a brand and have people call and find me." As an agent, you'll never have an iconic brand like Coca-Cola or McDonald's. Nor do you have those companies' marketing budgets. Instead, you can find tools that are inexpensive and that your brokerage may already provide.

Call capture . . . still effective

With the explosion of technology in the past 20 years, many new lead-generation systems have come and gone. However, interactive voice response (IVR) systems have stood the test of time. They're an important source of leads for champion agents. This type of system, when employed correctly, can quickly become part of your lead generation strategy.

Technology that works

Interactive voice response, or call capture, is a system that captures the phone number of an inbound caller to a predetermined phone number. The phone number is usually a toll-free number, and because you're paying for the call, you have a right to the phone number.

Within the toll-free number are extensions that connect to voicemail messages where you can record messages that callers can access. You advertise your toll-free number everywhere you normally advertise and market. This includes such things as your mailings, website, classified ads, and FSBOs or expireds campaigns. The goal is to create lead traffic in your system so you can capture phone numbers to call. More people will access information about homes if they think they're doing it anonymously.

One of the reasons buyers and sellers increasingly use the Internet to find real estate information is that it enables them to be stealthy. The problem with stealthy prospects is that they're dismally hard to convert. You need to focus on creating leads that you can then transfer to a fundamental sales channel, and IVR is one of the best technologies available to remove the stealth barrier between you and your prospects.

REMEMBER

When potential prospects contact you, you're able, via the rules of the National Do Not Call Registry, to call them back within a 90-day inquiry period — even if the prospect is on the registry.

By using an IVR system and legally gaining access to some Do Not Call Registry numbers, you're combining a limited-access strategy with a high-probability prospect. You won't have much competition for the business, and you'll be working with a prospect who has a demonstrated need.

IVR strategies to use

To make IVR work to its full potential, employ these strategies:

» **Contact each and every person.** The biggest mistake agents make with IVR technology is not contacting all the people who called in. We get busy, and we fail to schedule the time to return a prospect's call. It's as if the prospect called the office inquiring about a property, the receptionist took a hand-written message, and you just didn't call them back. I doubt you would do that, but countless agents, every day, fail to call their IVR leads.

If you're driving everyone from your ads and signs to your IVR number, you're combining into one large pool of warm and cold leads most of the people who would otherwise have picked up the phone and called you directly. The only way to find those golden, high-probability leads is to call everyone who uses your IVR system. I required my buyer's agent to call them all — no matter what. I watched and monitored her progress in this area. I didn't want to lose the easy ones. They can get mixed in with the more challenging ones.

» **Ask to sell the prospect's home.** You must be careful not to focus solely on buyers who call in. Some buyers must to sell, as well. I've seen agents secure the relationship with a buyer but lose the buyer's listing because they forget to ask for it.

» **Cut your message short.** Another mistake agents make is leaving long, rambling messages about their properties. Many of the IVR systems charge by the minute. The longer your message, the more money you spend to create the lead, whose number is captured in the first few seconds. A ten-minute message only runs up your monthly service bill.

Text-back strategies

Smartphones have created a whole new arena for real estate agents to pursue marketing possibilities. With more than 68 percent of cell-phone users owning a smartphone, this market base is a solid audience for creating leads. Many smart-phone users have dropped their landline, so their cell-phone number is the main way to contact them. How can you get your hands (or fingertips) on that number? The answer is text-back technology.

Text-back technology — with services like DotSignal — is a true game changer. This technology is the next step up from IVR. Prospects get more than a recording of you describing a home. They instantly get pictures and information delivered to their smartphone. It gains them access to a broad array of information and images in seconds. And, most importantly, you get what you want . . . the Holy Grail . . . their cell-phone number.

Using text-back technology enables you to capture leads. If you send prospects to your website, you may capture leads if they fill out your registration form. But with text-back technology you instantly have their phone number . . . boom!

TIP

If you want to see text-back technology in action, send a text to 35620 that says "Dummies" in the body of the text. In seconds you'll get information and pictures on a property just as a buyer would. You can see how powerful this type of service is in generating leads.

Some systems give you the ability to blast, as well. *Blast* is the techy term for sending the same message to multiple recipients at once. Let's say you have ten text leads on 123 Magnolia Way. You haven't sold it yet but have gotten the seller to reduce the price. You can craft a quick text message about the reduction and blast that out to all ten of your text leads on that property with a few keystrokes. You're getting a ten-to-one return. You also aren't wearing your fingers out on your phone to craft it. This can all be done with your computer or tablet, as well. It's a true game changer.

Targeting Your Marketing Message

Just as important as where you put your marketing dollars is how strong your message is. Agents turn off on the wrong marketing road when they try to take communication shortcuts by blitzing the market with their ad messages. This route leads to a dead end for two reasons:

>> You don't have the budget of a major national corporation, so you can't compete well in the mass-media environment.

>> Your prospective customer is already drowning in marketing messages. Simply lobbing another ad missile into the general market arena is hardly the way to target the person you're trying to reach.

WARNING

Because of the successful efforts of media salespeople, agents get roped into spending huge sums of money on image- or brand-building marketing campaigns that reach large, untargeted groups of consumers and that produce zero sales results. You have to establish a name and presence before this type of marketing works.

Agents at the top of their games may want to reinforce their dominant market positions and enhance their strong reputations by shifting some of their marketing dollars into image advertising. But if you're an agent just beginning to ascend the ladder of real estate success, image advertising isn't what you need. At this point in your career, you need to reach highly targeted prospects with messages about specific offerings that align perfectly with their interests and needs.

TIP

As you plan your marketing communications, think in terms of who, what, and why: Marketing communications is anything that you mail or email to the general public, your sphere of influence, or current and past clients. You must have a plan and an objective before you slap on that stamp or click Send.

>> **Who** is your target audience?

>> **What** are you offering to your target audience?

>> **Why** is the product you're offering a good fit for the wants, needs, and purchase abilities of your target audience?

In this section, I help you target your marketing audience, define your product, and determine the position your product fills in the marketplace.

Defining your target audience

Before you can choose how you're going to communicate your message and what you're going to say, you need to know who you're trying to talk to.

WARNING

The single biggest mistake in advertising — not just real estate advertising, but in all advertising — is that marketers create ads without a clear concept of the people they're trying to influence. As a result, they use the wrong media, say the wrong things, and fail to inspire the right outcome.

Before you risk a similar mistake, begin by answering these questions:

>> **Who are you trying to reach with this particular message?** Be specific: What age are your target prospects? How much money do they make? Where do members of this group currently live?

>> **Will this message be going to people you know?** If so, it can (and should) be more personal than an ad reaching brand-new prospects. People who already know you will most likely be the ones to consider doing business with you. Move them toward action by stressing your results and professional credentials while also conveying the benefits and features of the offer you're presenting.

>> **Is this marketing message targeted to specific buyer groups, such as first-time home buyers, empty nesters, second-home purchasers, or**

investors? If so, you need to focus your message toward the interests, needs, and motivations of that specific group.

» **Is the market for this message comprised largely of consumers in a specific age group or generational demographic?** If so, decide whether the offering you're promoting is of primary interest to one of the following groups of consumers:

- The Silent generation, born between 1925 and 1945

- Baby Boomers, born after World War II between 1946 and 1964

- The post-Baby Boom generation, born between 1965 and 1979, called Generation X

- People born between 1980 and 2000, called Generation Y or Millennials

REMEMBER

Prospects in the older generations still remember the Great Depression, World War II, JFK's assassination, the first moon landing, and Watergate. Younger audiences have never known a world without MTV, cell phones, and the Internet. Obviously, you should develop different messages and use different media approaches to reach each group.

TIP

The National Association of Realtors (www.realtor.org) and most of the large real estate companies have conducted extensive research to define how prospects in each of the various generational groups relate to real estate marketing, sales, and servicing. Training courses on this topic are ongoing. Watch for one, enroll, and invest a few dollars and a few hours to refine the strategies and tactics you use with consumers in each of these generational age groups.

Positioning your offering

In today's cluttered marketing environment, consumers are trained to tune out messages that don't seem to address their real and unfulfilled wants and needs. In other words, if your message doesn't clearly deliver a solution to your prospect's exact problem — if it doesn't position itself into an open slot in your prospect's mind — then your efforts, dollars, and time will go down the marketing drain.

Positioning is the marketing art of knowing what available space or position you and your offering fill in the market and then getting that message to exactly the people who want what you're offering.

TIP

By first figuring out the position your offering fills, you can easily decide who you want to talk to, what you want to say, and what marketing vehicles — from advertising to direct mail to online to personal calls — you need to use to reach the people you're targeting.

Positioning the property you're selling

Understanding your product position can make the difference between reaching your prospect and not, between motivating interest and action and not, and between making a sale and not.

REMEMBER

In real estate, price is the cornerstone of positioning. In my experience, 85 percent of your marketing strategy is set during the listing presentation when you and the seller agree on the right price and, therefore, the right market position for their home.

After you've worked with a seller to agree on the right listing price, your marketing strategy unfolds naturally following these steps:

>> Creating a description of the home's likely buyer

>> Listing the home's benefits and the reasons why likely buyers won't want to let the home go to anyone else

>> Selecting media channels or communications approaches that are most apt to get your marketing message in front of your target audience of likely buyers

USING POSITIONING TO YOUR COMPETITIVE SALES ADVANTAGE

Take time to look inside some of the other homes that compete for the same product position as your listing in terms of price and location. See how their features and benefits compare. Especially when handling ad and sign calls, this comparative information is valuable in two ways:

- By expressing with certainty your listing's benefits compared to the benefits of other available properties, you convince callers that they must see and consider the home.

- By offering information on other homes in addition to the one you've listed, you increase the odds of converting callers into buyer clients by establishing yourself as a skilled agent and valuable home-buying resource.

Knowing your product position and the nature of your likely buyer puts you in a better position to select the right media vehicles to carry your message to your market. Consider the following generalities in your planning:

>> **One segment of these buyers that is tech savvy is the first-time-buyer category.** Young buyers may have limited funds, but they spend those funds on gadgetry. They may be eating macaroni and cheese morning, noon, and night, but they have the latest smartphone.

>> **If you're marketing a home in the mid-price range, you can be fairly confident that your prospects are somewhat Internet savvy.** Studies show that more than 90 percent of middle-income home shoppers have Internet access and that most make the Internet their home-shopping starting point. To reach this audience, an effective Internet marketing strategy is essential.

>> **If you're marketing a high-priced home, one-to-one communications may be the most effective tactic.** Sometimes because of time constraints these buyers are using technology effectively but aren't on the cutting edge. In some cases they have people who do that for them. With one-of-a-kind, top-priced properties, you may find that mailing a high-quality brochure to carefully selected prospects nets greater success then your Internet marketing. Buyers for a property in this market position are likely too busy to spend hours on the Internet poring through properties. Additionally, many are connected with agents, so your other approach may be to market to agents directly.

Product positioning only works if the home you're selling is priced appropriately. If you give in to a seller's desire to set an unreasonably high listing price, your marketing task is vastly more difficult because

>> **You'll be forced to market to the wrong audience.** In order to reach buyers who can afford the price the seller is asking, you'll be talking to people seeking a higher-level home than the property you're offering.

>> **Your product will lose in competitive comparisons.** It won't take long for buyers to realize that the home you're offering is inferior to others they can buy with the same amount of money.

When you list an overpriced property, you have only two hopes for success: that the marketplace will heat up dramatically and lead to escalating prices, which brings your listing price in line with others, or that your seller will agree to a rapid price reduction.

Positioning yourself

Contrary to the opinions of consumers and a good many agents, not all agents offer the same or even similar services. It's safe to say that all agents work to bring real estate transactions to successful closings, but from there the differences in approach, style, and effectiveness vary wildly.

REMEMBER

As the owner of a real estate business, you must help prospects and clients realize the unique and beneficial position you hold in the marketplace. People need to know clearly why they should hire you. As you communicate your position through your marketing efforts, remember these three points:

>> **Tell and remind people that you're in the real estate business.** After your business achieves a high level of success, people will contact you based on your reputation. As a newer agent, however, you must notify everyone you know that you're in real estate sales, and then you must keep reminding them at regular intervals.

>> **Say and prove that you're good at what you do.** In a service business where all choices cost basically the same, as is the case in real estate sales, agents must differentiate themselves based on the expertise and service quality they provide. Client success stories, references from past clients, presentation of statistical advantages, results of satisfaction surveys, and glowing testimonials break you free from the crowd.

>> **Remind consumers that their choice of agent matters.** Agents need to band together to get this message into the minds of all real estate buyers and sellers. Agents as a whole haven't convinced clients that the right agent makes a difference in terms of down payment, sale price, net equity at closing, ease of transaction, level of satisfaction, after-sale service, and countless other benefits. Make it your job to convey to the public that the right agent makes a difference and that you're the best agent to make a difference in their deal.

Creating and Placing High-Impact Ads

When you're marketing, whether offline or online, the copy you write creates a powerful connection and engagement. You want prospects to experience the property. This section covers all the ins and outs of ad placement, paying special attention to what to say, where to say it, and how to achieve action.

Emphasizing benefits versus features

A large kitchen, spacious backyard, three-car garage, and air conditioning are all descriptions of features. Not one of these descriptions tells buyers what's in it for them. Not one conveys a benefit that the buyer gets from the feature. However, these terms fill most real estate marketing communications.

TIP

Add impact to your marketing by converting features to benefits:

>> Instead of simply announcing the feature of a three-car garage, advertise a three-bay garage with abundant storage space. Note in the ad that this feature makes a rental storage unit (with the accompanying $750 annual fee) a thing of the past and provides a workshop where the owner can fix kids' bikes and perfect shop skills.

>> Translate the feature of air conditioning into the benefits of comfort, coolness, and the restful feeling that results from a good night's sleep in an air-conditioned home.

Staying legal

Whether you're using offline or online strategies, certain words and phrases can land you in hot water. In marketing properties, agents can run into trouble by using terms or descriptive language that violates the Federal Fair Housing Act that governs the sale or rental of properties to individuals. These laws fall under the jurisdiction of the U.S. Department of Housing and Urban Development (HUD), which is serious about the ethical and honest treatment of all real estate consumers.

REMEMBER

The fair housing anti-discrimination stance applies to all public communications, including advertising. All the text on websites, in newspaper and magazine ads, on flyers, and in other printed materials must adhere to HUD guidelines.

WARNING

Following are a few words and phrases, often used in everyday conversations and considered normal real estate jargon, that can't be used in print advertising. The moment these terms appear in printed marketing materials, the ad is in violation of federal law:

>> Able-bodied

>> Adult community

>> Adult living

>> Bachelor pad

- Churches nearby
- Couple
- Couples only
- Empty nesters
- Ethnic references
- Families
- Newlyweds
- Traditional neighborhood

TIP

Ask your broker for a list of the prohibited words. However, when in doubt, the safest advice is to restrict ad copy to a description of the property for sale, while steering far clear of any descriptions of the type of people you think would be good buyers.

WARNING

Discrimination in housing because of race or color, national origin, religion, sex, family status, or handicap is illegal for both real estate agents and sellers and carries stiff penalties and fines. If you think a seller is discriminating, run, don't walk, away. For complete information, visit the Fair Housing website at `www.fairhousinglaw.org`.

Choosing the right media outlets

REMEMBER

You can create the most extraordinary marketing possible, but if it reaches the eyes or ears of people who aren't interested in or capable of buying your offering, your efforts are wasted. That's why media selection is so essential to effective real estate marketing.

For example, suppose you have a listing for a home that has specially built wheelchair access and an elevator and is on a golf course. You'll find very few people out there who are golfers, who have the need for wheelchair accessibility, and who have the assets required to buy a home with an elevator. If you place your marketing through media outlets that predominantly reach 20-somethings who are starting new families, you can bank on little to no response to your efforts.

On the other hand, if you place your marketing in golf publications, or if the golf course is private and you advertise in the monthly newsletter or send direct mailers to members, your marketing messages immediately reach the prospects in your target audience. You can buy a list of golf enthusiasts in your area . . . in our information age, you can find lists for everything and everyone. Even better, if you discover a magazine with a good many golfers with disabilities among its subscribers, you can safely bet your advertising dollars on the publication to serve as an ideal vehicle for sharing the targeted benefits of your listed property with the perfect target audience for this home.

TIP

The key to effective media placements is knowing the following:

>> **The profile of the target prospect you're trying to reach,** including the prospect's geographic location, demographic facts (which includes age, gender, ethnicity, income level, education level, marital status, household size, and more), and lifestyle characteristics, which includes personal interests and activities, behavioral patterns, and beliefs.

>> **How well the media vehicle you're considering reaches your target audience.** If you're targeting families with young children and income levels of $75,000 or more, ask the media representative what percentage of the publication's audience matches that description. The answer can help you determine whether an ad in that publication will be effective.

Converting ad interest to action

Your marketing needs to include a *response mechanism*, which is a fancy way of saying that you need to tell people what to do next and how to do it. Every single communication — whether through a Craigslist ad, pay-per-click campaign, mailer, website contact, open house, or any other outreach effort — needs to include a call to action that motivates prospects to take the next step. One call to action is having prospects give you contact information.

Enhancing Exposure via Virtual Tours

The term *virtual tour* applies to either a video presentation or a series of digital pictures "stitched" together to create a 360-degree panoramic view of the living space of a home.

With a virtual tour, a prospect in Nome, Alaska, can go online to experience the feeling of being inside a home in Palm Desert, California.

When the idea of virtual tours was introduced about 15 years ago, it was billed as the home-buying approach of the future. Technology forecasters said prospects would use virtual-tour capabilities to view their selected home and then simply click to make the purchase. Obviously, the sales predictions were wildly off course, but the popularity of virtual tours as a marketing device took off nonetheless.

At a time when consumers are demanding more information, more pictures, and greater ease of access, virtual tours are the fastest-growing innovation in real estate marketing. Studies of online home shoppers show that homes accompanied by virtual tours receive more hits, higher page views, and longer view times per page than homes featured in only a few grainy pictures. Virtual tours help your property get noticed.

WARNING

Be sure your listing is ready to show and that it competes well in its competitive environment before posting a virtual tour, or the tour can backfire on you and drive interest away. If your listing pales in comparison to competitive offerings, you won't get anyone into the home. Flip to Chapter 13 for advice on how to get a listing ready for showing.

Producing a virtual tour

WARNING

Whether your tour takes the form of video or stitched-together digital photos, my advice is "don't try this at home" unless you're willing to invest in some sophisticated equipment and training. Either way, consider this advice:

>> **Be prepared to invest some money.** You can piece together provided photos for practically nothing, but to produce a true virtual tour with a 360-degree visual presentation, you need to spend some upfront funds to purchase equipment and software if you plan on producing your own. Or if you can, hire a professional photographer to do the work for you.

>> **To create your own video tours, you need the right equipment.** If you don't already have video equipment, you will need a quality camera, a tripod with a ball head, special lenses, and software. Some retailers sell kits that come with everything you'll need. IPIX is the industry leader and is the provider of equipment used by the majority of professional producers of 360-degree tours.

After the virtual tour is over, put it to work. Feature it online, show it in your CMA presentations, use it when working with out-of-area buyers, and include it in the portfolio you use to present yourself to prospects and FSBO sellers.

Important questions to ask

Some agents are quick to spend money, even if they don't have a plan or set of objectives in place. Along the same lines, if not approached properly, virtual tours can cause agents to spend hundreds of dollars, without much return, for each of their listings. Each time you produce a tour, begin by answering these questions:

>> **What is your objective for the tour?** Will you use it to generate leads, close appointments, build your image as a real estate agent, or some other purpose?

>> **Who is your target audience?** Will the tour be shown primarily to low-end, mid-range, or high-end home buyers? The answer helps you match the presentation to audience expectations and arrive at your budget.

>> **What type of tour do you want to produce?** Choose either 360-degree video or digital photos.

>> **How much time and effort can you and your staff invest in producing and maintaining the tour?** Be aware that to produce your own 360-degree video tours, you'll need at least one in-house camera expert and one person to upload, create, and maintain the tours.

>> **Will you hire a professional company?** If so, be prepared to interview firms and compare resources based on company costs, the caliber of solutions the company provides, the way its services match your needs and expectations, and how easy the employees are to work with.

Mistakes to avoid

WARNING

The biggest mistake is to try to create virtual tours on the cheap. If you attempt to create your own virtual tours, chances are good that they, and by association you, will look cheap. They'll look cheap to potential buyers, potential sellers, and potential leads and prospects who see your work online from around the world.

REMEMBER

The quality of the production is interpreted as an indication of the quality of your character and your service. Aim high.

Resources to gather

Whether you're planning to do it yourself or hire professionals, the resources available are practically countless. Recently, I searched for the term "virtual tour" with an online search engine, and almost 97 million hits popped up.

TIP

Following are a few websites you may want to consider:

>> **FlyInside.com (www.flyinside.com):** This site provides a free digital slide show with audio capability. It delivers a pretty nice but basic product. It doesn't have enough bells and whistles for use with million-dollar homes.

>> **RTV (www.realtourvision.com):** You'll need your own equipment for this option, but it does offer a 360-degree solution. Options include their software or they can connect you with a local professional photographer and virtual tour provider.

>> **Paradym** (`www.paradym.com`): This company is probably the largest player in the virtual tour industry. For a reasonable upfront fee and monthly rate, this company produces a digital slide show with your photos "stitched" together to simulate a 360-degree view. It also includes dozens of marketing tools built into their system.

Leading prospects to your virtual tour

To drive prospects to your virtual tour, use these promotional channels:

>> When you produce outside-the-home flyers, include your web address and virtual tour information.

>> Include a virtual tour link on the MLS.

>> Arrange links or connectors from other sites that attract visitors who match your target prospect profile. This approach is especially effective in hot resort market areas where visitors are looking for in-depth regional information.

>> Feature the site address for your virtual tour in your print ads. Just be sure that your tour doesn't reveal the home address. Your aim is to generate interest so that prospects call you for additional information and home access.

>> Post to social media sites like Facebook, YouTube, Instagram, Twitter, and LinkedIn.

TIP

>> Use postcards as direct mailers to promote both the property and the virtual tour. Don't send a letter that may or may not be opened. Send a postcard that automatically makes an immediate visual impression.

Chapter **15**

Negotiating the Contract and Closing the Deal

truly believe that the secrets to creating true value for your clients are contained in this chapter. Most sellers think an agent's real work involves finding the right buyer, and most buyers think an agent's real work involves finding the right house to buy. In fact, the real work involves bringing the deal to a successful close, and that's what this chapter is all about.

Real estate consumers' wants are beginning to shift. In a recent National Association of Realtors (NAR) survey, only 50 percent of buyers reported that "help finding the right home to purchase" was the top service they wanted from an agent. That number was more than 65 percent in previous years.

Many buyers instead want the following: 11 percent most want help with price negotiations, and another 12 percent most want help with term negotiations. *Terms* include all other options besides the sale price, such as possession, condition, repairs, and the inclusion of personal property. When you combine the two, 23 percent of buyers cite negotiating skills or services as the top thing they want from real estate agents.

The public doesn't see the gyrations that go into reaching a contract agreement and closing a deal, but if the negotiation step goes awry, no other step in the real estate sales process matters. Buyers and sellers may feel the emotions during the negotiations, but everything else happens behind the curtain.

The process of negotiating a deal involves fiduciary responsibility, market knowledge, client relations, and enormous skill and tact. Sometimes success means your client is the one selected over other interested parties to buy a particular home. Sometimes success results in a negotiated reduction in a home's sale price. Always, success reflects the realities of the market and the best terms and conditions the buyers and sellers can achieve.

This chapter lays out the rules of negotiating, starting with knowing all there is to know about the market environment so you can convince your client to accept terms and conditions you believe are the best to be had at the present time, based on current market conditions. Often that persuasion needs to be administered to a less-than-enthusiastic client who is hoping for a better outcome. The following pages help you prepare for the task.

Preparing for the Task Ahead

TIP

At the listing presentation or buyer interview consultation, after you've gained commitment from the client through a signature on the contract, take a few minutes to outline the next steps. Cover the following two points:

>> Briefly describe how you'll work to represent your clients' interests when it comes to negotiating and closing their transaction. I use this final discussion to explain that my typical approach is to handle negotiations during an appointment in my office. Here are three ways you can conduct the meeting:

- Face-to-face meetings have advantages. They enable you to read the parties' full body language. Frequently I notice a disconnect between what the parties say and what their body language says.

- As an alternative, I provide documents to each party prior to an online meeting, during which we review the documents. Online meeting platforms are key tools the real estate industry needs to use more. Skype and Google+ are two options. I prefer a more robust platform like GoToMeeting (www.gotomeeting.com), WebEx (www.webex.com), or Zoom (www.zoom.us) type of platform because you can control what each party is looking at. The easiest and best, in my opinion, is Zoom.

- You can use a phone approach if necessary and then scan and send documents.

The question of which strategy to use is about efficiency versus effectiveness. While the technology creates significant efficiency for you and your clients, you lose some of the effectiveness that comes from face-to-face meetings. I find these three approaches to be most convenient for my clients and most time-efficient for me and for them. By explaining my process in advance, my clients know exactly what to expect. You can also uncover any potential technology-challenged clients in advance.

>> Advise your seller clients to expect that most initial offers will come in below the asking price. I always tell my clients that they should expect a below-list price offer, and that I rarely see a transaction that doesn't require a counteroffer. This adjusts expectations and averts disappointment.

Your objective is to set the stage for the negotiations that lie ahead. Preparing your client for what's in store is an imperative step that saves you time, emotion, and energy in the future. The truth is, negotiation is not a one-time event. There is an ongoing dialogue of negotiation at least through the home inspection contingency removal.

The right tone

Great real estate agents set an optimistic tone and create an expectation that all parties will work together to achieve a negotiated win/win outcome. This means that the sellers and buyers both need to feel as if they won in the final transaction. The agents for both parties need to feel they won, as well, not just in terms of commissions earned but also in terms of earning the satisfaction of their clients.

When a marketplace becomes unbalanced, it's harder for all parties to feel satisfied. Most of North America has experienced an unbalanced real estate environment during the past few years. The buyers' marketplace has left sellers feeling that they're at an advantage in sales transactions. Sellers have had the upper hand recently but it's only a matter of time before the market moves toward the buyer.

REMEMBER

One of your jobs throughout the transaction is to serve as a calming influence. When emotions run high — as they are sure to do — be the one to remain focused on the outcome and settle down the buyer, seller, and other real estate agents.

Take the approach followed by the best emergency-room doctors. They serve as a calming influence by displaying confidence and skill while reassuring their patients and other medical staff that everything is under good control. If the emergency room doctor flies into a frenzy, the entire clinical setting is likely to spin out of control on the tide of the unchecked emotion. The same is true in the final throes of a real estate transaction. Commit to yourself that you'll serve as the calming influence throughout the deal.

Keys to representing a seller

Sellers have plenty of reasons to be emotional during the final negotiation. They're undergoing change, making huge decisions, and dealing with a transaction that probably involves the largest investment they own. Your role in this environment, and the key to your success, is twofold: Be prepared and protect the seller at every step along the way.

Be prepared

TIP

By carefully preparing before you present a buyer's offer to your clients, you can shorten the meeting, craft a better counteroffer, keep sellers' emotions in check, and focus your clients on the next important steps. Follow this advice:

>> First and foremost, remain calm, no matter how high or low the initial offer.

>> Go through the buyers' offer carefully and note any key issues that need to be addressed.

>> Flag any contract points that merit your sellers' attention so you can easily reference them during the meeting. If you're emailing the document, also summarize the key points in the top of the email to which you attach the offer. This way your seller won't have to dig through every line of the contract. That's *your* job!

>> If your meeting will take place by online meeting or phone rather than in person, email the offer to the seller within minutes of your conversation. If your phone conference is set for 2 p.m., have the documents sent sometime between 1:30 and 1:45 p.m. You don't want the sellers to spend hours brooding if the price is low, and you certainly don't want them to call you with questions, concerns, and panic attacks half a dozen times prior to the scheduled phone conference. That can blow a hole a mile wide in your time-management strategy for the day.

Protect the sellers at all times

The worst thing that can happen to sellers is to have the transaction fall apart a few days before closing. By then, they're emotionally invested in another property. They've already made plans to move. They're excited about the future and then, wham, everything falls apart, and everyone — including you — loses market time, marketing momentum, and a considerable investment of time and money.

The biggest enemy of the seller is days on the market. If the property falls out of pending days before closing, when you place it back on the market to sell again, all those days it was not really for sale because it was pending still count. If the property sold right away, for example after three days on the market, and it fell apart 30 days later, when it comes back on the market it will show 33 days on the market . . . ouch!

In the aftermath of this kind of disastrous situation, I've had the chance to look at the contracts that were written, and I've seen examples that made me cringe. In most cases, the agent didn't protect the client, and all parties paid dearly for the mistake.

Even the most thorough approach results in a broken deal once in a while. But by taking these precautions, you can keep disasters to a bare minimum:

REMEMBER

>> Require prospective buyers to deposit enough earnest money to secure your clients' position. Set the earnest money high enough in your counteroffer to make it difficult for the buyers to purchase another home if they walk away from the deal after all contingent conditions are satisfied. You may be thinking that this advice conflicts with your objective to achieve a win/win outcome. In fact, it simply requires buyers to uphold their end of the deal or sacrifice their deposit. Remember, you're representing the sellers, and protecting your clients' interests is your fiduciary duty.

Not many buyers will walk away from a deal if an amount like $5,000 to $10,000 is at stake. Yet many agents allow initial deposits of as little as $1,000 or $2,000. The rationale is that buyers won't have the cash available to make a higher deposit, but if buyers need $15,000 to close in 30 days, depositing $5,000 to $10,000 upfront won't kill them.

>> If necessary, consider accepting part of the deposit in the form of a short-term note. Only do this if the buyers have no other way to increase the earnest money. If available cash is an issue, at least get a few thousand dollars deposited immediately and make arrangements to receive the balance within a few weeks, securing the latter portion with a note. Never secure the initial earnest money with a note for more than 24 hours. If you accept a note for the additional earnest money, be sure it's redeemed within a stipulated short period of time.

WARNING

Don't accept notes redeemable at closing. If the closing never happens, your seller can't redeem the note. It becomes a worthless piece of paper, because the transaction never closes and technically the note never comes due. Even legal action won't fix this agent mistake.

>> Another area of caution is financing. Require the buyers to provide proof of loan approval with no conditions. You want proof-positive that the buyers can and will perform within two weeks of acceptance of the offer. Lending institutions are notorious for writing loan-approval letters with conditions or weasel clauses that protect both the institution and the buyers. Make it clear on the counter offer that no contingencies or conditions will be acceptable after two weeks.

The prevailing rule in seller protection is to tighten the language every step of the way. Remember at all times that your job is to protect and secure the interests of your clients, the sellers. The broader the language of the contract, the greater the number of interpretable clauses — commonly known as "weasel clauses" — that make it into the transaction, each one endangering the level of security you provide your clients.

Keys to representing a buyer

The buyers' agent is responsible for crafting, presenting, writing a proper contract for, and prompting acceptance of a good offer. Follow these steps:

>> Your first step is to guide your clients toward a competitive offer. Perform at least a quick competitive market analysis, or CMA, to determine the value of the property. Among the factors you want to weigh are the home's current value based on the value of comparable properties, regional housing inventory levels, and the competitive nature of the current marketplace. Your findings help your clients arrive at a reasonable price decision and help you counsel them as they make a competitive offer.

>> After your clients have arrived at a competitive price to offer, your primary job as their representative is to properly prepare the contract you present on their behalf to the sellers. Your goal must be to protect your clients by writing terms and conditions that convey their intentions and meet their goals.

For most people, a home purchase represents the largest investment they make, the biggest purchase in their lives, and the greatest and longest-lasting debt they assume. The purchase agreement you write must protect them by addressing every issue — the price being offered, the items to be included in the purchase price, the amount to be deposited, the closing date, the date the offer becomes null and void, and any condition that accompanies the offer, including contingencies based on the outcome of inspections, approval of financing, and personal property transferring with the sale.

Work with your clients to understand all the terms and conditions that must be covered in the contract.

» When you're ready to present to the sellers, present the offer and your buyers as the best in the marketplace. Presenting the offer favorably to the sellers can mean the difference between your clients or other bidders buying the house. The more strongly you position your buyers by presenting their financial capacity, superior commitment, motivation, and even a human connection, the more you swing the negotiation in favor of your clients. The stronger the loan-commitment documents provided by the lender — preferably showing a valid loan approval and a commitment with no conditions — the more cashlike your buyers' offer will seem.

TIP

For some sellers, a human connection is the tipping point in choosing one set of buyers over another. For example, an offer from a family the sellers imagine will re-create their cherished memories in the home may trump another offer that is absent of the human connection, even if the offer results in equal or even slightly less money.

EDUCATING BUYERS ON TRUE MARKET CONDITIONS

One of the keys to negotiating in the real estate industry is knowing the market and educating the client on its true conditions. Using a market trends report, you can set a reasonable expectation of success. For example, you can convey to buyers that for the home they desire, others like it are selling for 97 percent of the asking price, and the market has only 2.4 months of inventory. Those numbers indicate a diminished leverage position for buyers.

Buyers who think they can "steal" a home in an environment of low inventory and high list-to-sale price ratios are frustrated easily when sellers yawn at their offers. This can cause frustration that is directed at you, the agent. The buyers may think your negotiating skills have failed, when really the marketplace just isn't in the buyers' favor.

The good news you have to convey is that based on 2.4 months of inventory and a 97 percent list-to-sale price ratio, the marketplace will continue to appreciate because there is not enough supply to meet demand. That's guaranteed to cause price increases.

Advice for partnering with the other agent

You and the other agent in the transaction are obligated to cooperate with each other; that's why you're called co-op brokers. At the same time, you're both obligated to represent the interests of your own clients, which works wonderfully when you both seek a win/win outcome but which is troublesome when the other agent comes to the deal with a we win/you lose mentality.

Before talking with the other agent at length, I suggest you do some homework. I always made it a point to learn in advance about the agent I'd be dealing with. Unless I already knew the agent personally, my staff would conduct some research. They'd start at the MLS computer, where they'd look at the number of listings and sales the agent had completed during the past few years. Also, you could quickly check Zillow (www.zillow.com) for reviews and production/sales in the last year and their present listing inventory. This also provides an indication of the agent's experience, which enables you to understand the role you might play in the negotiation. Are you likely to share power equally if the other agent is similar in experience?

TIP

When you're ready to talk with the other agent, cover these points:

>> Explain your desire to create a win/win transaction. Say that you'll be relying on the other agent to create a win for both the buyers and sellers, and that you intend to do the same. Some agents believe their job is to achieve a win only for their own clients. This discussion helps you spot these people.

>> If you're the listing agent, let the other agent know that the home is competitively priced — that it's at fair market value with no padding in the asking price. If your clients then counter a low offer at full price or close to it, the response won't be a surprise to the agent or prospective buyers.

>> If you reach a snag, challenge, or impasse with the other agent or with the agent's clients, test the situation by asking one of these questions:

"If you were representing my clients, would you counsel them to accept this offer?"

"If you were in my shoes, would you want your clients to accept these terms and conditions?"

If the answer is yes, then ask "Why?" or "How would you sell this to my clients if you were in my shoes?"

If the agent can't give you an answer, the silence will let you know that they know their offer is unreasonable.

If they can defend their position with cogent arguments, you know you must convince your client of the validity of the counteroffer.

BECOME YOUR OWN "OTHER AGENT"

The easiest other agent to work with is yourself. You know you. You know you want win/win outcomes. You know whether your listing price has padding or whether your purchase offer has room for negotiation. You know how you work and that your skills are up to the task. You probably know it's easier for you to work with you than with any other agent.

Make your real estate sales life easier by selling more of your own listings. Represent both the buyers and sellers and avoid the challenges of working with another agent to complete the transaction.

The biggest bonus: You don't have to split fees and will earn more for the sale.

Advancing or Accepting an Offer

When representing sellers, I always requested that offers be scanned and emailed rather than letting the buyers' agent personally present the offer to my clients. I was one of the first agents in the country to take this approach. Today it is commonplace. It gives the agent and the sellers time to consider the offer before responding to it.

That personal offer presentation has all but disappeared in real estate. It was common practice in the past. Most buyers' agents now scan in their offers and hope for the best, but that method doesn't truly represent your buyers or position them as the best buyers. I realize that listing agents want fast, easy, and effective offers, but that may not be best for your buyers. That's why using an online platform could be effective in time savings, but also buyer positioning.

More than 55 percent of communication is visual, so it's much harder to communicate when you can't see the agent or sellers in person. Instead, you simply have to be a better writer. Your case is made with words on the page. Hopefully you can get the other agent to show these words to the sellers. You may share a little bit of information about the buyers you represent, what they like about the home, and anything that creates a favorable connection between the sellers and your buyer. That also means you have to be cautious to not give away too much in their level of interest.

You can also express this information with a video that you send to the agent. This establishes you as a cutting edge, professional, knowledgeable agent. It also lets you advocate for your client with more than just words on the page.

Presenting a buyer's low offer

When you extend an offer that is under the asking price, be prepared to present offsetting benefits in an effort to make the offer attractive and valuable to the sellers. Alternate redeeming qualities include:

>> Solid earnest money

>> Buyers with impeccable credit

>> Buyers with good, solid employment history

>> Buyers with ample funds and a low loan-to-value ratio

>> Buyers with the flexibility to close quickly or to wait as long as 90 days

>> Explain how the buyers arrived at their offer price. Show current comps to validate their thinking. Perhaps the property was listed months ago and the market environment has changed considerably in the meantime. Presenting a current market analysis can help justify and win acceptance of the offer.

>> If appropriate, explain that the buyers have another home in mind, saying something like, "They wanted to try to work with you first."

>> If the offer is the highest one the buyers can make, then express that fact, saying something like, "The buyers would really love the home, but they understand if there isn't an opportunity for a win for everyone." This kind of statement defuses emotions before they arise.

Above all, when presenting a low price, convey that the offer is based on a realistic assessment of the market environment or the buyers' capability, not a personal reaction to the sellers or their home.

Receiving a buyer's low offer

If you did your job way back at the conclusion of the listing presentation, your sellers will be well aware of the likelihood of a low offer. When one comes in, here's what to do:

>> Call the buyers' agent to learn more about the buyers. Ask whether they have the funds to close, whether they've selected a lending institution, and where they are in regards to securing a loan. Learn whether they're just starting and haven't even met with a lender yet, or whether they have loan approval and are just working to find the right house.

>> Probing for the length of time they have been searching gives you some insider information. If they have been searching for some time, they are either very selective, they missed out on a few properties, or yours is just the right home. Try to determine from the other agent which of these might be the case.

>> If the buyers have already initiated the loan process, ask the agent what loan amount the buyers have been approved for.

TIP

- You may learn that the buyers can obtain a loan higher than the amount shown on their offer contract. This alerts you to the fact that they're qualified to pay more but are choosing not to. Your job then is to demonstrate that the home has a higher value than the price offered.

- If you learn that the buyers have been approved for exactly the loan amount listed on the contract, ask, "Is this the maximum they qualify for?" If they qualify for more, you want to know that fact.

>> If the agent can't or won't provide the loan answers you need, try presenting the same questions to the mortgage originators the buyers are working with. Elsewhere in this chapter, I give advice for working with lending institutions and other partners in the transaction.

Taking the insult out of an insulting offer

REMEMBER

When you're representing the sellers in a transaction, the first step toward taking the sting out of a low offer is assuring your clients that the offer is financial, not personal. Most likely the prospective buyers don't know your sellers or your sellers' family. They may not even know the rationale behind the number they presented. They may have relied on poor counsel, too much counsel, or an unskilled agent, in which case a well-presented counteroffer is in order.

On the flip side, the sellers' house may be overpriced, either because the sellers insisted on a high price or because the market environment changed between when the home was listed and when the offer arrived. If a home is radically overpriced, a fair offer can look insulting when it really isn't.

TIP

If your sellers' home is overpriced, you must get them to focus on the gap between the low offer and fair market value, not the difference between fair market value and their inflated listing price. Likely you'll remove tens of thousands of dollars of "insult" through this calculation alone. If that doesn't work, ask the cooperating agent to share the burden by getting them to write an explanation of the rationale behind their offer.

A good agent won't write an insulting offer. I was asked many times to write ridiculously low offers. I consistently refused to represent those, saying they were equivalent to fishing expeditions. One client chastised me, saying I was required by law to write whatever she wanted to offer. I corrected her misinterpretation of my responsibility. Agents are required by law in most states to present all offers they write, but nothing forces agents to write garbage that is embarrassing to present, wasteful of their time, and costly to their reputations.

Getting beyond emotion

People get emotional during the closing for a number of reasons. For one thing, a lot of money is at stake. For another, both parties are anxious to get the deal done, and time is ticking away. Third, home inspections and low-price offers reveal opinions about a home's value that can feel jarring to sellers who have viewed the home with pride and joy for a number of years.

The only antidote to an emotional uprising is a pragmatic focus on the goals the parties are trying to achieve and a renewed commitment to finding common ground and getting the deal done.

A few years ago, my father sold the family home I grew up in. My mother had died six months earlier, and he wanted to start a new life.

Fortunately, I didn't represent him in the sale, but he did call to discuss an offer he'd received. I took his call one night, and we talked for 45 minutes while I was driving through mountain passes on my way to a speaking engagement in Vail, Colorado. (FYI, I would never talk with anyone but my dad for 45 minutes about a contract.)

He was such a typical seller! His big issue was the sale price. I asked him the question I often pose to get to the core of what's affecting a negotiation: "Dad, is the reason you want this price for the house based on your ego, or do you really need the money?" There was silence on the other end of the phone. Of course, I knew he didn't need the $20,000 he was so emotional about.

I realize this was bold, but it was the right thing to say in this situation. As you advance your career, sometimes you will find that a seller's or buyer's ego is driving their decisions, not the money. From that point, he was able to find common ground with the buyers and get the home sold.

When you hit a buyer-seller impasse, find a way to ask: Is this about ego or income? Do they want the bragging rights that come with a high price, or do they need the money? Usually, you'll bring your client back down to earth in a hurry. You're asking, in essence, what are you really fighting for?

Turning concessions into victories

Buyer offers are usually accompanied by home-inspection conditions that require sellers to make concessions before the deal is closed. Usually these concessions take the form of repairs that the sellers need to make before the buyers take possession. The presentation of repair concessions is one of the toughest steps in the negotiation process. Buyers often use the home-inspection step to wring a bit more value out of their offer. Sellers, who feel they already gave at the office when they accepted the price offer, aren't in the mood to give more.

No matter whether you're representing the buyers or sellers, bring the focus down to the value of the requests. By itemizing the concessions and assigning value in terms of dollars, hassle factor, and time invested, you can maneuver a transaction to the end. Follow these steps:

>> If the list has ten items, select the six or seven easiest, least-expensive issues to act upon. By dealing with more than half the requested items, you demonstrate your clients' goodwill effort to meet the other party more than halfway.

>> Call the other agent and say, "I doubt I can be persuasive enough to get the sellers to handle all 10 requests. If your clients had to have a few of these concessions to keep the deal together, which ones would they be?" This strategy enables you to know which requests represent potential deal-killers.

>> Explain to the other agent that while you can't guarantee you'll get your sellers to agree, you'll see what you can do.

>> Focus the sellers on what they're gaining out of the deal. If they're pocketing an equity increase and the opportunity to open a new chapter in their lives, focus them on those facts. Urge them not to let $1,500 worth of repairs stand in the way of $300,000 cash in their pockets. Or, if they're moving to a terrific home in the perfect neighborhood for their family, focus them on that. Use a script like this:

> *"Mr. and Mrs. Buyer, we spent days and looked at more than 40 homes to find this one that you described as perfect. Do you really want to start that process over again?"*

To turn concessions into victories, focus your clients on what they're gaining rather than on what they're giving up.

Dealing with I win/you lose clients

Some clients, and some agents for that matter, only feel satisfied when they win and someone else loses.

The best way to handle I win/you lose situations is to avoid them. If you can't, then deal with them professionally, powerfully, and from a position of control. No matter what, don't back down. Most I win/you lose clients are perpetually testing the waters to see how much they can get away with.

I once took on an expired listing for a seller I knew had an I win/you lose personality. I thought I could overcome her tendencies, so I took the listing anyway. I got the price right and was confident I could sell and close quickly. What I didn't know was that I was dealing with what I call a toxic client.

I managed to sell her home to one of my own buyer clients in a reasonable time for full price and free rent back. She got a great deal. Then she called me three days before closing to inform me that she wouldn't close the transaction unless I cut my fee by $4,000.

I informed her that I understood her request but would not reduce my fee. I explained that she had the right not to sell. I indicated that the buyers probably would take legal action to force her to complete the sale if she didn't close the deal in a few days. I told her, "As your agent, I would advise you to close the sale as scheduled." Three days later she did what I expected her to do. She closed.

Closing the Deal

Most sellers and buyers think of the agreement as the tricky part of the transaction and the closing as the part they can take pretty much for granted. Agents know otherwise. As an agent, your work isn't done and your payment teeters in the balance until you successfully complete this final, challenging part of the real estate transaction.

The closing involves an army of people. Using a different analogy, you're like the conductor of an orchestra; control the instruments well and no wrong note will creep in.

Work diligently during the negotiating period to see that the loan, title work, and escrow or document preparation are handled by those on your own closing team.

Make it your objective to direct the business to companies and individuals you know will perform in a timely, professional manner. This assures your clients good service and fewer surprises and reduces the time you and your staff invest in closing the transaction.

Forming a closing team and working with the players

A good closing team can help you increase your prosperity by letting you efficiently wind up one deal and move on to the next. Following is the lineup of the players who make the closing a smooth process.

The loan officer

The loan officer holds a front-line position on your closing team. This is the person who secures the appraiser, verifies the deposit of funds, verifies employment, and, ideally, completes the loan package for the buyers within a few days of contract acceptance.

Make sure the loan officer on your team is a great salesperson backed by a team that is highly organized and able to push transactions through to a seamless close. A good loan officer can smooth out problems before you even hear about them, averting landmines and sparing you significant and time-consuming challenges.

Loan officers can add considerable value to your business even beyond the sales closing. After you form a relationship with a loan officer, you can work in concert to land clients. You can follow up on leads together. Or you can refer clients to each other, with both of you winning more business as a result of the relationship.

The home inspector

The home inspector is hired to evaluate the condition of the property, spot current or potential defects, and give guidance regarding the proper remedies.

WARNING

You want to work with home inspectors who are thorough and who fully disclose all defects and items in need of repair without throwing gasoline on potential problems. Beware of the home inspector who is an alarmist. Look instead for someone who resembles Joe Friday with his "just the facts, ma'am" approach.

You also want a home inspector who can quickly produce an easy-to-read report written in everyday, commonly understood language. If technical jargon is necessary, insist on plain-English translations. Nothing concerns buyers more than a problem they don't understand.

The appraiser

Because lending institutions often have the largest stake in a home — greater even than that of the borrowers — they hire appraisers to determine the value of the property.

TIP

The appraiser selection process is much different today than it was a few years ago. Banks and lending companies in the past could select the appraiser they wanted to use. Now appraisers are randomly assigned or put in rotation, so you may get assigned an appraiser who doesn't know the area well.

You must expect appraisal issues to come up periodically with transactions. You need to prepare for the possibility of an unfavorable appraisal.

Be sure to keep all your documentation on when you did the CMA, whether you represent the buyer or seller. You might need to show an appraiser comparables to increase value.

WARNING

Be aware that some appraisers have low-cost, limited-level memberships in the local MLS, and as a result some don't have lockbox keys. This saves them money but creates an inconvenience for agents on whom they have to rely for access to homes.

The escrow closer

An escrow closer is a neutral third party who coordinates the preparation and signing of documents, holds and distributes the funds, and records the documents and deeds. Some states are non-escrow states in which the real estate company provides these services or, in some states, an attorney prepares all the legal documents. Check with your broker to clarify the standard operating procedure in your area.

The escrow closing can also be associated with the title company. The title company researches the previous owners and searches for liens and encumbrances on the property. Most lenders require a title search to ensure that the title is clear before they issue a loan for a property. Lenders are in what's called first position. They take control if a buyer defaults on the loan.

Good escrow officers keep transactions on track for on-time closings. They also provide a second point of reassurance for your client, staying in close communication throughout the closing process, sharing updates that confirm things are going well, and underscoring what a great agent you are and how lucky they are to be working with you.

Avoiding derailment

Like a train, a transaction can get derailed at any point on the track. A closing can be hit by a clouded title, a home not appraising for its true value, a rapid change in interest rates, an undisclosed credit or income issue, or one of countless other unanticipated problems.

Choke points cause delays, and delays cause all kinds of problems for buyers, sellers, and agents. Moving plans get thrown into disarray. Interim housing or early-possession requests become necessary. Contingency plans need to be thrown together. Nerves get jangled. The resulting situation can be a nightmare, and a productivity killer, even for the most seasoned agent.

Most of the problems in closing transactions fall into three basic areas. Stay on the lookout for these problems and solutions to steer your transactions clear of as much trouble as possible:

1. **Documentation and verification:** Lenders need to assemble considerable paperwork and complete dozens of documents based on information submitted by the loan applicants. Then they need to verify all information for accuracy by checking the applicants' employment status, funds on deposit, and income level. The document preparation and information verification process takes time. Counsel your buyers that if they fail to submit the required information on a timely basis, or if they turn it in piecemeal, delays are certain to result.

TIP

2. **Repairs, repairs, repairs:** This is a choke point that good planning can avert. When you're representing the sellers, state clearly in writing that only lender-required repairs will be done. If you don't, you leave the sellers open to the risk that the buyers will come back with a laundry list of items.

A lender-required note usually limits repairs to structural, mechanical, or health and safety issues — with not a word about nicks in walls or non-matching doorknobs.

Also consider writing a dollar limit for repairs into the initial contract. The number isn't etched in stone, but it helps keep a lid on the potential amount for which your sellers are responsible. The buyers may still refuse to lift the home-inspection contingency until additional lender-required issues are dealt with, but the limit helps most of your sellers most of the time.

3. **Underwriting of the buyers' loan:** This is the stickiest of all closing choke points because the underwriter has complete power to approve the loan, approve the loan with additional conditions, or suspend the file until certain conditions are met, in which case the borrower starts the underwriting process all over again.

   Underwriters check to make sure the loan meets guidelines for debt ratio, loan-to-value ratio, credit score, employment history, and other qualifications. They also evaluate the loan based on whether it can be bundled with others in a big loan package that can be sold to Fannie Mae, Freddie Mac, or another entity that buys mortgages.

   Very few lending institutions hold their loans to maturity. Most write loans; realize profits through origination fees, document preparation fees, and margins on basis points; and then sell the loans within 30 to 60 days, recouping the loan amount to sell again as part of the next loan deal.

   If the underwriter approves a loan that can't be resold, the lending institution has to keep the loan in its portfolio. If that situation occurs too often and too many loans can't be resold, the lending institution runs out of money to loan, driving it out of business.

   Of all the choke points in a transaction, the underwriting process can cause the biggest delays. Expect that there will be times when underwriters slow things down with requests for second appraisals or additional documentation of value, especially if the home is in a high price range. After you clear the hurdle, the documents can be drawn up and sent to closing.

GETTING A CNE DESIGNATION

To really up your value to clients, consider going through a Certified Negotiating Expert course to get your CNE designation. This excellent course helps you understand strategy, raises your skills, and gives you a system to use when negotiating real estate situations.

The course is delivered all over the United States through local Boards of Realtors. With a CNE designation, you can market and position yourself to consumers who want an agent with top-notch negotiating skills.

5
Creating Ongoing Success in Real Estate Sales

IN THIS PART . . .

Check out how to build client relationships, develop client loyalty, deliver unbeatable service, and win client relationships that last a lifetime.

Discover how-to techniques and advice for generating the greatest return on the time you invest in your real estate career.

Chapter **16**

Keeping Clients for Life

Every businessperson wants to win clients for life — and there's good reason for that. It costs energy, time, and money to gain a prospect's awareness, win his attention, convince him of your benefits, and bring him into your business circle through an initial sale. If that first sale is the only sale you ever make to that client, then your sales investment has only a one-time payoff. But if that client keeps buying from you on a repeated basis — and refers others to you, as well — then your investment is amortized over numerous transactions and money-making opportunities.

The trick is to make yourself indispensible. Today's consumer has access to a broad array of real estate information. From an almost unlimited ability to search properties on websites such as agent sites, company sites, Zillow, Trulia, and Realtor.com, the public has gained a do-it-yourself mentality when it comes to real estate information. The traditional idea of using a real estate agent to "find our dream home" has shifted.

The do-it-yourself mentality has created a shift in referrals and repeat clients. Other factors contributing to that decline in referral-based business include economic shifts, job relocations, and a lack of equity that has caused many homeowners to get stuck with houses they must rent out rather than sell. More than ever, your past clients need the long-term service and value transfer that you can offer.

Some businesses have an easier time keeping clients in their business circles simply because they have more opportunities to see and serve their customers.

For instance, a car dealership sells a car and then, even if the buyer doesn't purchase another car for a decade, the dealership has the opportunity to see the customer face to face every time the vehicle is due for service, oil changes, or tire rotations.

A real estate agent also makes big sales on an infrequent basis to clients. The difference is that in real estate, after-the-sale service isn't automatic. You have to create strategies to keep in contact with your clients and continually remind them of the value you deliver. That's what this chapter is all about.

Achieving Relationship Excellence

As a real estate agent, your success depends on the quality and durability of the relationships you build with your clients, and the one and only way to build solid, enduring relationships is to deliver excellent, unrivaled service. To be an outstanding agent, you need to lavish your clients with service that exceeds their expectations — from the get-go and throughout a long business relationship.

REMEMBER

The key to winning clients for life is to avoid defections. When a former customer decides to buy or sell with another agent, you have a defection. When a client doesn't join your referral team, that's a defection as well. These defections can happen because of lack of communication consistency after closing. They also can happen due to commission discounting and someone offering a cheaper option when the marketplace heats up in sales.

WARNING

The challenge is that not all clients expect or want the same kind of service. What constitutes excellent service to one client may seem inadequate or even like overkill to another. It seems hard to imagine, but an agent can sell a client's home in less than a week, at full price, and still have a dissatisfied customer because of some action or oversight during the negotiation, inspection, or closing that simply didn't match with the client's service expectations.

TIP

To avoid service mismatches, learn each person's service expectations by doing something that few agents take time to do: Ask. Then put your findings to work, following these steps:

>> **Learn each person's service expectations.** Before you enter a new prospect presentation, make it a rule to learn everything you can about what your prospects are looking for in an agent and how they define excellent service.

>> **Customize and personalize your service delivery.** In your initial presentation and in subsequent contacts — whether you're working to make the sale,

service the client, build an after-the-sale relationship, or request a referral — refer to your initial research and highlight the service aspects that each client finds important. Weave in the words you heard them use to define great service. Highlight the communication points they described as essential service attributes. Let them know that you understand their needs and are focused on exceeding expectations.

>> **Never get complacent.** Don't assume that if your service falls a bit short your best clients will simply turn a blind eye. And by all means, don't think that if your clients want more or better service they will say something to you. They won't, because they don't want the confrontation. They'd rather just go away quietly and never come back.

I've met agents who are successful in spite of their "my way or the highway" approach to service delivery. Rather than focusing on customized service and long-term relationships, these agents prefer to serve a stream of here-today-gone-tomorrow clients that they acquire through relentless prospecting and high-volume lead development. These agents have a take-it-or-leave-it attitude about service. They practice what I call a fast-food hamburger-joint philosophy: "We sell hamburgers and fries, and if you don't like hamburgers and fries, pick another restaurant." The difference, of course, is that the number of people who want hamburgers and fries is huge and, if the fare is good, most customers automatically come back for more. The same is hardly true when it comes to home buyers and sellers.

As an agent, your prospect universe is limited, and your customers aren't apt to become repeat customers unless they're treated with the kind of unparalleled, consistent, and customized service that turns them into clients for life.

Using the Internet to generate leads may seem like a good move at first, and it can be, but in leveraging those new leads, it needs to generate relationships and referrals. Agents who use Internet lead-generation stealth systems like BoomTown, Real Geeks, TigerLead, and Zurple rely heavily on these systems to create new leads and have even more reason to develop quality referral systems. They are creating high-cost leads, so the big profit is the second sale, not the first.

I recently started working with a bright, young agent who has a great team. He is entering his eighth year in the business and closed more than 110 units last year. The sad part is that, when I analyzed his business, production, lead generation, and conversion, I discovered that 72 percent of his business was driven by Internet leads and only 6 percent was driven by repeat or referral business. The stability of this great agent's revenue is totally reliant on one source. If search engine algorithms change, pay-per-click campaigns become less effective, or consumer preferences shift . . . trouble.

Defining your service standards

When you deliver excellent service on a consistent and ongoing basis, your current client relationships will spawn repeat business and referrals that draw new clients into your business. As a result, your success will breed yet more success, your business will grow, and you'll need to provide superb service to an ever-growing group of people. At some point you'll face the important but difficult task of transitioning from an individual service provider to a service provider who works with a team to communicate with and serve clients.

WARNING

Making the shift from do-it-yourself service delivery to delivery that's leveraged through an agent team is an essential turning point in a successful agent's business. It's also a dangerous point, for these reasons:

>> Even though you know it's necessary to leverage your service ability by assigning tasks to others on your team, you may find it difficult to release ownership. This inability to let go can result in service lapses and frustration among both staff members and clients.

>> Unless you clearly establish and communicate your service philosophy and program to those on your team, you risk delivering an inconsistent or lower level of service to your clients.

The remedy to both of these pitfalls is to define and communicate the kind of service you stand for before you share responsibility for service delivery. To define the level of service you want your clients to receive, answer the following questions:

REMEMBER

>> How frequently do you communicate with sellers?

The number one complaint consumers have about real estate agents isn't that they charge or make too much money. The number one complaint is that they're bad or infrequent communicators. Especially if you're representing the seller, understand that your client wants consistent communication. If you're not making a weekly personal interaction, call, text, or instant message to provide an update on the process of the sale, you risk a poor customer relationship.

- How frequently do you make calls, texts, send emails, or email written reports?

- What is your process for sending sellers copies of your marketing pieces for their property?

- Do you provide sellers with links to virtual tours or websites promoting their property? Do you make it easy for them to see, feel, and touch what you're doing?

- How often do you meet face to face, and do the meetings take place in the sellers' home or in your office?

>> How do you receive and share feedback from showings?

  ● Do you call or text the showing agent once, twice, or three times in hopes of a response, or do you keep calling until you reach the agent and receive feedback?

  ● Do you have a showing site or other software that can give the seller feedback from agents in real time, and do you give sellers access to your marketing 24/7 just by going online? Examples of sites are www.homefeedback.com, www.feedbackcentral.com, and www.showings.com.

  ● Do you relay showing feedback to the seller right away, or do you collect feedback to share in a once-a-week meeting?

>> What marketing strategy do you employ for each property you list?

  ● What steps do you take to expose the home to cooperating agents?

  ● What tools or systems do you employ to raise awareness of your listed property within the real estate community?

  ● How do you generate awareness and interest within the public pool of real estate buyers?

  ● How do you promote the property online? How many sites is the property marketed to, and can you easily create a traffic report to share with the sellers?

  ● What marketing techniques and systems do you employ to attract qualified buyers to your seller's property?

  ● In what order do you execute your marketing plan?

Figures 16-1 and 16-2 toward the end of this chapter help you create checklists that everyone on your team can use and follow. When you're clear about what you stand for and how you deliver service to clients, you're in a position to train those on your team to deliver on your behalf and to your standards. At that point, your transition from a one-person service provider to professional service team is complete. Congratulations!

Promising, then flawlessly delivering

It's one thing to have a service delivery plan. It's another thing to implement your plan on a never-fail basis. I've seen marketing packages from countless agents. Most include 30-point, 50-point, or 100-point service action plans provided by the company the agent works for or created by the agent herself. I always ask, "Do you really do all of these things?" The sheepish response from most agents is that they implement fewer than 30 percent of the service tasks listed on their marketing plans.

The truth is, most agents don't follow through for two reasons: They over-promise, and then they lose track of what they said they'd do because they lack a system to follow.

TIP

My advice is this: Go through the multi-point action plan you currently provide to sellers and separate out the highest-value activities that you know you can perform with total consistency. Then commit to perform those tasks and be ready to execute flawlessly on your commitment.

Be ready to under-promise and over-deliver.

REMEMBER

The separation between marginal performance and stellar performance doesn't come from an abundance of magical extras. It's the result of keeping your commitments. For the vast majority of consumers, a professional who keeps commitments is a rarity.

Viewing the closing as a starting point, not a finish line

Great agents know the job isn't over when the transaction closes. After you achieve the sale, close the deal, cash the commission check, and spend the money, it's time to fortify your client relationship. Sure, you need to get on to the next income-producing activity. But as you cultivate your next deal, don't make the mistake of turning your back on the clients you just served.

TIP

In fact, your clients may need you more after their closing than at any previous point in your relationship for any of the following reasons:

>> After moving into their new home, they may discover repair issues that need attention. They may need the name of someone who can fix their roof, or they may need the names of service providers who are honest, trustworthy, and fair and who do quality repair work. Providing your clients with approved vendors, suppliers, and contractors is an excellent way to add value to your service.

>> Their home taxes may be high because of the correction in value over the past few years. They may need you to evaluate the marketplace, research comparable properties, and complete a report of your findings that they can use as they contest their property's taxable value. This puts real dollars back in your clients' pockets. I personally file appeals whenever any of my property values are out of alignment. My experience is that after the first year of ownership, if you've gotten a very good deal, the county doesn't automatically lower your assessed value to the purchase price. You have to appeal. The benefit is that most properties get revised by a percentage for the area. When you've won an appeal one time, it can pay off for years.

>> Your clients' home purchase may have sparked thoughts about building wealth through real estate investments. They may be thinking about how to secure their retirement or how to create a nest egg for their children's college educations. If your clients view real estate as a piece in their wealth puzzle, they may seek your advice about how to acquire and retain properties as a key step toward wealth creation.

>> Your clients may simply be interested in how the market around them is doing. When you call them to chat, you're likely to get the question, "How's the market?" or "What's happening in the marketplace?" Now that they're home-owners, your clients are vested in the local real estate marketplace. Become their resource and you'll be first in line when they're ready to make the next physical or investment move. You may want to provide an ongoing market update to all past clients. This market update should show inventory, supply and demand, and key opportunities in the marketplace. It truly affirms that you're a market expert.

WARNING

The National Association of Realtors completed a multi-year study to gauge the public's perception of real estate agents. It found:

>> About 84 percent of consumers rated the service they received from their agent as satisfactory or better. This is an acceptable number, and it indicates that, as a whole, real estate agents are doing an okay job during the course of the transaction. The study further broke down that 66 percent of consumers would "definitely" use the agent in the future, and 18 percent would "probably" do so.

>> About 23 percent of clients used the same agent on an upcoming deal that they had used on a previous transaction. The fact that fewer than one in four clients went back to the same agent, even though the majority felt that their previous transaction was handled satisfactorily, is a shocking testimony to the fact that agents aren't developing long-term relationships. And from here, the figures get even worse.

>> In 2015, the total number of real estate transactions was 5.1 million sales in a single year. Of those sales, 24 percent, or approximately 1.2 million, involved experienced buyers and sellers conducting investment or second-home transactions. When asked if they used an agent they had worked with previously, only 13 percent said yes. This clearly demonstrates the after-sales service issue in the real estate industry.

These stats reek of poor after-the-sale communication and woefully short relationship development. The only logical conclusion is that, in general, after-the-sale service in the real estate industry really stinks. The next section helps you break the stereotype.

Creating After-the-Sale Service

WARNING

If you don't plan for it, after-the-sale service won't happen. You'll get so consumed with the next deal and with the task of earning the next commission check that you'll overlook the opportunity to create long-term revenue through your past clients.

An after-the-sale service program is like most things in life: People get derailed before they take the first step, and if they don't take the first step — the step that involves establishing the program they commit to follow — they can't begin to meet the objective.

Use the upcoming section to guide you as you create your plan. It helps you define exactly what you need to do in the first 45 days after the sale and on an ongoing basis thereafter.

Laying the groundwork during the transaction period

When working a real estate transaction, you have three prime opportunities to develop interpersonal connections and high-grade referrals. The first is when you are actively working with them to sell their home or showing them homes to buy. In this timeframe their excitement for real estate is extremely high. They are telling everyone they know about looking for a new home. The second is during the transaction period when you're working with your client to close the purchase or sale. This timeframe is exciting but also stressful and hassle oriented because of documents, lending hoops and requirements, and repairs. The second is during the 30 to 45 days that follow the closing, where they are settling into their new home.

IN IT FOR THE LONG HAUL

According to the National Association of Realtors, only 10 percent of home buyers resell the home within three years. Another 12 percent sell within four to five years, and another 15 percent sell in years six or seven. In other words, more than 60 percent of homeowners wait at least eight years after the purchase to resell their home — and you want to still be in touch with them when they do. The median time to resell the home is at the nine-year mark. As agents, we must be focused on outstanding service before, during, and after the client moves into their home. The difference between a good agent and a great agent lies in the after-sales service and communication.

WARNING

If you do a poor job during the transaction, you'll be hard pressed to recover lost ground after the closing. An attorney who blows a case doesn't get a second chance from the client, and the same holds true for real estate agents. Your service during the transaction must be stellar, or you'll sacrifice the chance for repeat and referral business, which is the easiest and least costly business to acquire. If that isn't bad enough, you'll also lose the opportunity to collect client testimonials and generate positive word of mouth.

During the transaction period, you're in frequent contact with your clients and have ample opportunities to provide excellent service, make a strong, positive impression, and develop a long-term relationship by following these steps:

TIP

>> When you begin to work with clients to buy or sell a home, their enthusiasm is high. They fully anticipate and expect that they'll be able to find the perfect home and that you're the ideal agent to accomplish the task. During this initial period, your clients think about little other than their real estate hopes. Your presence becomes woven into the fabric of their lives and their conversations with friends and family members. This is an ideal time to ask for and win referrals.

WARNING

>> If the sale or purchase process drags on, expect your clients' level of excitement and energy to ebb. At the same time, expect their focus on their purchase or sale to intensify. The most important thing you can do during this potentially dangerous time — when your clients are experiencing concern and talking non-stop about their real estate issues with others — is to stay in frequent communication; offer solutions; provide calm, professional advice; and retain the clients' confidence in you and your abilities.

Flip back to the section titled "Defining your service standards" as you establish a plan that ensures frequent and professional contact throughout the transaction period.

Setting a service agenda for the first 30 to 45 days after the sale

If you did everything right during the transaction (and if you're using this book as a resource, I'm going to assume you did), then your clients were totally satisfied with your service when the deal closed. Now you have a decision to make: Do you wish your clients well and walk away, or do you begin an after-the-sale service program that turns them into clients for life? You've seen this chapter's title, so you already know the answer: You begin to turn them into clients for life.

>> **Begin by personally calling your clients at least four times in the 30 to 45 days after the closing.**

- Call in the first few days after closing to thank them for the opportunity to serve them. Say how excited you are for them to be moving into their new home. Share an anecdote about working with them that will make you all laugh and touch their hearts.

- After the call, send a handwritten thank-you note further expressing your thanks and asking for future business or referrals.

- By the end of the first week, call again. Again, express thanks for trusting you. Ask: How did the move go? Did anything get broken? How do the kids like their new rooms? Have they met any of the neighborhood kids yet? Did the seller leave the home properly? Is there anything that wasn't right that they need any help with?

   This last question can open a Pandora's box of issues, and that's exactly why to ask it. If there are problems you don't know about, you may be blamed for the mishaps without any opportunity to do anything about them. Most will be issues between the seller and the buyer, and the buyer's power over the seller — unless legal action is involved — is gone because the transaction has closed. Sometimes all you can do is provide a listening ear and sympathetic voice. Other times you can make a few phone calls to help right the wrong. The fact that you're willing to listen and see what you can do speaks louder than any demonstrable action. It shows that you care. Some of your most ardent fans will come out of an initial negative situation that you are able to resolve.

- At the conclusion of the second call, send another handwritten note. Express concern for the unresolved issue and again thank them for their trust and for taking time to talk with you today.

- Call again at the two-week mark. Ask how they are doing getting out of boxes and settling into their new home. Update them if you've made progress on the issue that was concerning them. Ask them about the kids and their transition. Before hanging up, ask if your service is needed. Also, ask them for referrals.

- On their 30-day anniversary in the home, call again. Congratulate them on their great decision in selecting this home. Check on the kids and their progress settling in to the house and neighborhood. Thank them again for the honor to serve them.

As simple as this approach sounds, it enables you to lock your clients in for life, plus it opens the door to referral business that flows freely.

>> **While you're at it, call the other party involved in your real estate transaction, as well.**

Every real estate deal involves a buyer and a seller. In most cases you represent only one of the two parties, but why not call and offer after-sale service to both? Do you think the other agent is doing this? For your answer, you only have to look at the National Association of Realtors' finding that only 18 percent of buyers and 23 percent of sellers use an agent they had used previously to represent their interests. My estimation is that fewer than 15 percent of agents actually call their clients regularly after closing.

When calling to follow up with the party represented by the other agent in your transaction, be ready for a response of surprise and great appreciation. The fact that you're calling four times in a month, while the agent who got paid to represent their interests hasn't called even once, will positively awe most people. By the end of your 30-day after-sale service period, the names of the other agent's clients will be in *your* database, and you'll be the one receiving their referrals.

» **Deliver or send a gift to your client.**

WARNING

This gift is usually called a closing gift, but even if you attend the closing, don't take the gift with you, for two reasons:

- At the closing, your clients will be focused on the transaction and thinking about their impending move and all the challenges that lie in front of them. Your gift will be lost in the shuffle.

- The papers at the closing put the amount of the real estate commission in writing, causing your clients to focus on exactly how much money you made from the transaction. If you give your gift at the same time, they may make a negative comparison between the value of the gift and the money you received.

In choosing your gift, don't go overboard. Save any over-the-top gestures you want to extend until after your clients have settled in and after your commission has long-since been paid. The more you deliver after you get paid, the more your gift communicates that you care about your clients, not your commission check.

Find a closing gift that reminds clients of you and your service. Give them something that can be used rather than consumed. A great bottle of wine or gift basket quickly disappears. A customized mailbox, door knocker, or yard plant will last almost forever.

By delivering your gift to your clients' new home, you put it in their hands at a time when it can create the most significant feelings of good will and warmth — and the best likelihood of referrals. If you still want to give them something at closing, hand them a thank-you note instead.

Another nice gesture is to help your clients notify their friends of their move. Offer to create a postcard with a picture of their new home on the front and to print up a few hundred for their use. Then offer to mail them out on your clients' behalf. You'll save them the cost and enlarge your database to boot.

THE PROBLEM WITH COMMISSIONS . . .

When closing time arrives, sellers basically receive a bill for the agent's services right there on the closing papers. By the time they see that big 6 percent figure staring them in the face, chances are they've already forgotten the risk you took with your time and money to market their home and the many services you provided. Plus, you made countless efforts they never knew about — such as calls to lenders, title companies, attorneys, repair contractors, other agents, appraisers, and all the other partners involved to achieve the sale of the home.

Although clients don't understand the hours of work it took to create a smooth transaction, they most certainly understand how much you got paid: The number is presented in black and white at the closing. And because most agents do little after the sale, the clients' parting memory is how much you got paid, which isn't exactly a great way to launch a long-term relationship.

I really believe that the way we collect our income or fee makes it more difficult to achieve a high level of warm feelings from our clients, and I think it hardly encourages customer retention. I'm not advocating changing the compensation structure. In fact, I'm a true believer in the plan. But I caution you to remain aware of its inherent challenges and to make doubly sure that your last contact with your clients isn't on the day you get paid. After-the-sale service is the best antidote.

You may even call people on the list to make sure they received the card you sent for your client. You can then ask them if they're committed to another agent. If not, you've opened the door to a new client relationship.

Establishing an ongoing communication strategy

After your clients have completed their moves and put their real estate transactions behind them, you still need to be in touch at regular intervals if you want to remain on their radar screens.

WARNING

Unless you develop a pattern of frequent communication with phone calls, emails, direct mailings, and other forms of contact, too many clients (even your best ones) won't remember you at the important moment when they need real estate counsel or when their friends need it. You need to constantly remind them that you're still in the business and ready to be of assistance.

I have a coaching client in New Jersey named Joe Simone, who happens to be one of the best agents in his state. During a recent conversation, he shared his disappointment with the number of referrals he was receiving from past clients. He follows a good system to communicate with them frequently, but when it came to referrals the results were not what he wanted. He encapsulated his frustration by saying that he had been in the business for seven years and had not gotten a single referral from his own mother!

I followed up with an obvious question: "Have you ever asked her for a referral?" Joe's response was similar to the one I hear from most agents: "She's my mother. She knows I'm in real estate. I didn't think I had to ask."

You can replace the word mother with best friend, little brother, older sister, favorite cousin, aunt, father, wife's boss, accountant, attorney, pastor . . . you get the idea. The lesson is exactly the same. You may think that the people you know should remember your business and assume that you welcome referrals, but they don't. That's why ongoing communication is essential.

Now here's the rest of Joe's story. He agreed to add to his upcoming week's action plan a call to his mother, during which he'd ask for a referral. The next time we talked, he seemed subdued. When I asked if something was wrong, he answered sheepishly, "I called my mother. A day later, she called me with a referral. I've already listed and sold that home. She called me yesterday with another, and I'm going out tonight to list that home." He'd waited seven years to get his first two listings and sales from his mother's referrals.

If Joe's mother can forget to recommend her own son because he lacked an ongoing communication strategy, anyone can forget you're an agent.

Using direct mail

Direct mail is still an effective way to generate business, but only if it gets to the right people and only if it gets opened and read. Let me state further, I think direct mail is more effective today because of the social-media revolution. Our mailboxes are no longer stuffed with direct mail; it's our email inboxes that are overflowing. Direct mail puts your message in a smaller group where it can have more impact.

Check out the U.S. Postal Service program called Every Door Direct Mail, which can really save you money. A regular postage stamp is $0.49, but this program can cut the per-piece cost down to $0.16. You simply identify a geographic area you want to target and develop and print your marketing pieces. The post office gives your pieces to the postal carrier who serves your target area, and they get delivered to every address in your target area based on the routes . . . no stamping, licking, sticking, or address labeling . . . and less money!

Direct mail is also effective with your past clients and sphere of influence. You can't use Every Door Direct Mail for them, though. To get your mail to the right people, create a carefully developed list that includes the addresses of past clients and people within your sphere of influence, which basically consists of people you know.

To get your mail opened, make it look personal. People sort their mail with the garbage can close by. They rifle through the pile and within seconds put pieces into an A pile that will definitely get attention, a B pile that has a 50/50 chance of getting opened, or the trash. You want to get into the A pile.

TIP

To get your mail into the A pile, try putting these tips to work:

>> Send your correspondence on notecard-sized pieces.

>> Handwrite the envelope address. Avoid computer labels or, if you must use labels because your writing resembles hieroglyphs, use clear labels that are almost invisible and at a glance allow your address to appear typed onto the envelope.

>> Send special-occasion cards. Use the clients' anniversary, the anniversary of the day they moved into their home, Mother's Day, Father's Day, and birthdays to reinforce your connection with the clients and remind them that you care. Also send thank-you or "just thinking about you" cards.

>> Send mail to their children. Separate yourself from nearly all of your clients' other business contacts by taking an interest in their children. I didn't understand the value of this connection until I had children. Now I know firsthand that someone who transfers value, service, and kindness to my kids is someone who will get my business forever. Send your clients' children birthday cards. Include a certificate for a treat at the local ice-cream parlor and you'll really get your mailer noticed, by both the kids and their parents.

WARNING

Don't expect your direct-mail program to just happen spontaneously. Plan it out a year in advance. Select about half a dozen times over the course of the year to send handwritten cards to past clients or people in your sphere. Program the dates and the nature of the mailers into your database to remind you when to do it. And then do it.

Staying in touch via email

Email provides an easy and cost-effective way to deliver your correspondence to your prospects and clients, so long as you create a good list full of recipients who want and have given permission to send them your mailings.

I suggest that you establish at least two databases of email addresses:

>> One database should include the names and addresses of all prospects who have given you permission to send them email messages. When mailing to these people, you're trying to generate interest and confidence and to coax

them into a relationship with you. The text in their messages is sales oriented and articulates reasons they should take action in the real estate market now. Mailers may focus on appreciation rates, inventory levels, interest rates, and projections of future rate increases. Additionally, each mailer should include a concise statement about the value of doing business with you, why they should hire you, and the benefits they will receive from working with you over the competition.

>> A second database should include the names and addresses of past clients and those in your sphere of influence, which includes friends, family members, and professional associates. When mailing to this group, tone down your sales message. You still want to provide an update on current and emerging market conditions, and most certainly you still want to convey the value you deliver, you just want to do it all with a softer, more personal approach. Your purpose when mailing to this group is to generate referrals. By sharing marketplace facts, you provide them with information they can use in their conversations with friends.

TIP

When compiling your databases, make sure you obtain and include email addresses for each person you want to reach in a home or business. For instance, my wife, Joan, and I each have our own email addresses. If you only send a mailer to my email address, she'll never see it because I won't take the time to forward it on to her. I guarantee that we're not unusual in this respect.

When mailing to your databases, put the following advice to work:

>> I still believe a newsletter has value in today's blog-centered world. Send a monthly newsletter. Choose a template from your word-processing program or one of countless third-party resources. Then all you have to do is fill in the text area with a customized message.

>> Develop content that is solid, helpful, positive, and valuable. It doesn't have to be earthshaking in terms of news value. And it doesn't have to be written in award-winning prose. It just needs to be current, customized to your local market conditions, and capable of making a good impression over the few minutes between when it's opened and when it's deleted.

WARNING

>> Avoid email blasts that send identical messages to a long list of addresses. The exception is when you're sending a newsletter or news flash to your full list, but in all other cases, work to personalize the notes you send. Your clients are well versed in email and know exactly how much (or little) time and effort goes into a communication that involves absolutely no personalization. Subconsciously, they'll translate the mass mailing as a definition of the quality of your relationship with them. For that reason alone, use mass emails sparingly.

A FEW NECESSARY WORDS ABOUT SPAM

Spam, or unrequested, unwanted email, is the scourge of the online world. In 2003, the U.S. government passed the CAN-SPAM Act, requiring, among other things, that anyone who sends unsolicited email must follow some clearly stated rules. The sender must be clearly identified, the email must include a valid physical postal address, the message must present a means for the recipient to opt out or unsubscribe, and the person or organization sending the mailer must honor unsubscribe requests within a specific timeframe. Be sure your mailings comply.

TIP

When emailing market updates, don't get lazy about relaying market facts. When the MLS shares that the average home price has gone from $205,458 to $221,497 over the last year, the numbers really don't mean much to clients or prospects. But if you take the time to do some math, you can tip off your email recipients to the fact that home prices in the local market area increased by 7 percent in the past 12 months. That kind of figure is memorable and gets passed along, with your name as the source.

Picking up the phone

In your effort to stay in touch, add value, and generate referrals, you want to pick up the phone and call some of your contacts weekly, some monthly, and maybe some only one time each year. To organize the effort, create phone lists that are segmented by the level of connection and frequency of contact you have with each group.

>> Your star clients and closest friends and associates deserve star treatment. These people are sold on you and the service you provide. They want to help you advance your career. They're happy to hear from you, and they're likely to send you more referrals than you'll get from any other portion of your contact list. It's okay to treat them differently than everyone else. In fact, it's good business. Call those in this category monthly or at least one time every other month, and weave a referral request into each conversation.

>> Past clients and those in your sphere of influence should be called at least once a year. Unless you have an enormous database, anyone you have serviced in your career should hear from you personally at least once every 12 months.

Don't hesitate to pick up the phone and make calls to thank people for their business, see how they're doing, and ask if there's anything you can do for them. Most consumers, when called by a service provider, are delighted and honored by the contact. If you got a friendly call out of the blue from your insurance agent, attorney, accountant, or financial advisor, you'd be both surprised and pleased. The same is likely the case when you call your clients.

Showing appreciation

The National Association of Realtors has about 1 million members. Obviously your clients have a choice! Do you thank them enough for choosing you?

I have to admit that I've become aware of how little common courtesy is extended in our society as the result of our efforts to instill the "magic" words "please" and "thank you" into the conversations of our children, Annabelle and Wesley. I'm amazed at the positive responses we receive from waiters, grocery-store clerks, bank tellers, and other service providers who heap praise upon our polite children — even though they're simply displaying courtesies that should be standard fare in everyday exchanges.

From watching the reactions to my kids, I'm more certain than ever that you can set yourself apart by conveying courtesy and appreciation to your clients on an ongoing basis. Express thanks several times during the transaction and again after the closing. Say "thank you" every time clients sign anything like a listing agreement, buyer agency contract, or offer or counteroffer. Frequently affirm that they've made a good decision in working with you or choosing to buy their home. Because of the recent housing crisis, other people in their lives may still feel that they've made an unwise decision to buy now. You may be one of the few people saying, "Good for you!" Constantly confirm that you appreciate their business.

Writing the thank-you note

I truly believe the most powerful force in the business world is a handwritten thank-you note. That may sound terribly "old school" to tech-savvy agents, but it's exactly what you need to send if you want to set yourself apart.

I remember my mother sitting down with her three boys at the kitchen table each year after Christmas to write thank-you notes for the gifts we received. Over our protests, she insisted that by accepting the gifts we had accepted the responsibility to write thank-you notes.

Back then, writing thank-you notes was a standard operating procedure. Today, thank-you notes arrive rarely, and as a result they carry far more weight. They convey, in essence, "You matter so much that I took the time to craft a message with my own hand."

Exceeding expectations

REMEMBER

The keys to exceeding expectations are few and pretty obvious: Extend courtesy. Say thanks. Show appreciation. Always be professional and remember that little gestures go a long way to building strong relationships.

You don't have to go overboard. Small gifts like ice-cream certificates for the children, movie tickets for the adults, or coffee-shop coupons make the point that you appreciate working with your contacts and receiving their referrals, whether they result in business or not.

WARNING

My only caution is to be sure that every gesture you make further enhances your professional reputation. A few years back, the *Wall Street Journal* featured a profile on the service styles of three real estate agents. One bought groceries for out-of-town clients before they arrived to enjoy their vacation homes. Another personally mowed the lawns of out-of-area sellers. A third reduced his fees to accommodate client requests. Each exceeded expectations in a way that lowered the professionalism and status of the real estate agent community. One is a personal shopper, one is a lawn boy, and the last is a discounter. I can't think of a doctor, dentist, attorney, or accountant who would provide these types of services to exceed expectations.

TIP

Keep your efforts in line with your professional image. Getting groceries for out-of-town clients is thoughtful but inappropriate for a professional; helping arrange for a personal shopper is thoughtful and professional. Mowing the lawn is thoughtful but unprofessional; arranging for a professional yard crew is thoughtful and professional.

Customizing your messages

REMEMBER

From an early age, every child learns the Golden Rule: Treat others the way you want to be treated. Customer service pros replace the Golden Rule with the Platinum Rule: Treat others the way they *wish* to be treated.

The Platinum Rule was coined by speaker/trainer Tony Alessandra, who explains that a salesperson's job is not to treat and serve clients as *you* want to be treated but as *they* want to be treated.

The only way to know how a person wants to be treated is to ask and observe. Different kinds of customers have different values and service expectations. A one-time client expects a different level of attention than is expected by a long-time client. A busy executive expects more efficiency than is expected or even desired by a person with a fairly empty calendar.

TIP

Know yourself. Understanding your natural style and strategy for sales and business is imperative. We all follow some basic individual patterns. If you want to know more about yourself, try a behavioral assessment. I have one on my website that you can take for free (www.realestatechampions.com/freeDISC). By discovering and recognizing your communication style, decision-making style, and expectations, you can supercharge your business. You can modify your service and selling style and strategy to better meet the needs of your clients and prospects.

Visit www.realestatechampions.com to learn more about this customized approach to business building and client building.

Understanding the difference between unique and one-size-fits-all communications

The difference between junk mail and personal mail boils down to one question: Is the message targeted and tailored to the interests of the recipient, or could it just as easily be addressed to "occupant"?

The more you segment your database, the better you'll be able to customize the messages you send. Prospects, clients, and those in your sphere have different information needs. Likewise, those with various interests will respond to different kinds of messages.

TIP

Segment your mailing list by the nature of your relationship with the contact and also by the recipients' lifestyle facts such as children or no children, age group, special interests, and faith, to name a few categories. Then with a few keystrokes you can pull up address lists of people with shared interests and information needs. You can send a great article on golf to all the golfing enthusiasts in your database. You can send an invitation to a family-oriented event to all prospects with children. You can be sure that every mailer that leaves your office conveys that you know and care enough about the recipient's interests to send appropriately tailored information.

Dealing with one-time or transactional clients

A transactional client isn't looking for a long-term relationship with a business or service provider. Transactional clients simply want to complete a deal. Their eye is on the bottom line, and their decisions are based on dollars and cents. When the real estate marketplace is robust, expect to encounter a good many transactional clients.

In their book *Rethinking the Sales Force* (McGraw-Hill Education, 1999), Neil Rackham and John Vincentis outline the key characteristics of transactional clients:

>> Transactional clients view service as standard and readily substitutable.

>> The transactional buyer's primary concerns are the price and ease of acquisition.

>> The timing of a transactional purchase is triggered by a specific event, rather than by a whim.

>> The key nature of the relationship is cost-based, and the relationship can be contractual.

WARNING

In serving transactional clients, ask yourself whether you can turn enough of a profit off this single transaction to make the effort worthwhile, because the chance of repeat business is slim. You may, with your stellar service, turn a transactional client into a relationship client, but the odds are long. This kind of client is primarily motivated by the cost of your service. If the numbers don't fly, the level of your relationship won't matter.

Dealing with long-term or relationship clients

Relationship clients are clients who give you the opportunity to serve them on a repeated basis. Unlike transactional clients, relationship clients view their contact with you as part of an ongoing relationship. Unlike their transactional brethren, relationship clients expect to do business with you again. You can also expect referrals to their friends.

When dealing with relationship clients, be aware of what matters most:

>> They are focused on how your characteristics are different from others and how your services are customized and unique. They want the benefits that you provide to help them solve their problem.

>> The price of your service is not their highest concern. The solution you provide carries equal or more weight than the cost.

>> They are willing to consider price and performance trade-offs to arrive at a lower-risk, higher-probability outcome.

>> They respond favorably to the service and communication aspects of your business.

>> They expect and require a high level of customer service.

>> They have a cooperative attitude and want to work together with you toward a common goal.

You can wish all you want, but the truth is that not all clients fit into the relationship category. You'll meet agent trainers who tell you to work only with people in this category, but I think you'd be foolish to limit your business so significantly.

REMEMBER

If you place your service emphasis on buyer clients, odds are good that you can win a preponderance of relationship clients. But if you're a listings agent who works primarily with sellers, get ready to deal with a good many transactional clients. The difference: Sellers pay the fees to real estate agents, so they're more focused on the price than the service. Stay in the business long enough and you'll watch relationship-oriented buyer clients adopt the traits of transactional clients. As your buyer clients become sellers, their purchasing traits shift, too.

Establishing Awesome Service

A service encounter happens any time a consumer interacts with a servicing organization. Every website hit or incoming ad or sign call is a service encounter. When a prospect talks to you, your staff, your company receptionist, your closing coordinator, or your broker, owner, lender, escrow or title attorney, or anyone on your service team, that person is having a service encounter.

WARNING

If one person in the long chain of people who help you get your job done says or does anything negative, it affects the impression of the nature of the service you provide. There's no way to separate yourself from your colleagues if they mess up. It's even possible for your service to be tainted by those outside your service team. For example, say that a buyer uses a lender other than the one you recommend. If the transaction closes late and with a higher interest rate than originally quoted, that client will leave with a bad impression about the whole transaction and everyone involved in it. Your future business and referral opportunities are affected by the actions of someone entirely outside your influence.

To direct your service encounters toward superb outcomes, follow these steps:

» Control service encounters by using your own people to conduct transactions. Direct and drive as much business as possible to the best providers. Work hard to convince the client to use people on your team when securing a mortgage or closing the deal. Some may call this "steering," but I view it as taking care of your clients.

» Make sure your clients work with lenders who know their stuff and are responsive. Be aware that the lender triggers the choke point in most transactions. Take time to counsel your clients toward a resource you know will perform.

» Have a plan for recovering from service disasters if necessary. If your client is reasonable, no situation is too far gone to salvage. In fact, handle the problem well and you're apt to turn a disgruntled client into one of your most vocal supporters. Take these steps:

- Do what is necessary to right the wrong.

- Find out from the client what it will take to turn the unsatisfactory situation into a satisfactory outcome. Ask what it will take for them to be delighted. Be cautious here. I don't really believe that forgoing a fee or reducing a cost ever creates a more satisfied client. The service and the cost are not linked at this stage of customer satisfaction.

- Avoid the blame game. If you point out that it was the client's decision to use the service provider who caused the problem, you only make the situation worse. Conveying that "I told you so" is never a way to soothe feelings.

- Follow up. Eventually sore feelings will wane, but the only way to replace the negative impression is to make a better one through continuous, professional contact. In the early stages after the mishap you may not see many referrals, but when they start to come through you'll know your service recovery plan was a success.

- If you can't turn the situation around, don't concede your profit. Some clients only feel placated if they get into your pocketbook and win cash compensation. If you did something that caused them to be hurt finan-cially, you may have to buck up. Most of the time, though, that won't be the case. I caution you, before you ever give up your hard-earned money, ask yourself three questions:

  1. Will offering cash really turn this client into a raving fan?

  2. Is there another way to turn this client into a raving fan?

  3. Is there a reasonable chance that I'll win future business and referrals from this person?

     If your answers don't cause you to feel confident that giving up money will net a future return at a low risk, keep the cash in your pocket.

I'm an ardent supporter of Hyatt hotels, and a good part of the reason is that years ago they took a bad situation and turned it around. I'd flown to Tampa, Florida, from Bend, Oregon, which entailed leaving at 6 in the morning and arriving in Tampa sometime after 7 at night. I was tired and hungry and faced a full schedule the next day. From the airport, I called for the shuttle van three times before it showed up 45 minutes later. My last call had gotten through to the manager on duty. She was sympathetic to my weary travel story, but I expected only a listening ear.

When I arrived at the hotel, which was less than ten minutes from the airport, the manager greeted me as I stepped off the bus. She told me she had already person-ally checked me in. She walked me to a wonderful room where wine, cheese, and fruit were waiting. While walking to the room, she took a genuine interest in my day and travel trials. She later sent up a tray of desserts. She knew how to create a raving fan out of what could have been a lost situation.

Developing a service plan

The best way to provide the level of service you and your client agree upon is to create two checklists, a New Listing Checklist that details the steps you will follow when accepting a listing and a Sale Agreement Checklist that details all the steps that happen from contract to close.

Figures 16-1 and 16-2 present samples of each of these checklists to guide you as you develop forms that work for your own business. Standard procedures vary from state to state and MLS board to MLS board. Although the samples included in this book will be 90 percent accurate for your situation, you need to customize them to fit the requirements of your state, region, municipality, and code of ethics.

Extending extra touches that create gold

A whole book could be written on the topic of customer service. I find that a little extra service goes a long way.

Ask the agents in your office what extra touches work for them. Ask your broker what she thinks falls into this category. Following are two of my favorites: one that is extended right after the closing and one that works well for long-term clients:

» Right after closing, arrange for two hours of complimentary handyman repair work. The cost of this much-appreciated added value is only about $100, and the perceived value is huge. More often than not, clients use more time than the amount covered by your gift, so the handyman acquires new clients and as a result will probably give you a great deal on the time he sells to you.

Also, by sending in a handyman, you help the clients resolve small issues the seller didn't handle before they fester into something bigger that leads to frustration with the transaction, which leads to frustration with you. This idea is an inexpensive win/win.

» For long-term clients, consider buying four season tickets to an event series you enjoy in your town — perhaps the symphony, theater, or professional or college sports games. Be sure the events are ones you enjoy attending and that the activity is consistent with your professional image. (Tickets to WWE wrestling probably won't make your list.)

Shortly before each event date, invite clients to attend the event with you. Don't issue invitations when you first buy the tickets. Wait until a few days or a week before each event. At that point, your invitation will seem spontaneous and genuinely friendly. Some of your invitees will already be booked and will have to decline. You may have to call six to ten people to give the tickets away. If so, you'll win their appreciation, and you'll still have the tickets to share with another long-term client.

NEW LISTING CHECKLIST

Seller _____

Address _____

Within Two Days of Listing

At the House:

☐ Make duplicate key   ☐ Take photo

☐ Install lock box   ☐ Put up and fill flyer box

☐ Place directional signs as needed

In the Office:

☐ Order sign up

☐ Submit listing to office for MLS input

☐ Fill in information on listing folder

☐ Log listing in current listing log book with copy of listing

☐ Obtain and keep:

  – Original lead-based paint disclosure

  – Property disclosure/disclaimer

  – LP siding claim, if applicable

☐ Create Flyer

☐ Add property to Internet ad

☐ Ad Client to database or change ID/Status to "Current Listing"

☐ Communicate with sellers

  – Send thank you note

  – include:

  ☐ MLS listing   ☐ Sellers agency disclosure

  ☐ Copy of all their listing forms   ☐ Property disclosure or disclaimer

  ☐ Listing agreement   ☐ Lead-based paint disclosure

☐ Send "Just Listed" cards

☐ Check listing in MLS for accuracy

☐ Place home Office Tour ___ Confirm _____ Date Toured

☐ Place home on Realtor's Tour ___ Confirm _____ Date Toured

☐ Include listing on Pre-Scheduled Ad form

In the Future

☐ Keep track of showings   ☐ Send copies of ads to clients

☐ Track when and where ads run   ☐ Follow up with agents

☐ Keep copies of ads on file   ☐ Follow up with clients

© John Wiley & Sons, Inc.

FIGURE 16-1: Customize this checklist to reflect the steps you follow when acquiring a new listing.

EARNEST MONEY CHECKLIST

Close Date _____ Sales Price _____

Seller _____

Buyer _____

Property Sold _____

Open Escrow

☐ Complete sales transaction sheet

☐ Complete earnest money agreement.

    Submit ☐ Original (listing side) or ☐ Copy (buyer's side) to office administrator.

    ☐ Send originals to listing agent, if applicable

☐ Earnest money $_____ ☐ Note ☐ Check Held by: _____

☐ Complete buyer/seller agency disclosure forms. Submit original to administator.

☐ Submit "Sale Pending" addendum to the office

☐ Send copy of property disclosure to ☐ Seller ☐ Buyer

☐ Receive fully signed property disclosure

    Submit ☐ Original (listing side) or ☐ Copy (buyer's side).

☐ Note deadlines in calendar.

☐ Record information on agents, lender, escrow, and buyers or sellers on file folder.

☐ Send escrow letter to clients with copies of their paperwork.

☐ Send copy of earnest money agreement and preliminary title report to lender

☐ Print copy of MLS (if representing the buyer)

Escrow

☐ Check the MLS to make sure the property is listed as "Pending"

☐ Schedule inspections/appraisals:

    Inspection date _____ Completed _____

    Appraisal date _____ Completed _____

    442 _____ Completed _____

☐ Receive copy of preliminary title report.

☐ Review preliminary report

    ☐ Note concerns on transaction file

    ☐ Schedule follow-up to resolve concerns prior to closing

☐ Removal of Contingencies

    ☐ Home sale/close. Date to be removed: _____

    ☐ Financing: Date to be removed: _____

FIGURE 16-2: Customize this checklist to reflect the steps you follow from contract to closing.

(continued)

☐ Lender Arrangement
    ☐ Loan Application: Completed _____
    ☐ Credit Report: Completed _____
    ☐ Verification of Deposit (VOD): Completed _____
    ☐ Verification of Employment (VOE): _____
    ☐ FICO Score: Completed _____
    ☐ Loan Documents: Ordered _____
☐ Put up sold sticker
☐ Request copy of closing statement prior to closing. Review Go with seller or buyer

Sale Closes
☐ Receive Paycheck
☐ Remove lock box and directional signs
☐ Deliver keys to buyers
☐ Order post sign down
☐ Submit "Sold" addendum to office.
☐ Update buyers and sellers information in database to "Past Clients" category
☐ Send thank you note to seller and/or buyer

Following the Closing
☐ Contact past client one day after closing of escrow to ask for referrals
☐ Contact past client three days after closing of escrow to ask for referrals
☐ Contact past client seven days after closing of escrow to ask for referrals
☐ Prepare closing statement letter
☐ Contact past client 30 days after closing of escrow to ask for referrals

Commission Due _____ + _____ (Processing Fee)= _____

Remember to follow up weekly with lenders and agents

FIGURE 16-2:
continued

© John Wiley & Sons, Inc.

Chapter **17**

Maximizing Your Time

The most significant challenge in an entrepreneurial business like real estate sales is managing time effectively. The daily battle against procrastination, distractions, interruptions, low-priority activities, and ingrained customer expectations of instant accessibility can exhaust even the most energetic agent and can derail the plans of all but the most disciplined time manager.

This chapter helps you take control of your calendar, giving you the time you need to build skills, prospect, follow up with leads, plan and make quality presentations, market properties, and position and present yourself successfully. Your ability to manage your days and invest your time for the highest return will separate you from the other agents who are vying for top-producer status and also enable you to earn your desired income.

Spending Less Time to Accomplish More

Many real estate agents invest too much time and too little urgency in their businesses. They commit well over 40 hours to the job, and they put themselves on call seven days a week. They spread themselves thin, and then, in order to sustain themselves over this endless schedule, they dilute their intensity. No other professional works so many hours. Even doctors have a lighter on-call schedule than most agents choose to accept. This is even truer in today's technology-based world of instant communication.

A real estate agent lives in an over-stimulated world. The sensory overload of smartphones, emails, text messages, websites, and social media makes the time-management challenges more acute than ever.

I suggest that you commit right now to become more effective in way less time each week. Consider this advice:

REMEMBER

>> **Set aside at least one day a week to recharge and refresh yourself.** Before you say you can't afford the day off, realize this truth: Work expands to fill the time you give it. Reduce your work hours and you'll automatically squeeze more productivity into shorter spans of time. The day off should be a true day off. That means you shut down access (your smartphone, email, social media, and so on) and enjoy your family and other activities without interruption.

>> **Increase your productivity by increasing your intensity.** Give yourself deadlines with no procrastination options. If you know you need to accomplish a lineup of goals over the course of a five-day workweek, your focus automatically zooms in, you sweep away distractions, and you get the job done in the time allowed.

   I watched my own focus and productivity intensify as I went from a seven-day workweek to a six-day workweek to a five-day workweek. The largest production increase I experienced, though, was when I moved to a schedule of four days of work followed by three days off, with no correlating reduction in my income or success objectives. Given my goals, I knew I had to work with incredibly high intensity and no options for procrastination. What's more, I couldn't change my mind and add a work day to my schedule because my wife, Joan, and I were constructing a vacation home some three hours away in Bend, Oregon, and we had to be on site every Friday to check the progress. Joan was the general contractor, and she allowed no reneging over the eight-month construction schedule. The amazing outcome? When the home was done, I saw no need to revert to a long workweek schedule and stayed on that four-day workweek pattern.

>> **Take away your time-wasting options.** Commit to time off and force yourself to work during established, reasonable work hours. Automatically, you'll force yourself to eliminate time-wasting activities.

>> **Give yourself no option to add hours back to your workweek.** If you allow yourself the option to add time back to your workweek, you leave yourself open to time-wasting choices.

Begin to treat time as your most valuable asset. Real estate agents are too casual with their time, leading to career, relationship, or bank-account casualties that could be avoided by treating time as life's most precious resource.

Applying Pareto's Principle: The 80:20 Rule

In the late 1800s, an Italian economist named Vilfredo Pareto observed that in Italy a small group of people held nearly all the power, influence, and money, which they used to create a significant advantage over the rest of the population. He theorized that in most countries about 80 percent of the wealth and power was controlled by about 20 percent of the people. He called this a "predictable imbalance," which eventually became known as the 80:20 rule.

In the 1900s, researchers realized that the theory of a "vital few and trivial many" — 20 percent of the participants accounting for 80 percent of the results — applies across many fields of expertise. Most certainly, it's true when it comes to time investment, and here's what that means to you:

>> Eighty percent of your results are generated by 20 percent of your hard-fought efforts. Conversely, 20 percent of your results are generated by 80 percent of your mediocre efforts. In other words, one-fifth of your time-consuming activities delivers four-fifths of your gross sales or gross commissions.

>> You can increase the productivity that results from your time investment by assessing which activities achieve the highest-quality results. Too many agents allow their time to be consumed by activities that generate a mere 20 percent of their revenue. The moment they shift their time investment into higher-return activities, they see dramatic income results.

REMEMBER

The 80:20 rule holds true across a spectrum of life activities. Whether you're investing in your career, relationships, health, wealth, or personal development, 20 percent of your efforts deliver 80 percent of the results you seek. The secret is to figure out which activities deliver the highest-quality returns and invest your time accordingly.

My 11-year-old daughter, Annabelle, loves to play games, read books, and especially have tea parties. I've discovered that an hour spent having a tea party with her gives her real joy and contributes greatly to our relationship. It's a minor time investment, clearly fitting into the 20 percent category, yet the results are significant in proportion.

Do you make time for the few activities that return the most significant results? Or are you, like most people in the world, giving your time to the time-gobbling 80 percent of activities that deliver a meager return?

Top performers in nearly any field quickly identify which actions account for the great majority of results, and they weight their time toward those activities, performing them with great regularity and intensity.

Following is the list of the half-dozen important activities that I share with all my real estate coaching clients:

1. Prospecting or direct lead generation
2. Lead follow-up
3. Listing presentations
4. Buyer interview presentations
5. Showing property to qualified buyers
6. Writing and negotiating contracts

TIP

If you dedicate yourself to these six activities, you'll see high returns on your time investment. I've studied the time allocation of agents for nearly 30 years. I know for certain that on average real estate agents spend fewer than two hours a day engaged in the activities on this list. Instead, they work long hours, often putting in more than ten hours a day, spending 80 percent or more of their time on activities that generate less than 20 percent of their revenue. Flip the principle to your advantage. Begin spending more and more of your time on the activities that are proven to deliver results, and refuse to be crushed by the weight and waste of those that don't.

Making time for the things that impact your success

If controlling time and gaining discipline to invest hours in better, higher-value activities were easy, everyone would be making big money in real estate sales. Facts prove otherwise. On average, newer agents make less than $20,000 a year. Almost certainly the low-income statistics correlate with poor time-allocation choices.

TIP

To allocate larger amounts of time to success-generating actions, follow what I call the four Ds:

1. **Decide** that your time-management skills, habits, and activities are going to change.

   This is a challenging first step for most people. That's because changing behavior isn't easy, and time usage is a behavior. To avoid change, people search for solutions that enable them to keep doing what they've always done. In doing so, they waste yet more time by vacillating between the change they know they must face and the hope that they won't have to face it.

   I believe that the biggest waste of time occurs from the moment you know you need to do something and when you actually set out to do it. That's why it's so important to make an immediate commitment to change your time-management patterns and habits. Make the decision to change today!

2. **Define** what needs to change. This step involves two phases. First you have to determine the specific activities that are causing you to waste time or sacrifice productivity. Then you have to figure out how you can remedy the situation.

   For example, do you need to get to your office earlier each day? Does that mean you need to go to sleep earlier each night? Do you need more prospecting time or more time for lead follow-up? Does that mean you need to turn off your email and text access and social media platforms to minimize distractions when you're trying to undertake these activities?

   What is barring your success?

   I worked with a client a few years ago who had difficulty getting into the office early enough to begin his day. We tracked it back to the fact that he was going to bed too late to be able to reach his office consistently by 8 a.m. when he needed his day to start.

   We further determined that he needed a certain amount of time in the evening to have dinner with his family, play with his children, put them to bed, and then have time with his wife before their bedtime. He needed to be home from work by a certain hour for all of this to happen efficiently and consistently for him.

   After he made the necessary changes, by coming in earlier and leaving the office on time, his income shot up dramatically. The quality of life with his children and wife skyrocketed, as well, all the result of defining the problem, designing a solution, and managing time accordingly.

3. **Design** a time-management plan. Get proactive rather than reactive. Typical day planners, smartphone scheduling apps, and Google Calendars are reactionary time-management tools. They enable you to schedule time for client needs, appointments, and limited activities, but they don't help you take control of time for your own priorities and purposes. You need to do that part on your own.

   To master your time, you need to adopt a time-blocking system that dedicates predetermined periods of time to your most valuable activities. The upcoming section describes time blocking in detail. The key point is that you can't leave your days vulnerable to the time needs of others. You must block out periods of time for your own priority activities. Otherwise, you risk giving your days away to the appointment or time requests of clients and colleagues, leaving yourself no time for your own needs. No wonder so many agents feel like they're being pulled like taffy.

4. Just **do** it! Growing up in Portland, Oregon, and graduating from Beaverton High School, I lived my early life down the street from a famous company's world headquarters and within constant earshot of the famous marketing slogan. Nike urged the world to take action now — to *Just Do It!* I interpret its three words as a life-success slogan.

Don't wait to analyze every aspect of every problem and design the absolutely perfect solution before taking action. Waiting promises only unrealized income, unfulfilled potential, and limited wealth. Instead, decide what to change, define how to change, design a time-management plan that allows for change, and then just do it.

Weighting your time to what matters

In order to achieve success, any newer agent must commit a minimum of 15 hours a week to DIPA, or direct income-producing activities. That means that you need to dedicate 15 hours every single week — three hours every day — to prospecting, lead generation, and lead follow-up. Do that, and you assure your success and income. Fail to do so and your success is in question.

WARNING

Don't cheat by trying to replace DIPA tasks with what I call IIPA, or *indirect income-producing activities.* IIPA tasks include things like making client-development marketing pieces, producing direct mailings, creating or fiddling with your website, optimizing your search-engine placement, publishing newsletters, and a near-endless list of other efforts that agents invest in to indirectly produce income.

The vast majority of social media is IIPA. Yes, you read that correctly. Although social media is valuable to your business, the truth is that far too many agents expect social media to replace all other forms of lead generation. Too often agents think they can sit behind their computers and generate large volumes of quality leads.

Social media is a wonderful way to communicate with, engage, and listen to clients, past clients, and prospects. But balancing your time is essential. You can spend hours checking posts and private messages, but you're faking yourself out if you think that's a productive use of your time. The key is to invest just 30 to 60 minutes a day in social media.

The exception is the use of Facebook or instant messaging. You can create a dialogue in real time with instant messages. If you invest a portion of your time using instant message to communicate with people each day, it will bring results.

The problem is, IIPA activities are difficult to control in terms of the time, effort, energy, and dollars they require, and they're almost impossible to measure in terms of outcome. Often, countless hours of your work result in marketing pieces that go straight to the trash bin, emails that are deleted with a single keystroke, or social-media posts that don't reach the right audience.

REMEMBER

Indirect marketing efforts result in a high *quantity* of contacts. Direct marketing efforts result in high-*quality* contacts — and sales success is the result of quality and quantity.

TIP

Aim to spread your time between DIPA and IIPA tasks on at least a four-to-one ratio: For every hour you spend in IIPA, spend at least four hours in DIPA. Veer from that ratio and you risk dramatic income swings rather than consistent revenue growth.

Keeping PSA time in check

Agents spend an undue amount of time on production-supporting activities, or PSAs. These activities include all the steps necessary to support such direct income-producing activities as prospecting, lead generation, following up on leads, taking listings, and making sales. You can't avoid the administrative functions that support your sales and customer-service efforts, but you can and should handle them in the fewest number of hours possible.

Using your time wisely

PSA functions surrounding sales tend to be recurring — requiring weekly or even daily attention. Here are several ways to keep these supporting tasks on a firm leash:

>> **Streamline the process.** Determine whether you can create a system to make it faster, possibly eliminating some unnecessary steps. Instead of doing it once for each prospect, can you do several at once, batching the work for greater efficiency? It takes almost as much time to assemble one set of marketing-material packages and brochures as it does ten. Invest the time to create the ten and have nine ready to go out the door.

>> **Create templates.** Don't craft a sales or lead follow-up letter from scratch each time. The same goes for proposals. You can take a basic format and customize it for individual use.

>> **Batch your work.** Make your PSA calls one after another. Bunch together the PSA actions as much as possible so you can move quickly from one similar call or action to another.

>> **Eliminate the step.** Sometimes your examination of process may uncover that a particular function doesn't need to be done at all.

>> **Delegate.** Is there administrative help somewhere in your sales department? Can you find someone to lend a hand? Are there internship programs that might provide some eager business students who want to learn the business from the ground up? A talk with your sales manager may help.

>> **Hire help.** If you can't get support within your department, are you willing to pay a few bucks for it? Maybe you can hire a college or high-school student, a stay-at-home parent, or a part-timer who just wants a low-pressure opportunity to earn a little money. For many of the PSA tasks that aren't proprietary, the work can be done off-site.

A part-time virtual assistant is another viable option. There are skilled people you can hire part time to fulfill administrative functions. Companies like My Out Desk (www.myoutdesk.com) or Best Agent Business (www.bestagentbusiness.com) have assistants ready to help your efforts.

Asking for referrals to turn PSA into DIPA

When you must turn to PSA work, you can often take the opportunity to get in a little DIPA action at the same time. For instance, customer-service follow-up calls are part of your production-supporting activities. Checking to confirm that the prospect or client has received expected materials or information is a routine task that doesn't relate directly to income generation.

TIP

But don't stop there — get some extra mileage from this PSA effort by turning your customer service call into a prospecting call: Ask for a referral.

It's never too early in a sales relationship to begin building a referral base. A truly qualified referral request, however, takes a little time and attention. Be ready to invest at *least* five minutes in conversation to avoid appearing like a hit-and-run referral driver. You may use a great segue statement like:

> *"I have a very important question to ask you."*

This statement forces a pause, builds anticipation, and sets the tone for a meaningful conversation. And it requests permission to explore client or prospect contacts. You may use a script like this to help you:

> *"I'm delighted that I've been able to serve you. I was wondering about others you might know who would also benefit from my service. Could we explore for a few minutes other individuals you believe I might be able to serve?"*

Managing Your Day

How often do you exclaim at the end of the day, "Where did the day go?" It's as if we've gotten nothing of significance done in the last eight hours on the job. When you feel that way, go back and review the mix of PSA, IIPA, and DIPA. How much time was spent in each category?

If you find that your time investment was a little off-balance, accept that today is gone, but tomorrow can be a new opportunity to get it right. Spend a few minutes figuring out where the day *did* go. Did you put off tackling your DIPA tasks until your day was derailed by interruptions? Were you so engrossed in IIPA tracking that you spent more time than you intended in analyzing the results? Did you lose momentum by jumping back and forth between prospecting, lead follow-up, and administrative activities?

Pinpoint the problems, plan for the next day, and nail down a schedule that ensures maximum productivity and keeps you on the path toward success.

Knowing the power of the 11 a.m. rule

REMEMBER

The 11 a.m. rule goes like this: The world around a real estate agent gears up at 11 each morning. Attorneys, title officers, loan officers, other agents, appraisers, home inspectors, repair contractors, and clients will most likely call you after or close to 11 a.m.

Because of this, it's imperative that you start in your home office or real estate office early and complete your prospecting and lead follow-up before the clock strikes the hour.

TIP

I even suggest the extreme approach of not answering your phone until 11 in order to minimize the chance of being distracted during your most important production hours.

Tracking your time

It's hard to know exactly how much time you spend on DIPA, IIPA, and PSA functions unless you've tracked your activities over a period of time to determine an average. This is very important, and it supports an undeniable truth in sales: When performance is measured, performance improves. By tracking your time usage, you're guaranteed to increase your time effectiveness.

Figure 17-1 is a form I use at Real Estate Champions to help our clients record and report how they utilize their time in half-hour increments. Most people have between 16 and 20 half-hour increments to invest at work daily. Here's how this form can help you make the most of those increments:

>> Keep the form with you and fill it out as you go. Don't wait until the end of the day to complete it — you're bound to forget something.

>> Track yourself for at least a week — longer is better. This allows for daily anomalies and helps create more of an "average" work flow.

TIP

Repeat this tracking process at least every six months. Over time, habits and behaviors may creep into your routine to diminish your time effectiveness. A routine check-up keeps you on track.

Activity Tracking by the Half-Hour

7:00-7:30	_____	DIPA	IIPA	PSA
7:30-8:00	_____	DIPA	IIPA	PSA
8:00-8:30	_____	DIPA	IIPA	PSA
8:30-9:00	_____	DIPA	IIPA	PSA
9:00-9:30	_____	DIPA	IIPA	PSA
9:30-10:00	_____	DIPA	IIPA	PSA
10:00-10:30	_____	DIPA	IIPA	PSA
10:30-11:00	_____	DIPA	IIPA	PSA
11:00-11:30	_____	DIPA	IIPA	PSA
11:30-12:00	_____	DIPA	IIPA	PSA
12:00-12:30	_____	DIPA	IIPA	PSA
12:30-1:00	_____	DIPA	IIPA	PSA
1:00-1:30	_____	DIPA	IIPA	PSA
2:00-2:30	_____	DIPA	IIPA	PSA
2:30-3:00	_____	DIPA	IIPA	PSA
3:00-3:30	_____	DIPA	IIPA	PSA
3:30-4:00	_____	DIPA	IIPA	PSA
4:00-4:30	_____	DIPA	IIPA	PSA
4:30-5:00	_____	DIPA	IIPA	PSA

DIPA Payoff Hours _____

IIPA Payoff Hours _____

PSA Payoff Hours _____

Total Hours _____

FIGURE 17-1: Productivity form for recording time spent.

© John Wiley & Sons, Inc.

You must monitor the mix of total hours in each category. The goal is to spend at least 40 percent of your hours in DIPA, with more than half of the 40 percent spent in prospecting, lead generation, and lead follow-up.

Dealing with time-consuming fires

Time-consuming fires are the hot issues that result from the emotional turmoil involved in many real estate transactions. Sometimes they require calm and caution; other times you need to put on a fireman's hat and start dousing the flames of a delayed closing; emotionally frustrated buyer or seller; problem co-op agent; or slow-moving inspector, appraiser, or loan officer. Let the following rules guide your responses:

>> **Rule #1: There is no closing issue that can't wait an hour.** When your transaction hits a snag, don't let it dramatically change your day's schedule. Wait to resolve the issue during the time you've blocked for administrative tasks.

>> **Rule #2: A frenzied reaction only adds fuel to the fire.** More often than not, when one closing party gets riled it's because someone else in the transaction is riled — and hysteria is catching. Aim to serve as the calming influence in the transaction. If the problem arises two hours before your predetermined administrative time slot, inform the parties that you have prescheduled appointments that you can't change, but that you'll be able to take action when you get out of the appointments in two hours.

>> **Rule #3: Fires often burn themselves out.** Rather than jump into the mess, give the issue a bit of time to simmer down. Remember that your prospecting and lead follow-up tasks are appointments to which you've committed. Sticking with your daily plan may give the issue time to cool or even resolve itself.

>> **Rule #4: Don't wait for a three-alarm fire to call for the pump truck.** If the fire becomes hot, suit up your broker right away. Before the transaction flares out of control, ask for help. The longer you delay, the more effort you'll spend getting the situation cooled down.

Time Blocking Your Way to Success

A time-blocked schedule reserves and protects slotted time segments for pre-planned, pre-determined activities. The objective of time blocking is to increase the amount of time you can invest in direct income-producing efforts.

In more than 30 years as a business owner, I've yet to run across a more reliable method for seizing control of time and boosting productivity than time blocking.

Many people have heard of time blocking, but few master its use. The challenge isn't in creating the schedule; that's the easy part. The challenge is keeping on the schedule. That's the hard part, because most people set their time-blocking expectations very high, reserve large portions of time, and then can't maintain the schedule. The good news, though, is that even if you need to compromise your time blocks, you still come out ahead.

One of my coaching clients increased the number of units she sold by more than 100 in one year, at the same time increasing her sales volume by more than $17 million. Pretty amazing performance. I asked her how much of her time she spent on her ideal time-blocking schedule. Her answer: "About 50 percent of the time." She is proof that even maintaining half of your blocked-out time can produce incredible results.

Setting your schedule in time blocks

Good time blocking starts with a schedule grid. See Figure 17-2 for a good sample to follow. In the beginning, create a grid that breaks your schedule down into 30-minute segments. As your skill progresses, you may shift to a 15-minute grid format.

TIME BLOCKING SCHEDULE

	MONDAY	TUESDAY	WEDNESDAY	THURSDAY	FRIDAY	SATURDAY	SUNDAY
6AM	Personal Development	Personal Development	Personal Development	Personal Development	Personal Development		Day Off
6:30	+	+	+	+	+		+
7:00	Workout	Workout	Workout	Workout	Workout		+
7:30	+	+	+	+	+	Breakfast with Family	+
8:00	Breakfast	Breakfast	Breakfast	Breakfast	Breakfast	+	+
8:30	Flex time	Flex time	Flex time	Flex time	Flex time	+	+
9:00	Prospect	Sales Meeting	Prospect	Prospect	Prospect	Prospect	+
9:30	+	+	+	+	+	+	+
10:00	Lead Follow-Up	Office Tour	Lead Follow-Up	Lead Follow-Up	Lead Follow-Up		+
10:30	+	+	+	+	+	Lead Follow-Up	+
11:00	Flex time	+	Flex time	Flex time	Flex time		+
11:30	Return Phone Calls	Return Phone Calls	Return Phone Calls	Return Phone Calls	Return Phone Calls	Flex time	+
12PM	+	+	+	+	+	Appointments	+
12:30	Lunch	Lunch	Lunch	Lunch	Lunch	+	+
1:00	+	+	+	+	+	+	+
1:30	Administration	Administration	Administration	Administration	Administration	+	+
2:00	+	+	+	+	+	Flex time	+
2:30	+	+	+	+	Planning Time	Appointments	+
3:00	Flex time	Flex time	Flex time	Flex time	+	+	+
3:30	Marketing Activities	Marketing Activities	Marketing Activities	Marketing Activities	+	+	Day Off
4:00	+	+	+	+	Return Phone Calls	+	+
4:30	Return Phone Calls	Return Phone Calls	Return Phone Calls	Return Phone Calls	+	+	+
5:00	+	+	+	+	Evening Off	Evening Off	+
5:30	Appointments/ Prospecting	Appointments	Flex time	Appointments	+	+	+
6:00	+	+	Evening Off	+	+	+	+
6:30	+	+	+	+	+	+	+
7:00	+	+	+	+	+	+	+
7:30	+	+	+		+	+	+
8:00			+		+	+	+
8:30			+		+	+	+
9:00			+		+	+	+
9:30			+		+	+	+
10:00			+		+	+	+

FIGURE 17-2: Use a schedule grid such as this one to block your time and manage your day.

As you complete the grid, I strongly suggest that you block your entire daily schedule, not just your workday. Follow these steps:

>> **Block time for your personal life first.** If you don't, you'll be hard pressed to squeeze in personal time after scheduling everything else.

Decide which are the most important personal activities in your life and block them out before you allow any other obligations onto your calendar. Set aside a date night with your spouse or significant other. Block time for exercise, quiet time, prayer time, personal-development time, and family time. If your daughter has soccer games on Tuesday and Thursday evenings, put those in your schedule. If someone wants to see you during those times, say you're booked with a previous appointment.

For my personal schedule, I reserve a weekly date night with my wife, Joan. I block workout times. I have Wednesday afternoons for men's golf day at my club.

>> **Decide which full day you'll take off each week.** No ifs, ands, or buts. You must take at least one day off. The reaction of new agents is, "Oh! I couldn't do that." Give me a break; even God took the seventh day off.

WARNING

A few words on the definition of a day off: It means no real estate calls, no answering your cell phone, no negotiating offers, no taking ad calls, no taking sign calls, and no meeting with clients or prospects. The minute you do any business activity, it's a workday, even if it's just for five minutes. Honor yourself and your family with one day a week away from real estate. The 24/7 approach leads to family frustrations and burnout. It's hard to receive the love you need from a pile of money.

>> **Decide which evenings you will and won't work.** Again, set boundaries. I suggest that you make no more than three or four nights a week available to clients. Designate them during the time-blocking stage and then move prospects only into those evening time slots. I limited my own evening work to Tuesdays only. Every other night of the week my wife could expect me home no later than 6:30 for dinner if I had a 5:15 listing appointment.

>> **Begin blocking time for DIPA,** or direct income-producing activities.

- Block time for prospecting and lead follow-up first, and preferably early in the day. I know what you're thinking: "Don't more people answer their phone in the afternoon and evening?" Probably so. But will you prospect consistently if you do it in the evening? After almost 30 years in real estate, I know for a fact that the answer is no. The fact that more people are freer at night doesn't matter if that's not when you're calling to engage them. Schedule calls for morning hours when you can and will make the contacts.

- Schedule time slots for appointments next. Determine how many appointments you need to hold and how long they need to run. How long do you need for a listing presentation? How much time do you need to show a buyer homes in a specific area?

I scheduled appointment slots in one-hour increments, which worked because after my second year in the business I didn't work with buyers. When you work with buyers, you need to plan on longer appointments. With sellers, I figured that my typical listing presentation lasted about 45 minutes. The hour block gave me at least 15 minutes of drive time to reach my next appointment.

I scheduled appointments in the afternoons at 3:15, 4:15, and 5:15 Monday through Thursday. Tuesdays I worked late, and I scheduled appointments at 6:15, 7:15, and 8:15. Whenever I didn't have a 5:15 appointment, I transferred that block to prospecting time, so I could catch up with people after work.

The reason I scheduled appointments at a quarter after the hour was strategic. It demonstrated to the prospect that I was exact with my time, and that my time was valuable. Also, it was a unique time, so it was more memorable, and the prospect was less likely to forget the appointment.

TIP

When you block appointment slots, you know exactly when to ask people to meet with you. You can emulate a doctor's nurse or dentist's reception-ist, saying, "I have an opening at 5:15 on Tuesday or 4:15 on Wednesday. Which would be better for you?"

>> **Schedule time for administrative tasks.** This includes phone calls, office meetings, company property tours, and the like. Make a list of your regular, necessary activities and then put them into your time-blocked schedule.

>> **Finally, block some flextime.** Flextime helps you stay on track. It allows you to put out fires, make emergency calls, handle unscheduled but necessary tasks, and still stay on your schedule.

WARNING

Most agents who are new to time blocking create schedules that are too rigid. The lack of flexibility causes them to be off their schedules before 10:30 in the morning. From that point, they're off schedule for the rest of the day.

TIP

As you start out, block about 30 minutes of flextime for every two hours of scheduled time in your daily grid. You can always reduce or remove the flextime blocks as your skills and discipline increase.

Avoiding time-blocking mistakes

Sales professionals in the top 10 percent of their industries share a common trait: They control, use, and invest their time more wisely and effectively than their lower-performing associates. Among sales professionals, time usage determines income.

The most significant challenge for most sales professionals is time control. Through years of study and coaching sales professionals, I've compiled the following list of challenges that most salespeople experience when trying to master their time–block schedule.

1. **Mistake #1: Making yourself too available.** The biggest error that salespeople make is getting sucked into the interruption game. You need times in your schedule that are free of interruptions, during which you bar access to all but those to whom you grant exceptions. Follow this advice:

   - Use an effective gatekeeper to screen your calls, redirecting all minor issues, problems, challenges, and interruptions that can be handled by an assistant or some other person.

   - Use your voicemail to screen and inform. Record a new voicemail greeting daily. Tell the listener when you're in appointments and when you'll be returning calls. This sets the standard that you're busy and valuable but also available.

   - Employ auto-responders for email and text. When you are busy or unavailable, at least the person who is inquiring will get a touch from you.

   - Limit the number of people who have unfiltered access to you. Create a short list of the important few people who can interrupt your schedule at any time of the day, and don't let anyone else in during time blocked for interruption-free activities. My short list includes my wife, my father, my attorney, and a few key associates. Period. As you make your own list, include only those who are extremely important to your personal life. Very few clients find their way onto the short lists of truly successful people.

2. **Mistake #2: Choosing the wrong office location and setup.** The nature of your physical office has a dramatic effect on your time management and productivity. Give serious consideration to the following two issues:

   - See that the size of your work environment matches the size of your practice. If you don't have enough square footage for yourself and your staff, your production will be stunted.

     I had a coaching client a few years back who worked out of 150 square feet of office space with three associates. Amazingly, even as they were tripping over each other they managed to do 150 transactions a year.

     But when they moved into a new 500-square-foot office, they watched their production soar. Each team member could control time better, limit interruptions, access files, and hold meetings. The expanded space allowed for an increase in discipline, talent, skill, and production.

     Don't let your physical space limit your growth opportunities. If you're crowded and not able to be productive or creative, you're in the wrong physical location.

- Your personal office must be private. A home office in your home's hub central doesn't offer the privacy needed. If your work area at the real estate office enables you to leave everything going on around you, it's likely you will have a loss of productivity. The only way to control your planning and prospecting environment is to locate your work environment in a private location away from distractions.

3. **Mistake #3: Failing to operate on an appointment-only basis.** Too many agents are willing to meet at all hours of the day and night and on a moment's notice. By time blocking, you can create appointment slots and drive prospects into those slots, just as your doctor, dentist, or attorney does.

   Studies show that 80 percent of all prospects are willing to fit into the schedules of their professional advisors. But when they aren't alerted to a schedule, they take control on their own, dictating the appointment time and leaving an agent like you juggling your schedule to adapt to their needs. Realtors accept this knee-jerk scheduling approach as a necessary aspect of a "service-oriented" business, as if total availability equals service.

   TIP

   Operate as a professional on an appointment-only basis, with all appointments scheduled during time-blocked periods when you know you'll be available, focused, and uninterrupted by any issue other than the one your client is sharing.

4. **Mistake #4: Bowing to distractions.** Real estate sales is among the most interrupted and distracted professions on the face of the planet. Realtors are distracted by the constant jangle of cell phones, texts, emails, and personal messages.

   TIP

   If the phone isn't ringing, you have the distraction of email, usually interrupting you with some unsolicited miracle offer or, less often, with a new lead opportunity. Here's a tip: Don't derail your day just because your tablet or smartphone tells you that you've got mail.

   Control distractions following this advice:

   - Block time in your day for the distractions you know you'll encounter. If you want to socialize with other agents, plan a set time to do that. Just remember to keep it short and limit the coffee klatch to the time you allocated for it.

   - Create a list of no more than five people who are granted instant access during your workday. Have your assistant memorize the names. If you don't have an assistant, work with your receptionist so that only those few people are granted unfiltered access.

REMEMBER

Position yourself as an agent-in-command versus an agent-on-demand. Block your time and maintain your schedule. Rather than putting yourself at the beck and call of others during all hours of the day and night, work on an appointment basis, eliminate distractions, and take control of your days, your business, your income, and your life.

Killing the Time Killer Called Procrastination

The number-one obstacle between real estate agents and higher production is interruptions. A close second is procrastination.

REMEMBER

Procrastination is the direct result of a lack of urgency to do what needs to be done and to do it *now*. Urgency is directly linked to success. You can increase your output by 30 percent if you work with urgency in mind.

My friend Brian Tracy shared with me years ago the *law of forced efficiency*. It's based on the premise that you'll never have enough time to do everything you want or need to do, but that in every day you'll always have enough time to accomplish the most important tasks. Obviously, you won't get to the most important tasks if you're bogged down with tasks of low importance that can easily wait until later. Nor will you get to the most important tasks if you procrastinate.

An upcoming section in this chapter helps you set priorities. After you set your priorities, take action without procrastination by following these two pieces of advice:

>> Limit the time in which you can get the job done. Too much time to work can lower urgency and lead to procrastination. By identifying days off and time off, you raise the efficiency and effectiveness of your production on the days you're working.

>> Give yourself deadlines. Have you ever noticed how much gets done when you're leaving on vacation in a day or so? I've seen people double or triple their work output in the days leading up to a vacation. What if you operated every day at that pace and urgency? Your income and quality of life would explode to heights you never imagined.

Moving forward with a clear vision

A good deal of procrastination results directly from the lack of a clear vision or clarity about what to do. If you don't know what you want, you can't possibly achieve it. You can hardly hit a target you can't see.

REMEMBER

Clarity of purpose kills procrastination, yet fewer than 3 percent of all people define and write down their goals.

Answer these questions:

>> What do you want to be?

>> What do you want to do with your life?

>> What do you want to have?

>> Where do you want to go?

I know you want to be financially independent. Otherwise, you wouldn't be in real estate sales. But what does financial independence mean to you? How much money do you need to live the lifestyle you dream about? The famous success motivator Napoleon Hill explains the importance of identifying your goal when he says, "There is one quality that one must possess to win, and that is definiteness of purpose . . . the knowledge of what one wants and a burning desire to achieve it."

Clarify your desires. When you're certain about what you want to achieve, you'll find it far easier to set and follow an action plan that isn't hindered by the problem of procrastination.

Knowing your objectives

You'll set annual goals, of course. But also view each day that you work or play in terms of daily objectives. What do you want to accomplish today? What result do you want to effect by day's end?

Setting your priorities

REMEMBER

Your priorities are the most important actions or steps you must take in order to achieve your objectives for the day. Objectives and priorities aren't one and the same. Objectives are results you intend to achieve. Priorities are steps you take to achieve success.

By prioritizing the importance or value of the tasks on your to-do list, you greatly increase the probability that you'll be motivated to overcome procrastination and get the job done.

Most people go about creating task lists in the wrong way. They write down all the things they must do each day and then go to work, proudly ticking off items as they are completed and equating their level of success with the number of items they check off the list. Success, though, doesn't result from how many things you get done. It results from getting the *right* things done. In other words, you need to know your priorities.

Following is an outline for the prioritization system I've used with success for years:

1. **Create your daily task list as you normally would.** Don't think at all about what is most important. Just think about what needs to get done over the course of the day. Put yourself in brainstorming mode and get your thoughts down on paper.

2. **When you have your list, create task categories.** You're not prioritizing during this step. This isn't about what to do first, second, or third. All you're doing is sorting tasks into these categories:

    A. You'll suffer a significant consequence if you don't complete these tasks today. If it means you have to work all day and all night, these items must get done.

    B. These tasks trigger a mild consequence if they aren't completed today. You probably wouldn't stay late to finish them.

    C. These tasks have no penalty at all if they aren't done today.

    D. These tasks can be delegated. They involve low-value activities that should be performed by someone who has a lower hourly dollar value than you.

    E. These tasks can and should be eliminated. They probably made their way onto your list out of tradition or habit. They aren't necessary, so you need to figure out a way to get them off the list. I call it *pruning*.

    My late friend Zig Ziglar used to tell a story of a little boy who asks his mother as they are preparing a holiday meal why she cuts the ends off the ham. She says, "I don't know. My mother always did it this way." Now this 4-year-old boy (I know he is four because my son, Wesley, would say the exact same thing when he was 4) says, "Let's call Grandma right now and find out." So they call Grandma and ask why she always cuts the ends off the ham. Her reply: Her roaster is too small for the whole ham! Break out of the habit of doing things a certain way because you have always done it that way. You need to be constantly looking to eliminate nonproductive activities.

3. **When your list is categorized, prioritize the tasks.** Begin with your A category and determine which item deserves A-1 status. Follow by designating A-2, A-3, A-4, A-5, and so on. Then repeat the process for the B, C, and D categories. Go to work in the order of these priorities, and you'll be amazed at how you can accomplish more in less time without falling into the procrastination trap.

As you master the art of prioritizing, expect to see fewer cross-offs or check marks on your task list. By undertaking your most important tasks first, you'll complete fewer but more important activities.

WHAT'S AN HOUR OF YOUR TIME WORTH, ANYWAY?

Your hourly rate or hourly value is one of the most important numbers in your life, yet only one out of a hundred real estate agents can say what their time is worth.

Ask members of a real estate agency's administrative staff, and you can find out the answer down to a penny. They know exactly what they're paid on an hourly basis. Your broker manager, who is on salary, can answer the question, as well. And certainly most people in the world around you, including your clients, can tell you what an hour of their time is worth.

It's time that you get with the program!

Most respected professionals, including doctors, dentists, accountants, and attorneys, fundamentally sell time for a price. The higher their professional skills and the greater their reputations and success levels, the more they're able to increase their hourly rates in order to earn even more income. A successful attorney can decide to charge $500 an hour instead of $250.

As an agent, you can't simply decide to start charging, say, an 11 percent commission rate rather than the rate that is deemed normal or standard in your marketplace. But you *can* raise your income and the value of each hour invested in your business by increasing your productivity.

To calculate your hourly value, follow this formula:

- Add the number of hours you work in a typical day. Multiply that by the number of days you work a week. Then multiply that by the number of weeks you work in a year. This gives you the total hours you work each year.

Hours worked per day x days worked per week x weeks worked per year = total hours worked

- Calculate the gross commission income you earn in a year. If you're a new agent, use your income goal instead of actual income.
- Divide your total income by the total number of hours you work a year. The result is your hourly rate or value per hour.

Gross commission income ÷ total hours worked = hourly rate

If you're a full-time real estate agent, you probably work somewhere between 2,000 and 4,000 hours per year. If the number is closer to 4,000, then I'm safe to wager that your hourly rate is very low.

I've met with agents who make $400,000 a year by working practically round-the-clock, and their hourly value barely reaches $100 an hour. Other agents limit their work hours and maximize productivity, earning hourly rates well over $1,000 an hour — better than a surgeon's rate!

To raise your hourly rate, raise the productivity of each hour you invest in your business.

Watch your hourly value as a key indicator of your business success. Use your current hourly rate as a benchmark and then set a goal to double, triple, or even quadruple the value you wring out of each hour.

TIP

Consider every day that you achieve closure on all your A category items a terrific success. If you complete your A items on every single one of the days you work this year, I guarantee that you'll see your production and income explode.

Giving yourself deadlines and rewards

It's human instinct to move away from pain and toward the pleasures of life. That's why you have to link deadlines with rewards if you want to keep yourself motivated to complete your work in a sustained way. Without a reward, it's darned hard to face the rigor of a difficult task.

Each day when you set your objectives and priorities, set deadlines as well. Then link completion of your tasks with a clearly defined reward.

For example, set a deadline to get all of your prospecting, lead generation, and lead follow-up calls done by 11:30 a.m., and then reward yourself with a trip to your favorite coffee shop or lunch restaurant. Beyond that, promise yourself that if you meet your deadlines and complete all your priorities for a full week, you'll reward yourself with a massage, facial, or special evening out.

Realize these two truths about rewards:

>> You have to give them to yourself. Don't expect to receive them from your broker, clients, prospects, staff, or even family.

>> You have to set interim goals to keep you moving forward on a consistent basis. If your reward is financial independence, your payoff may not arrive for 10 or 20 years. That's way too long to wait for a pat on the back.

Sales involves high pay, for sure, but also a fair amount of rejection and discouragement in between. Rewards encourage you to do the things you know you should do even when you don't feel like doing them.

Carpe Diem: Seizing Your Day

One of the most identifiable characteristics of high performers is that they're action-oriented. They don't wait around to see what will happen or how things will turn out. They seize each day, wringing all the possibilities, performance, and profit out of every encounter. They treat each moment as a gift. As the saying goes, that's why we call today the present!

Stop wasting time

To quote Napoleon Hill again: "Do not wait; the time will never be 'just right.' Start where you stand and work with whatever tools you may have at your command, and better tools will be found as you go along." In other words: Get to work!

If you're a newer agent, don't waste time fretting over the fact that your skills or tools aren't at the level of other agents. Work with what you've got and know that your abilities will improve with use. At the worst, you'll make a mistake from which you'll learn a good lesson. Finding out early in your career what *not* to do delivers value that pays off again and again in your future.

I accepted a newer agent as a coaching client a year ago. Recently, he made an exception to the policy of making a client sign a buyer's agency contract. His client was the younger sister of his wife's best friend, and so he didn't insist that the client-agency relationship be formalized in writing. After three offers were written and many hours were invested, his client chose to buy through a discount broker. My client was out time and money, the result of his lack of experience.

I told him this was the best thing that could happen to him. He'd been burned by someone he never expected would let him down, and he'd learned a good lesson. I told him to get back to work and *never* make that exception again!

Stop letting others waste your time

Too many consumers feel no loyalty or obligation to agents. They have the idea that agents are well paid through commissions, but they don't seem to acknowledge that we're not paid at all if no sale occurs.

REMEMBER

For that reason, it's very important that you work with clients who are serious about buying or selling and who agree to work exclusively with you to accomplish their real estate objectives. Otherwise, you're letting real estate shoppers waste your time.

The biggest loss that most agents experience is lost opportunity. Each time you invest in helping a prospect who fails to take action or, worse yet, leaves you for another agent, your investment results in absolutely no financial compensation. That's like a personal injury attorney losing all his cases. He will be out of business soon.

Manage interruptions

The best way to handle interruptions is to stop them from happening in the first place.

TIP

Especially when you're conducting direct income-producing activities — when you're prospecting, lead generation, or doing lead follow-up — turn off unnecessary access points like your email, private messages, and even texts if you need to stay focused. Tell the receptionist to hold your calls and take messages instead if you are working in the real estate office. Turn off your email program so the "you've got mail" icon doesn't blink onto your computer screen. Sign out of your online instant-message program. Hang a sign on your office door advising that you aren't to be interrupted.

Follow the same rules when you're with a client. Nothing is more impolite than an agent who handles phone calls while driving around showing clients property. At the very least, set your cell phone to vibrate rather than ring when you're doing buyer interviews, showing properties, or attending listing appointments.

Eliminate distractions for your own good and for the good of the relationship with the client you're trying to serve.

Handle intrusive clients

In real estate, we're in a customer-service business. We place a high level of value on our customers. But the thought of "the customer is always right" can be taken too far.

You know that in order to provide the best service to each customer, you have to seek some balance. If the "squeaky-wheel" clients take up more than their share of your time and resources, you won't be able to give the attention to other deserving customers.

It's important to educate customers about your availability. Let new customers know your schedule and the best times to reach you — as well as how to leave a message when you can't be reached. As part of this education, you also want to establish how quickly they can expect a response from you after they leave a message: 24 hours? The same business day?

As for existing clients and customers, be sure to update them whenever your availability circumstances change. If you make changes to your schedule, notify them of the schedule revisions and your new availability. Depending upon the importance of the client and the immediacy of the situations you deal with, you may even want to let customers know when you're on vacation or on a business trip so they know your response time will be longer.

REMEMBER

Creating reasonable expectations is key in good customer relations. It may not be unreasonable to take 24 hours to return a client's call — but not if the client is used to and expects to hear from you within an hour.

TIP

You can also reinforce this through your voicemail message. When you leave your availability and response details as part of your message, callers are more likely to recall and retain. For example:

> *"You've reached Dirk Zeller. I'm out of the office today, Tuesday, September 2. Please leave a message, and I will return your call by end-of-day Wednesday, September 3. If you need immediate assistance, please call . . . Until then, make it a great day!"*

I've set the scenario: The caller should not expect a return call from me today. And, in fact, because I'll be returning to an inbox filled with calls, emails, and correspondence, I may not be able to get back until as late as the end of the day. I've offered, however, a back-up plan if the situation is more urgent. This should satisfy virtually anyone who calls.

WARNING

Don't be tempted to include, as many agents do, "If it's an emergency, call me on my cell phone," unless you're prepared for lots of interruptions. After all, isn't *interruption* exactly what you're trying to avoid?

Keep phone calls short

Especially when you're making or taking transaction-servicing calls or production-support calls, you need to conduct business in the shortest time period possible. Otherwise you'll erode the time you need for high-value income-producing activities. To keep calls short, employ these techniques:

>> Establish an indication of the time available as you begin the call. For example, say something like, "I have an appointment in 15 minutes, but your call was an important one, and I wanted to get back to you as quickly as I could." This technique alerts the call recipient to your time limitation. It says, nicely, "Get to the point quickly." It underscores that you value the caller and made a special effort to make time for the conversation.

If you're on a time-blocked schedule, everything is treated as an appointment, including times for returning phone calls, so you'll be speaking the truth. You *do* have another appointment in 15 minutes. This technique is particularly appropriate for prospect or client calls.

» Offer an alternative to a short phone call. If you think your client or prospect wants or needs more than a short return phone call, follow the above technique but then go one step further: Assure the other person that 15 minutes should be more than enough time, but if it's not you can schedule a phone conference when you'll be available for an appointment later in the day. I've made this offer many times, and I've never had to talk with the client later. We've always managed to resolve the issues during the short conversation.

» When possible, handle production-support calls with voicemail messages. You don't want to rely on voicemail with prospects, because you want to establish personal relationships that lead to face-to-face meetings. But when you're handling service calls, voicemail is a time-effective option for both you and the other party. Make a call, leave a message, and offer the option to call you back with the assurance that if your message resolves the issue then there is no need for a return call. Follow a script such as this one:

"Bob, I know that you're busy. I believe that this resolves the issue. If you agree, there is no need for you to call me back. If you do need to speak with me, I'll be available later today between 3:30 and 4:15. Please call me then."

Use your car to gain efficiency and career advancement

One of my greatest assets in my early career was my car. It wasn't because I had such a glamorous vehicle. It's because I turned it into my skills-development classroom. I never turned on the engine without listening to something that would teach me something (except when I had clients with me, of course).

TIP

I'm a firm believer in the auto university. You have a large learning curve ahead and plenty of drive time during which you can "go to school" with downloads and podcasts that help you improve your business, sales, and personal skills. Connecting your iPod or MP3 player to your car to engage in auto university will explode your income.

Use your drive time as educational time. You're success-oriented or you wouldn't have invested in this book and read thus far. Keep acquiring new ideas by turning your commute into skills-development time, and get ready to watch your career take off.

6

The Part of Tens

Gain access to a treasure-trove of tools that are essential for any real estate agent's success.

Behold the top keys to making great listing presentations.

Find out how working on teams can confer various advantages in real estate sales.

Be safe out there — check out some important safety tips for real estate agents.

Chapter **18**

Ten Must-Haves for a Successful Agent

To be a successful agent, you need to be focused, determined, and organized. You also need a few items to keep you on the path to success. Keep the following things in your agent arsenal and you'll be well on your way to achieving your goals.

Good Contact Management System

As a salesperson, you have to be able to keep in touch with prospects and clients easily and effectively. You must be able to put your hands on names, addresses, phone numbers, and email addresses in an instant.

You can track people and prospects the old-fashioned way, on spreadsheets or your phone contacts, but you'll soon outgrow that method. My advice is to get a customer relationship management (CRM) software package. Many, such as Sage ACT, GoldMine, and Salesforce, are specifically designed for salespeople. These programs automate your client database, sales, and more.

Another option is to buy something that is specific to the real estate industry. The programs that are specific to real estate agents hold many advantages over general sales programs. They're usually programmed with letters and correspondence an agent can use. They also have pre-created lead follow-up and client follow-up plans already built in. Most have plans to apply when marketing a property. They also have plans you can launch after you've secured a buyer for a listing.

I recommend real estate-specific software like Top Producer, Wise Agent, or Real-tyJuggler. Most of these programs are web-based, which means they can be accessed from anywhere or from any tool, such as a computer, laptop, tablet, or smartphone. Additionally, most charge a monthly fee. This allows you to pay as you go rather than budgeting for a large upfront cost, and you get the updates for free.

WARNING

A good contact management system is a must for any serious agent. Most agents attempt to use Outlook . . . mistake! In my opinion, Outlook doesn't have the necessary power and lacks the "cascading action plans." You need to be able to set a lead follow-up or contact sequence and automate the process of reaching out to clients and prospects.

Online Lead-Generation Software

Buyer and seller prospects are searching for homes online before they contact a real estate agent. According to NAR, last year over 33 percent of buyers found the agent online that they used to help them buy a home. If you're not working to generate leads online you are losing a third of potential buyer prospects.

Buyers want to be able to search properties, gather information about properties, areas, and school districts, and even compare and save properties for future reference. Your ability to "push" properties out that match their predetermined criteria is also essential.

Many MLS systems offer a basic version of data exchange for the agent to provide the consumer. There are more advanced systems, like Real Geeks, Commission Inc., Real Estate Webmasters, Kunversion, and Agent Jet. These systems will aid you in capturing and communicating directly with buyer and seller prospects. You will be able to see what properties they viewed, how frequently they have searched, and what properties they have saved or favorited. You gain an inside view of their habits to help you better understand their purchase timing.

Enhanced CMA Software

Listings are becoming more competitive than ever. The value of a listing to an agent's business has grown exponentially in the last five years. This is due to the lower listing inventory in most markets, the buyer shift to online research, and third-party websites like Zillow, Trulia, and Realtor.com commanding so many eyeballs. Your listing presentation has to be better packaged, especially in your analysis of their property and its value.

The basic CMA software that is provided inside most MLS software is lacking. You need powerful images, charts, graphs, and marketplace analysis that create a differentiation for you compared to the other agents. Most agents use the basic MLS-provided software. That means that for the part of the presentation where you discuss the value of their home, market conditions, and what price to start at initially, your presentation in that segment will look largely the same as other agents' unless you use something different.

Using software like Cloud CMA (www.cloudcma.com) or Touch CMA (www.touchcma.com) will give you the edge when discussing the marketplace and value of their home. In addition, if you use Cloud CMA, they have a "What is my home worth?" campaign built right into the software. This allows you to use your email lists, Facebook ads, and pay-per-click campaigns to attract seller leads through a "What is my home worth?" campaign.

BombBomb

One of the most revolutionary software programs I have seen in the past 20 years is BombBomb (www.bombbomb.com). BombBomb is a video email program that enables you to create video emails from your web camera, smartphone, or video camera. You can quickly make a video within the software application or upload an existing video into the program.

The program delivers your video right to the inbox of the prospect, client, or past client. It's not a link they have to click but an actual compressed video with a big still image of your smiling face greeting them.

BombBomb is ideal for breaking the ice with a prospect you haven't reached via phone or who hasn't returned your calls. It's perfect to create that ongoing relationship with your past clients and sphere of influence. You can create individual customer video emails or create a drip campaign that automates the relationship you're trying to build. A *drip* campaign is a pre-created series of emails that go out to prospects via an autoresponder feature at specific intervals.

The company also has a product called Playbook, in which all emails, videos, and sequences are designed for you. You don't have to figure out what to say or write. All you have to do is record, upload, and send — it takes mere minutes. Check out www.bombbomb.com/rechampions to try it out.

Tablet Computer

To keep up in the real estate market, you need to be technologically driven. One essential tool is a tablet computer, such as an iPad.

A tablet is critical because of the mobile environment in which real estate agents work. The sleek design and portability of the tablet is perfect for the real estate industry.

You must have a tablet with both wi-fi and 4G capabilities. Being able to show clients real-time property listings, including videos and pictures, can make a big impact. Use a tablet for open houses, listing presentations, and buyer consultations, whether at your office, at a client's home, or at the local coffee shop.

Showing such information to prospective clients who walk into your open houses expands their options, enhances their knowledge base, and creates an opportunity for them to linger at the open house longer — and get to know you better.

Tablet computers also create opportunities for a paperless process, which is an attractive option in the real estate industry.

DocuSign or Dotloop Software

The ability to serve your clients and prospects faster and more efficiently without paper is a key service. These types of software save you time in not having to transport documents and instead putting documents immediately into the hands of your clients digitally. DocuSign was one of the first software packages to be universally accepted on purchase agreements. It allows your clients and prospects to sign documents electronically with a few clicks. They can approve agreements and contingency-removal documents and in some areas even close a transaction.

Dotloop offers a full suite of paperless storage options for your key documents.

Facebook Business Page

Facebook has become an effective tool for service-based businesses, such as real estate agents. The balance between your personal Facebook page and a business Facebook page is delicate. Both need to be used to communicate with your sphere of influence. Agents can make the mistake of posting too many listings and other business topics on their personal pages. The sooner you can establish a business presence on Facebook, the more muted you can be on your personal page.

The goal is to establish yourself as an expert and a portal of key real estate information for your area. You can highlight market trends, share national and local real estate articles, and even promote real estate best buys and opportunities.

Personal Website

With more than 91 percent of buyers using the Internet to search for properties, your website is an essential tool for generating leads and promoting your sellers' homes.

You don't need the fanciest, most expensive website you can find. A lot of companies make solid template-based websites. These sites are extremely economical, considering the low initial investment and monthly hosting fees. Many of these companies build cost-effective sites and earn most of their income when they charge monthly fees for hosting your site.

You want to work with a company that builds template sites as well as custom sites. Most new agents start on a budget, so you may start with a template site and then as your business grows move to a custom site. You also want a company that has the ability to place you higher in search-engine rankings. This is how you'll generate traffic and leads.

KEEPING LOW-COST CONTACT WITH "IFFY" PROSPECTS

Sometimes you want to maintain relationships with moderately motivated prospects, in hopes that they choose to work with you when they're finally ready to buy or sell.

A good, low-cost way to stay in touch with these contacts is to send an email version of your real estate newsletter or some other form of cyber-correspondence that costs you nothing for delivery or printing. Don't expect a high percentage of these long-term prospects to convert into listings or sales based on this contact technique, but your cost is almost nonexistent, so any success is nearly pure profit. However, be reasonable with your expectations. If you achieve a 3 percent return, consider yourself fortunate.

There are numerous WordPress-like website-building companies that specialize in the real estate industry. As a newer agent with a more modest budget, you might take a look at Placester (www.placester.com) or WebsiteBox (www.websitebox.com) as options for your site.

A Phone Headset

I'm a huge proponent of prospecting, and a headset makes it much easier for you to prospect effectively. It enables you to stand while you're making phone calls and keeps your hands free. That way, you can engage your whole body in your communication or type notes directly into your contact manager while talking. A headset improves your posture, position, energy, and enthusiasm. It's the only way to do it.

WARNING

Don't go the cheap route. You can get cheap headsets for $50, but they sound like cheap headsets. Make the investment of a couple of hundred dollars and get a good one. I prefer wireless headsets because I'm completely free to walk my whole office when talking to someone.

Sales Scripts

Knowing clearly what to say in every situation really separates the high earners from the low earners in real estate sales. My best advice is to find scripts that have worked for others. Invest several hours each week practicing those scripts to perfection, preferably with a role-playing partner. A word of caution: Practice does *not* make perfect, as the old saying goes. Practice makes *permanent*. Only perfect practice makes perfect. To achieve perfect delivery, be sure to have the right attitude, an expectation of success, appropriate pauses, and enough repetition to master each script.

Find a role-playing partner who is as committed to your success as you are. My best role-playing partner was my wife, Joan. I know there were times when she was thinking "not again," but she never showed it.

Chapter **19**

Ten Tips for Listing Presentations

Representing sellers and taking listings is the best way to leverage your business and create future business. A listing creates more leads and opportunities for any agent. Although an agent's marketing ability and online presence can somewhat make up for a lack of listing inventory, the bottom line is that listings are always king! Your marketing and lead generation will be more effective on listings because a percentage of buyers want to work directly with the listing agent. They believe they can save money. This chapter helps you nail your listing presentations and win more clients.

Winning the Seller with Preparation

What you do before you arrive at the listing presentation sets the tone for your engagement with the sellers. What you ask before you meet them can be the difference between success and failure. Ask questions about when and how they're going to choose an agent. What's important to them in service and outcome? What are their wants and needs? What prior experience do they have with buying or selling real estate? Whom else are they considering? The agent who has the most information about the sellers and their thought processes has a huge competitive advantage. It enables you to adjust your presentation to fit their needs, wants, and desires.

Knowing Your Competition

The percentage of referral-based and non-competitive business is dropping. Consumers are shopping agents both online and in direct interview situations. Technology has given consumers the ability to search multiple real estate companies and read through numerous online reviews about agents. Competition is increased, and referrals are decreased. When you access a prospect, it's just as important to gather information about your competition as it is to find out the prospect's buying or selling needs. Ask which other companies and agents they're interviewing. This way you can do some research and find out how to plan your presentation based on your competitive points of difference.

Sticking with Your Strategy

Some flexibility is essential during a listing presentation. However, a wholesale strategy change usually doesn't end well. When preparing for a listing presentation, choose either a one-step or two-step strategy:

>> A one-step process has you go to the home or meet with the seller once. You don't go out in advance to see the home and connect with the seller. You prepare your CMA (comparative market analysis) in advance and deliver your sales presentation at the one visit. The goal is to walk out after this meeting with a signed listing contract in hand.

>> A two-step process has you meet the prospect and see the home. Then you complete your value analysis, or CMA. You then meet again to deliver your findings and tell the seller why you're the best for the job.

Your preparation is determined by the process you select. Deviating from that strategy alters your presentation and goals — not a good idea. Select a path that you feel comfortable with and stick to it. If a seller tries to have you speed up or slow down your process, let them know in no uncertain terms that to ensure high quality, you've found your chosen process to be best.

Forgetting about a "Be Back" Listing

A "be back" listing is when the seller stalls, objects, gives brush-offs, and doesn't sign before you leave the presentation. When you walk out the door, the odds that you'll secure this listing have been cut in half. If you're in competition with other agents, the seller probably won't remember all or even most of the differences between the agents. She is more likely to select the agent who gives the highest list price or lowest commission fee. All the presentations start to run together in sellers' minds after a few days of decision delay. If you don't get a signed contract at your listing presentation, you need to act fast to stay in your client's mind. What you do after the presentation is vital to the seller's decision. Be sure to assertively follow up after your presentation; call, email, text, and send handwritten notes.

Using Technology to Impress a Prospect

In today's technological world, a flip chart or a presentation without visuals won't cut it. You need a tablet or laptop computer to make your presentation sleek, tech-savvy, and visually stimulating. Show them something innovative, creating a single moment during your listing presentation.

TIP

With a technology tool like Dotsignal (www.dotsignal.com), you can demonstrate the text-back feature, which sends listing information and pictures directly to a buyer's smartphone. Your phone receives a text showing that a potential buyer sought information about that listing, allowing you to contact the prospect within seconds. Demonstrating this technology at a listing presentation impresses seller prospects — it shows that you can capture buyers and aligns with sellers' needs to get people into their home.

Conveying Your Benefits Clearly

Too many agents sell features instead of benefits. A seller buys benefits but yawns at features. Your presentation has power and punch when you showcase benefits that answer the question, "Why should I hire you?" What's in it for them? If you can connect your company, technology, personal service, and whatever you're selling to a specific set of benefits, the seller will respond and see how you're different from other agents.

If you're a newer agent, sell your company's benefits more than your own. For example, if you're with a company that has large production or market share, that is a feature of the company's service. The benefit is lower risk in working with you and your company because you produce more leads, which increases showings, increases urgency with more buyers creating competition, and leads to higher, speedier initial offers. Additionally, you reduce the risk of the home not selling. All of these are key benefits that you can sell as a result of being with a strong company.

Inserting Trial Closes Strategically

Most agents go through their listing presentation without doing any trial closes at all, so they arrive at the end of their presentation uncertain about whether the seller is tracking with them or leaning their way. Because of the potential rejection, they frequently fail to close at the end of their presentation, as well. If they do close, it's more along the lines of, "Hey, what do you think?" That is clearly not professional, but it's used more often than not. You want to place trial closes after every few benefits and services you highlight for the seller. Use powerful statements like "Do you see how this creates an advantage for our sellers?" or "Is this the type of service you desire?" These lead the seller to confirm that you're heading in the right direction — that your service and value are aligned with what they expect.

Talking about Value Rather than Price

The real purpose of a CMA is to determine the value of the home based on today's market conditions. It's not to determine the price. The price of the home or anything else you sell is a marketing decision. It determines how many people will be interested. The value doesn't change just because your sellers want to overprice their home.

If you focus on the word "value" rather than "price," you can shift the discussion to how the value is determined by the marketplace, the replace-ability of the property (meaning how many other similar homes are available on the market), and competition from other sellers, rather than what the sellers want or hope to get. Everyone always wants to price their home higher than the actual value of the property. Your goal is to delay the discussion on price until you gain agreement on the value of the home. The truth is that homes can be priced at any price, but it will not change the value.

Being Willing to Walk Away

If a seller is demanding, confrontational, and unrealistic in his expectations of your service and the value of the home, it's probably better to walk away from the listing. In taking thousands of listings in my career, I made some errors. The biggest ones were working with people I should have passed on. The amount of emotional energy you invest to service an overly demanding and unrealistic seller isn't worth the commission or aggravation. The empowerment you receive by saying no is unmatched. And the look on most sellers' faces when you turn down the business is priceless.

WHEN THE PHILOSOPHY GAP CAN'T BE BRIDGED

Sometimes, a prospective client relationship just doesn't feel right. That doesn't mean the prospect is a bad client. It means the prospect is a bad client for you. The only way you'll know is to do your homework.

Enter the listing appointment with a clear understanding of your own service approach and philosophy and use that as the basis for determining whether the prospective client is a good match for your business.

- If your minds meet easily, proceed full steam ahead.

- If you uncover philosophical differences, work to iron them out by presenting the benefits of your approach and seeking agreement to proceed along the path you know will result in success.

- If you can't find common ground, walk away from the opportunity if it doesn't feel right. I think you should walk away from a bad client match at least one time to see how it feels to take control of your life and career. Sadly, most agents are too scared to do so. Instead they plow ahead through nightmarish situations with toxic clients.

Clarifying Service and Next Steps

After being at the listing presentation for 45 minutes or more, the typical agent wants out of there as quickly as possible. But when you complete the signing of the listing agreement, disclosure forms, and other documents, you need to pause to debrief sellers about the next steps.

Spend even just five to ten minutes sharing the following information:

>> What your service steps will be in the first 14 days

>> When the listing will go live

>> When to expect showings

>> How communication and feedback systems work

>> What happens if you haven't secured a buyer in a specified timeframe

When you invest five to ten minutes to go through these steps, you'll have clients who are less stressed out and more satisfied. They'll be less likely to call you or feel that you're not calling, texting, or emailing enough. You'll deter them from Monday-morning quarterbacking everything you do.

Chapter **20**

Ten Advantages of Teams

The concept of real estate *teams* has been around for more than 30 years. I added my first team member to my business in 1991, in my second full year in real estate sales. Teams have become more common and influential in the real estate industry in the last five years with the expansion of lead-generation systems and strategies inside brokerages themselves. There are key reasons why: Some reasons are based on economy of scale in gathering a group together to spread the business costs of service, marketing, and lead generation over a larger number of sales producers. Other reasons are based on owning an actual business, quality of lifestyle, and freedom. Production is usually reflected under the team or team leader. This creates a larger production level to market the successful results to sellers and buyers. When you can say that you sold, or your team sold, 100, 200, or even 500 homes last year, that shows higher level of success. You demonstrate a better system and lower risk in working with your team.

Increased Skill Improvement

As a newer agent, if you join an existing team you will gain more experience in real estate sales more quickly. A good team will provide you listing inventory to hold open houses, create online buyer leads, and gain more listing opportunities as well. Because you have more leads and lead-creation opportunities, you will build your sales skills, time management, and negotiating skills faster through real application of those skills with actual buyers and sellers. The learning curve for a newer agent is very steep and can be even steeper if you don't have leads to work. The best way to build your skills is through sales opportunities or practice opportunities. I suggest role playing, as well as learning on live prospects that could buy or sell with you.

Lone Wolf Syndrome

Sales can be a lonely business, especially when you are an independent contractor salesperson. There is limited camaraderie in the real estate business. Because most agents work remotely from a home office or Starbucks, the agents of today don't come into the office 9–5. When you join or build a team, creating a culture of camaraderie is important. Agents are joining teams to be part of something bigger than themselves — to work in a community of other people to accomplish the vision of the business that aligns with their personal vision. People enjoy and want to be part of a community. A team can create that community and caring atmosphere.

Lead Coverage

Because prospective buyers and sellers have access to real estate information and properties 24/7, the agent of today is on the treadmill of always being connected to their phone, email, text, and business 24/7 as well. The typical agent has family time interrupted with inquiries at all hours. There is no substitute for *speed to lead.* Your response time in today's world to a lead will determine more than 68 percent of your success. Failing to get back to an online lead until the next day will dramatically lower your conversion rate. You don't want to waste leads by being non-responsive, but you, like anyone else, need down time to recharge your batteries. This is the quandary and fine line we walk in the real estate business. A team can help lead coverage opportunities, whether you are the team leader or team member.

Quality of Life

I would not have sold more than 150 homes annually and taken Friday, Saturday, and Sunday off each week without my team. A team leader can achieve a better quality of life because of the leverage of other people and the coverage they have from the team. A team leader can create their own schedule and know that their clients and prospects will be serviced while they are not working. This is especially true during vacation time. Most agents who are not part of a team end up working their phone, email, and text message while they're on the beach trying to relax. It's hard for an agent who is not part of a team to shut down work and really relax with the family. Giving your family the 100 percent attention they deserve is one of the biggest challenges for most agents not part of a team.

Stability of Income

One of the challenging areas for agents is the feast-or-famine nature of their real estate business. They have a couple stellar income months, followed by a month or two of low or no income. The cycles of income make it difficult for most agents to control cash flow, spending, investment, and savings. The outcome is overspending in the good months and limited funds left for the lower months. A team of other sales producers can smooth out the income swings that can happen in real estate sales. When your personal production is having a lower level month, one of your team members could be having a really strong month. Because you are the team leader, you are getting a piece of their production. If you have a number of sales-producing team members, your income will likely be more consistent from month to month.

Leverage

Leverage is a hot topic in the real estate industry. How do you leverage your business to create more revenue from your effort, capital, and time? The greatest leverage in real estate is listings. You can create leverage by securing a listing, and all the other agents in your MLS have access to sell that listing. You are employing all agents without pay until they bring you a valid buyer and offer. The second-best leverage is to have your own sales team working to sell that listing or use it to create buyers to sell other properties. That is human leverage: the ability for sales to be made without your effort or limited effort by you. A team leader who has more leads than they can personally work can create a strong leverage position. This increases sales and reduces expenses on a per-sale basis. That creates more net profit on each sale.

Specialization

Most of us are only really world-class at a few things, and most highly skilled salespeople are not very skilled in administration. That's been my personal discovery too. I was not, and am not, skilled in the administrative aspects of business. It takes me much longer to perform administrative functions, and I don't enjoy them. I do enjoy sales and creating sales. The key to success in business is doing more of what you are good at. Then delegate other activities to people with a higher level of competency in your weak areas. In teams, you can build in transaction coordinator and listing coordinator positions. These are the administrative areas in real estate sales: buyer's agents, listing agents, and even inside sales associates. Having people who specialize in working with buyers and sellers can yield better results. The inside sales position creates and nurtures leads through prospecting and lead follow-up.

Coaching and Training Others

For any profession, being able to do it well is one thing. Being able to communicate and teach it is a whole different level. In the last 20 years, coaching and training and writing about how to be more successful in real estate sales have refined my philosophy, mind-set, attitude, and skills. If I went back into active real estate sales armed with having coached and trained people to put into practice the skills and strategies that create success, that time invested would make me a better agent by far. It's rewarding and gratifying to help and teach others how you created your success and how they might achieve theirs. We truly receive by giving more to others. There is no greater reward than helping a team member craft and achieve the life they desire for themselves and their family. To have the honor of a front row seat in someone else's success show is truly the greatest.

Increased Income and Increased Leads

If you require a team member to work to create leads themselves as well as work the leads you give them, you both will increase their income and sales. Use the 1/3, 1/3, 1/3 Principle. One third of the leads and sales come from opportunities that you create for them — from past clients and the sphere of influence out of your database that you turn over to them, and from your online leads that they follow up on. Another third of their sales comes from their prospecting efforts to lead opportunities, such as working your listing inventory holding open houses. They work to use the team inventory to create leads apart from the ones you create online. The final third comes from working their past clients or sphere of influence. This creates a right balance between your efforts to create business for them as part of the team and their right effort to create income for the benefit of themselves and the team.

Saleable Business

Because most agents' business is so personal to them, it can be difficult for them to sell. A team can be better set up, like a dentist, doctor, or attorney practice, where the book of business is transferred through sale at retirement of the principal or one of the partners. The purpose of any business is to create a strategy, system, or process that can be replicated by others. This in turn enables the owner to step away or sell the business. By creating a team, you move the business beyond just yourself to become a future saleable asset.

Chapter **21**

Ten Tips for Agent Safety

Safety has always been an issue for real estate salespeople. Meeting people at homes as standard practice of service has made agents easy targets for a criminal element. It has been a back burner issue that got put on the front burner due to the death of a few agents who were targeted in the last few years. Developing a system and strategy for your personal protection is a necessary part of being a successful agent.

Trust Your Gut

The greatest safeguard you have is to trust yourself. If a particular situation doesn't feel right, it probably isn't. When it feels wrong, treat it that way.

WARNING

Let me be clear: The opportunity to serve someone or create income can never override that uncomfortable feeling of something not being right. If you have any doubts about meeting a prospect, don't. One of our best defenses is fear. If you are even a little fearful, flee the situation. Each of us is responsible for our own personal safety. Nothing is worth taking unsafe actions.

"Talk Time" Leads to Higher Security

How long did you get the prospect to talk? You have to increase the talk time with the prospect. When you talk longer with a prospect on the phone, you gain more information about them. You can secure information that will allow you to research them before you meet by asking questions about them and finding out more about why they are looking at this time. You can find out where they work, where they live presently, and how long they have been there. You can check their responses and verify their information.

Create Your First Appointment Strategy

As agents, our job is to get face to face with a prospect while maintaining our safety and security. According to NAR, 67 percent of buyers buy through the first agent they meet with. Our job is to get face to face with a prospect and upsell them to becoming a client. The right strategy is essential in being safe: to sell the prospect on the value of an in-office appointment. That in-office appointment, during normal business hours, creates safety because of the number of other people present in the office with you. If you can't get them to come to the office, then offer to meet them at a neutral public location. A Starbucks or other coffee shop is a wonderful neutral site. It's public and if it doesn't feel right, you can safely remove yourself.

TIP

I firmly believe first appointments should be either at the office or neutral site. If you have to use the actual safety issue in our world to convince a prospect to meet at the office or neutral site, you might use a script like this:

> *I realize that you would like to meet at the home on __. There is nothing more than I would like to do than show a buyer this great property. Because at this point, I don't know you and you don't know me, there is a safety risk for both of us to meeting a stranger at a private location. I am sure we both want to be safe . . . let's meet at __.*

> *I can appreciate your excitement to meet and to see this wonderful home. Based on the nature of our marketplace, this home will probably not last long . . . Let's set an opportunity to meet. Because of the world we live in . . . for personal security reasons, my first appointments with (prospective clients, buyers, and online buyers) are at my office. I have appointment openings at __ or __. Which would work best for you?*

When You Meet at a Home

There are a few steps you should take before you meet someone for the first time at a home. Because there is greater safety in numbers, be sure to use the word "we" in describing the meeting. As in: "Let me doublecheck to make sure we can meet you at that time." Or: "We look forward to showing you that property." It creates a clear indication that it won't just be you there.

If you are meeting a new prospect at a home, take someone with you. It could be another agent, your boyfriend or spouse, or a friend who comes with you to the showing. I would not advise bringing young children, even if they remain in the car. The risk of stranger danger is too great. The second option is to arrange for the listing agent to meet you at the property. This again would create safety in numbers. You could also have the seller present as well. The buyer would not have much privacy to express their true emotions about the home, but it's better to ensure your safety.

Trail Behind When Showing a Home

When showing a home, always have the buyer prospect walk in front of you. This allows you to keep any potential threat or dangerous situation fully visible and in front of you. It will also allow you time to react, rather than getting caught by surprise. Don't lead someone through a home. You want to direct them; be sure to make clear gestures for them to go ahead of you to each area and room of the home.

Inform Others and Check In

If you are showing a property to a previously unmet buyer, inform your office, buddy agent, and family members. You can't inform too many people. Set a time to check back with them. The clearer you are in communicating in advance, the greater your safety. You could also provide them with the information on the buyer prospect you are meeting.

Distress Code for Safety

You want to be able to alert the cavalry without bringing attention to the fact you have called them in. Create a voice or text distress code, secret word, or phrase to alert your need for help right away. Some offices use a predetermined phrase like, "Can you bring me the *red* file for the property on XYZ Street?" (*XYZ Street* being the address you are currently at for the showing). This would alert the office or other agent to call 911 and leave right away for the property as well to help you. Another option is a code name like "Henry Miller," which stands for "help me." You call and say, "Please let Henry Miller know I will be running late from my showing on XYX Street." This code clearly informs the office you need help right away.

Taking a Self-Defense Class

Being able to defend yourself and break free of an assailant could save your life. Self-defense classes are offered by community colleges, the YMCA or YWCA, health clubs, and martial-arts studios. The investment in your personal safety is well worth a few dollars and a few hours of your time.

Arrive Early and Plan for Your Exit

Always arrive before the buyer you are showing the home to. This gives you ample time to evaluate and observe the neighborhood. Does anything seem sketchy, out of place, or out of the ordinary? Is there anyone loitering around the home or property? Is it unusually quiet? Is there anyone who shouldn't be there or who is unexpected? In planning your exit strategy, walk through the home to determine the floor plan and the flow. Evaluate each room to see if there are two "escape" routes. You want to have options in case one route is blocked. Be sure to unlock all doors and deadbolts so there is no hindrance to your outside exit. You do all of that before the buyer shows up at the property. This removes the nervous fumbling to open locks to escape if you need to.

Practice Your Excuse

You must be ready to create and talk through your "out." If you are present with a person who makes you uncomfortable, you need to communicate your excuse and leave. Don't worry about the house — worry about yourself. Prepare your responses in advance and even practice them so they sound real and credible. Your cell just went off and you need to call the office. Your son just texted and needs you to call him right away. You left brochures and other information in your car for them. Anything that gets you out of the home and immediately. Anything that is common and logical will do. This practiced script could save your life.

Index

About the Author

Dirk Zeller has been a licensed Realtor, speaker, coach, investor, and real estate industry expert for more than 25 years. As an agent he rose to the top of the real estate field quickly. Throughout his sales career, Dirk was recognized numerous times as one of the leading agents in North America. He has been described by industry insiders as the most successful agent in terms of high production with life balance. His ability to sell more than 150 homes annually, while only working Monday through Thursday and taking Friday through Sunday off weekly, is legendary in the real estate field.

Dirk turned his selling success into coaching significance by founding Real Estate Champions (www.realestatechampions.com), the premier coaching company in the industry, with clients worldwide. Dirk has created custom performance improvement programs for Century 21, Coldwell Banker, and ERA that are taught worldwide. These programs and others like them have changed the lives of hundreds of thousands of real estate agents worldwide.

Dirk is one of the most published authors in the areas of success, life balance, sales training, and business development in the real estate field. He has more than 1,000 published articles to his credit. His blog and newsletter *Coaches Corner* is read by over 200,000 subscribers. He has authored eight books, including a number of *For Dummies* titles: *Your First Year in Real Estate, Telephone Sales For Dummies, The Champion Real Estate Agent, The Champion Real Estate Team, Successful Time Management For Dummies, Thriving in the Marketplace For Dummies, Selling All-In-One For Dummies, and Running a Great Meeting in a Day For Dummies.*

Dirk is also one of the most sought-after speakers in the real estate arena. He has been the keynote speaker for real estate and sales conferences on five different continents. Besides contributing to the real estate agent community, Dirk and his wife of 27 years, Joan, are very active in their church. They live with their 15-year-old son, Wesley, and 11-year-old daughter, Annabelle, in Bend, Oregon.

Dedication

So many people have contributed to my success in life, from my parents to my two brothers, my mentors and coaches, and now my two children, Wesley and Annabelle. No one, however, has contributed to my success in the real estate field more than my wife, Joan. I dedicate this book to her: my supporter, encourager, coach, role play partner, accountability partner, and best friend. The success that has been achieved in real estate sales, writing, speaking, training, and coaching was achieved only through our partnership. We did it together! Some 27 years later, I'm still amazed at God's grace in giving me a wife without compare.

Author's Acknowledgments

Just as a successful business is always a collaborative effort, so is a book. While I receive the unfair lion's share of the credit, countless others are behind the scenes making me look good. To the team at Real Estate Champions, an incredible group of people who change people's lives each day, you are the best. Thank you to our support staff of Julie Porfirio, whose loyalty all these years means so much to me. To Wende Fletcher, who also has been with me for a couple of tours of duty between family responsibilities, and Julie Tracy, whose addition to the team has been transformational. You three ladies are unmatched in your value. Thank you.

To our coaches and salespeople, who really change the lives of everyone they touch. I also need to thank the team at Wiley. Tracy Boggier, acquisition editor, and Corbin Collins, project editor. You are truly pros at what you do. A big thank you to Alec Hagerty, my technical editor, who helped shape this book into the best it could be. It was a pleasure working with you, friend!

Finally, I must thank my personal clients and our Real Estate Champions clients. With you constantly challenging us and wanting passionately to improve, you drive us to work so hard to stay ahead, to build new programs and intellectual property to enhance your business and lives. It would be easy to become complacent, but you don't let us. Thanks!

Publisher's Acknowledgments

Acquisitions Editor: Tracy Boggier
Editor: Corbin Collins
Technical Editor: Alec Hagerty

Production Editor: Antony Sami
Cover Image: ©David Malan/Getty Images

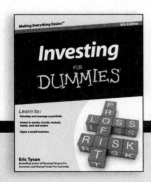
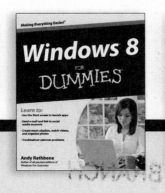

Math & Science

Algebra I For Dummies, 2nd Edition
978-0-470-55964-2

Anatomy and Physiology For Dummies, 2nd Edition
978-0-470-92326-9

Astronomy For Dummies, 3rd Edition
978-1-118-37697-3

Biology For Dummies, 2nd Edition
978-0-470-59875-7

Chemistry For Dummies, 2nd Edition
978-1-118-00730-3

1001 Algebra II Practice Problems For Dummies
978-1-118-44662-1

Microsoft Office

Excel 2013 For Dummies
978-1-118-51012-4

Office 2013 All-in-One For Dummies
978-1-118-51636-2

PowerPoint 2013 For Dummies
978-1-118-50253-2

Word 2013 For Dummies
978-1-118-49123-2

Music

Blues Harmonica For Dummies
978-1-118-25269-7

Guitar For Dummies, 3rd Edition
978-1-118-11554-1

iPod & iTunes For Dummies, 10th Edition
978-1-118-50864-0

Programming

Beginning Programming with C For Dummies
978-1-118-73763-7

Excel VBA Programming For Dummies, 3rd Edition
978-1-118-49037-2

Java For Dummies, 6th Edition
978-1-118-40780-6

Religion & Inspiration

The Bible For Dummies
978-0-7645-5296-0

Buddhism For Dummies, 2nd Edition
978-1-118-02379-2

Catholicism For Dummies, 2nd Edition
978-1-118-07778-8

Self-Help & Relationships

Beating Sugar Addiction For Dummies
978-1-118-54645-1

Meditation For Dummies, 3rd Edition
978-1-118-29144-3

Seniors

Laptops For Seniors For Dummies, 3rd Edition
978-1-118-71105-7

Computers For Seniors For Dummies, 3rd Edition
978-1-118-11553-4

iPad For Seniors For Dummies, 6th Edition
978-1-118-72826-0

Social Security For Dummies
978-1-118-20573-0

Smartphones & Tablets

Android Phones For Dummies, 2nd Edition
978-1-118-72030-1

Nexus Tablets For Dummies
978-1-118-77243-0

Samsung Galaxy S 4 For Dummies
978-1-118-64222-1

Samsung Galaxy Tabs For Dummies
978-1-118-77294-2

Test Prep

ACT For Dummies, 5th Edition
978-1-118-01259-8

ASVAB For Dummies, 3rd Edition
978-0-470-63760-9

GRE For Dummies, 7th Edition
978-0-470-88921-3

Officer Candidate Tests For Dummies
978-0-470-59876-4

Physician's Assistant Exam For Dummies
978-1-118-11556-5

Series 7 Exam For Dummies
978-0-470-09932-2

Windows 8

Windows 8.1 All-in-One For Dummies
978-1-118-82087-2

Windows 8.1 For Dummies
978-1-118-82121-3

Windows 8.1 For Dummies Book + DVD Bundle
978-1-118-82107-7

ℓ Available in print and e-book formats.

WEST WINDSOR BRANCH

Available wherever books are sold. **For more information or to order direct visit www.dummies.com**